THE REVOLVER 1889–1914

Also by A. W. F. Taylerson

REVOLVING ARMS
THE REVOLVER: 1865–1888

By A. W. F. Taylerson, R. A. N. Andrews and J. Frith

THE REVOLVER: 1818–1865

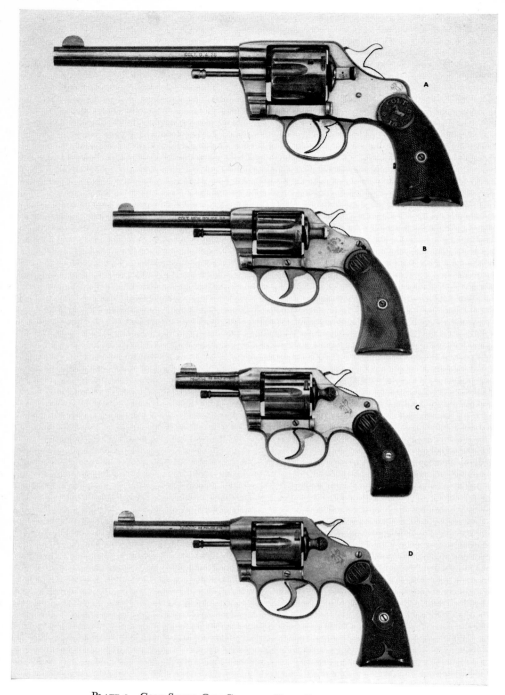

PLATE I   COLT SWING-OUT CYLINDER HAND EJECTING REVOLVERS
A. Six-shot Colt "New Double Action Army" revolver, Model 1892 (civilian version), in ·38 centre-fire calibre, with 6-inch barrel. Serial number 10519.
B. Six-shot Colt "New Police" double-action revolver, in ·32 centre-fire calibre, with 4-inch barrel. Serial number 33710.
C. Six-shot double-action "Pocket Positive" revolver, in ·32 centre-fire calibre, with 2½-inch barrel. Serial number 71186. Embodies the "Colt Positive Safety Lock" shown in Figure 5, which was protected in England by the Br. Pat. 13,680/1905 of O. IMRAY (q.v.).
D. Six-shot Colt "Police Positive" double-action revolver, in ·32 centre-fire calibre, with 4-inch barrel. Serial number 153020. Embodies the "Colt Positive Safety Lock" mentioned in respect of "C" above. *Tower Collection.*

THE REVOLVER

1889–1914

By

A. W. F. TAYLERSON
M.A., F.Inst.D

BARRIE & JENKINS
LONDON

First published in 1970 by
Barrie & Jenkins (Herbert Jenkins Ltd.)
2 Clement's Inn
London, W.C.2

COPYRIGHT © A. W. F. TAYLERSON 1970

ALL RIGHTS RESERVED

S.B.N. 0 257 65116 0

Printed in Great Britain by Cox & Wyman Limited, London, Fakenham and Reading

CONTENTS

CONTENTS

LIST OF PLATES

LIST OF PLATES

LIST OF FIGURES

LIST OF FIGURES

ACKNOWLEDGEMENTS

IN writing this book, I received friendly assistance from many people, whom it is my pleasure here to acknowledge, but before naming those who responded to my letters, it is necessary first to identify the literary sources upon which some of this text depends. To that end a Bibliography appears as Appendix III and in that order by which the relevant reference or material is embodied in these pages; normally, the only textual reference is to an author, but a glance at Appendix III will then establish that book, magazine, or paper, to which recognition is due.

My greatest debt, however, is undoubtedly to a handful of people, without whose help this book would not have been written at all. John Bell, John Darwent, Douglas Fryer, Pierre Lorain, Rolf H. Müller and Ray Riling gave me encouragement and unselfish assistance in the widest sense, and I have also to thank both Messrs. Wallis & Wallis (the well-known firm of Lewes-based arms auctioneers) for those Plates acknowledged to them, and A. N. Kennard, Esq., for granting fresh access to the Armouries at H.M. Tower of London.

Upon individual or specialized subjects of inquiry, I most gratefully acknowledge (by that author's standby, the alphabetical listing) assistance given by:

R. A. N. Andrews, Esq.

Mr. F. Askgaard, *Chief Curator, Tøjhusmuseet, Copenhagen.*

Tenente Joaquim Almeida Monteiro de Azevedo, *Museu Militar, Lisbon.*

Cav. Capt. C. A. I. Belfrage, *Curator, Kungl. Armémuseum, Stockholm.*

Mr. Harry Bergenblad, *Director, Stadsmuseum Husqvarna, Sweden.*

H. L. Blackmore, Esq., F.S.A., F.G.A., *President, The Arms & Armour Society.*

C. Blair, Esq., M.A., F.S.A.

Lt. Ph. M. Bosscher, R.Ned.N., *Koninklijke Marine, Nederland.*

A. G. Briggs, Esq.

General Giovan Battista Calogero, *Museo Storico dei Bersaglieri, Rome.*

Mr. W. H. J. Chamberlain, Lakewood, Ohio.

T. Col. Gran. SPE Ubaldo Perrone Capano, *Associazione Nationale Granatieri di Sardegna, Rome.*

Doctor L. P. Clarke, *National Rifle Association, Bisley.*

I. McW. Davidson, Esq.

J. R. Dineen, Esq., A.L.A., *Librarian, Royal United Service Institution, London.*

Major W. C. Dowell.

T. W. Eagle, Esq.

Brig.-Gen. H. Engin, *Armed Forces Attaché, Turkish Embassy, London.*

Senhor João de Figueiredo, *Lisbon.*

E. B. Ford, Esq., *Messrs. Wallis & Wallis, Lewes.*

Mr. K. B. C. Gorlitz, *Head, Armentarium, Legermuseum, Delft.*

Capt. A. Gundeid, *Armourer, Haermuseet, Oslo.*

J. D. Hall, Esq.

Mr. Akira Hattori.

S. B. Haw, Esq.

The Director, *Heeresgeschichtliches Museum, Vienna.*

B. Hinchley, Esq., B.A.

Lt.-Col. S. Jeffrey, *Curator, The Loyal North Lancashire Regimental Museum, Preston.*

Major J. Wilkinson Latham, T.D.

Monsieur J. R. Leconte, *Le Conservateur en Chef, Musée Royal de l'Armée et d'Histoire Militaire, Brussels.*

R. P. Lee, Esq., *Proof Master, The Birmingham Gun Barrel Proof House.*

Mr. J. Lenselink, Ryswyk, Nederland.

Library Council, *Hispanic & Luso-Brazilian Councils, London.*

T. Col. s. S. M. Luciano Lollio, *Stato Maggiore dell 'Esercito, Ufficio Storico, Il Capo Ufficio, Rome.*

Mr. C. O. Maris, West Glacier, Montana.

Monsieur Robert Marquiset, *Conservateur du Musée de la Manufacture Nationale d'Armes de Saint-Etienne.*

Mr. Carlos H. Mason, Bristol, Connecticut.

Colonel Victor Militaru, *Muzeul Militar Central, Bucharest.*

Excmo. Sr. Don Jose Luis Morales, *Subdirector, Museo Naval, Madrid.*

Mr. H. P. Muster, Basel.

The Keeper, *National Reference Library of Science and Invention, Holborn Division, London.*

The Director, *Museo Nazionale di Castel S. Angelo, Rome.*

F. Peel, Esq.

Messrs. Phelps & Marchant Ltd., *Photographers, Reigate.*

Edward Reeves, Esq., *Photographer, Lewes.*

W. Reid, Esq., F.S.A. (Scot.).

Joseph G. Rosa, Esq.

G. W. P. Swenson, Esq., *Messrs. John Wilkes.*

Director Torriani, *Eidg. Waffenfabrik, Berne.*

Major G. Tylden.

R. Z. Watts, Esq., *Managing Director, Messrs. Accles & Shelvoke Ltd.,
Birmingham.*

Colonel Wemaere, *Conservateur, Musée de l'Armée, Paris.*

F. Wilkinson, Esq.

Yushukan, *Yasukuni Shrine, Tokyo.*

Finally, my grateful thanks to Mrs. B. A. Ewing, of Reigate, who
typed the manuscript of this book, and to Malcolm Pendrill, Esq. (of
Malcolm Pendrill Ltd., Reigate), who photographed so many of the
weapons illustrated in these pages.

INTRODUCTION

LIKE its predecessor (*The Revolver, 1865–1888*, Herbert Jenkins Ltd., London, 1965), this book deals with the revolving arms available to Britons in a specific period, but is not (for reasons made clear in the text) limited to a study of British arms only. Conclusion of such study in the year when the First World War commenced may cause momentary puzzlement, but reflection should concede that 1914 was a turning-point in the art, since (as the major conflict bred needs for ever-increasing quantities of small-arms) one attitude to manufacture and design flourished, but another necessarily died.

In these pages, as before, two substantial Appendices are used to simplify the story, with Appendix I listing all relevant British patents (and Chapter V explaining the nature of the protection thus secured), and Appendix II constituting a "Who's Who" of patentees in question, and a summary of the inventions so protected. Thus, whenever a name is mentioned in capitals, this fact directs the reader to an entry in Appendix II, and reference to a British patent by number and year only (as, for example, to "Br. Pat. 17520/1899") should prompt recourse to Appendix I, for details of its subject and duration of protection. However, where reference is made to any British patent not directly relevant to this book, the citation is then made *in extenso* (as, for example, "Br. Pat. No. 14269 of 18th June, 1912") to warn the reader that the patent is not included in Appendix I, either because it antedates the period or because it is not a revolving arms patent. The object of these Appendices is to tell a coherent account of the art in the first four Chapters of the book, by sifting-out biographical and other detail irrelevant to the purpose of those Chapters, whilst ensuring that this is available for reference, at need.

Regarding two fields of endeavour, this book differs from its precursor, in omitting direct mention of both crew-served machine-guns and weapon-systems competing with that revolving ammunition-feed

B

principle of primary concern here. The first exclusion arises from the fact that such constructive work as was done upon revolving-barrel machine-guns in the relevant years (and these weapons remained in wide service), has been admirably covered by Wahl and Toppel, whilst in the second category too much occurred in the development of self-loading arms for any useful summary to be attempted here.

Even casual study of Appendix II will show that this book is not confined to a study of "the revolver" as that term is generally applied, namely to a single-barrelled pistol in which a rotating cylinder (longitudinally-bored with cartridge-containing chambers) turns for the successive discharge of cartridges through that barrel, *via* the medium of a lock-mechanism operated by the user.

References to such pistols, of course, abound in these pages, and their lock-mechanisms are described as "single-action", or "self-cocking", or "double-action" in operation. The first can only be cocked, for firing, by drawing back the hammer with the thumb; the second type is operated simply by pulling the trigger to raise and drop the hammer; the last may be operated single-action or self-cocking, as the firer chooses.

However, the study of such arms is joined with that of other small-arms which used the same principle of a revolving or rotating ammunition-feed. We thus have the rifles of F. VON MANNLICHER (*q.v.*) or A. W. SAVAGE (*q.v.*), whose rotary magazines are shown, respectively, in Figure 51 and Plate 35, as we have, for example, those "automatic" revolving pistols of G. V. FOSBERY (*q.v.*) or H. F. LANDSTAD (*q.v.*) shown in Plates 31 and 33, and the radial arms of L. F. TAVERNIER (*q.v.*) or J. E. TURBIAUX (*q.v.*). In addition, there were many improvements of detail, either to the mechanism of existing firearms, or to accessories for use with them, and reference to the Index will acquaint the reader with Appendix II entries relating to holsters, sights, stocks, air-rifles, and other such side-issues. Trivial as these inventions may seem, today, they evolved in a period when some weapons were built as carefully as a watch, and thus are indicative of an owner's attitudes to such arms.

As to the general background for our period, in the U.K. Queen Victoria reigned until 1901, was succeeded by Edward VII (1901–10), and George V ruled for the remainder of those years in point. Preceded by that decade of economic depression which had terminated in 1886, the era was one of only partial recovery, for although a number of new industries were successfully established, those (like the Birmingham gun-trade) which had been damaged by the recession did not regain their former pre-eminence.

Thus, taken over the whole industry, our years 1889–1914 were not those when the entire British gun-trade prospered, although firms manufacturing military rifles and machine-guns did well enough (even against Government competition) out of the demands for new magazine rifles, to re-equip the British armed forces at large, or to fight the South African War. For those parts of the gun-trade which manufactured shot-guns or sporting arms, however, American and Continental competition became severe in some traditional markets, whilst to others the export of all arms was entirely banned by parent European governments. Moreover, the infliction of import duties (like the M'Kinley Tariff, in America) made profitable British export to some formerly successful markets almost impossible. Such tariffs did not greatly affect the exporters of quality arms (American buyers, for example, remaining willing and able to pay the higher prices caused by such duties), but the effect upon exporters of cheap arms was crushing. As a result, *Artifex & Opifex* recorded, Birmingham gun-trade exports to America fell from $349,000 in 1890 to less than $20,000 in 1905 (where, in 1882, such exports had totalled $1,169,000), and G. C. Allen reported that Census figures showed a fall in numbers of persons employed in the industry from 5,500 in 1881 to 4,100 in 1911.

Moreover, it must be pointed out that no comparable tariffs were levied upon arms imported into Britain at that time, and therefore the mere fact that the M'Kinley Tariff made export of cheap pistols and revolvers to America so difficult, meant that those Belgian and German manufacturers who specialized in such arms, of every type, began to penetrate the British market instead, with weapons (of a kind shown in Plate 9) offered at prices against which few British workshops could hope to compete. So keen, indeed, were these prices, that British firms could buy arms in quantity to retail individually at a profit, and this practice spread to embrace importation of Continental components for completion and assembly in England (see A. ARBENZ), to the further detriment of British makers. Another major discouragement to any British would-be manufacturer of revolvers, if any was needed, came with the Pistols Act, 1903 (3 Edw. 7, c. 18); this was pathetic legislation, aimed at limiting the sale of pistols with barrels less than nine inches in length (though it omitted to cover the ammunition for them), but poor as it was, it further inhibited interest by any British manufacturer in this field.

The case in relation to relevant commercial rifles and pistols of better quality was similar, and again need not concern us here. It can be stated generally, as to the former, that buyers in the U.K. (or any other important market), wishing to use rifles with rotary magazines, were able to meet their needs, without reference to a British manufacturer, by purchases of arms noticed in Appendix II (with remarks upon M. H. DURST; O. H. J. KRAG and E. JÖRGENSEN; C. and F. VON MANNLICHER: the OESTERREICHISCHE WAFFENFABRIKS-GESELLSCHAFT; H. PIEPER; A. W. SAVAGE; O. SCHOEN-AUER; and J. SCHULHOF), whilst, in regard to revolvers, British products noticed in Chapter III had to compete with American and Continental arms described in Chapters I or II.

As to the techniques of arms manufacture during this period most British and Continental revolver-makers hardly deviated from those methods used prior to 1889, although iron did become generally replaced by steel, for the barrels and cylinders of all but the cheapest arms. In America, on the Continent, and even in the U.K., military-rifle manufacture had become extensively mechanized decades earlier, but this practice was now everywhere intensified in that industry by the introduction of more sophisticated machinery, by use of the new electric motors to power such plant, and by improved methods and metals for use in making the milling and drilling tools used with such equipment. Several Continental sporting-gun and revolver-makers (notably H. PIEPER (q.v.), A. Francotte, and the Swedish Husqvarna Arsenal) also took up such methods in their respective fields, and the American manufacturers did likewise. Because such a course was expensive, however, other manufacturers took little advantage of these improvements, since skilled labour to do the work by hand or on simple machinery was readily available. Thus L. NAGANT (q.v.) in Belgium, or P. WEBLEY & SON (q.v.) and their successor companies in Birmingham, for example, may increasingly have worked upon components cast, rough-forged, or stamped-out by the elaborate equipment of others, yet those simple lathes, drills and profiling millers used by them to manufacture revolvers from such components would have been instantly recognized by men who had made such arms in the 1850s, and their weapons would almost certainly have been rifled by hand, perhaps even by out-workers situated away from the factory.

Opportunities for the use of revolving arms during our period were as plentiful as those suitable to the deployment of other small-arms. In America, for example, some former devotees left the scene, whether by wilful act or circumstance, with the deaths of such stalwarts as Belle Starr and Bob Younger (in 1889); Bob Dalton, and others, during the Coffeyville raid in 1892 (the year Bob Ford also died); and Cole Younger (1902), "Judge" Roy Bean (1903) or Geronimo (1909). However, others as testy came forward, for these were the years of the assassin (President McKinley falling to Leon Czolgosz, in 1901, and

Theodore Roosevelt being wounded by John Schrank, in 1912); of the 1890 Indian risings in the "Badlands" of S. Dakota (which finished at the Wounded Knee Creek), or by the Chipewa and Navajo in 1892/93; and of the Carroll County Courthouse massacre, in 1912, when six Virginians died as the defendant (and his relatives) disputed a verdict.

In Europe, assassins were also busy (though the bomb was favoured as frequently as the pistol), taking amongst many the lives of President Carnot of France (in 1894); King Humbert of Italy (in 1900); Alexander I of Serbia (in 1903); King Charles and the Crown Prince of Portugal (in 1908); the Archduke Ferdinand of Austria, and Jean Jaures of France, in 1914.

Such incidents, of course, caused misery to many, but there were also larger events, rich in both the infliction of suffering and opportunities for the use of small-arms of every kind.

1890	Field operations in the Sudan.
	Revolution in Argentina.
1892–93	First Matabele rebellion.
1892–94	Dahomey conquered.
	Armenian massacres.
1894–96	Revolutions in Brazil, Colombia, Cuba, and Peru.
	Sino-Japanese War.
	Field operations in Chitral.
	Jameson Raid into the Transvaal.
	Conquest of Madagascar (1896–1901).
	Italian campaign in Abyssinia.
	Spanish field operations in the Philippines.
	Second Matabele rebellion.
	Field operations in the Sudan (1896–99).
1897	Uganda rebellion.
	Greco-Turkish War.
	Tirah campaigns (1897–99).
1898–99	Spanish-American War.
1899	Philippine Rebellion against the U.S. (1899–1901).
	South African War (1899–1902).
1900	Boxer Rising in China.
	Colombian Civil War (1900–03).
1902–03	Macedonian rebellions.
1904–06	Lhasa expedition.
	Russo-Japanese War.
	Tanganyika rebellion.
	Natal rebellions.

Second Cuban rebellion.
French and Spanish field operations in Morocco (1904–11).

1908–09   Persian rebellion.
Turkish rebellion.

1910–13   Portuguese rebellion.
Mexican rebellions and U.S. border operations against Pancho Villa (1912–14).
Italo-Turkish fighting at Tripoli.
Turkish counter-rebellion.
Balkan Wars.

1914   Outbreak of the First World War.

In some of these events, revolving arms played little part. British service rifles in South Africa, for example, were of a type lacking any rotary ammunition-feed, and British officers frequently altogether abandoned the practice of carrying revolvers, because their visible possession tended to attract the attention of Boer marksmen. However, the products of O. H. J. KRAG (*q.v.*), F. VON MANNLICHER (*q.v.*), the OESTEREICHISCHE WAFFENFABRIKS-GESELL-SCHAFT (*q.v.*), O. SCHOENAUER (*q.v.*) and J. SCHULHOF (*q.v.*) were carried in considerable numbers by opponent forces of the period, and few readers will be unaware of the side-arms produced by such firms as THE COLT'S PATENT FIRE ARMS MANUFAC-TURING CO. (INC.) (*q.v.*), P. WEBLEY & SON (*q.v.*), or SMITH & WESSON (see remarks to D. B. WESSON), for both the above and more private conflicts.

CHAPTER I

AMERICAN ARMS

AMERICA's contribution to our field of study was considerable, and the following entries in Appendix II relate to British patentees of stated U.S. domicile, namely, M. V. B. ALLEN (improvements to revolvers); W. H. BOFINGER and W. J. TURNBULL (magazine pistol); THE COLT'S PATENT FIRE ARMS MANUFACTURING CO. (INC.) (charger, sight and safety-devices, all for revolvers), through O. IMRAY and H. E. NEWTON; C. A. DAVIS and W. W. HERRON (revolver stocks); M. H. DURST (rifle); F. M. FERGUSON and J. O. FITZGERALD (sights); P. H. FINNEGAN (revolver); G. E. GARDNER and V. DE MARAIS (sights); IDEAL HOLSTER CO. (holster stocks), through W. P. THOMPSON; O. JONES (revolver extractor), through W. R. LAKE; C. A. LEWIS (sights); S. N. McLEAN (magazine pistol); J. T. MOMNIE and T. MONT-MENY (rifle); A. B., B. F., and F. L. PERRY (rifle); C. W. RANDALL and I. H. RODEHAVER (rifle/shot-gun); G. B. REID (improvement to revolvers); J. RUPERTUS (improvements to revolvers); J. SABO (rifle magazines); E. A. SALVATOR (rifle); A. W. SAVAGE (rifle); T. THORSEN (rifle), through H. H. LAKE; and D. B. WESSON (improvements to revolvers).

Solely as a matter of convenience, six other patentees from the same Hemisphere, noticed in Appendix II, are also listed here, namely, Canadians, I. BELAIR and J. B. A. GUINDON (rifle), D. E. GRANT (rifle), H. M. KIPP and M. C. LISLE (whose "gas-seal" revolver is later described, with other such arms, in Chapter IV), and the Mexican B. REYES (revolver-sword).

Although several of those ideas above-mentioned were both ingenious and well-conceived, only three of them achieved real commercial success, namely, the COLT Company's "Positive Safety Lock" (described later in this Chapter), A. W. SAVAGE's rifle (see Plates 34 and 35), and two revolver crane-latches by D. B. WESSON (see Figs. 70

and 71), so that concentration merely upon Appendix II entries could give a misleading impression of activity over the period in point here.

Accordingly, it is the purpose of this Chapter to demonstrate other successful ideas, which were developed (and solely patented, as a rule) in the United States of America, but nothing further will be said here regarding longarms. Those entries, in Appendix II, relating to M. H DURST, O. H. J. KRAG, F. VON MANNLICHER and A. W. SAVAGE sketch adequately other rifle designs (embodying rotary ammunition-feeds) which found favour with American buyers, either as native manufactures or by importation.

As to revolvers, four firms dominated the American market, whilst two others figured substantially in it, and the products of other minor manufacturers are also relevant to our study. Some revolvers noticed in Chapter III were also imported into the U.S. from England but, for reasons suggested by the Introduction (with remarks upon the M'Kinley Tariff of 1891), imported arms were not an important element in U.S. sales over most of the period. Total annual American imports of fire arms, from Birmingham, in the years 1901–05, for example, averaged about $21,800 value each year, according to *Artifex* & *Opifex*. It is doubtful if many British revolvers contributed to those totals, which largely related to sporting arms of good or superior quality.

Accordingly, this chapter deals (in alphabetical order) with those revolvers made by THE COLT'S PATENT FIRE ARMS MANUFACTURING CO. (INC) (*q.v.*), Harrington & Richardson Arms Co., Iver Johnson's Arms & Cycle Works, and Smith & Wesson (see D. B. WESSON), as the four leading manufacturers in America, whilst also noticing the products of lesser makers, as shown.

"AETNA" revolvers

See "Suicide Specials", below.

"AMERICAN ARMS CO" revolvers

A small revolver manufacturer of our period used the trading-style "American Arms Co., Boston, Mass.", and apparently had a sales office at 103 Milk Street, Boston (until 1893), and manufacturing premises at Chicopee Falls, Mass. (until 1897) or Milwaukee, Wis. (1897–1904). Double-, single-action, and self-cocking pocket revolvers were manufactured by this company, under the U.S. Patents of A. F. and F. W. Hood (see "Hood" revolvers), G. H. Fox, and H. F. Wheeler; the two last-named mentioned Boston domicile in their patents.

Arthur Freeman Hood (of Hopkinton, Mass.) specifically assigned to the company his U.S. Patent No. 391612 of 23rd October 1888, for a revolver cylinder-bolt; George H. Fox held U.S. Patent No. 342507 (of 25th May 1886) for an ejector-lever; and Henry F. Wheeler secured U.S. Patents Nos. 430243 (of 17th June 1890) for a revolver lock-mechanism, and 458687 (of 1st September 1891) covering a cylinder-bolt, which protected features of a self-cocking weapon described below.

As to the actual weapons, Sell illustrated a five-shot hinged-frame single-action pocket revolver by this maker, which was in ·38 centre-fire calibre, and similar in appearance to the revolver version of a Smith & Wesson pistol shown on Plate 38; the arm in question had, however, a manually-operated extractor, in place of an ejector.

Another "American Arms Co." revolver was both tested by A. C. Gould (as described in the 1894 edition of his book) and illustrated by Farrow, ten years later, with the comment that "the single, double-action and hammerless revolver combined . . . is noted for its safety and perfect action. It can be changed from absolute safety to active use in an instant and while drawing from the pocket. It can also be changed to single action for target practice with equal facility." The weapon illustrated by Farrow (as available in ·32 and ·38 centre-fire calibres) was a five-shot concealed-hammer, hinged-frame, self-ejecting weapon, with double locking-notches at the rear circumference of its half-fluted cylinder. The principal distinguishing feature visible in Farrow's draw-ing of this revolver (which otherwise strongly resembled an arm shown in Plate 4) was a large circular plate in the left side of the action, bearing a switch-button sliding to-and-fro in an arcuate slot, and it is this feature which establishes the design as made under H. F. Wheeler's U.S. Patent of 1890 above-mentioned.

As Gould described this "American Arms Co." lock-mechanism, pressure on the trigger cocked the hammer, and (after aim had been taken) the lock-mechanism permitted a second pressure to fire the weapon; transposition of the switch-button in the side-plate, from one side of its arc to the other, altered the lock-action so as to operate in a conventional self-cocking manner. Gould tested ·32 and ·38 calibre versions (both abominably sighted, but well made), to find that recoil in the specimen of heavier calibre was sufficient to move Wheeler's switch-button involuntarily; subsequent attempts "to cock the revolver by the only way provided to do it" led, of course, to accidental dis-charges.

"BACON MFG. CO" revolvers

See "Suicide Specials", below.

"CHICAGO FIRE ARMS CO." revolvers

See Appendix II–FINNEGAN, P. H.

"COLT" revolvers

For general remarks upon this manufacturing company, see Appendix II—THE COLT'S PATENT FIRE ARMS MANUFACTURING CO. (INC.); O. IMRAY; and H. E. NEWTON.

Unlike its major competitors, this Company manufactured no hinged-frame self-ejecting arms, and cartridges were expelled from solid-framed Colt revolvers either singly, by rod-ejector, or simultaneously (from a side-swinging, crane-mounted cylinder) *via* a manually-operated star ejector. All pistols were of excellent quality.

In the first, or rod-ejecting, category there were five principal models available, between 1889 and 1914, all of which could be purchased in a variety of calibres, barrel lengths and finishes. Not all of those were in continuous manufacture by the Company, but it is true to say that only one of them (the "Bisley" Model) was not in widespread use over the whole period of concern here. Various names were applied to these arms, by dealers and retailers, but their most widely-catalogued names, in Great Britain, were "Colt's Double Action Government Army Revolver", "Colt's Bisley Model Revolver", "Colt's Double Action Constabulary Revolver", "Colt's Frontier Single Action Revolver", and "Colt's House Revolver", in which order they are considered below.

"Colt's Double Action Government Army Revolver" is widely known to modern collectors as the "Model 1878", from the year in which it was reputedly introduced. Frame and butt were forged as a single component, into which barrels of $3\frac{1}{2}$, 4, $4\frac{3}{4}$, $5\frac{1}{2}$ and $7\frac{1}{2}$ inches were screwed, and the trigger-guard, lock-mechanism components, spring-loaded ejector-rod, ejector-rod housing, loading-gate, side-plate and lanyard ring were inserted or attached as separate components. This arm (which was six-chambered, and provided with *three* bents to the hammer) was offered in ·476 Eley, ·455 Eley, ·450 Eley, ·45 Colt, ·44–40 WCF, ·44 S & W, ·41 Long and Short, ·38–40 WCF, ·38 Long and Short, and ·32-20 WCF calibres, and weighed about 2 lb. 5 oz. (unloaded), in the version with $5\frac{1}{2}$-in. barrel. It could reasonably have been noticed as semi-obsolete, from the viewpoint of this book, were it not for an unexpected revival of interest in the design, during a Filipino rebellion.

Following cession of the Philippine Islands, by Spain to the U.S., in 1898, a native leader, Emilio Aguinaldo, rose against the American military government, and intermittent fighting occurred between 1899 and 1901. Due to combination of tribal tastes with ground conditions, hand-to-hand combat was a fairly common occurrence over those years, and service revolvers then carried by American forces involved (being ·38 calibre swing-out cylinder designs, in Colt or Smith & Wesson models later described) often proved incapable either of dropping or stopping frenzied attackers. Excellent heavy-calibre Colt or Smith & Wesson revolvers existed at that time (nearly 15,000 obsolete Colt single-action Model 1873 U.S. Army revolvers, in ·45 calibre, having been refurbished by Springfield Arsenal in 1897/98), and such arms were hastily procured by many American combatants, either as issues from second-line stores, or by private purchase. The U.S. Ordnance Department merely studied these events (and actually purchased ·38 calibre Smith & Wesson revolvers, as later remarked, whilst fighting continued), but the Bureau of Insular Affairs took positive action, and Lieut.-Col. R. C. Kuhn has recorded that, on 20th September, 1901, the Bureau ordered 5,000 double-action ·45 centre-fire revolvers, through the Ordnance Department, for issue to the Philippine Constabulary in 1902.

These arms were, in fact, Model 1878 Colt revolvers in ·45 Colt calibre, with 6-in. barrels, an enlarged trigger-guard and long trigger, and fifty more of them were subsequently ordered for the Bureau, on 28th October, 1904. Grounds for choosing such a miserable weapon have never been formally disclosed, but (as was the case with other governments) a policy decision may have been made that arms issued to subject races must be inferior to those held by occupation forces.

The lock-mechanism of both Colt M/1878 and 1902 revolvers is that shown in Figure 1, and it was not of satisfactory design; as may be seen from the Figure, single-action operation is effected by use of a long sear "a" (pivoted beneath the hammer "h") which engages bents cut at the heel of the hammer, and is disengaged by pulling back the trigger "t", until this pivots the sear from engagement with the bents. Self-cocking operation is achieved by a lifter "d" (pivoted in the tumbler "e") which engages a notch across the rear face of a channel cut behind the hammer-breast. Pressure on "t" pivots "e", raising "d" to thrust back the hammer, on its axis, by engagement in that notch. Eventually, "d" escapes from the notch into the channel, and the hammer is free to fall, "a" being by then held clear of the bents as in single-action fire.

The pawl "p", loosely pivoted on "e", is held against the cylinder-rotating ratchet by engaging a "T"-shaped head on the front limb of a V-spring (the other limb of which is pinned to "d") in a semilunar cut

on the inner surface of the pawl; the V-spring thus serves both to hold
the lifter "d" into the notch on the hammer, and as a pawl-spring.
Since it is of frail construction, this V-spring often breaks in use and,
since its twin duties are important ones, the revolver is then unserviceable.

Removal of the circular side-plate (secured by a hammer-axis screw
with a thread turning *anti*-clockwise), from the left side of the action-
body, gives access to this lock-mechanism, *via* an aperture so small that
no one but a watchmaker can either do or learn anything of value, by
use of it.

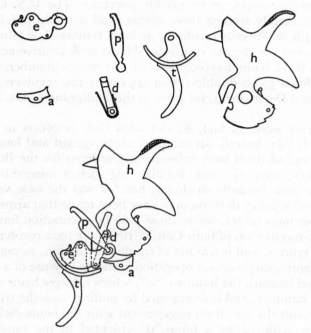

FIG. 1. *Colt's M 1878/02 revolver lock-mechanism.*

Origins of this mechanism are obscure, since Model 1878 weapons
(unlike most relevant Colt pistols) acknowledge no U.S. patents
amongst their markings. William Mason secured U.S. Patent No.
247374 of 20th September, 1881, for an improvement to such arms, and
assigned this protection to the Colt Company, laying claim to use of a
projection on the loading-gate (bearing against the cylinder-rotating
ratchet) as a cylinder-bolt, and such an improvement is found in

production Model 1878 arms. It is noteworthy, however, that (only three years after the weapon was introduced) Mason's Specification had specifically disclaimed any novelty in the basic lock-mechanism.

Later in the same year (as U.S. Patent 248190 of 11th October 1881), Mason also secured protection for a complicated double-action revolver lock-mechanism, which may have been considered as a replacement for that used in M/1878 revolvers, but no specimen arm embodying it has been traced; Carl T. Ehbets, too, attempted to base a self-cocking concealed-hammer revolver lock-mechanism upon this design (by his U.S. Patent No. 306596 of 14th October, 1884), but that venture was as unsuccessful as Mason's had been. The Model 1878 lock-mechanism was, and remained, one of those design-errors afflicting even the best manufacturers.

A study of serial-numbers suggests that a total of some 50,000 Model 1878 and Model 1902 arms were made, all of which were numbered in one serial-range, with the lowest serial-number reported to this writer being 408 (·450 Eley calibre, with 5½-in. barrel), and the highest (·44-40 WCF calibre, with 4¾-in. barrel) as 49289. Because it has a large trigger-guard suitable for gauntleted hands, the Model 1902 Colt revolver is sometimes called "the Alaska Model"; in fact, however, this version of the weapon was probably made only in the Philippine Constabulary production-run mentioned above, with serial-numbers in the approximate range 41000 to 47000.

A "Colt's Bisley Model Revolver" is shown at Plate 2, and has, like the "Frontier Single Action" arm later described, been so admirably discussed by John E. Parsons or James Serven, that little new can be said of it here.

The model was introduced in 1895 (and sometimes catalogued as "Colt's New '95 Model Military Target and Frontier Revolver In One"), but manufacture ceased in 1912. Unlike most Colt revolvers of this period, a "Bisley Model Target" version was introduced first, and followed by the shorter-barrelled "Bisley Model" self-defence sidearm, but both were merely improved versions (by use of low hammer-spur, improved butt, pawl, and trigger, and reduced pull-off) of those "Frontier Single Action" Model 1873 pistols later described. Obtainable in thirteen different calibres or chamberings, and with barrel lengths between 3½ and 7½ inches readily available, some extremely fine shooting was made with these weapons, but neither the standard version (with common sights and rounded frame-top) nor the original target arm (with special sights and flat frame-top) ever achieved that degree of popularity which it appeared to warrant. Serial-numbers for these weapons were taken from a range used for "Colt's Frontier Single

Action" models, and a total "Bisley Model" production of about 45,000 weapons has been estimated, falling in the approximate serial-range 159000–325000.

"Colt's Double Action Constabulary Revolver" is better known to modern collectors as the "Lightning" model, and bears a superficial external resemblance to that "Double Action Government Army Revolver" first described. The lock-mechanism was basically similar to that used in such Model 1878 and 1902 arms, but complicated by addition of a conventional Colt cylinder-bolt (which engaged locking-notches in the rear face of the "Lightning" cylinder) and use of a smaller and more complex sear than that shown in Figure 1. The two designs had also in common a separate trigger-guard, but the "Lightning" component was part of a complete butt-assembly, which was both held together and united to the frame by screws.

Introduced at about the same time as the Model 1878 arms, Colt discontinued manufacture of "Lightning" weapons only in 1910. Since specimen arms are all too frequently found with unserviceable lock-mechanisms (disabled by spring-failure), and the design was as viciously difficult to strip or reassemble as it was to repair, the reason for such a long production-life (when better Colt designs were readily available) remains to be established. The calibres offered were ·38 and ·41 Long or Short Colt (although a few revolvers in ·32 calibre were also produced), and barrel lengths from $2\frac{1}{2}$ to $7\frac{1}{2}$ inches could be secured, with or without rod-ejector; a blued or nickel-plated finish was common, but presentation arms in full silver-plate, engraved and with mother-of-pearl or ivory grips (in place of those in hard rubber or chequered walnut) are not uncommon.

A serial-range distinct from that used on the Model 1878 and 1902 pistols, was applied by the Colt Company to these "Lightning" arms, and has been observed (by this writer) to run from a number as low as 1044, up to one as high as 163940; a ·38 calibre weapon (with $4\frac{1}{2}$-in. barrel) has been recorded as shipped to The Continental Tobacco Co., of New York, on 15th July, 1904, and its numbering at 151302 may give some indication of serials achieved by that year.

It is also fair to remark that this writer's low opinion of the "Lightning" revolver was clearly not shared by those with access to supplies of it. Arms bearing markings and domestic numbering of the American Express Company survive today, as does a ·38 calibre revolver (numbered 111659, with $3\frac{1}{2}$-in. barrel) carried by Constable T. H. Holyroyd, of the North West Mounted Police, and four times notched by him to record the passing of criminals who resisted arrest.

"Colt's Frontier Single Action Revolver" (also widely known as "the

Model 1873", "the Single Action Army", "the Peacemaker", or "the Frontier Six-Shooter") will require no introduction to the reader, however slight his experience with such arms. Described in innumerable books and magazines, featured so prominently by cinema and television, the weapon has also been the subject of countless specialist articles or letters in learned journals, and has been exhaustively described in John E. Parsons' definitive work.

Sufficient to say of it that this was a six-chambered, gate-loaded, rod-ejecting, single-action revolver, similar to the "Bisley" variant shown on Plate 2, and that (having been an issue sidearm to the American Army from 1874 until around 1903) it was in continuous production over the whole period in point here. In a standard commercial model, twenty different calibres were available, and barrel lengths from $3\frac{1}{2}$ to $7\frac{1}{2}$ inches (with or without rod-ejector) could be purchased more or less direct from stock; given suitable notice, the factory would supply arms with longer barrels, with detachable carbine-stocks, or in exotic finishes, or a Target Model (distinct from the "Bisley" arm) was also to be had, with $7\frac{1}{2}$-in. barrel, target sights, flat frame-top, and target butt. Prices for the standard arm, retail in Great Britain, were about £3 2s. 6d. in 1896 and £3 10s. 0d. in 1910; equivalent wholesale prices were about £1 less, in either case.

Serven and John E. Parsons have both published data to establish the likely year of manufacture, for any specimen arm, by reference to serial-numbers, and show a spread between serial-number 128001 at the beginning of 1889, and 329500 at the close of 1914. However, estimates of total production for the Model 1873 revolver must, as earlier mentioned, have subtracted from them about 45,000 "Bisley Model" revolvers numbered in the same serial-range.

Shipping records of the Colt Company are particularly rich in data upon this Model 1873 weapon, both as to the identity of many buyers (to whom the factory shipped special arms direct) and to quantities produced in particular years. In the latter context, however, it was left to G. Charter Harrison, Jr., to express the annual production totals in graphic form and, from the curves thus created, clearly to demonstrate the extraordinary fact that two all-time production-peaks were actually achieved for this elderly design during those years in point here.

Thus, between 1899 and 1907 an average annual output of 13,555 Model 1873 revolvers was maintained (18,000 arms being made in 1902 alone), where only in 1873 and 1883 had individual production-peaks previously exceeded that average figure. Bearing in mind that (as Lieut.-Col. R. C. Kuhn has demonstrated) the U.S. Ordnance Department alone purchased over 37,000 Model 1873 revolvers prior to the year

1890, and that the period previous to that year is traditionally regarded as one when American expansion into the West created a heavy demand for small-arms, the record output in 1902 (and a lesser production-peak, of 160,000 Model 1873 revolvers, in 1907) remains to be explained. It is certainly probable that the Alaskan gold-rushes, around 1900, stimulated the demand, but they cannot be held accountable for all of it.

As to "Colt's House Revolvers" (the last rod-ejecting revolver in point here), the reader is directed to later remarks upon "Suicide Specials". Inclusion of these neat Colt arms in such a category may seem to do them less than justice, but their design (and use, in our period) properly consigns them to that place.

In turning now to the series of swing-out cylinder, simultaneous-ejection revolvers, which the Colt Company also made on a solid frame, it is reasonable to point out (though unnecessary to dwell upon it) that a line of excellent self-loading pistols, outside the scope of this work, was undertaken during that period covered by this book. In 1895, the Company became interested in producing such arms under the patents of John M. Browning, in 1896 the first of such licences was executed, and by 1910 (for example) no less than six different models of Browning self-loading pistols were available from the Company. Since none had ammunition-feed principles relevant here, such arms cannot be discussed. However, they formed an increasingly substantial and profitable part of Company activities after 1900 (in 1911, for example, one such pistol was approved for issue to the U.S. Army), a success possibly responsible for its rather conservative attitude to new revolving-pistol design in the twentieth century.

Before considering those swing-out cylinder manually-ejecting revolvers which were the other Colt line in point here, it should be emphasized that the Company appears to have arrived at that design (first launched in 1889) only after a careful examination of alternatives. As early as 1881 (see his U.S. Patents Nos. 249649 of 15th November, and 250375 of 6th December), W. Mason had proposed a side-swinging crane-mounted cylinder which would automatically eject the cartridges from its chambers, at the completion of its arcuate travel out of the frame, and three U.S. Patents of 1884, namely, Nos. 303135 and 303827 (Carl T. Ehbets), with 303172 (by H. Lord), also explored radically different approaches. As early as 1882, also (see U.S. Patent No. 263551 of 8th August), Mason had investigated a revolver lock-mechanism for swing-out cylinder arms, in which the mainspring was the only spring used, and which had a rebounding hammer and latch-retracted pawl to operate off that spring.

However, though internal changes and improvements occurred over our whole period, Plate 1 can be accepted as typifying the external appearance of those Colt manually-ejecting swing-out cylinder revolvers actually produced and sold throughout it, all of which were double-action arms. Between 1889 and 1914, in fact, the Company from time to time catalogued six basic models of this type (and could supply spare parts for lines discontinued), namely:

The "New Navy" ('89 Model) revolver.
The "New Army", "New Navy", "Marine Corps Model", and "Officers Model Target" revolvers; see Plate 1.
The "New Pocket" and "New Police" revolvers; see Plate 1.
The "New Service" and "New Service Target" revolvers; see Plate 2.
The "Pocket Positive", "Police Positive", "Police Positive Target", and "Police Positive Special" revolvers; see Plate 1.
The "Army Special" revolver.

Colt's "New Navy" ('89 Model) revolver was apparently manufactured for only three years, and is a rarity today. Serven records that the U.S. Navy purchased 5,000 of these weapons (in ·38 Colt centre-fire calibre, with 6-in. barrels), and that civilian versions were also made, in ·38 and ·41 centre-fire chamberings, with a choice of 3-, 4½-, or 6-in. barrels; in either version, this was a six-chambered, double-action revolver, with its cylinder mounted upon a crane pivoted at the front of the frame. By drawing back a sliding latch (mounted on the left side of the pistol-frame, beside the hammer), the cylinder could thus be freed to swing outwards from its position in the frame, and left suspended on the crane parallel to, but slightly below, the aperture in which it normally rested. Here, its chambers could be loaded, or all cartridges simultaneously ejected, by manually pressing to the rear a rod projecting from the front of the cylinder; this rod (which was spring-loaded, so as to project forward when "at rest") passed entirely through the cylinder, and ended in a star-shaped ejector resting beneath the rims of any cartridges in the chambers. After loading or ejection, the cylinder was swung up and inwards, on its crane, and once more latched into the pistol-frame, by engagement of an internal latch-pin (connected to the external latch) which engaged a depression in the centre of the cylinder-rotating ratchet, to hold the cylinder *in situ*.

Frame, trigger-guard and butt were formed as one unit, into which a separate barrel was screwed, and access to the double-action lock-mechanism could be achieved by removal of a large side-plate, secured by screws on the right side of the frame. Cylinder-rotation was (apparently at the insistence of U.S. Navy experts) anti-clockwise, contrary to

c

Colt practice in any of those rod-ejecting arms above-described, which detail had one unfortunate effect in that thrust of the pawl, against the cylinder-rotating ratchet, tended to push the cylinder outwards from the pistol-frame, so misaligning chamber and bore at discharge.

The double-action lock-mechanism need not be discussed here (save to remark that its pawl was intended to act also as the sole cylinder-bolt), since it was essentially that used in "New Army" (or associated) revolvers next to be described, and can be most conveniently scrutinized in conjunction with subsequent improvements to it (see Fig. 2).

Barrel markings on these Model 1889 "New Navy" revolvers embody reference to U.S. patents dated 5th August, 1884, and 6th November 1888, covering certain design-features used in the arms, but positive identification of the earlier protection is difficult, since two possibly relevant patents were secured at that 1884 date. The marking may therefore relate either to the earlier-mentioned Carl T. Ehbets' U.S. Patent No. 303135, or to H. Lord's U.S. Patent No. 303172, or to both; these patents actually covered two cartridge-ejection systems, for revolvers, that were never commercially developed by the Colt Company, but either might fairly be regarded as covering the principle of using a manually-operated star-shaped cartridge ejector in such arms. The 1888 patent reference, on the other hand, was undoubtedly to U.S. Patent No. 392503, which was secured by Carl T. Ehbets (a patent attorney) and assigned to the Company; subjects claimed as novel included the trigger-lock, hammer rebound and cylinder-latch used both in these Model 1889 arms, and in the "New Army" (and associated) revolvers next to be described.

Total production of this "New Navy" ('89 Model) is difficult to estimate, but cannot have been large in such a short production-life. Serial-numbers between 729 and 19334 have been noted by, or reported to, this writer.

The "New Army" revolver appeared in 1892 (when manufacture of the Model 1889 "New Navy" arm ceased), and production was discontinued in 1908; improved models of 1894, 1895, 1896, 1901 and 1903 are recognized, but it was also sold as a Model 1895 "New Navy" revolver, as a Model 1905 "Marine Corps" arm (with slightly modified butt), and as an "Officers Model Target" pistol. Originally offered in ·38 or ·41 Colt centre-fire calibres, versions were later introduced in ·32-30 WCF and ·38 Special centre-fire calibres, but all were six-shot double-action weapons, for which barrel lengths of 3, 4½ or 6 inches were available (see Plate 1).

Parentage of this arm lay with the "New Navy" ('89 Model) of which 100 had been issued for test by the U.S. Army (alongside Smith &

Wesson "New Departure" revolvers later described) in 1890, and their design subsequently recommended for adoption, if the trigger-spring was strengthened and a separate cylinder-bolt embodied. Colt complied with these requirements, whereupon 5,000 arms so improved were purchased by the U.S. Army (in ·38 Colt calibre, with 6-in. barrels) and issued in 1893; at that time, commercial versions were also available, as the "New Army" Model of 1892, and all bore patent markings identical to those mentioned above, in relation to the "New Navy" ('89 Model) revolver.

Experience with Model 1892 arms showed the original design as now substantially improved, but still to be sufficiently short of perfection for the Colt Company to examine a "safety" double-action lock-mechanism feature covered by Carl T. Ehbets's U.S. Patent No. 469465 of 23rd February, 1892; this was intended to prevent accidental damage to the lock-mechanism, if the hammer slipped from under the user's thumb, in single-action fire.

However, the prime defect in "New Army" revolvers was that they could be fired when their cylinder was not fully swung home into the frame, and this was a shortcoming aggravated by counter-clockwise cylinder rotation, tending anyway to unseat a cylinder that had not been properly latched.

In 1894, therefore, yet another improved Colt swing-out cylinder model was introduced, which had an extra lock-component within it, to render such accidents theoretically impossible; all Model 1892 issue arms were recovered from the U.S. Army, replaced with Model 1894 revolvers, and then altered to take this new component. Like most good ideas, this improvement was simple, and consisted in milling a vertical groove into the left-hand wall of the pistol-frame, and securing within it a safety-lever (pivoted at its top) which was acted upon by the internal latch-pin of the external sliding cylinder-latch. When the cylinder was properly home in the frame, the latch-pin was so situated that it held the safety-lever clear of the lock-mechanism, and permitted firing; if, however, the cylinder was not fully seated, the latch-pin was so situated that the safety-lever was tilted into a position where it bolted the trigger, and the weapon could then be neither thumb-cocked nor discharged by trigger-pull.

Subsequently, F. B. Felton secured U.S. Patent No. 535097 of 5th March, 1895 (which he assigned to the Colt Company) for a safety-lock of this type, and a reference to that patent-date thereafter appeared upon the barrels of these arms, with the two dates of 1884 and 1888, earlier mentioned. In Felton's Specification, this safety-feature was such that the cylinder could not be swung out if the hammer was cocked, nor (if by some mischance this had been accomplished) could an opened cylinder be swung into the frame of a cocked revolver.

The lock-mechanism of these "New Army" (and associated) revolvers is shown in Figure 2, where "a" is the hammer; "b", the trigger; "c", the hammer rebound; "d", the cylinder-bolt; "e", the pawl; and "f" and "g" are, respectively, the main- and rebound-springs; Felton's safety-lock is concealed behind "a" and "b".

In single-action fire, "a" is pulled back by the thumb, until the bent, at its toe, engages the nose of "b", when it is held at full-cock; in pivoting backwards, "a" has (by the action of its toe against the nose of "b") also been tilting "b" upon its pivot, thus causing "e" to rise and rotate the cylinder, and disengaging "d" from the cylinder locking-notches. When "b" is pressed, "a" is released and driven forward on to a cartridge by "f" and, on releasing "b", "g" causes "c" to pivot about its axis; this movement rebounds the hammer "a" slightly, by bearing against its underside, and at the same time tilts the trigger "b" forward again, to its "at rest" position. Self-cocking fire follows the same general course, with the nose of "b" tilting back "a" on its pivot, by engaging the strut or hammer-catch pivoted on the breast of the hammer "a". When this hammer-catch eventually escapes from the trigger-nose, "a" falls as before, and upon "g" restoring the trigger "b" (as above described), the trigger-nose passes the spring-loaded hammer-catch without difficulty.

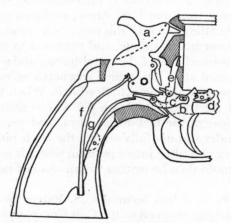

FIG. 2. *Colt's M/1894 revolver lock-mechanism.*

In Figure 3 is shown the original trigger-lock claimed by Carl T. Ehbets's U.S. Patent of 1888, which was recognized in the markings

upon these weapons; here alignment of trigger and cylinder-crane pivot
were turned to advantage, in a somewhat similar manner to that discussed under the Br. Pat. 6184/1894 of D. B. WESSON (*q.v.*). Where,
however, Wesson proposed to cam his trigger-lock into operation,
Ehbets merely juxtaposed a vertical slot in the rear face of the crane
pivot with a "safety-nib" formed on the trigger. In relevant Colt arms,
therefore, the trigger could only be pressed to operate the lock-mechanism if "safety-nib" and vertical slot were truly aligned, and this
obviously could not occur if the cylinder-crane was not also vertical, i.e.
with cylinder latched fully home into the frame.

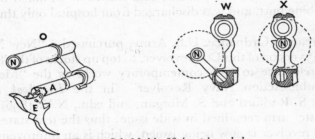

FIG. 3. *Colt Model 1889/92 trigger-lock.*
(After C. T. Ehbets' U.S. Patent No. 392503.)

A slot in the rear face of pivot "A", upon which the cylinder may be swung
outwards on its crane "N", lies on the arc of travel for a safety-nib on the
trigger "E" when (as shown at "O", with the slot partly cut away) the trigger
is pulled rearwards from the "at rest" position. Thus, if "E" is pulled when the
crane is vertical (as at "X"), that nib rides in the slot and encounters no
resistance. The hammer is therefore raised by "E", in the normal fashion. If,
however, the crane is not vertical (as at "W") the slot is likewise not vertical
and any attempt to pull "E" will engage the safety-nib with the side of the
misaligned slot in "A", locking "E" as shown at "O". Equally, "A" cannot
rotate (to permit swinging out the cylinder from the weapon) if the action is
cocked and the safety-nib on "E" is protruding into the vertical slot.

It must be conceded, however, that this trigger-lock was never
infallible, for the contemporary *Firing Regulations for Small Arms for the
United States Army*, S. E. Blunt (Chas. Scribner's Sons, New York)
specifically records those symptoms to be found in revolvers where such
a safety-device has been negligently or wilfully overridden, and this
weakness was grounds for including that Model 1894 safety-device
earlier mentioned.

Serven records that the U.S. Army ordered 68,500 "New Army"
revolvers between 1892 and 1903, and these were officially categorized
as Model 1892 (7,490 arms subsequently modified to Model 1894, as

mentioned); Model 1894 (with Felton's safety-lock); Model 1896; Model 1901 (with butt-swivel for lanyard, and thinner butt cheeks); and Model 1903 (reduced-diameter bore); during such service-life, a change from black to smokeless powders occurred in relation to the ammunition. It was arms of this type which performed so badly during the Philippine rebellion, by their inability to stop a determined assailant in his tracks, which was a failure ultimately leading to adoption of heavy-calibre Colt or Smith & Wesson revolvers later described. That their failure was real is borne out in such stories as that reported by Major J. S. Hatcher, of the attempted escape by Antonio Caspi, from Samar Island, in the Philippines; shot three times in the chest with such a ·38 calibre revolver, this prisoner had still to be subdued by a blow from a carbine butt, and was discharged from hospital only three weeks later.

The Bureau of Ordnance, U.S. Army, purchased a "New Navy" or Model 1895 version of this Colt revolver, to top up stocks of the '89 Model arm, but reference to such contemporary works as the "Manual for Colt's Double-Action Navy Revolver" (in the *Handbook of Naval Gunnery*, C. S. Radford and S. Morgan, 2nd edn., N.Y. 1896) suggests that the latter arm remained in wide issue; thus the text states that "a new Colt's revolver is now being issued, which is an improvement over the old, insomuch as the cylinder can only be revolved by cocking the piece, and the pistol cannot be fired until the cylinder is in place". A civilian "New Navy" Colt pistol was also sold, but it is probable that the only discernible difference between it and either civilian or service versions of the post-1892 "New Army" revolvers lay in their barrels, where the Navy preferred a five-groove rifling, to the Army's six.

At about this time, the Company examined two more improvements for use in these arms; J. Peard's U.S. Patent No. 680274, of 13th August, 1901, proposed the use of a safety-sear to hold the hammer (against an accidental blow) in its rebounded position, and Carl T. Ehbets' U.S. Patent No. 734524, of 28th July, 1903, covered the use of a cylinder-latch which also locked the crane. However, although (as earlier mentioned) Model 1901 and Model 1903 "New Army" revolvers are recognized, they did not embody these improvements.

Turning to "Marine Corps Model" and "Officers' Model Target" versions of "New Army" Colt revolvers, the first was manufactured from 1905 until 1908, whilst the second was introduced in 1904 and discontinued in 1908; both were in ·38 Special calibre chamberings (although they would also, of course, accept ·38 Colt service cartridges), had 6-in. barrels, and were merely modifications to the Model 1903 "New Army" weapon. The "Marine Corps" arm was offered in both

commercial and service versions (the latter with a lanyard ring) and
had a rounded butt, whilst the "Officers Model Target" had hand-
chequered walnut butt-cheeks and special target sights. The latter were
adjustable, at both front and rear components, and were produced
under J. J. Peard's U.S. Patent No. 671609; the relevant patent date of
9th April, 1901, was added to the above-mentioned patent references of
1884, 1888 and 1895, in the markings of target arms. Total production
of "New Army" (and associated) revolvers has never been publicly
stated, so far as this author is aware, and study of specimen arms has
not established whether all models were numbered in a single serial-
range.

Quite early in the manufacture of "New Army" revolvers, it became
clear to the Colt Company that their design had certain defects capable
of abatement, but never of elimination. The small calibre apart, these
weapons had (as indicated earlier) a lock-mechanism capable of serious
abuse in clumsy hands, and their cylinders were rotated in a direction
contrary to that desirable in this particular swing-out cylinder arm.
Since the U.S. armed forces apparently liked the design, and the Company presumably had a substantial investment in tools and equipment
for making it, there was (as demonstrated above) no precipitate withdrawal of the "New Army" line, and what could be done to improve
such arms was conscientiously done. However, a Company decision was
early taken to produce revolvers lacking those features criticized above,
and the first model of an alternative series appeared in 1893 or 1894.

At a casual glance, this "New Pocket" revolver (and other arms of
similar design, which followed it) gave no visible indication of improvement, but more detailed examination revealed that cylinder-rotation
had now reverted to that clock-wise direction desirable in a swing-out
cylinder revolver opening to the left, and that an entirely different
double-action lock-mechanism had been adopted; in addition, the
removable side-plate (by which access to that lock-mechanism was
gained) had been switched to the left side of the frame, and all models
produced after mid-1905 embodied a really fool-proof hammer-lock.

The lock-mechanism thus adopted was neither new nor of Colt invention, but came from Europe; it was, in fact, that "Schmidt-Galand"
lock-mechanism used by P. WEBLEY & SON (q.v.) in all of their post-
1887 British service revolvers; it is shown in Figures 12 or 33, and was
also adopted for use in Europe (see Fig. 12), as described at Chapter II.
This design was quite old (having been patented by a Liège gun-maker,
Charles Francois Galand, in 1872), but very strong and reliable, and
there is no indication that the Colt Company ever had subsequent
cause to regret their choice of it.

The Colt version of this lock-mechanism is shown at Figure 4, where "a" is the hammer, "d" the trigger, "n" the rebound lever (or "mainspring auxiliary", in British parlance), "e" the mainspring, "f" the pawl, and "g" the cylinder latch-pin; the cylinder-bolt is (from this aspect) concealed by "a", and shown at Figure 5, when dealing with that safety-device embodied in revolvers made after mid-1905.

In single-action fire, "a" is drawn back with the thumb, until the nose of "d" engages a bent at the toe of "a"; this movement has, by engagement of "a" and "d", drawn back the trigger "d" on its pivot, and raised the pawl "f" to rotate the cylinder. The tip of "n" is engaged in a notch on the inner side of the pawl "f", and therefore the raising of

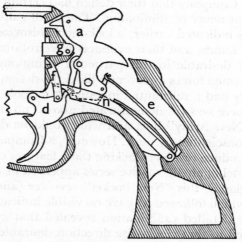

FIG. 4. *Colt's "Schmidt-Galand" lock-mechanism.*

"f" lifts the rebound lever "n" on its pivot, and compresses the mainspring "e"; initial movement of "n" has caught the tail of the cylinder-bolt, tipped the latter out of engagement with the cylinder locking-notches, and permitted "f" to rotate the cylinder until the cylinder-bolt escapes from "n", and re-bolts the cylinder with a chamber in line with the bore.

Pressure on "d" releases "a", which is pivoted smartly forward (by action of the top limb of "e") to strike a cartridge; on release of "d", the mainspring "e" throws down the rebound lever "n" which (being engaged in a component "f" that is pivoted on the trigger "d") returns the trigger "d" to its forward position. In this movement of the trigger "d", its nose readily pushes by the spring-loaded hammer-catch, on the breast of "a", and a surface on the rebound lever "n" strikes the heel of the hammer "a", and pivots this slightly, backwards off the cartridges in the cylinder.

Self-cocking operation follows the same general course, with the nose of "d" engaging the tip of the hammer-catch on "a", to tilt the hammer backwards (until it escapes the trigger, and falls) as the trigger "d" is pressed back.

As earlier mentioned, this lock-mechanism was introduced by the Colt Company in a six-shot "New Pocket" revolver, which was offered in three ·32 centre-fire calibre chamberings, and with a choice of 2½-, 3½- or 6-in. barrel lengths; Serven appears satisfied that introduction occurred in 1895, but it is noteworthy that A. C. Gould noticed this "latest product" of the Company, enthusiastically, with the 1894 edition of his book. In 1896, a slightly heavier version (with conventional Colt butt, where the "New Pocket" had a rounded handle) appeared, and was sold as the "New Police" revolver visible in Plate 1. This weapon later chambered a slightly more potent ·32 calibre centre-fire cartridge, named after it, and was offered in barrel lengths of 2½, 4 or 6 inches; a target model was also available, from 1897 onwards.

These ·32 calibre arms were successful enough, but the Colt Company now also launched a heavy-calibre "New Service" revolver with the same mechanical features, which eventually proved to be one of their most successful swing-out cylinder arms, and which also saw extensive use during the First World War. With this weapon (shown in Plate 2), chamberings for the most powerful of centre-fire pistol cartridges were featured from the start, so that revolvers in ·476 Eley, ·455 Eley, ·450 Eley, ·45 Colt, ·44 Russian, ·44-40 WCF, ·38-44, ·38-40 WCF, and ·38 Special calibres were available during our period; standard arms could be had with 4½-, 5½ or 7½-in. barrels, but a "New Service Target" revolver (with flat frame-top, hand-finished action, chequered trigger-guard, straps and trigger, and target sights) was only available as a 42-oz. pistol, with 7½-in. barrel. The latter model, in and after 1901, embodied adjustable sights of a type covered by the claims of J. J. Peard's U.S. Patent No. 671609 earlier mentioned.

Opinion as to the exact date of introduction for Colt "New Service" revolvers is divided, but most authorities appear to recognize that original model as appearing in 1897; certainly, the name "New Service" was registered as a Colt Company trade-mark, in America, during 1899. It is noticeable, however, that arms with quite low serial-numbers carry a patent date of 1900 amongst their markings, to suggest that initial production was not large, if this model was really introduced in 1897. Clearly, too, the "New Service Target" revolver appeared early in the series, even before Peard adjustable sights (of 1901) were available for use with it.

Markings on the early "New Pocket", "New Police" and "New Service" revolvers included only one patent reference, namely, to the date (5th August, 1884) of those two patents mentioned in respect of "New Navy" ('89 Model) arms, covering the principle of their ejectors; the 1888 patent reference found upon "New Army" weapons was, for obvious reasons, not used, and no patent reference relevant to the new lock-mechanism appeared before 1900. At 5th June, 1900, however, Carl T. Ehbets and J. J. Peard secured U.S. Patent No. 650931 (for improvements to such double-action lock-mechanisms), and thereafter that date also appeared upon the barrels of these arms.

U.S. Patent No. 650931 claimed two methods for operating the cylinder-bolts of double-action revolvers. One method was applicable to arms with lock-mechanisms of the Warnant type (as used in French Model 1892 service revolvers, described in Chapter II), where the lower limb of a V-shaped mainspring formed the hammer-rebound, and it was proposed to use a projection upon that limb, to rock the cylinder-bolt from engagement with the cylinder locking-notches; the other patented method employed a separate hinged rebound lever ("n", in Fig. 4) to carry out such a task, and this was, of course, the device taken up by the Colt Company.

In fact, it is doubtful if the Ehbet/Peard rebound-lever was actually used for "New Pocket" and "New Police" revolvers, although it was employed for the larger lock-mechanism of "New Service" arms; thus Colt Company illustrated parts-lists, of post-1905 vintage, show rebound-levers for the smaller arms that are devoid of any "lever fly", where such a component is clearly shown in spares lists for the "New Service" line. This "lever fly" was actually a small component, pivoted on the right sight of the rebound-lever, which operated the cylinder-bolt, as the rebound-lever was lifted by the act of cocking the hammer. Experience proved that a cam-surface formed on the rebound-lever was effective, though not as smooth-working as the "lever fly", and the fly was ultimately abandoned, even for "New Service" revolvers. Reference to the date of U.S. Patent No. 650931, upon arms not embodying the "lever fly", was probably justified by a view that the cam-surface principle was also envisaged by the claims of that patent.

In 1905, manufacture of "New Pocket" and "New Police" revolvers ceased, but they were respectively replaced by "Pocket Positive" and "Police Positive" arms shown in Plate 1; originally, each differed from its parent only by the addition of a lock-mechanism improvement next to be described, but the "Police Positive" line was expanded considerably, in years prior to 1914. Initially offered either as a standard arm (with 4-in. barrel) or target revolver (with 6-in. barrel) in ·32 Colt or ·32 Colt New Police chamberings only, target versions for the ·22 Long Rifle rim-fire or ·22 WRF cartridges were also available by 1911, along with standard arms chambered for ·38 Colt New Police or ·38 S & W cartridges; around 1907, too, a "Police Positive Special" standard revolver was also introduced, with chamberings for the authoritative ·38 Special or ·32-20 centre-fire cartridges. This pistol had a frame and cylinder slightly longer than those same components in "Police Positive" arms, and it could be had in barrel lengths of 4, 5 or 6 inches; the weight-increase arising from this modification was slight, so that the "Police Positive" with 4-in. barrel weighed 20 oz. against 22 oz. for the equivalent "Police Positive Special".

This "Positive" name given by the Colt Company to its new models stemmed from U.S. Patent No. 793692 of 4th July, 1905, which G. H. Tansley secured, and assigned to the Company. In England the equivalent protection was Br. Pat. 13680/1905 (secured by O. IMRAY; *q.v.*) and similar patents were secured in other countries, but all protected the "Colt Positive Safety Lock", which was embodied in both the new models, and in those "New Service", "Army Special", and "Officers' Model Target" revolvers made in or subsequent to that year. A reference to the date of this U.S. Patent thereafter appeared upon the barrels of all the above-mentioned models, beside the patent dates of 1884 and 1900, earlier described.

Oddly enough, the Specifications to both Tansley's and Imray's patents of 1905 showed this "Colt Positive Safety Lock" as it could be applied to the obsolete Model 1894 Colt "New Army" double-action lock-mechanism, but, being perfectly adaptable to the now-favoured Schmidt-Galand design, the device was in fact never applied to late "New Army" (and associated) models.

The "Colt Positive Safety Lock" is shown in Figure 5, but should be studied in alliance with Figure 4, showing the basic lock-mechanism to which that improvement was applied; Figure 5 also illustrates the configuration of cylinder-bolt used in revolvers of post-1905 vintage, other than certain "New Service" arms earlier-mentioned, which still used the short cylinder-bolt and "lever fly" from the Ehbets/Peard patent of 1900.

In Figure 5, "d" is the trigger, "h" the cylinder-bolt, "i" the safety, and "l" the safety-lever; the "Colt Positive Safety Lock" consists of "i" and "l" (in conjunction with "d"), and has as its objective preventing the hammer of a revolver from accidentally striking a cartridge, unless the hammer has first been cocked (by thumb or trigger-pressure) and the trigger has been drawn to the rear literally as far as it will go.

This "i" is an L-shaped component (sliding in a slot milled in the right-hand wall of the pistol-frame), linked to the trigger "d" by a lever "l" which turns upon the same pivot as the hammer; for clarity, the latter is omitted from Figure 5. The short arm of "i" is a hammer-block, and extends across the front of the hammer to prevent it from reaching any cartridge, except when that hammer-block is aligned with a suitable notch cut across the breast of the hammer; see Figure 4. In fact, the only way in which such a juxtaposition can be effected is by pulling the trigger completely to the rear, and well past that position at which it releases the hammer.

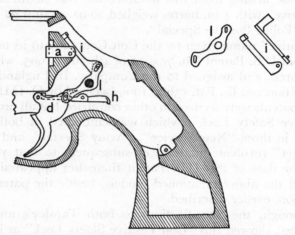

FIG. 5. *The "Colt Positive Safety Lock"*.
(After U.S. Patent No. 793692/1905.)

In Figure 5, it will be seen that pressure upon the trigger "d" will turn "l" upon its pivot, dragging "i" downwards in the frame, and eventually (as the hammer is literally falling) aligning the hammer-block on "i" with the notch in the hammer-breast, so that the firing-pin reaches a cartridge. Thus no inadvertent blow upon the hammer (as by dropping a pistol), or slipping of the hammer from under the thumb in single-action fire, can in any conceivable way discharge the cartridge accidentally.

Although such a point was not made in the Specifications either to Tansley's or Imray's patents for the "Colt Positive Safety Lock", this contrivance also acts as a trigger- and hammer-lock when the cylinder is not properly latched home into the frame. In such an event (as may be seen in Figure 5), the cylinder-latch pin "a" is forced back into the frame-cavity, by the extractor head, and protrudes sufficiently into that cavity to block the downwards movement of the hammer-block (on "i", in Figure 5) if any attempt is made to cock the weapon.

Altogether, this is an excellent safety-device, and deservedly successful from the date of its introduction. Serven teaches that it was embodied in "New Service" revolvers from serial-number 21000 onwards, and in "Pocket Positive" revolvers (which were apparently numbered in sequence with their "New Pocket" predecessors) at serial-numbers above 30000; the point of introduction for "Police Positive" arms is uncertain, but assumed to have occurred *ab initio*. The serial-numbers of these "Police Positive" revolvers are notably confusing, in any event, with considerable indication that the ·22 target and "Positive Special" arms, for example, had their own separate serial-ranges.

The next events of importance to the Colt Company, in relation to its swing-out cylinder revolvers, occurred in or shortly after 1908, when the last two models relevant to our study were introduced, namely, the "Army Special" and new "Officers' Model Target" revolvers. The first was merely a replacement for the unsatisfactory "New Army" design (by now in its Model 1903 incarnation), but embodying both the Schmidt-Galand lock-mechanism and improvements of 1900 and 1905; the second (as its name suggests) was a similar replacement for that old Model 1904 "Officers Model Target" version of the "New Army" design.

Colt "Army Special" revolvers were initially offered in ·32-20, ·38 Special and ·41 Colt centre-fire chamberings, with barrel lengths of 4, 4½, 5, or 6 inches, at choice; it was hoped to interest the U.S. Army in adopting this model, but (with Philippine memories still comparatively fresh in official minds) a calibre of less than ·45 was unattractive, and no official interest was aroused.

However, the "Army Special" line (which was rechristened "Official Police", a decade after the First World War) sold well to police officers or marksmen, and its substantial frame, so necessary in a revolver handling the relevant cartridges, also made it a superb platform for the construction of target revolvers; a resultant "Officers Model Target" version had all those refinements earlier noted for "New Service Target" arms, and could be had (with barrel lengths of 4½, 6 or 7½ inches) in ·38 Colt, ·38 Colt Special or ·38 S & W Special chamberings.

Finally, the Colt Company (which must have remarked, with some irritation, service purchases in 1901 and 1902 of a Smith & Wesson revolver later noticed) were successful in securing orders for swing-out cylinder revolvers to replace or supplement those obsolete "New Army" (and associated) Colt arms in the hands of U.S. forces. The weapon selected was Colt's "New Service" revolver (see Plate 2), in what is now called a "1909 Army Model" version, and Lieut.-Col. R. C. Kuhn has recorded the following purchases as relevant to our period:

1st U.S. Army contract 10th February, 1909—	7,200 revolvers
1st U.S. Marine Corps contract 7th July, 1909—	500 revolvers
2nd U.S. Marine Corps contract 14th October, 1909—	700 revolvers
2nd U.S. Army contract 16th December, 1909—	3,000 revolvers
3rd U.S. Army contract 30th June, 1910—	2,000 revolvers
4th U.S. Army contract 8th December, 1910—	6,703 revolvers
U.S. Navy contract 12th April, 1911—	1,000 revolvers

When war was declared by Great Britain, on 4th August, 1914, Colt "New Service" pistols in ·455 centre-fire calibre were available here from a number of retailers, and were privately purchased (as was then the practice) by many officer volunteers; in years subsequent to 1914, the purchase of such arms in quantity, by a British Purchasing Commission sent to the United States, was officially arranged, but it is not believed that any really significant operations of that type occurred in the last year relevant to this book.

"COLUMBIAN" revolvers

Although quite rare in Great Britain, two revolvers bearing the "Columbian" trade-name were marketed in America, and we have Mathews as formidable authority for the view that one version at least was made at a "Columbia Arsenal", in Tennessee. It is noticeable, however, that such evidence as may be surveyed upon the point does not necessarily support that view for their origins.

The "Columbian Double Action" revolver illustrated by Mathews was a ·38 centre-fire solid-framed pistol, with chambers individually loaded or unloaded, which had no apparently patentable features, and was marked "New York Arms Co.". MacFarland's researches reveal that brand-name as one used by the Crescent Firearms Co. (see below) upon arms which it supplied for sale by Garnet Carter & Co., of Chattanooga, Tenn.

The "Columbian New Safety Hammerless" revolver, on the other hand, seems principally to have been sold by Maltby, Henley & Co., a firm of New York jobbers later mentioned, and although also solid-framed, it varied from the double-action "Columbian" arm in using patented design-features. These were the work of John T. Smith (at Rockfall, Middlesex County, Conn.), another designer mentioned below, and the weapons acknowledged relevant patent dates, of 24th January, 1888 (U.S. Patent No. 376922) and 29th October, 1889 (U.S. Patent No. 413975), amongst their markings.

In the first of these patents, Smith had proposed to mount his self-cocking lock-mechanism upon a butt-cum-trigger-guard component, and to hinge the latter to the barrel and shrouded-hammer lock-case of his revolver. By these means, access for repair or cleaning of the complete lock-mechanism could readily be obtained. In the second patent, both frame-construction and lock-mechanism were slightly refined, a wheel-shaped safety-device (blocking the hammer, when suitably rotated) was provided in the rear butt-strap, and a combined cylinder-bolt and cocking-indicator was mounted in the top frame-strap. Such features were all embodied in "Columbian New Safety Hammerless" revolvers, and the composite frame-construction (though solid enough) did give these arms an external appearance of being hinged-frame self-ejecting revolvers, in better quality than was actually the case.

Alongside their ·22 rim-fire and ·32 or ·38 centre-fire "Columbian New Safety Hammerless" line, Maltby, Henley & Co. sold versions under their house name (see Plate 6), and may also have sold the similar "Parker" or "Scott" weapons later described. There is no reason why that firm should not itself have arranged licensed manufacture of such arms under the Smith patents, but it does seem more logical to propose that Smith (earlier connected with revolver-making, as mentioned below) could actually have handled that end of the operation, and himself marked the weapons sold, with such "Columbian" or other legends, as his various customers required.

"CRESCENT FIREARMS CO." revolvers

Research by Harold E. MacFarland has established the Crescent Firearms Co., of Norwich, Conn., to have been an important manufacturer of cheap firearms after 1892, selling shot-guns, rifles and pistols (either wholesale or by mail-order) through a sales-outlet trading as the H. & D. Folsom Arms Co., of New York. Over ninety different brand-names were impressed upon Folsom arms (although some thirty names appeared upon weapons actually purchased from Belgian, British or other American manufacturers), but most were exclusively used upon products supplied for sale by large hardware companies trading in various parts of the United States, and never impressed upon weapons sold through the Folsom mail-order outlet.

Although MacFarland does not refer to this matter, it seems probable that the Crescent Firearms Co. was actually launched by George W. Cilley, a former associate of the Hopkins & Allen Manufacturing Co. (see below) at Norwich, who purchased stocks and equipment valued at about $14,000, from the moribund Bacon Manufacturing Co. of that town, in 1892.

Mathews clearly identifies double-action self-ejecting revolvers as sold under the "Crescent" name (which accounts for their mention here), but MacFarland's more recent investigations suggest that such arms emanating from that source would more probably have been sold under brand-names like "Empire", "Howard Arms", or "New York Arms Co." (elsewhere mentioned), rather than by reference to their manufacturer's name. MacFarland does list certain brand-names as used by the Crescent Firearms Co. upon its own products (as well as some names used on arms sold only through the Folsom mail-order outlet), but this writer has not encountered revolvers marked with such names, save as elsewhere indicated in these pages.

"EASTERN ARMS CO." revolvers

This name appeared upon cheap hinged-frame, self-ejecting revolvers (with double-action or concealed-hammer self-cocking lock-mechanisms), of a type shown at Plates 3 or 4; five-shot, ·32 centre-fire calibre arms, with 3¼-in. barrels, have been observed, and the source for these arms is suggested (by Mathews) as that Meriden Fire Arms Co. later discussed.

"EMPIRE" or "EMPIRE STATE" revolvers

As noticed by Mathews, five-shot "Empire State Hammerless" hinged-frame, self-cocking, self-ejecting revolvers (with 3¼-in. barrels) were offered, during our period, in ·32 or ·38 centre-fire calibres, and their manufacture ascribed by him to the Meriden Fire Arms Co. later mentioned. It should be pointed out, however, that MacFarland lists the Crescent Firearms Co. as users of the brand-name "Empire", and also as suppliers of arms under the brand-names "Empire Arms Co." and "State Arms Co." respectively to Sears, Roebuck & Co. and J. H. Lau & Co. for sale by them under such names.

"FEDERAL ARMS CO." revolvers

These were inexpensive ·32 and ·38 calibre hinged-frame, double-action revolvers and are also believed to have been made by the Meriden Fire Arms Co. (q.v.).

"THE FOEHL & WEEKS FIRE ARMS MANUFACTURING CO" revolvers

Charles Foehl was a Philadelphia gun-maker, who died in 1912. Prior to years of concern here, his U.S. Patent No. 139461 of 3rd June, 1873 (for an improved cylinder-rotation pawl) had been briefly used by I. J. Clark, to manufacture small single-action revolvers sold under the trade-name "Deringer". It is not definitely known if Foehl had operated from the Clark plant on Tamarind Street, Philadelphia, prior to its closure in 1879.

At about 1889, The Foehl & Weeks Fire Arms Manufacturing Co. was formed, in Philadelphia, and Foehl both secured and assigned to it his U.S. Patent No. 417672, dated 17th December in that year; subsequently, he and C. A. Weeks jointly secured U.S. Patent No. 444823 of 20th January, 1891, which they also assigned to the Company. The first patent related to a hammer-rebound for self-cocking, solid-frame revolvers, and the second to an arbor-latch and cylinder rotation-damper suitable for such arms.

In fairly rapid succession, Foehl and Weeks thereafter jointly secured U.S. Patents Nos. 447219 (of 24th February, 1891), 468243 (of 2nd February, 1892), and 471112 (of 22nd March, 1892), which respectively claimed a firing-pin retractor and hammer-rebound for solid-framed, self-cocking, concealed-hammer revolvers, another hammer rebound, and a barrel-latch for hinged-frame arms. The only Foehl & Weeks revolver likely to be encountered today was apparently sold (under the trade-name "Perfect") as a 5-shot ·32 calibre, self-cocking, solid-frame weapon, with a concealed hammer, which acknowledged the above-mentioned date of U.S. Patent No. 447219 in its markings, but may have embodied other patented features. However, hinged-frame pistols may also have been manufactured by this firm.

It is probable that The Foehl & Weeks Fire Arms Manufacturing Co. existed for only a few years, since it is noticeable that Foehl's later U.S. Patent No. 530759 of 11th December, 1894 (in which he claimed a cylinder-retainer and cylinder-bolt for hinged-frame revolvers) was not vested in the Company, but assigned, as to half, to one Henry Ruhland, of Philadelphia. At all events, Weeks appears to have left the scene at about this time, and Foehl thereafter to have engaged in other activities, until the occurrence of those events, later described, relating to KOLB revolvers.

"FOREHAND" revolvers

The "Forehand" trade-name was applied to revolvers made by a Forehand Arms Co., at Worcester, Mass., in years between 1890 and about 1902; however, it is convenient also to consider with such arms those made by Sullivan Forehand and Henry C. Wadsworth, who traded as Forehand & Wadsworth, between 1871 and 1890, using the Worcester plant and assets of their late father-in-law, Ethan Allen, who had been a noted revolver-maker until his death, in 1871.

The degree of active participation by Wadsworth in this firm is

D

uncertain, for some authorities place his retirement as early as 1880, and it is noticeable that assignments of patents relevant to partnership business were taken by Forehand alone from 1886, a date well before that relevant in these pages. However, there seems no doubt that (as U.S. Vice-Consul at Santos, Brazil) Wadsworth died of yellow fever in 1892, and that Forehand had reorganized the venture, as his own Forehand Arms Co., less than two years earlier; he did not long survive his partner (dying at Worcester, on 7th June, 1898) and the business then passed to the Hopkins & Allen Manufacturing Co. (at Norwich, Conn.), whose activities are mentioned below. This transfer apparently occurred in 1900, and use of the Forehand Arms Co. name was finally abandoned about two years later.

In years prior to 1889, Forehand & Wadsworth had specialized in the manufacture of solid-frame revolvers, which were offered in a wide range of sizes. There were single-action "Suicide Specials" (sold as "The Terror", in ·32 calibre, "The Bull Dog", in ·38 calibre, and "The Swamp Angel", in ·41 calibre), and ·32 or ·38 calibre double-action and self-cocking "Automatic Police" revolvers (some of which had folding hammer-spurs), all of which continued to be available in years of concern here, and embodied minor features patented by Sullivan Forehand or the partners jointly, in years between 1871 and 1877. It is likely, too, that such obsolete models as the double-action "British Bull Dog" and single-action "Army" revolvers (of ·44 calibre) remained in wide use.

When they turned to the manufacture of hinged-frame self-ejecting revolvers, it would appear that the partners envisaged production of a quite novel arm, since Forehand took assignment of J. C. Howe's U.S. Patent No. 373893 (of 29th November, 1887) for an unusual self-cocking design, which embodied both grip- and latch-safety devices, together with M. Bye's U.S. Patent No. 375799 (of 3rd January, 1888) for a hammer-lock for concealed-hammer revolvers. In the event, however, such hinged-frame revolvers as were actually produced in that period when the partnership name was impressed upon them were quite conventional in appearance, although use was made of ejector improvements patented by Howe, on 7th December, 1886 (U.S. Patent No. 353948) and by Sullivan Forehand himself on 11th January, 1887 (U.S. Patent No. 355761), in such arms.

For obvious reasons, "Forehand Arms Co." revolvers differed little from their predecessors (early models are frequently found with "FW" monogrammed grips), and were made in ·32 or ·38 calibre hinged- and solid-frame versions, with self-cocking or double-action lock-mechanisms. The self-ejecting arms (in barrel lengths of 3¼ or 5 inches) acknowledged the Howe and Forehand patents of 1886 and 1887, earlier described, whilst solid-frame weapons were marked with the patent-date (2nd June, 1891) of H. M. Caldwell's U.S. Patent No. 453421, covering a pivoted arbor-latch used in them.

Understandably (since considerable good-will must have existed in it), the Hopkins & Allen Manufacturing Co. produced revolvers under the "Forehand" name after the Forehand Arms Co. had been absorbed, and "Forehand Model 1901" or "Forehand Double Action" revolvers, for example, will both be found with the Norwich maker's name and address impressed upon them. Indeed, an assignment of A. C. Wright's U.S. Patent No. 615467 (of 6th December, 1898), covering a revolver cylinder-bolt, is actually recorded to the Forehand Arms Co., and not to Hopkins & Allen, although there is no clear evidence that the patent was worked by the new-comers.

"FYRBERG" revolvers

Andrew Fyrberg was a prolific patentee of improvements to revolvers, either alone or in association with others, in those years between 1886 and 1910, but most of his ideas (one or two of which must have been extremely valuable to those controlling them) actually benefited others, rather than himself. Conveniently regarded, therefore, his career falls into two parts, namely, those years from 1886 to 1900 when his ideas were at the disposal of others, and a period between 1900 and 1910, when he endeavoured to work on his own account.

In the first period, Fyrberg resided at Worcester, Mass., and assignment of his patents (or his joint securing of them with such men as Reinhard T. Torkelson, or Iver Johnson) show his work benefiting either the Harrington & Richardson Arms Co. (as it then was), or Iver Johnson's Arms & Cycle Works, in respect of inventions later described in remarks upon those beneficiaries.

In the second period, Fyrberg either promoted or participated in a firm called Andrew Fyrberg & Co., at Hopkinton, Mass., which name appeared upon hinged-frame, self-ejecting pocket revolvers (in ·32 or ·38 calibres) similar in external appearance to those arms shown at Plate 4; such arms acknowledged the date (4th August, 1903) of Fyrberg's U.S. Patent No. 735490, covering a frame-latch and a cylinder-retainer used in them. The possibility that these revolvers were manufactured by others, for the Fyrberg Company, has to be considered.

In years between 1907 and 1910, Fyrberg secured U.S. patents covering "safety" lock-mechanisms for double-action revolvers, and also revolver cartridge-ejection systems not based upon the use of a hinged frame; weapons embodying the latter systems had cylinders either pivoted to the top of their solid frame, or turning diagonally to the bore-line, and this writer has not encountered specimen arms.

"HARRINGTON & RICHARDSON" revolvers

In 1874, Gilbert Henderson Harrington and William Augustus Richardson had begun to manufacture revolvers together, at Worcester, Mass., and had branched into the production of shot-guns about six years later. Around 1888, the Harrington & Richardson Arms Co. was incorporated, and in 1894 transfer to a larger plant at Park Avenue commenced, an operation barely concluded in 1897, when (within a few months of each other) the two founders died. The Company underwent a corporate reorganization around 1905, but continued its operations most successfully through the remainder of our period, as it has continued to do to this day.

Although some solid-frame double-action revolvers were produced by the original partnership, their handguns were predominantly cheap single-action "Suicide Specials", of a type later described; however, shortly before incorporation of their Company, the partners signalled a real transfer of their attention to more sophisticated arms, by jointly securing U.S. Patent No. 360686 (of 5th April, 1887) and by taking an assignment of H. M. Caldwell's U.S. Patent No. 370926 of 4th October in the same year. These patented ideas were not ambitious, with the first protection relating to a "safety hammer" for use with double-action revolver lock-mechanisms, and the later patent to a cylinder-retainer for hinged-frame arms, and (between 1888 and 1914) the Company subsequently took by assignment only about a dozen more patents in the revolver-field, but during that period the Harrington & Richardson Arms Co. quite rapidly achieved a most important position within the industry. Indeed, by 1907 (Sell records) more than three million modestly-priced revolvers had left the Worcester plant, and there were few major countries in the world where such arms were unobtainable.

Company production of double-action revolvers probably commenced with "The American Double Action Revolver", a solid-framed weapon quite similar in appearance to that shown as Plate 3 (lower), which could be had in ·38 (five-shot) or ·32 (six-shot) rim- or centre-fire versions, and with barrel lengths of 2½, 4½ or 6 inches. A variant was marketed as "The Safety Hammer Double Action" and lacked any hammer-spur to catch in the user's pocket; instead, the upper face and tip of what appeared to be a self-cocking hammer were roughened and concaved so that (first starting the hammer rearwards, under gentle trigger-pressure) the user could thumb-cock his pistol, if he wished to do so. This safety-hammer feature was the subject of U.S. Patent No.

360686 above-mentioned, and the line was so popular that (in conventional or safety-hammer versions) "Young America", "Bull Dog" and "Vest Pocket" models, in ·22 rim-fire and ·32 rim- or centre-fire calibres, were added to it.

At about the time that its founders died, the Company introduced a series of "Automatic Ejecting" revolvers, of that double-action hinged-frame self-ejecting type shown at Plate 3 (top), which could be had in six-shot ·32 centre-fire (16 oz.) or five-shot ·38 centre-fire (15 oz.) versions, with 3¼-, 4-, 5- or 6-in. barrels, and which acknowledged patent dates of 14th May, 1889, 6th August, 1889; 2nd April, 1895, and 7th April, 1896. The first of those dates in fact related to the date for registration of that trade-mark (a bullet-riddled target) on the grips of each weapon, but the other dates respectively referred to H. M. Caldwell's U.S. Patent No. 408457 (for an improved pawl, mounted on the lifter), to A. Fyrberg's U.S. Patent No. 536618 (for the ejector-mechanism), and to G. Harrington and W. A. Richardson's U.S. Patent No. 557814 (for a refinement to the ejector-mechanism); one version of this model had a folding blade beneath the barrel, and is quite rare today.

At about the same time, a line of similar "Premier" double-action hinged-frame revolvers (of the pattern shown at the top of Plate 3) in 7 × ·22 rim-fire (13 oz.) or 6 × ·32 centre-fire (12 oz.) models were also introduced, together with a short-barrelled "Bicycle" variant, and these also became very popular. The weapons acknowledged only one patent date, that of 8th October, 1895, which related to F. Smith's U.S. Patent No. 547525 covering an ejector-mechanism used in them.

Although "Automatic Ejecting", "Premier" and "Bicycle" models could all be had in a "Police" version (embodying that safety-hammer above-described), there was a substantial demand for "Hammerless" revolvers (i.e. concealed-hammer, self-cocking arms) of the kind shown at Plate 4, and the Company therefore met that demand with 13-oz. 7 × ·22 rim-fire or 5 × ·32 centre-fire and 6 × ·32 centre-fire (18 oz.) or 5 × ·38 centre-fire (17 oz.) revolvers with such shrouded hammers. The lighter models could be had with 2-, 3-, 4-, 5- or 6-in. barrels, and the heavier arms in barrel lengths of 3¼, 4, 5 or 6 inches, and although they normally acknowledged only the 1895 date of Smith's patent, it is believed that many embodied a frame-mounted firing-pin covered by W. A. Richardson's U.S. Patent No. 552699 of 7th January, 1896.

Later, too, loading-gates were an optional extra for the solid-framed series (under W. A. Richardson's U.S. Patent No. 565692 of 11th August, 1896), and "Model 1904" (Plate 3; lower), "Model 1905", and "Model 1906" revolvers, barely distinguishable from each other but, respectively, in 6 × ·32 or 5 × ·38 centre-fire (16 oz.), 5 × ·32 centre-fire (11 oz.), and 7 × ·22 rim-fire (10 oz.) versions, with barrel-lengths of 2½, 4½ or 6 inches were added to the solid-framed range. With a 6- or 10-in. barrel, and oversized grips, the Model 1906 frame did duty in "Trapper Model" and "Hunter Model" ·22 rim-fire kit-guns, for sale to campers, hunters and trappers.

As mentioned earlier, the Company secured (by assignment) only a dozen or so U.S. patents in our period, for improvements to revolvers, although it numbered such stalwarts as Homer Caldwell, Martin Bye, and Andrew Fyrberg, amongst its "stable" of patentees. Indeed, with those exceptions noted above, there is little evidence that the Company used (or even needed to use) these patented ideas to maintain its position as a leader in the production of inexpensive pocket arms. A lock-mechanism barely distinguishable from that shown at Figure 32 (but lacking, of course, the patented cylinder-bolt of J. CARTER) served in almost all Harrington & Richardson revolvers relevant to these pages, whatever patented refinements of detail might sometimes be added to it, from time to time.

"HOOD" revolvers

Freeman W. Hood (whilst based in Norwich, Conn., during the 1870s) had been associated with companies which were prolific manufacturers of cheap single-action solid-framed "Suicide Special" revolvers, of a type described below; his Norwich operations had apparently ceased in 1881 or 1882, but he is known to have secured a half-interest in A. F. Hood's U.S. Patent No. 304731 (of 9th September, 1884) covering a cylinder-bolt used in double-action revolvers made by the American Arms Co. (q.v.). Arthur F. Hood had himself assigned U.S. Patents Nos. 391612 and 391613 (of 23rd October, 1888) respectively to the American Arms Co. (q.v.) and the John P. Lovell Arms Co. (q.v.); the former may have used the protected cylinder-bolt, or made such revolvers for sale by the inventor.

"HOPKINS & ALLEN" revolvers

The Hopkins & Allen Manufacturing Co. had been formed at Norwich, Conn., in 1867 or 1868, and later occupied a factory at 132 Franklin Street during the whole period in point here; Samuel S. Hopkins, Charles W. Hopkins, and Charles H. Allen gave their names to that Company, but others were associated with the organizing of it, and this circumstance eventually had unfortunate effects upon the fortunes of most participants. Thus Charles A. Converse had sold his share in the Company to Merwin, Hulbert & Co. (a substantial firm of

New York sporting-goods jobbers, later mentioned) in 1874, and the Hopkins & Allen Manufacturing Co. had thereafter become over-dependent upon that type of sales outlet; not only had a large part of the Company's output been sold through these particular jobbers, but revolvers to a design patented by that customer (or others like it) had been produced in quantity, and no real attempt made, as a result, to establish sales contact and a Company reputation with the public at large.

As early as 1880, Merwin, Hulbert & Co. had (through the failure, for $100,000 of the Evans Repeating Rifle Co.) slipped into serious financial difficulty themselves and involved the Norwich firm in that affair, but because of the New Yorkers' share-holding in the Hopkins & Allen Manufacturing Co., this association and dependence was not terminated. In 1896, however, Hulbert Bros. & Co. (as the New York firm had become) failed completely, and could pay a dividend of only 10 cents in the dollar on the debt of $90,000 due to their Norwich associates.

Following that collapse, the Hopkins & Allen Arms Co. was incorporated, in 1898, and only then was an attempt made to sell the out-put of revolvers, shot-guns, rifles (introduced in 1888) and bicycles (a line belatedly attempted in the early 1890s) direct to the public, as well as to wholesalers. Regrettably, the Franklin Street factory was gutted by fire, on 4th February, 1900, and irreplaceable sales lost in the time spent on re-equipment of it, so that although a takeover of the Forehand Arms Co. (see above) ensured the existence of some products to sell, the Company never regained that eminence which it had un-doubtedly enjoyed prior to 1880. Charles W. Hopkins died in 1914, and although the Company did manufacture some rifles for the Belgian government, this was merely a prelude to its takeover (in 1915) by the Marlin Rockwell Corporation, of New Haven, Conn., and ultimate extinction.

In addition to single-action revolvers of good quality, the Hopkins & Allen Manufacturing Co. had commenced production of cheap single-action solid-frame "Suicide Specials" almost from the date of formation, and those arms (sold under such trade-names as "Blue Jacket" or "XL") remained a staple until just before the period in point here, when a decision was taken to introduce double-action revolvers in both solid- and hinged-frame models; indeed these single-action arms were still catalogued by mail-order specialists like Hartley, Graham & Co. (at $1 or $1.25 each) as late as 1900, and the successor Company itself only ceased to catalogue parts for them in 1902.

The point is not entirely clear, but it is probable that an "XL

Double Action" series were actually the first double-action Hopkins & Allen revolvers, being solid-frame pocket arms, available in ·22 rim-fire and ·32 or ·38 centre-fire calibres. These weapons had folding hammer-spurs (permitting an unhampered quick-draw from the pocket), and acknowledged patent dates, of 28th March, 1871, and 5th January, 1886, amongst their markings; the first date recognized Samuel S. Hopkins's U.S. Patent No. 113053, covering their arbor, and the second J. Boland's U.S. Patent No. 333725, for use of a coiled pawl-spring, carried by the trigger in that fashion shown at Figure 6. Oddly enough, those markings were not always extended to include reference either to Samuel S. Hopkins's U.S. Patent No. 311323 of 27th January, 1885 (for the folding hammer-spur) or, upon the occasions when such a refinement was fitted, to his U.S. Patent No. 297801 of 29th April, 1884, covering a combined arbor and spring-loaded ejector-rod. The case was similar for later solid-framed arms, like the "Universal Model Double Action" (which was sold under a model-name related to the calibre as, for example, the ·32 centre-fire "Double Action No. 6" revolver), the "XL Bulldog" double-action series (in ·22, ·32 or ·38 calibres) offered with conventional or folding hammer-spur, or the concealed-hammer self-cocking "Acme" model; this latter arm (manufacture of which ceased around 1903) was available in ·22 or ·32 versions, and had a safety-catch in the rear of the hammer-shroud.

In a hinged-frame self-ejecting series, Hopkins & Allen pistols were sold under the model-names "Automatic" (·32 or ·38 centre-fire) and "Safety Police" (·22 rim-fire, ·32 or ·38 centre-fire), which were of very sound quality for their price.

The "Automatic" revolvers were available in both concealed-hammer (self-cocking) and double-action versions, the latter with the folding hammer-spur, if desired, and all used the spiral pawl-spring embedded in the trigger, as claimed by U.S. Patent No. 333725 earlier-mentioned. The lock-mechanism of the "hammerless" version (which differed only in detail from that used for the double-action model) is shown at Figure 6, from which it will be seen that a hammer-rebound and safety-catch were fitted to such arms. The frame-mounted firing-pin was designed to the claims of C. W. Hopkins's and J. Boland's U.S. Patent No. 505569 (of 26th September, 1893), which also claimed the safety-device.

The Hopkins & Allen Arms Co. "Safety Police" revolver was possibly the best double-action self-ejecting pocket revolver of its day, and was matched in the ingenuity of its safety lock-mechanism only by an equivalent Iver Johnson design later described, for it was genuinely impossible to fire this weapon by any accidental blow to the hammer, or mishap in cocking.

Protected by John J. Murphy's U.S. Patent No. 829082 (of 21st August, 1906), which had been assigned to the Company, and the date of which was acknowledged upon these revolvers, the lock-mechanism was publicized as having a "Triple Action Safety". Essentially, the design consisted in using a separate frame-mounted firing-pin and ensuring that the hammer could only strike that firing-pin when the trigger had been fully pressed to the rear. In any other circumstance, the hammer rested upon or struck only the frame.

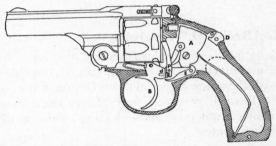

FIG. 6. *"Hammerless" lock-mechanism used in Hopkins & Allen "Automatic" revolvers.*

"A" is the hammer, "B" the trigger, and "D" the safety-device (shown rotated to block the hammer if the trigger is pulled), and "E" the hammer-rebound, which is forced up on its pivot by "B" (*via* the trigger-spring) to engage the rear of the hammer and force this back off the firing-pin. Note that the pawl-spring is a coiled component, nested in the trigger at "d", and bearing upon the lower end of the pawl "p".

Murphy accomplished this highly desirable feature by mounting the hammer rotatably upon a pivoting hammer-mount, which itself rocked eccentrically upon yet another axis fixed in the frame-wall. The effect of this eccentrically-hung hammer-mount was that mainspring-pressure on the hammer normally kept this hammer-mount on the upper position of its eccentric (with the hammer-nose resting on the frame above the firing-pin, as a result), and full trigger-pressure was needed to rotate that hammer-mount down into a lower position where, on falling, the hammer turned thereon to strike the firing-pin instead of the frame.

Over and above this safety-feature, "Safety Police" revolvers had an unusual barrel-latch, in which wear was automatically taken up by engaging (under spring-pressure) wedge-shaped dogs with suitable frame-cuts, to accomplish the latching.

In concluding these remarks upon Hopkins & Allen revolvers, the reader's attention is drawn to arms discussed under the names

"Forehand", "Imperial Arms Co.", "Merwin & Hulbert", and "Thames Arms Co.", which may all be considered as "Hopkins & Allen" pistols, in a general sense.

"HOWARD" revolvers

The name "Howard Arms Co." appeared upon ·32 and ·38 calibre centre-fire double-action hinged-frame self-ejecting pocket revolvers made in our period. Mathews ascribes these arms to the Meriden Fire-arms Co. (see below), but MacFarland notices "Howard Arms Co." as a brand-name used by the Crescent Firearms Co. above-mentioned, upon weapons supplied by it for sale by Messrs. Fred Biffar & Co., of Chicago, Ill.

"IMPERIAL ARMS CO." revolvers

A self-cocking hinged-frame self-ejecting revolver (with shrouded hammer) was manufactured by the Hopkins & Allen Arms Co. (q.v.), but marked with the name Imperial Arms Co. As in the parallel cases of "Eastern" or "Howard" revolvers, for example, the sales outlet for these "Imperial" revolvers was presumably a large hardware firm in another part of the United States.

"IVER JOHNSON" revolvers

A partnership formed at Worcester, Mass., in 1871, between Iver Johnson and Martin Bye, had begun to manufacture single-action solid-frame "Suicide Special" revolvers (see below) at 50 Central Street, in 1873. The business was successful, but Bye sold his interest to Johnson (in 1883), and became associated with Sullivan Forehand, and later with the Harrington & Richardson Arms Co. (q.v.), although his inventions were never seriously developed by either recipient of them.

Iver Johnson re-styled the Worcester business as "Iver Johnson's Arms & Cycle Works", but moved his plant to Fitchburg, Mass., in 1891, and died there on 3rd August, 1895. Until his death (Sell reports) all firearms were marketed exclusively through the John P. Lovell Arms Co., of Boston (q.v.), but this dependence was then wisely ended, and thereafter the firm sold to all comers. Iver Johnson's son, Frederick I. Johnson, was deeply involved in the business after his father's death, but the firm was apparently legally controlled (during most of those years in point here) by Mary Elizabeth Johnson, Iver Johnson's widow, acting first as Executrice and subsequently as Trustee of her husband's estate. By 1914, sales of "Iver Johnson" revolvers from the Fitchburg plant had become very large indeed (as they continue to be, even today), but the firm also sold excellent shot-guns in various qualities, together with

stock blanks, wrenches, gun- and rifle-swivels, bicycles, and (after 1910)
a line of cheaper revolvers which were marketed under the trade-name
U.S. Revolver Co.

Even prior to 1889, Iver Johnson marketed solid-framed double-
action revolvers (in all readily available rim-fire calibres up to ·44
Short) in addition to his single-action arms, the last of the "Suicide
Specials", a "Defender '89" model, not being dropped from his catalogues until 1895. Further, a simultaneous-ejecting double-action solid-
frame weapon (in which the cylinder swung out sideways, through 90°,
on a vertical pivot) had been briefly produced under the U.S. patents of
Andrew Hyde, but manufacture was not continued into those years
relevant here.

Until 1900, the principal solid-framed double-action Iver Johnson
revolvers were the "Boston Bull Dog" and "American Bull Dog" arms
(resembling that comparable Harrington & Richardson arm shown on
Plate 3, lower) offered in a choice of rim- or centre-fire calibres, and in
various barrel-lengths. These weapons had no patented features, but
were highly successful. In 1900, this series was lightly remodelled, and
thereafter offered as the "Double Action Model 1900", in 7 × ·22,
5 × ·32 rim-fire, or 5 × ·32, 6 × ·32 and 5 × ·38 centre-fire calibres,
with which a 2½-in. octagonal barrel was standard, but 4½- or 6-in.
barrels available at extra cost. A 7 × ·22 rim-fire "Target" version
with 6- or 9½-in. octagonal barrel was introduced at the same time, but
all wholesalers and retailers were forbidden to describe these two
models as "Iver Johnson" arms, since they lacked the patented safety-
device later described. A cheaper "U.S. Revolver Co." version of the
Model 1900 line was also marketed, with round barrel and unfluted
cylinder and, for a comparatively short time, the firm later offered
(possibly as a competitor to the Kolb revolvers, described below) a
solid-framed concealed-hammer self-cocking "Petite" revolver, in ·22
rim-fire calibre and with folding trigger; this arm embodied a hammer-
rebound protected by T. F. Bowker's U.S. Patent No. 898717 of 15th
September, 1908 (which had been assigned to Mary Elizabeth Johnson),
but was never very popular.

Undoubtedly, the best known and most successful Iver Johnson
revolvers in our period were hinged-frame self-ejecting models (in
double-action or self-cocking concealed-hammer versions shown on
Plate 4) which were, admittedly with certain detailed improvements,
marketed for over fifty years before it was thought necessary to vary
their basic lock-mechanism. Arms of that type shown on Plate 4 should
be clearly distinguished, however, from "Swift" or "U.S. Revolver
Co." weapons quite similar in external appearance, which were also

manufactured by this firm. The "Swift" weapon need not detain us here, since it is discussed in later remarks upon the John P. Lovell Arms Co. (*q.v.*), and "U.S. Revolver Co." arms are described at the conclusion of these remarks.

A self-cocking Iver Johnson "Safety Hammerless" revolver shown at the top of Plate 4 bears patent dates of 6th April, 1886, 15th February, 1887, 10th May, 1887, and 26th December, 1893; it also bears the notation "Pats. Pending", and may conveniently be discussed here (by reference to those improvements covered by the relevant patents), as personifying hinged-frame arms first introduced at about the time of Iver Johnson's death. It was with revolver No. 463344 of this model, that Leon F. Czolgosz shot President McKinley, at Buffalo, on the 6th September, 1901; his victim died eight days later.

The patent date of 6th April, 1886, referred to U.S. Patent No. 339301 (which was secured by Iver Johnson, R. T. Torkelson and A. Fyrberg, with the two latter patentees assigning their interest to Johnson), amongst the claims of which was one relating to the "safety trigger" used in these self-cocking models. This device is visible in Plate 4 (top), as a component hinged into the upper part of the trigger; it operated to bolt that component (by fouling the rear bow of the trigger-guard) unless the user first displaced it by applying deliberate finger-pressure to the trigger, in that fashion normal when firing.

The patent date of 15th February, 1887, related to J. C. Howe's U.S. Patent No. 357710, which claimed a method for retaining the cylinder upon its arbor (when the pistol was broken open for loading) by means of a male thread, cut around a small collar at the front of the cylinder, which had to be withdrawn through a female thread cut into the barrel-lug, before the cylinder could be removed.

The patent date of 10th May, 1887, referred to U.S. Patent No. 362631 (secured by Iver Johnson and A. Fyrberg, the latter assigning his interest to Johnson), which covered an ejector-mechanism used in these revolvers; save that the version illustrated has a coiled spring, instead of a flat spring proposed by these patentees, the ejector shown in Figure 7 is the subject of this protection.

The patent date of 26th December, 1893, related to O. F. Mossberg's and Iver Johnson's U.S. Patent No. 511620 (for which Mossberg assigned his interest to Johnson), which covered the rather complex barrel-latch visible in Plate 4; this latch was released by raising the small thumb-piece protruding on the left of the barrel-strap.

The legend "Patents Pending", stamped upon these revolvers almost certainly referred to then-pending U.S. patent applications which ultimately became H. M. Caldwell's U.S. Patent No. 561963 (dated

16th June, 1896) and A. Fyrberg's U.S. Patent No. 566393 (dated 25th August, 1896); the first of these was assigned to Mary Elizabeth Johnson, and the second, presumably whilst still an application, to Iver Johnson himself. The earlier protection related to that detachable hammer-shroud visible in Plate 4, and the later (which was by far the most important) to an ingenious safety lock-mechanism later described.

Early double-action hinged-frame Iver Johnson "Safety Hammer" revolvers marketed with the self-cocking arms (and of a pattern also shown on Plate 4) normally bore the dates of the above-mentioned U.S. Patents Nos. 339301, 357710, and (once it had been granted) of 566393. However, reference to the date of the ejector patent (No. 362631) was sometimes omitted from these markings, and the date 13th March, 1888, will be encountered on all weapons fitted with the simple barrel-latch visible in Plate 4 (lower), which was covered by Iver Johnson's and A. Fyrberg's U.S. Patent No. 379225 (assigned to Iver Johnson), prior to introduction of the more complex latch covered by the Mossberg/Johnson patent of 1893 earlier described. As with self-cocking arms, such markings concluded with the notation "Pats. Pending".

Figure 7 shows the details of Iver Johnson double-action revolvers developed by the close of our period, but the reader's attention is here specifically drawn to a safety feature embodied from the outset in that mechanism, which was the subject of Andrew Fyrberg's U.S. Patent No. 566393, which was vigorously promoted by the description of pistols embodying it as "Hammer the Hammer" revolvers (because no accidental blow upon the hammer could possibly fire weapons embodying it), and which met a richly-deserved success for many years after 1914.

In Figure 7 "v" is the hammer, "w" the trigger, "x" the lifter, "y" the pawl, and "z" the sear; it will be noticed that a separate frame-mounted firing-pin "a" is used, which the hammer cannot (in normal circumstance) actually strike. Basically, the lock-mechanism is to that French design (described in Chapter II, and illustrated at Figure 15), so that the hammer "v" is raised in self-cocking fire by pressure on "w" raising the lifter "x", which is in turn engaged with a tooth on the breast of "v". Eventually, the hammer escapes from "x" (and can fall because "w" has pressed back the sear "z"), when the tip of "x" is aligned with the firing-pin and transmits the hammer-blow to it. When the trigger "w" is released, the trigger-spring forces it forward, drags the lifter "x" downwards to re-engage the tooth on the hammer, and so frees the firing-pin to retract into the frame, under pressure from a coiled spring. The sequence of single-action fire may be deduced from Figure 7, and presence of the sear "z".

The lock-mechanism shown in Figure 7 actually embodies certain design-features available only at the close of our period, but serves well enough to demonstrate ideas introduced by earlier models. As study of the cylinder locking-notches in Plate 4 will show, for example, the first arms had no separate cylinder-bolt, indexing chamber and bore instead by means of a lump on top of the trigger, which engaged the locking-notches only when the trigger had been pulled sufficiently far to the

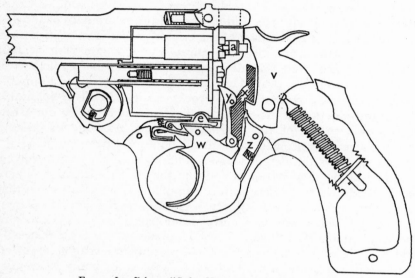

FIG. 7. *Iver Johnson "Safety Hammer" double-action revolver.*

rear. In Figure 7 is shown that positive cylinder-bolt "e" covered by the claims of O. W. Ringquist's U.S. Patent No. 968691 (of 30th August, 1910), which was assigned to Mary Elizabeth Johnson, who had earlier secured rights to R. T. Torkelson's U.S. Patent No. 903919 (of 17th November, 1908) for the self-retracting and readily removable firing-pin "a" shown in Figure 7. One other distinctive feature of later lock-mechanisms was the use (in place of flat springs) of draw-tempered piano-wire springs, which were introduced under Frederick I. Johnson's U.S. Patent No. 1004172 of 26th September, 1911. It will be observed from Figure 7, that tension of the coiled mainspring may be adjusted by placing the adjusting-bar (against which it works) in a series of mounting-notches in the frame, and it would be interesting to know if the patentee was aware of Br. Pat 10072/1905, by W. J. WHITING (*q.v.*), when this U.S. protection was sought.

Although their hammer rested upon the frame below the firing pin, and not as shown in Figure 7, the lock-mechanism of concealed-hammer self-cocking "Safety Hammerless" revolvers also operated as above described, and later arms embodied the same improvements as double-action models. Some improvements to the "Hammerless" line were ones of omission rather than addition, with the separate hammer-shroud (covered by U.S. Patent No. 561963) being discarded in favour of a one-piece frame, and the complex side-lever barrel-latch (covered by U.S. Patent No. 511620) being dropped in favour of the type of latch shown upon the double-action arm in Plate 4.

By 1914, these improved Iver Johnson hinged-frame revolvers had discarded the use of patent dates upon their barrels, and were marketed in six basic models, namely, the "Safety Hammer Automatic", the "Special 32 Safety Hammer Automatic", the "Safety Hammerless Automatic", the "Special 32 Safety Hammerless Automatic", and the "Safety Cycle Automatic" (hammer and hammerless) pistols; "Special 32" arms were six-chambered 19 oz. revolvers, with sufficient extra metal in them to handle ·32 S & W Long or Colt New Police cartridges, whilst the other models could be had in 7 × ·22 rim-fire and 5 × ·32 or 5 × ·38 centre-fire versions, with the "Cycle" arms available only with 2–in. barrels.

Hinged-frame "U.S. Revolver Co." pistols have only been observed by this writer in a concealed-hammer self-cocking model, available in 5 × ·32 or 5 × ·38 centre-fire calibres with 3- or 3¼-in. barrel respectively; introduced around 1910, these arms had the one-piece hammer-shroud of later Iver Johnson "Safety Hammerless" revolvers, but lacked Fyrberg's "Hammer The Hammer" safety lock-mechanism, and used flat springs instead of the coiled variety. An earlier Iver Johnson venture of this kind is noticed in later remarks upon "U.S. Arms Co." revolvers.

"KOLB" revolvers

Following those events recorded in earlier remarks upon the Foehl & Weeks Fire Arms Manufacturing Co., Charles Foehl became associated with Henry M. Kolb, of Philadelphia, and was joint-applicant with the latter (between 1902 and 1907) for U.S. Patents Nos. 702735; 818177; 826788; and 847011; the patents related to revolvers of a pattern (like Colt arms earlier described) in which the cylinder was swung outwards from the solid frame, on a crane, for loading or ejection of cartridges.

There is no evidence that Foehl and Kolb achieved production for such arms, but Kolb was also involved in the manufacture of another type of revolver, which achieved a limited popularity prior to 1914, and it may be that Foehl (until his death, in 1912) was a party to this production. At any rate, Foehl's last U.S. revolver patent, No. 1019446 of 5th March, 1912, related to an automatic cartridge-ejector for solid-frame revolvers (similar in effect to the devices of H. A. SILVER and W. FLETCHER, or F. PRAUNEGGER and L. P. SCHMIDT; *q.v.*), which was shown in the Specification as fitted to a revolver of that type next described.

The "Kolb" solid-frame arms were self-cocking, concealed-hammer pocket weapons (similar in external appearance to an Iver Johnson "Petite" revolver, earlier mentioned), which had 1½-in. barrels, paired cylinder locking-notches, folding triggers, and could be purchased either as the 6 × ·22 rim-fire pistol shown at Plate 8 (lower), or as a 5 × ·32 calibre centre-fire model, which is now quite rare.

On 5th April, 1910, Kolb took out two U.S. patents (Nos. 954190 and 954191), covering firing-pin and arbor-retainer improvements to such arms, which protection was recognized in a marking "Pats. Apr. 5. 10. Model 1910" found upon such weapons. U.S. patents of 24th May, 1910, and 13th June, 1911 (numbered 959229 and 995156), were also granted to Kolb for design-features applicable to hinged-frame arms (similar in appearance to his solid-frame models), but although some authorities recognize such pistols as actually made by Kolb, this writer has not been fortunate enough to encounter specimens for description here.

"LOVELL" revolvers

As mentioned in remarks upon "Iver Johnson" revolvers, the Boston-based John P. Lovell Arms Co. were exclusive distributors of such arms until around 1895, and during the later years of this relationship manufacture of a "Swift" model revolver was also commenced by the Iver Johnson Arms & Cycle Works, to a design dictated by that Boston company. After exclusive access to "Iver Johnson" arms had ended, production of the "Swift" model at Fitchburg, for the Lovell company, apparently continued, and the weapon is therefore mentioned here as a specific "Lovell" arm, rather than as simply another "Iver Johnson" revolver.

The John P. Lovell Arms Co. took an assignment of Arthur Freeman Hood's U.S. Patent No. 391613 (dated 23rd October, 1888), relating to an improved ejector-lever apparently used in the hinged-frame "Swift" model, but the name itself seems to have come from Captain Eben Swift, of the Fifth U.S. Cavalry, to whom Farrow attributed the design jointly with a "Mr. Lovell".

This writer has not secured a specimen arm for illustration here, but A. C. Gould (in the 1894 edition of his work) described a ·38 calibre double-action "Lovell (Swift)" revolver as having been provided for test by him, with the comment that it appeared to be a well-made arm, but that ". . . it was discovered to be too large in the bore to shoot any of the ammunition provided, and was withdrawn". It is not clear from Gould's use of that term whether he used the description "double action" in the American (i.e. self-cocking) or British manner, and it is therefore uncertain if the "Swift" weapon had a "Hammer" or a "Hammerless" action.

"MALTBY HENLEY" revolvers

Maltby, Henley & Co. was a firm of New York sporting-goods jobbers, which was earlier mentioned in relation to solid-frame self-cocking "Columbian" revolvers, made for the firm under U.S. Patents Nos. 376922 and 413975 secured by John T. Smith. In addition to those weapons, a very similar type of pistol was marketed under the firm name, in ·32 or ·38 centre-fire calibres, but acknowledged the date of yet another Smith lock-mechanism patent (in place of that relating to U.S. Patent No. 376922), namely, 17th March, 1885, the date of U.S. Patent No. 314067.

Arms bearing these revised patent dates were sold by this firm as both the "Parker Safety Hammerless" revolver in ·32 centre-fire calibre, and as the "Maltby, Henley & Co. Hammerless Model 1892", in either calibre; both versions were five-shot arms, but the heavier "Model 1892" arm had a detachable side-plate which the lighter "Model 1892" pistol had not. An example of the latter, shown at Plate 6, ended the life of Mrs. Lucy Packham (at Brighton, on 1st March, 1900), in circumstances leading to a verdict of manslaughter against its user.

In years prior to 1889, the predecessor firm of Maltby, Curtis & Co. (at 34 Reade St., New York) had organized a revolver manufacturing company at Norwich, Conn., called the Norwich Falls Pistol Co., which had produced revolvers, roller-skates, and tools, under the U.S. patents of William H. Bliss; manufacture had been suspended in 1887 or 1888, but the possibility is mooted that stocks of such arms were inherited by Maltby, Henley & Co. (for sale in the early years of our period), and that manufacturing plant from the assets of the Norwich Falls Pistol Co. could have been available for use in production of the "Columbian" and associated model revolvers, if John T. Smith's resources at Rockfall were, for any reason, inadequate.

"MARLIN" revolvers

John Mahlon Marlin had been a self-employed out-worker to the New Haven, Conn., gun-trade during the early 1860s, but had begun to

E

manufacture cheap single-shot derringers and single-action rim-fire revolvers (of which "XXX Standard", copies of Smith & Wesson arms became the best-known) for sale under his own name, around 1872. Shortly afterwards, he had begun to produce single-shot Ballard rifles at New Haven, and in 1881 the Marlin Firearms Co. was incorporated, and the first of a most delightful line of lever-action tube-magazine rifles was introduced. During 1898, the first Marlin shot-gun appeared, and by its founder's death (on 1st July, 1901), the Company was a well-established firearms manufacturer, with product-lines outside the scope of these pages. There had been, however, two earlier periods of activity by the Company which are in point here, involving manufacture of a rifle with rotary magazine (noticed in remarks upon A. W. SAVAGE; q.v.), and an unsuccessful attempt to vary the Company's revolver-making activities.

Thus, between 1884 and 1889, Marlin had secured seven U.S. patents for cylinder-bolt, ejector, and barrel-latch features applicable to hinged-frame self-ejecting revolvers, and the Company had taken assignments of David H. Rice's U.S. Patents Nos. 366794 (of 19th July, 1887) and 385009 (of 26th June, 1888) for cylinder-retainer and ejector improvements to such arms. In 1886, production of single-action revolvers was ended, preparatory to introducing a double-action line under this protection, and five-shot hinged-frame self-ejecting revolvers of this type, embodying a lock-mechanism closely modelled upon that shown in Figure 9, were then briefly manufactured in ·32 or ·38 centre-fire calibres, and sold from 1887 until about 1900.

For reasons not wholly clear (when the uniform excellence of other Marlin arms is considered), this double-action revolver venture was never successful and, in an 1894 edition of his book, A. C. Gould actually criticized specimen double-action Marlin revolvers (submitted to him for test) as positively dangerous to handle through careless manufacture. If quality-control in that particular section of the factory eluded Marlin executives, the cesser of such production was a wise decision.

"MERIDEN" revolvers

Both double-action and concealed-hammer self-ejecting revolvers (of small calibre) were sold under the name Meriden Fire Arms Co. during our period, and Frank de Haas has described this manufacturer as owned by Messrs. Sears, Roebuck & Co., a large American mail-order firm. In addition, Mathews credits the Meriden firm with manufacturing "Eastern Arms Co.", "Empire State", "Federal Arms", "Fyrberg", and "Howard Arms" revolvers although, as earlier indicated, at least two of these identifications may be questioned.

A surviving catalogue, of 1914, however, simply refers to the Meriden Firearms Company (of Meriden, Conn.) on both the cover and on the arms illustrated in it, and mentions only the Meriden Firearms Mfg. Co. at its page headings. Further, this text lays no claim whatsoever to use of patented features in those lines of inexpensive firearms shown upon its pages, which comprise shot-guns (hammer, hammerless and slide-action), rifles (slide-action or single-shot, in ·22 rim-fire calibre), and ·32 or ·38 centre-fire revolvers similar in appearance to those Iver Johnson arms shown at Plate 4. Over-stamped upon the catalogue in question is the name of H. A. Astlett & Co., of 113–117 Pearl St., N.Y., presumably as a distributor of the Meriden company's products.

Since these arms are clearly illustrated in the Meriden catalogue, it is possible to point out that most of the long-arms closely resemble lines also offered at that time by the J. Stevens Arms & Tool Co., of Chicopee Falls, Mass., and the suggestion is therefore offered that some "Meriden" arms, at least, were actually made up from components supplied by the Stevens company. As to "Meriden" revolvers, it is true that the Stevens company is not now remembered as a manufacturer of such arms, but the reader's attention is drawn to later remarks upon patents secured by it, and the suggestion again made that components could have been supplied from Chicopee Falls, for working and assembly at Meriden into some or all of the pistols shown in the 1914 catalogue.

Whilst it is true to state that the catalogue text contains nothing in support of these proposals, it can also be said that it is equally silent upon those connections suggested by de Haas and Mathews, for ownership by Sears, Roebuck & Co. and access to the patents of Andrew Fyrberg, respectively.

"MERWIN HULBERT" revolvers

Enough has been said (in remarks upon "Hopkins & Allen" revolvers) to avoid need for description here of the activities of Merwin Hulbert & Co., or the successor Hulbert Bros. & Co., during our period.

As to the revolvers sold by this New York firm, three basic types should be noted, as single-action "Suicide Specials", and two types of double-action revolver; the first were unremarkable solid-framed rim-fire weapons (sold under the names "Ranger", "Dictator", "Czar" or "Blue Jacket"), manufactured by the Hopkins & Allen Mfg. Co. until 1898, and part of the second category consisted of solid-frame "XL" or hinged-frame double-action self-ejecting "Automatic" Hopkins & Allen revolvers sold (with and without folding hammer-spurs) as standard

Hopkins & Allen lines. The quality of workmanship in these arms was criticized by A. C. Gould, in the 1894 edition of his book.

In the third category, however, were self-extracting (rather than self-ejecting) arms of a type almost unique in America, which the Hopkins & Allen Mfg. Co. made exclusively for the New York house (under patents controlled by the latter), where the barrel was not hinged to the frame for operation of an ejector, but had to be unlatched, turned over on its arbor to free cuts in the top-strap from engagement with an inverted "L"-shaped joint on top of the standing-breech, and then pulled straight forward. This straight-pull movement operated in a manner also used by another American inventor (O. JONES, *q.v.*), and withdrew the cartridge-cases from their chambers, as the cylinder moved forward in train with the barrel, by a star-shaped extractor fixed to the standing-breech.

First introduced by J. Merwin, M. H. Hulbert and W. A. Hulbert around 1877, in substantial single-action "Army" revolvers of heavy calibre, this type of frame-construction and cartridge-extraction was (during our period) normally applied to double-action pocket models, often fitted with the S. S. Hopkins folding hammer-spur, in 5 × ·38 or 7 × ·32 centre-fire calibres; however, ·44 centre-fire calibre revolvers (in both single- and double-action versions) could also be purchased by those needing such substantial 36/41 oz. pistols, and a spur-trigger single-action pocket revolver was available to conservative buyers. Although not always acknowledging the source of their manufacture, such double-action weapons were of adequate quality, and some versions were sold with interchangeable $3\frac{1}{2}$- and $5\frac{1}{2}$-in. barrels.

Amongst earlier patents, the double-action "M. H. & Co. Automatic Ejecting Revolvers" (as they were marketed) acknowledged patent dates of 14th March, 1882, and 9th January, 1883, respectively relating to U.S. Patents Nos. 254798 and 270204 held by George W. Cilley, of Norwich, Conn. These were patents relating to improved double-action lock-mechanisms suitable for such arms, and Cilley held three other U.S. lock-mechanism patents (Nos. 263684; 336894, and 339149) in which the Specification drawings showed that frame-configuration peculiar to Merwin Hulbert Arms. It is not known if revolvers were produced under those patents, however.

"MINNEAPOLIS F. A. CO." revolvers

See Appendix II—FINNEGAN, P. H.

"NEW YORK ARMS CO." revolvers

See "Columbian" revolvers.

"PARKER" revolvers

See "Maltby Henley" revolvers.

"REID" revolvers

See Appendix II—REID, G. B.

"REMINGTON" revolvers

Although a noted revolver manufacturer in the years 1857–88, the Remington Arms Co. had drifted into financial difficulties by the opening of our period, and a reorganization of that Company (by a majority shareholder) led to the discarding of this type of firearm, as a serious part of its production-line, after 1889.

It is probable that single-action "New Line" rim-fire and "Model 1875" ·44 or ·45 calibre centre-fire Remington revolvers continued to be sold for some years, whilst stocks lasted, but this Company's small efforts in the hand-gun field were, after 1889, concentrated upon the production of double-barrelled derringers or single-barrelled rolling-block target pistols, almost to the exclusion of revolvers. A lightened version of the single-action "Model 1875" revolver was produced and sold (as the "Model 1890" arm) from 1891–94, but the Karrs estimate total production at only about 2,000 pistols, and so Remington's contribution to these pages must therefore be dismissed as negligible.

"RUPERTUS" revolvers

See Appendix II—RUPERTUS, J.

"RYAN" revolvers

Thomas E. Ryan died in 1891, after manufacturing cheap single action "Suicide Special" revolvers, of a type described below, for nearly a quarter of a century. He was based at Norwich, Conn. (where Wm. Paul Smith credits him with forty-five employees and a monthly output of 30,000 revolvers, in 1887), but marketed arms through his Ryan Pistol Manufacturing Co., in New York.

It is possible, but not established, that he began to manufacture double-action revolvers, between 1885 and the time of his death.

"SCOTT" revolvers

A brass-framed revolver similar to the "Columbian New Safety Hammerless" weapon was sold, in ·38 centre-fire calibre, with the marking "J. N. Scott Safety Hammerless". This pistol acknowledged the dates of those John T. Smith U.S. Patents Nos. 376922 and 413975 earlier mentioned in remarks upon the "Columbian" arms, and it was presumably made at the same plant, but possibly to the order of another principal.

"SMITH" revolvers

In studying arms relevant to the period 1889–1914, the reader may encounter two obsolete revolvers with the name "Smith" upon them, which strictly date from preceding years, but may still have been marketed into the early 1890s.

Otis A. Smith (at Rockfall, Conn.) had produced a series of solid-framed single-action rim-fire revolvers, which should be distinguished from "Suicide Special" arms later mentioned, by their superior workmanship and use of a quick-dismount device for their cylinders, covered by his U.S. Patent No. 137968 of 15th April, 1873. The patentee manufactured such arms in ·22, ·32, ·38 or ·41 rim-fire calibres, until 1890 or 1891.

Moreover, on 20th December, 1881, Otis A. Smith and John T. Smith had jointly secured U.S. Patent No. 251306, and produced a five-shot ·32 calibre single-action hinged-frame "Model 1883 Shell Ejector" revolver under that protection. This arm was still available during our period (resembling the Smith & Wesson revolver shown as a catalogue illustration on Plate 38, save that it had a stud-trigger), and was later joined by other John T. Smith designs earlier described in remarks upon "Columbian" and "Maltby, Henley & Co." revolvers.

"SMITH & WESSON" revolvers

In view of later notes upon the firm (under D. B. WESSON, q.v.), and of excellent specialist works detailing the course by which such arms evolved, remarks here will be limited to describing those "Smith & Wesson" revolvers available during our period. Thus the Springfield, Mass., factory of this firm produced both hinged-frame self-ejecting and solid-frame swing-out cylinder arms between 1889 and 1914, the latter having manually-operated ejectors of a type earlier described in remarks upon similar "Colt" revolvers.

The hinged-frame Smith & Wesson arms covered by our period were:

The Safety Hammerless, or "New Departure" models; see Plate 36.
The Double Action models; see Plate 5.
The Single Action pocket models; see Plate 38.
The No. 3 New Model or Target models;

whilst the solid-frame arms of that period, with swing-out cylinders, were:

The Model (1) ·32 Calibre Hand Ejector; see Plate 5
The Model ·38 Hand Ejector Military & Police
The Model ·32–20 Hand Ejector Winchester
The Model (M) ·22 Calibre Hand Ejector; see Plate 36
The Model ·44 Hand Ejector (New Century); see Plate 38

Dealing first with hinged-frame arms, the Safety Hammerless design had been introduced as a five-shot ·38 centre-fire weapon (with barrel

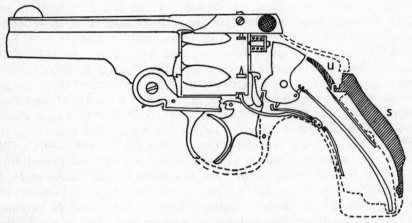

FIG. 8. *Smith & Wesson "Safety Hammerless" self-cocking revolver lock-mechanism.*
"s" is the safety-lever, and "u" the safety-latch; both are hinged at the lower end, and a flat spring normally holds "u" in such a position as to block the hammer from any rearward movement. When the butt is gripped, the upper end of "s" is depressed and, in turn, tilts "u" upwards to clear the hammer for cocking by the trigger. The self-cocking lock-mechanism is conventional, using the mainspring stirrup to rebound the hammer, and having an ordinary lifter mounted upon a common pivot with the pawl. The cylinder-bolt is unusually long, however, and is operated by a projection beneath the hammer, which strikes a split-spring component as the travel of the hammer occurs, in cocking.

lengths of 3¼, 4 or 5 inches) in 1887, and followed next year by a smaller ·32 calibre version; these were self-cocking concealed-hammer revolvers (with that lock-mechanism shown in Figure 8), using hinged-frame cartridge-ejection, and with a press-in safety-lever in the butt-strap, which blocked all movement of the hammer unless that lever was first depressed, by gripping the butt in a fashion normal for firing.

Publicized as the "New Departure", this design was popular until many years after 1914, and hundreds of thousands of such arms (in the two different models) were manufactured during our period alone.

Indeed, the ·38 calibre arm was so highly regarded that nearly one hundred pistols were extensively and seriously field-tested by a U.S. Ordnance Board, before that Board eventually secured adoption, by the U.S. Army, of a Colt "New Army" double-action revolver (Model of 1892) earlier described.

The ·38 calibre Safety Hammerless revolvers made between July 1888 and August 1890 embodied features covered by five U.S. patents, respectively secured on 20th February, 1877; 18th December, 1877; 11th May, 1880; 4th August, 1885; and 11th October, 1887. The patents in point were Nos. 187689 and 198228 (D. B. WESSON and J. H. Bullard) covering the cylinder-retainer and hammer-rebound, 227481 (J. H. Bullard) covering the ejector-cam, 323839 (D. B. & J. H. WESSON) covering the grip-safety, and 371532 (D. B. WESSON) covering the rather complex press-button barrel-latch. In 1890, this line was extended to include a version with 6-in. barrel, and three design-improvements were also embodied, in respect of a hardened steel abutment shoulder on the barrel-latch post (D. B. WESSON's U.S. Patent No. 377878 of 14th February, 1888), hardened steel inserts on the wearing side of each cylinder locking-notch (D. B. WESSON's U.S. Patent No. 401087 of 9th April, 1889), and a simplified press-button barrel-latch; this latter feature was described in the claims of D. B. WESSON's U.S. Patent No. 429397, of 3rd June, 1890, as then already in use, although the design feature claimed in the patent (a hammer-block working off the barrel-latch) was never embodied in production arms. Finally, late in 1898, this model was again modified, by replacing the 1890 press-button barrel-latch with a lift-up design, having knurled side-surfaces for gripping between thumb and forefinger.

The ·32 calibre Safety Hammerless model (see Plate 36) was first offered with a 3- or 3½-in. barrel, but the longer barrel was discarded around 1900, shortly after a "Bicycle" model, with 2-in. barrel, had been introduced. These smaller weapons are regarded by most authorities as having undergone only one design change during our period when (in September, 1900) a press-button barrel-latch was replaced with the lift-up device adopted in 1898 for ·38 calibre arms. On this contention, however, it is worth recording that pre-1900 Smith & Wesson catalogue illustrations of the ·32 calibre pistol show a press-button barrel-latch of the type introduced in 1890 for the ·38 calibre arms, rather than the earlier press-button design covered by D. B. WESSON's U.S. Patent No. 371532 (above-mentioned) which would presumably be the design feature to be reckoned upon if the ·32 calibre model in fact underwent only this 1900 design change.

In turning to Smith & Wesson Double Action revolvers of a type shown at Plate 5, it should be emphasized that these hinged-frame self-ejecting models were quite elderly at the opening of our period, ·32 and ·38 centre-fire calibre versions having been introduced in 1880, and a ·44 centre-fire calibre pistol in the following year; however, a third version of the smallest pistol appeared in 1889, the ·38 calibre weapon underwent design-changes in 1894 and 1909, and the heaviest models were only discontinued in 1910 and 1913, so that such arms may be legitimately noticed here.

A lock-mechanism shown in Figure 9 was used in Smith & Wesson Double Action models of our period (other than a "Perfected" model, later noticed), and may be seen as little more than a cleverly modified version of that European service revolver mechanism discussed in Chapter II, and illustrated in Figure 15; the two smaller versions of this mechanism used that type of cylinder-bolt shown in Figure 9 (which had been patented by J. H. Wesson as U.S. Patent No. 251750 of 3rd January, 1882, and as Br. Pat. No. 5569 of 20th December, 1881), but the ·44 calibre arms clung to a more complex rocking cylinder-bolt requiring two rows of locking-notches around the cylinder, which was protected by D. B. WESSON's U.S. Patents Nos. 222168, of 2nd December, 1879, and 228009, of 25th May, 1880. The ejector mechanism in all three models was that covered by the Bullard patent of 1880 noted in remarks upon Safety Hammerless revolvers, whilst cylinder-retaining and lift-up barrel-latch devices were to the D. B. WESSON/J. H. Bullard patents of 1877 also noticed with "New Departure" arms.

A most noticeable change in the two smaller models, during our period, involved elimination from the trigger-guard of a reverse curve (at the rear) visible in Plate 5, and this refinement occurred in 1889 for the ·32 calibre pistol, but was not introduced for ·38 calibre arms until 1894 and was never applied to the arms of heaviest calibre. All three versions, however, eventually embodied both the steel-shimmed cylinder locking-notches covered by D. B. WESSON's U.S. Patent No. 401087 (mentioned in relation to Safety Hammerless weapons), and hardened steel bearing-bosses fitted into the frame-walls and side-plates, to reduce friction incurred by rubbing of hammer and trigger surfaces against the sides of a pistol.

Between 1889 and 1914, the five-shot ·32 calibre revolvers could be bought with barrel lengths of 3, 3½, or 6 inches, and ·38 calibre arms (in "Double Action" or the late "Perfected" models) with a barrel 3¼, 4, 5 or 6 inches long; the ·44 calibre pistols (sold by "New Model Army", "New Model Navy", "Double Action", "Wesson Favourite", and "Frontier" names) were offered in ·44 Russian or ·44–40 WCF chamberings, with barrel lengths of 4, 5, 6 or 6½ inches. "Perfected" ·38 calibre revolvers were introduced in 1909, apparently in an attempt to prolong demand for hinged-frame arms, and differed markedly from any predecessors, since their lock-mechanism was that later described in remarks upon "Hand Ejector, Model 1" pistols, and not the mechanism shown at Figure 9. Further, the barrel was double-latched (on a principle covered by D. B. WESSON's U.S. Patent No. 684150 of 8th October, 1901), so that the user raised a lift-up barrel latch, of the type visible in Plate 5, only after he had pressed forward a sliding thumb-piece, on the left of the frame, to unseat a longitudinal bolt of a kind indicated in remarks upon D. B. WESSON's Br. Pat. 6184/1894. "Wesson Favourite" ·44 calibre revolvers differed from other hinged-frame arms in that calibre, only by the ingenuity expended upon machining all surplus metal from them.

Standard "Double Action" revolvers of our period were generously stamped with patent dates, some referring to those few lately-patented features described above and others to past glories of design dating as far back as 1865, but the "Perfected" model was, for obvious reasons, an exception in this respect. Patent dates in this case were 4th August, 1896 (D. B. & J. H. WESSON'S U.S. Patent No. 565245, covering hardened steel bushings for the sliding cylinder-latch, and a "hand lever" which operated the pawl), 8th October 1901 (D. B. WESSON's U.S. Patent No. 684150 above-mentioned), 6th February, 1906 (J. H. Wesson's U.S. Patent No. 811807, covering the sliding hammer-rebound later described in remarks upon post-1905 "Hand Ejector" revolvers), and 14th September, 1909 (C. M. Stone's U.S. Patent No. 933797, covering means later described for increasing the arc of the hammer-throw during self-cocking fire), instead of the other markings earlier mentioned.

As to Smith & Wesson single-action hinged-frame revolvers of the period, and whether as pocket arms or as "No. 3 New Model" and Target pistols, it must again be said that these were designs of an earlier period; their beautiful workmanship and mechanical excellence ensured sufficient demand for production to continue, but their undoubted contribution to any state of the art had been made many years before 1889.

During our period, there were actually three single-action hinged-frame self-ejecting centre-fire Smith & Wesson revolvers marketed; the $5 \times$ ·32 calibre Model No. $1\frac{1}{2}$ had a bird's head butt and spur-trigger (with available barrel lengths of 3, $3\frac{1}{2}$ or 6 inches), whilst the $5 \times$ ·38 calibre Model 1880 had a flat-bottomed butt and spur-trigger, with barrel lengths of $3\frac{1}{4}$, 4, 5 or 6 inches available. Manufacture of both these models had ceased by 1892 (a weapon shown at Plate 38 having rendered them superfluous, on its introduction in 1891), although the Model 1880 revolver continued to be catalogued for some years after that date. As can be seen from Plate 38, the ·38 Single Action Model 1891 revolvers had a trigger-guard in place of an earlier spur-trigger but the weapon embodied no mechanical improvement over its predecessors, and was chiefly remarkable for the fact that, as may be seen in Plate 38, a single-shot target barrel (of 6, 8 or 10 inches in length) could be used interchangeably with the centre-fire barrel and cylinder and was available in ·22 rim-fire and ·32 or ·38 centre-fire calibres. In the event, this weapon proved a better target pistol than pocket arm, and although manufacture of the Model 1891 revolver was not discontinued until 1911, a single-shot target pistol incapable of conversion to a revolver was introduced in 1905, and (with further modifications in 1909) continued in most successful use for decades after 1914.

As to the big "No. 3 New Model" and Target single-action hinged-frame revolvers, in our period, the Smith & Wesson catalogues of those times offered such arms in ·32–44, ·38–44, ·38 WCF, ·44 Russian, ·44 WCF, and ·450 Eley calibres, with barrel lengths of from 4 to 6½ inches available for all calibres (but with an 8-in. barrel also manufactured for the superbly accurate ·44 Russian cartridge), and with special sights fitted to target arms. All barrels were impressed with patent dates, but (as with most "Double Action" revolvers) these related to protection secured in the 1860s and 1870s, when Smith & Wesson had led American arms manufacturers into the era of hinged-frame self-ejecting weapons.

These models had, in years relevant here, little to commend them save their superb workmanship and accuracy, for they had been early rendered obsolete by double-action swing-out cylinder arms next to be described. Thus manufacture of the big Single Action models ceased around 1910, although dealers continued to catalogue them for some years afterwards.

In turning now to consider solid-frame "Smith & Wesson" revolvers with swing-out cylinders and manually-operated ejectors, it should be noticed that (for good and sufficient reasons) the Springfield firm here proceeded at a rather more leisurely pace than had been adopted by its principal competitor. Thus, it will be recalled, the COLT'S PATENT FIRE ARMS MANUFACTURING CO. (INC.) (q.v.) introduced a "New Navy" revolver of this type as early as 1889, but that Company's hand-gun line then comprised obsolete solid-frame rod-ejecting pistols only, and some sort of fillip to the range must have been seen as an urgent need; at Springfield, on the other hand, excellent hinged-frame self-ejecting revolvers had long been a "Smith & Wesson" staple, so that

little real need for the adoption of a competing design could be demonstrated during the 1880s or 1890s, and such an arm was not actually
introduced until nearly seven years after the Colt venture.

Catalogued as the "·32 Hand Ejector, Model 1896" by its makers,
this first Smith & Wesson swing-out cylinder design is today frequently
referred to as the "Hand Ejector, Model 1", and shown at Plate 5 (top);
it is a double-action revolver, chambered for six ·32 S & W Long cartridges, and was available in barrel lengths of 3¼ inches (17¾ oz.), 4¼

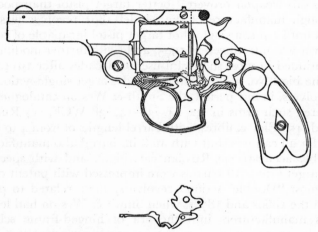

FIG. 9. *Smith & Wesson double-action lock-mechanism for hinged-frame revolvers.*
The firing-cycle of this lock-mechanism is the same as that for the French design
described in relation to Figure 15, but the cylinder-bolt (shown separately,
below, in the Figure above) is peculiar to the American weapon.

inches (18½ oz.) or 6 inches (20 oz.), with a choice of blued or nickel
plate finishes, and target sights as an optional extra. The lock-mechanism is shown at Figure 10, and will be seen to have a superficial similarity
to the Colt mechanism shown at Figure 2 (save for the use of a cylinder-
bolt, mounted in the top frame-strap, which is rocked in or out of
engagement with the cylinder by the hammer-nose), but to be a most
ingenious design in its own right, when examined. The cylinder was, of
course, crane-mounted to swing sideways out of the frame (when loading or ejecting cartridges) and latched home in that manner later
described with remarks upon D. B. WESSON's Br. Pat. 6184/1894.

In Figure 10, "A" is the hammer, "B" the trigger, "C" the cylinder-
bolt, "D" the pawl, "F" the trigger-lever, and "G" the rebound-lever;
the pawl "D" (pivoted on "B") is held forward into engagement with a

rotating-ratchet on the cylinder by means of "E", a small "hand lever", later protected by D. B. & J. H. Wesson's U.S. Patent No. 565245 of 4th August, 1896. This "hand lever" rocks in a longitudinally-cut chamber at the top of the trigger and is tensioned, by a minute coiled spring, to bear upon a pin projecting (from the left side of the pawl) into the hand-lever chamber, *via* an arcuate slot cut in the right side of the trigger. Hammer and trigger movements follow a cycle described for that Colt mechanism shown at Figure 2, in self-cocking or single-action fire, but with the hammer of this Smith & Wesson design operating the

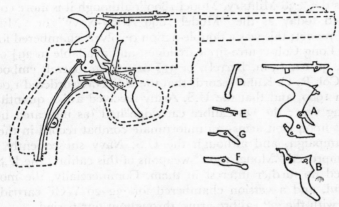

FIG. 10. *Smith & Wesson double-action lock-mechanism, Model 1896.*

"A" is the hammer, "B" the trigger, "C" the cylinder-bolt, "D" the pawl or hand (tensioned by the hand-lever "E"). "F" is the trigger-lever, and "G" the rebound-lever.

cylinder-bolt, and with the long trigger-lever "F" returning the trigger "B" to rest, after firing, and operating the rebound-lever "G" to turn the hammer-nose back off the cartridges.

Engraved upon the Model 1896 Hand Ejector revolver shown in Plate 5 are references to patent dates of 1st July, 1884, 9th April, 1889, 27th March, 1894, 29th May, 1894, 21st May, 1895, and 16th July, 1895, some of which present problems in identifying those American patents to which they were intended to refer. Thus, W. Trabue secured U.S. Patents Nos. 301180 and 301181 on the first-mentioned date, and that reference was probably directed to both patents, as proposing use of a manually-operated star-shaped ejector (in a swing-out cylinder), although not in the manner actually used here; the second date was that of D. B. WESSON's U.S. Patent No. 401087 (earlier mentioned) for the steel-shimmed cylinder locking-notches. The succeeding dates respectively related to U.S. Patents Nos. 517152 (D. B. WESSON) covering those cylinder-latch and hammer-block features described in Appendix II remarks upon this patentee's Br. Pat. 6184/1894; 520,468 (D. B. WESSON), which was an obscure reference for this particular model, but could be cited for use of anti-friction bosses in the frame-walls; 539497 (D. B. & J. H. WESSON), again obscure since the patent claims related to a sliding cylinder-latch not used in the weapon illustrated; and 542744 (D. B. WESSON) covering the trigger-lever "F" and rebound-lever "G" shown at Figure 10.

Smith & Wesson's next Hand Ejector revolver was catalogued by them as the "·38 Military, Model 1899", although it is more commonly described today as the "Model 1899 Army-Navy" or "Military & Police" model; this was a double-action revolver, chambered for six ·38 calibre Long Colt centre-fire cartridges, and available in 29¼ oz. (4-in. barrel), 30 oz. (5-in. barrel), or 31¼ oz. (6½-in. barrel) embodiments. Lieut.-Col. R. C. Kuhn records that the U.S. Navy ordered 1,000 of the arms in 1900, and that the U.S. Army received a like quantity in the following year; the ·38 calibre cartridge had (as indicated in earlier remarks upon Colt arms) an unfortunate combat record in the Philippine campaign, and although the U.S. Navy subsequently ordered 1,000 improved "Model 1902" weapons of this calibre, the U.S. Army displayed no further interest in them. Commercially, the model was successful, and a version chambered for ·32–20 WCF cartridges was offered with the ·38 calibre arms, throughout our period.

Although larger, the Model 1899 revolver was quite similar in appearance to Model 1896 pistols, and patent dates marked upon it recognized design features earlier described, in remarks upon U.S. Patents Nos. 301180; 401087; 539497; 542744; and 565245. However, those markings also recognized further improvements to the 1896 design, by reference to patent dates of 22nd December, 1896 (D. B. & J. H. WESSON'S U.S. Patent No. 573736, for using the sliding cylinder-latch to bolt the hammer, if full latching of the cylinder had not occurred), and 4th October, 1898 (D. B. & J. H. WESSON'S U.S. Patent No. 611826, for a rocking cylinder-bolt situated over the trigger, in place of the Model 1896 cylinder-bolt in the top frame-strap), although regard was not had to the sliding cylinder-latch (operated by a thumb-piece on the right of the frame), which had replaced the pull-rod system of the 1896 weapons.

In 1902, one of the few Smith & Wesson design features open to criticism was eliminated from "Military & Police" revolvers, by provision (in a new model) of fore-and-aft locking for the cylinder-latch, in accordance with D. B. WESSON's U.S. Patent No. 689260 of 17th

December, 1901. The date of this improvement was added to the markings upon such arms, and it was accomplished in that manner shown at Figure 71, and for those reasons mentioned in remarks upon the patentee's Br. Pat. 24597/1901; the refinement introduced a heavy barrel-lug (in which the front latching-nib was located), which remains a distinctive feature of Smith & Wesson revolvers to this day. Other changes in the 1899 construction involved use of anti-friction surfaces upon the hammer and trigger, as claimed by D. B. WESSON's U.S Patent No. 520468 of 29th May, 1894, and chambering for the potent ·38 S & W Special cartridge.

1902 was also the year in which Smith & Wesson's first ·22 rim-fire calibre Hand Ejector revolver was introduced. Known to collectors as the "Model (M)", this was a seven-shot pistol, offered in barrel lengths of 2¼, 3 or 3½ inches, had its cylinder-latch operated by a large press-button on the right of the frame, and was produced in quite modest numbers.

Between 1903 and 1906, a number of detailed changes were made to existing Smith & Wesson Hand Ejector arms. The Model (1) ·32 calibre model of 1903 had a conventional sliding cylinder-latch (located on the left of the frame) and, save for a brief period between 1904 and 1906, the rocking cylinder-bolt covered by that U.S. Patent No. 611826 earlier mentioned was embodied in it for the remainder of our period. The ·38 calibre Military & Police arm, after more minor changes in 1903 and 1905, was fitted with a rebound-slide of the type shown in Figure 11; this was an important modification (covered by J. H. Wesson's U.S. Patent No. 811807, of 6th February, 1906), eliminating the weaker flat-spring-operated trigger-lever and rebound-lever shown in the Model 1896 mechanism at Figure 10, and is used in Smith & Wesson revolvers even today.

In Figure 11, "r" is the hammer, "s" the trigger, and "t" the rebound slide; in self-cocking fire, pressure on the trigger "s" pushes back "t" to a point where the rebound lump on top of it is sufficiently far to the rear for the hammer not to strike that lump in falling. On release of the trigger, a coiled spring within "t" pushes the rebound-slide forward (which movement, by a linkage shown in Figure 11, also restores the trigger to its "at rest" position) and the rebound lump strikes the base of the hammer "r", and turns this back off the cartridges. An accidental blow upon the hammer, when it is down, should not drive "r" forward on to the cartridges, since the base of the hammer will strike the rebound lump on "t", and prevent forward movement of the hammer. Similar results will occur, where the hammer accidentally slips from under the firer's thumb, in single-action cocking.

The year 1906 also saw some redesigning of the Model (M) ·22
rimfire revolver, from which the side cylinder-latch was now removed.
To replace that device, a system quite similar to the Model (1) latch
was embodied, where a knob in front of the barrel-lug (which is
visible on a later version of the Model (M) shown in Plate 36) was
pulled forward by the user, as claimed by J. H. Wesson's U.S. Patent
No. 743784, 10th November, 1903. In the same year (1906), ·32 calibre
Hand Ejector revolvers also received the rebound-slide shown in
Figure 11.

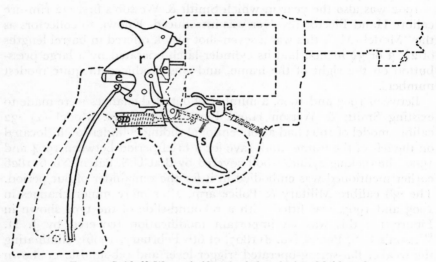

FIG. 11. *Smith & Wesson double-action lock-mechanism, Model 1906.*
"a" is the cylinder-bolt, "e" the inner part of the sliding cylinder-latch (which
fouls the tail of the hammer, to prevent cocking, if the cylinder is not properly
latched into the frame), "r" is the hammer, "s" the trigger, and "t" the
rebound-slide; the pawl and hand-lever are shown only in outline, but function
as described in relation to the lock-mechanism shown in Figure 10.

In 1907, the firm produced its first heavy-calibre Hand Ejector
revolvers, in the shape of a "New Century" pistol (of that type shown
at Plate 38), which is now more popularly known as the "Triple Lock"
model, since it embodied a three-point cylinder-latch covered by the
U.S. Patent No. 688141, of D. B. WESSON, discussed in remarks upon
that patentee's Br. Pat. 24588/1901 and shown in Figure 70. Offered in
barrel lengths of 4, 5, 6½ or 7½ inches, and in versions chambered for the
·44 Russian, ·44 S & W Special, ·45 Colt, and ·450 or ·455 Eley centre-
fire cartridges, this was a superb revolver. Early models carried patent

dates acknowledging U.S. Patents Nos. 565245 and 573736 earlier noticed, but specimens likely to be encountered by British collectors (purchased for the British Army, in 1915) are marked also with the patent dates of 8th October, 1901 (D. B. WESSON's U.S. Patent No. 684150, covering use of the "Perfected" revolver's sliding cylinder-latch), 3rd December, 1901 (D. B. WESSON's U.S. Patent No. 688141, covering the cylinder-latch shown at Figure 70), and 6th February, 1906 (covering J. H. Wesson's U.S. Patent No. 811807) for the rebound-slide shown in Figure 11.

After minor modifications to the lock-mechanism of ·32 Calibre Model (1) arms (in 1909 and 1910), an important improvement to that mechanism was introduced in 1910, under C. M. Stone's U.S. Patent No. 933797, earlier mentioned in remarks upon hinged-frame "Perfected" revolvers. This improvement (which was applied to both "Military & Police" and ·32–20 Winchester Hand Ejector pistols, in the same year) improved self-cocking fire greatly, by providing a backward throw of the hammer through an arc as great as that for single action fire, to improve cartridge ignition *via* a heavier hammer-blow, and by imparting a smoother motion to the hammer in the last moments of its self-cocking travel to the rear. Stone actually accomplished these aims by shaping hammer-toe and trigger-nose to engage at that moment when the hammer-catch slipped off the trigger in self-cocking fire (which stole the extra bit of hammer-travel), and by realigning the pivots of hammer and trigger to yield a last point of engagement, between hammer and trigger, in a straight line drawn between those pivots.

Finally, in May and June of 1911, Smith & Wesson issued two ·22 rim-fire revolvers, which were the last arms relevant to these pages. The first of these (see Plate 36) was an improved version of the Model (M) Hand Ejector, with square-bottomed butt and C. M. Stone's lock-mechanism improvement, under U.S. Patent No. 933797 earlier mentioned; the second (known as the "·22/32 Target", or "Bekeart Model", after a dealer who suggested its design) was actually a six-shot pistol, built upon the frame and components of the 1910 Model (1) ·32 calibre revolver, with 6-in. barrel and target sights.

"STEVENS" revolvers

The J. Stevens Arms & Tool Co. had been incorporated, in 1888, to take over a twenty-five-year-old private firm. It was based at Chicopee Falls, Mass., and manufactured considerable quantities of small-arms during our period, in lines which latterly embraced pump-action and double- or single-barrelled shot-guns, target pistols, single-shot or

F

repeating rifles, sights, and cleaning or reloading accessories; most of these products were sold to U.S. dealers and to overseas agents (the pre-1914 London sales offices being located at 15 Grape St., off Shaftesbury Avenue), and the Company is still operating today.

As remarked in relation to "Meriden" arms, the Stevens Company is not now remembered as a revolver manufacturer, but it is a fact that assignments were taken by it (from the patentee, Oscar F. Mossberg) of U.S. Patents Nos. 778500 and 778501 relating to revolving arms; the first of these patents (both of which were dated 27th December, 1904) related to a self-cocking lock-mechanism, for use in a hinged-frame revolver with grip-safety, and the second to a double-action lock-mechanism.

This writer has never seen revolvers marked with either the relevant patent date or the Stevens name, but a possibility clearly exists that such arms were produced by this maker.

"SUICIDE SPECIAL" revolvers

This name was used by Donald B. Webster, Jr. to describe those inexpensive single-action, solid-frame, stud-trigger and predominantly rimfire pocket revolvers to which his trail-blazing book was devoted, and is here also extended to cover weapons of similar appearance, but better quality, which were made by the Colt and Remington firms.

In terms of that period studied here, such arms were obsolete, and superseded by inexpensive double-action or self-cocking designs made by firms like the Harrington & Richardson Arms Co., or Iver Johnson's Arms & Cycle Works, for example, but large stocks held by manufacturers formerly specializing in them, and a demand for revolvers selling at prices as low as 60 cents apiece, ensured a traffic in "Suicide Specials", even years after 1914.

By 1889, indeed, most of those manufacturers wholly dependent upon "Suicide Specials", as their stock-in-trade, were out of business, but it is believed that the following firms were ready to supply such revolvers (although sometimes producing more modern designs, at the same time) to wholesalers and mail-order firms, during our period:

Aetna Arms Co., New York (until 1890)
Bacon Manufacturing Co., Norwich, Conn. (until 1891).
Colt's Pt. F. A. Manufacturing Co. (Inc.), Hartford, Conn.
    N.B. Colt "New Line" House or Police revolvers were of superior quality, and still carried by some American police officers until the

1890s; late models tended to be centre-fire arms, and British dealers still catalogued them (priced at around thirty shillings, retail) until about 1900.

Forehand & Wadsworth, ⎫
Forehand Arms Co.,   ⎬ Worcester, Mass. (until 1902).

Harrington & Richardson Arms Co., Worcester, Mass.

Hopkins & Allen Manufacturing Co., Norwich, Conn. (until 1902).

Iver Johnson's Arms & Cycle Works, Fitchburg, Mass.

N.B. MacFarland indicates that a "U.S. Arms Co." revolver was made by Iver Johnson for a "Folsom" selling organization (noticed in remarks upon "Crescent" revolvers), who supplied it to the Supplee-Biddle Hardware Co.

Remington Arms Co., Ilion, N.Y.

Rupertus Patent Pistol Manufacturing Co., Philadelphia, Pa. (until 1890).

Ryan Pistol Manufacturing Co., New York (until 1891).

C. W. Turner & Ross, Boston, Mass.

N.B. A "Czar" model revolver was made for this firm, by the Hopkins & Allen Manufacturing Co.

"THAMES" revolvers

Mathews illustrates ·32 and ·38 calibre centre-fire, double-action, hinged-frame, self-ejecting revolvers, as made by the Thames Arms Co., of Norwich, Conn., under J. Boland's U.S. Patent No. 333725 (of 5th January, 1886), and G. W. Cilley's U.S. Patent No. 350346 (of 5th October, 1886), the dates of which were marked upon such arms. The earlier protection was, of course, assigned to the Hopkins & Allen Manufacturing Co., who used the subject invention as shown at Figure 6, a fact which may indicate that those revolvers illustrated by Mathews were actually manufactured for the Thames Arms Co., by the Hopkins & Allen company.

Later, however, mesne assignments of J. D. Robertson's U.S. Patents (Nos. 708078, 710008 and 816125) to the Thames Arms Co. were also recorded, and Mathews lists revolvers made under the first two patents as another product of this company. The earliest patent (dated 2nd September, 1902) proposed use of a split spring-steel arbor for retaining the cylinder of self-ejecting revolvers; the second patent (dated 30th September, 1902) covered an ejector mechanism for use in such arms, as did the third, which was dated 27th March, 1906.

One noticeable feature of "Thames Arms Co." hinged-frame revolvers is their marked external resemblance to such weapons sold under that "Fyrberg" name earlier mentioned; whether a common manufacturing background can be traced for these brand-names remains to be established.

"UNION" revolvers

Charles F. Lefever (of Toledo, Ohio) secured U.S. Patent No. 944448, of 28th December, 1909, for a recoil-operated revolver similar in principle to that discussed in remarks upon G. V. FOSBERY (*q.v.*); he proposed use of a double-action lock-mechanism, and cylinder-rotation by means of zigzag grooves about the circumference of the cylinder, which were engaged by a yielding rotation-pin in the frame-floor, as barrel and cylinder recoiled (on firing) along the top of the action-body.

A small-calibre version of Lefever's pistol was made by the Union Firearms Co., of Toledo, Ohio, but little is known of this company, save that it also sold repeating rifles and double-barrelled shot-guns.

"U.S. ARMS CO." revolvers

See "Suicide Special" revolvers.

"U.S. REVOLVER CO." revolvers

See "Iver Johnson" revolvers.

CHAPTER II

ARMS OTHER THAN AMERICAN OR BRITISH

THE following entries in Appendix II are of parallel interest to the subject of this chapter, namely, L. ARMANNI (magazine pistol); the AUSTRIAN SMALL ARMS MANUFACTURING CO. (rifle magazine); B. BEHR (pistol); J. VON BENKÖ and E. TATAREK (magazine); CLAIR FRÈRES (gas-operated pistol); J. COURRIER (rifle); H. DANNER (rifle); E. FABRE and A. TRONCHE (magazine pistols); T. A. FIDJELAND and J. A. SCHWARZ (rifle): E. JÖRGENSEN and O. H. J. KRAG (rifles); C. KRNKA and G. ROTH (rifle); K. KRNKA (magazine pistol); J. LAUBER (rifle); A. LINDNER (rifle); C. VON MANNLICHER (rifle); F. R. VON MANNLICHER (rifle magazines); F. R. VON MANNLICHER and O. SCHOENAUER (rifle magazine); A. MUND (alarm); A. G. NOLCKEN (rifle); the OESTERREICHISCHE WAFFENFABRIKS-GESELLSCHAFT (rifle magazine); P. A. PHILLIPPIDES (rifle magazine); H. PIEPER (rifles); E. REIGER (magazine pistol); C. RICCI (rifles); G. H. SCHNEE (magazine firearms); O. SCHOENAUER (rifle magazine); J. SCHULHOF (rifle and rifle magazines); and H. SUNNGÄRD (rifle magazine).

Although some of those inventions were of real importance (notably in the development of military and sporting magazine rifles), lack of space inhibits embroidery upon the notes of Appendix II, and this Chapter instead sketches only those types of revolver available in countries alphabetically listed, and in areas upon which that Appendix casts little light. The Appendix II entries relevant to such a field of study are those relating to W. DECKER (revolver); H. DIMANCEA (revolver); K. DOBSLAW and P. SCHMIDT (sights); M. DOZIN (ejector); G. ENVALL (revolver); G. V. HAEGHEN (revolver); O. HAGEN (aiming improvement); M. HASSELMANN (revolver); B. KREITH (revolvers); H. F. LANDSTAD (revolver); H. LANGENHAN (revolver); P. P. MAUSER (revolver); P. MONNERAT (revolver sword); E. PAUL (revolver); PIRLOT & TRESART (revolver safety); F. PRAUNEGGER and L. P. SCHMIDT (ejector); H. RENFORS (revolver mounts); J. TAMBOUR (revolver safety); R. TARGAN and the W. T. G. "WESPI" (sights); T. F. TÖRNELL (cylinder-bolt); G. TRESENREUTER (revolver); J. E. TURBIAUX (revolver); W. T. UNGE (revolver).

AUSTRO-HUNGARIAN revolvers

During our period, a number of self-loading pistols were field-tested for possible adoption by the Austro-Hungarian armed forces, and two such arms (the Roth M/1907 and Steyr M/1912 designs) were in limited issue by 1914. However, as a result of this forward-looking concern with competing hand-gun designs, Austrian service revolvers in issue between 1889 and 1914 comprised but three models (only one of which actually appeared during those years), namely, the Gasser Model 1870–74, the Gasser-Kropatschek, and the Rast & Gasser Model 1898 pistols.

A rare Naval model of the M/1870–74 Gasser is shown at Plate 7 (top), but differs from the more common Army version only by use of a barrel-securing wedge (passing through both barrel-lug and arbor) omitted from the latter weapon; both revolvers were six-shot arms of 11-mm. centre-fire calibre, with an overall length of over $12\frac{1}{2}$ inches (320 mm.), a $7\frac{1}{4}$-in. (184-mm.) barrel (rifled with six grooves, twisted to the right) and weighing over 3 lb. (1370 g.) unloaded. They were, moreover, gate-loaded (so that each cartridge had to be separately ejected from its chamber, by use of a rod-ejector visible in Plate 7), and this M/1870–74 pattern really differed from the original M/1870 issue only by its use of a steel action-body, in place of an original iron component. The double-action lock-mechanism, with its distinctive leaf-spring half-cock device lying along the right side of the frame, was a relic from the past, and is sufficiently described and illustrated in another place.*

The Gasser-Kropatschek *Infanterieoffiziersrevolver* may be seen at Plate 7 (lower), as merely a scaled-down version of the M/1870–74 arm, chambering six 9-mm. centre-fire cartridges, weighing slightly over $1\frac{1}{2}$ lbs. (770 g.) unloaded (with $4\frac{4}{5}$-in. (120-mm.) barrel) and an overall length of about 9 inches (230 mm.)

The Rast & Gasser M/1898 revolver is shown as Plate 12 (top), and was an eight-shot, gate-loaded, solid-framed, rod-ejecting, double-action weapon, having a frame-mounted firing-pin and that "Schmidt Galand" lock-mechanism (sketched as Fig. 12), the basic operation of

* *The Revolver, 1865–1888.* A. Taylerson. Herbert Jenkins. London, 1965.

which is described at p. 40; intended for issue to infantry officers and
N.C.O.s, this arm was chambered for an 8-mm. centre-fire cartridge,
had an overall length of about 9 inches (226 mm.), with a 4½-in. (117-
mm.) barrel rifled by four grooves twisted to the right, and weighed just
under 2 lb. (900 g.) when unloaded. Though of curious appearance to
modern eyes, these were beautifully-made pistols, with an improved
loading-gate safety-device (based upon the Portuguese "Abadie"
system, later mentioned) which not only disconnected trigger from

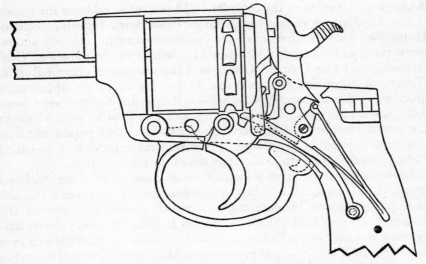

FIG. 12. *Double-action lock-mechanism of Austrian M/1898 service revolver.*

hammer, when the gate was swung open, but also bolted the latter.
They were, however, defective in stopping power, since the hardened
lead bullet (propelled by a charge of smokeless *Jagd-und Schieben-
pulver No. 2*, at a muzzle-velocity of about 750 f.p.s.) had a penetration rather than a knock-down value. One excellent feature was the
take-down system, by which the trigger-guard (the rear end of which
was normally latched into the frame) could be pulled down, on a pivot
at its front, to release the hinged left-hand side-plate affording access to
the lock-mechanism. Total production of Model 1898 revolvers is
difficult to estimate; this writer has seen serial-numbers only as high as
122432, and believes that all weapons marked "Rast & Gasser" were
consecutively numbered.

Writing in 1903, Leleu alleged that an improved version of the
M/1898 revolver was then to be issued to Austrian cavalry, embodying

"un extracteur collectif", and using a charger for loading all chambers simultaneously; the latter, presumably, of a kind similar to those devices mentioned in relation to W. DE C. PRIDEAUX or A. J. WATSON (*q.v.*). It is tempting to interpret Leleu's "extracteur collectif" as reference to a major reshaping of the M/1898 arm, by provision of a crane-mounted swing-out cylinder, or even a hinged-frame and self-ejection. In fact (although no specimen arm could be located, to clarify this point), any such improvement probably consisted in mounting a manually-operated star-shaped push-rod ejector in the cylinder, which could be operated after the cylinder had been removed from the frame.

For an Empire containing a large small arms industry, Austro-Hungarian manufacturers of civilian revolvers remain curiously anony-mous (save as indicated in Chapter IV), with only the names of Vien-nese suppliers like Leopold Gasser and the associated firm of Rast & Gasser, or Springer, now seeming to survive upon an appreciable quantity of arms. Possibly new self-loading pistol designs were more fashionable after 1900, with designers and public alike but, whatever the actual reasons, Austrian civilian revolvers of our period are now best remembered in the shape of one particular pattern, a so-called "Montenegrin" weapon of the type shown in Plate 8 (top).

Such pistols were arms which all male subjects of King Nicholas (1910–18) were required by law to purchase, so the story went, and this to a pattern made by companies in which (again by rumour) the sovereign himself held shares. Although Belgian revolvers (both self-ejecting and solid-frame) of an appearance similar to that pattern now to be described will be found in some numbers, examination of surviving arms does suggest that certainly two (and possibly three) models of a relevant type of revolver were made in Austria, and that if a "Montene-grin" pattern ever formally existed then Austria was the logical source from which to secure supplies of such arms.

For the purposes of these pages, "Montenegrin" revolvers are large, gate-loaded, rod-ejecting, double-action revolvers which, though solid-framed and of heavy calibre, appear unduly frail in construction. They have the "broom handle" butt and lock-mechanism of that Model 1870–74 Gasser weapon shown at Plate 7, and are usually decorated with bone grips, coarsely engraved or chiselled frames and cylinders, and nickel- or silver-plating. The cartridge used in them is (save that it was centre-fire) disputed amongst collectors today, and variously de-scribed as of 11, 11·75 or 12 mm. calibre. For many years, however, Kynoch Ltd. catalogued a "·44 Revolver (Montenegrin Model)" cart-ridge, with 30 grains of black powder propelling a 300 grain solid lead bullet, and the fact that an ammunition manufacturer of that status should list such a round until as late as 1926 suggests (to this writer, at any rate) that a large number of "Montenegrin" revolvers must have been chambered for it.

Today, the most sought-after "Montenegrin" model is a 3¼-lb. (1475 g.), six-shot monster shown at Plate 8, measuring 15 inches (375 mm.) overall, and with a 9¼-in. (232-mm.) barrel; markings are profuse, and may embrace "Guss-Stahl", "Akers Patent", "Kaiser's Patent", or "Rast & Gasser", amongst others, but normally always include the words "Vero Revolver Montenegrino", or "Vero Montenegrino". Another version has only five chambers, and measures 10 inches (250 mm.) overall, with a 5-in. (125-mm.) barrel; markings here may include the words "Extra Montenegrino", "Guss-Stahl", "Excelsior", and "S. Marke", together with the legend "L. Gasser, Wien, Ottakring, Patent". A third (six-chambered) version, of similar dimensions to the second, is illustrated by Blair, who notes the same markings as allied with a crown over letters "N.I.".

BELGIAN revolvers

As later remarks upon M. DOZIN, L. NAGANT, H. PIEPER, and PIRLOT & TRESART (*q.v.*) should confirm, the Belgian firearms industry was heavily concentrated, in or around the town of Liége, and it was of surprising size for such a small country. The Liége manufacturing pattern was confused, in that part of the trade was in the hands of firms (like those mentioned in remarks upon L. NAGANT, *q.v.*) who operated conventional factories of their own, whilst another section (dominated by such houses as Frères Dumoulin et Cie, Raick Frères, or Théate Frères) consisted of factors and merchants, who maintained warehouse premises rather than factories. The latter sold firearms, but occupied themselves also in arranging the necessary manufacture (from components which they supplied) by independent craftsmen, who carried out the various processes of filing, assembly, or finishing, often by hand, in their own homes. Indeed, even true factories frequently used the services of these out-workers for certain products, with some weapons entering and leaving their premises as many as thirty times (for the attention of various outside specialists) before completion.

Due to the effect of increasing mechanization upon Liège (from the late 1890s), it is impossible, in the compass of these notes, to detail that course followed by revolver manufacturers during our whole period. Clearly, however, when taken with the Belgian manufacturer or merchant's normal intention to supply improved models, as frequently and as cheaply as possible, the system enabled that industry to provide a very wide range of revolvers for those markets which it served. Indeed, that outlay (for adapting machine tools) or simple factory-floor dis-organization which would, for example, have deterred any large American manufacturer amongst those mentioned in Chapter I, from producing non-standard models in any but a production-run involving hundreds of arms, barely existed for a Belgian manufacturer or merchant. Foundries at Herstal (a Liège suburb) made components for a variety of industries, and would both manufacture rough revolver parts from foundry patterns or forging dies supplied by their customers, and treat cast material to make it malleable enough for filing. If necessary, these establishments were fully equipped to machine and bore cylinders, lock-frames, or barrels (although the latter would be rifled, elsewhere, by firms or craftsmen specializing in that trade), so that the principal could pass amongst his chosen out-workers, revolver components in a wide range of production stages, and leave to hand-work those details of barrel length, shaping of frames, and so forth, which machine tools could never so cheaply have tackled for small quantities of arms.

Even by American standards, the output of Belgian revolvers was respectably large, having regard to those diffused methods of manu-facture used in many cases, and Cmd. 2683–14 mentions (but does not break down, by type) an average annual Liège revolver *and* self-loading pistol output of about 500,000 weapons, the figures for 1904 being 549,669, and those for 1905, 629,376. Moreover, it is no exaggeration to say that Liège both could and would supply revolvers of almost any pattern and quality, to almost any market in the world where such imports were permitted at all, and in rim-, pin-, or centre-fire embodi-ments.

Plate 9 shows one British firm's range of the cheapest Belgian revolvers and, bearing in mind that prices shown include both the Liège sup-plier's margin and Chas. Osborne & Co.'s mark-up, it will be appre-ciated how cheaply such arms could be produced in Liège, around 1900; it is significant that the same catalogue features only one American revolver of this type, the U.S. contribution being otherwise confined to ejector revolvers of far better quality. The lock-mechanism used in Belgian revolvers of that kind shown at Plate 9, was double-action, normally embodied a hammer-rebound, and was almost the ultimate in simplicity, as may be seen at Figure 13; here, "p" is the hammer, "r" the trigger (on which the pawl "m" is pivoted) and "s" a hammer-rebound; in self-cocking fire, "p" is lifted by "r" acting on the hammer-catch (pivoted in the breast of "p"), until it escapes and falls to fire a cartridge, whilst in single-action fire, thumbing back "p" rocks the trigger "r" to the rear (by engagement of trigger-nose with hammer-toe) until the nose of the trigger engages a bent cut at the toe of the hammer, to hold "p" at full-cock until "r" is pressed. When "r" is released, after double- or single-action firing, the trigger-spring rocks "r" forward again on its pivot; when "s" is fitted, this movement (since "r" rubs against "s", as it moves forward) raises the rear end of the rebound which, in turn, presses against the heel of the hammer, and turns this back off the cartridges.

As will be noted, by reference to Plate 9, such pistols were offered in small calibres, and another weapon in this category (though of marginally better quality) is shown at Plate 6 (lower), and known to modern collectors as the "Velo Dog" model; Spanish competition for the

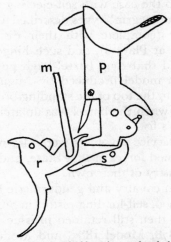

FIG. 13. *Cheap Belgian double-action revolver lock-mechanism.*
N.B. All springs have been omitted to isolate the main components.

market in these arms was keen enough to be felt even by Belgian manufacturers, and although such concealed-hammer, self-cocking, solid-framed, rod-ejecting pocket revolvers were normally chambered for that long 5·5 mm. centre-fire cartridge after which the model was named, versions were also offered in other small-calibre centre-fire chamberings. Another line of arms, with which the Belgian and Spanish makers competed for African and South American markets, was in double-action rod-ejecting pin-fire revolvers of very large size; these models (some of which were in calibres as heavy as 15 mm.) were of an obsolete pattern first introduced in the 1860s.

Liège also produced hinged-frame self-ejecting and swing-out cylinder revolvers during our period, although it was with the first

mentioned that the factories really excelled, prior to 1914; swing-out
cylinder designs then tended to be limited to such arms as the French
M/1892 service revolver shown at Plate 14 (or to Pieper and Nagant
arms mentioned in Chapter IV), although a few "hammerless" pocket
weapons of undistinguished type were produced. Many Belgian hinged-
frame self-ejecting revolvers were literal copies of Smith & Wesson
"Double Action" (see Plate 5), "New Navy" or "New Departure" (see
Plate 36) lines described in Chapter I, whilst others were copies of that
"Pryse" weapon (with press-button tong barrel-latch) illustrated at
Plate 24 (lower); however, smaller hinged-frame revolvers, with folding
triggers, had no extensively manufactured American or British counter-
part, and this was also the case with self-ejecting arms similar to solid-
framed Austrian "Montenegrin" types described above. The latter were
also copied at Liège (complete with their distinctive Gasser lock-
mechanism, as shown at Plate 8), and such hinged-frame self-ejecting
variants normally used that tong barrel-latch popularized in "Pryse"
revolvers. However, a model produced by Auguste Francotte & Cie
had the barrel hinged to the top of the standing breech, and operated its
ejector automatically, when the barrel was unlatched and tipped backwards over the holder's fist.

Finally, of course, service revolvers were also manufactured in Belgium, both for the armed forces of that State, and for use by countries
lacking any arms industry of their own.

By 1914, the Belgian cavalry and gendarmerie had been issued with
a Browning, Model 1900, self-loading pistol (in 7·65 m/m. calibre), but
service revolvers were then still retained in issue by the artillery, and
consisted of Model 1878, Model 1883, and Model 1878–86 arms; all
were well-made, six-shot, solid-framed, rod-ejecting weapons (chambered for 9-mm. centre-fire revolver cartridges, with 12·2 g. lead
bullets and a charge of 1 gramme of fine-grain artillery black powder),
having $5\frac{3}{5}$-inch. (140-mm.) octagonal barrels, rifled by four grooves
twisted to the left, and weighing just over 2 lb. (950 g.) when unloaded.
The Model 1878 pistol had originally been issued as an officer's sidearm,
with rod-ejector, take-down, and frame-construction details patented
by Emile Nagant; see, for example, his British patent No. 4310 (of 22nd
October, 1879), which had expired in 1882.

The Model 1878 double-action lock-mechanism is shown as Figure
14, and there compared with the Model 1883 single-action lock-
mechanism subsequently developed from it; the latter was a rather
unusual single-action lock-mechanism, in that the hammer rebounded
slightly, after discharge.

The double-action Model 1878–86 lock-mechanism design also had a hammer-rebound, and had been arrived at by eliminating five components from the Model 1878 lock-mechanism (namely, sear, sear-spring, trigger-spring, pawl-spring, and mainspring stirrup), and by using the mainspring also for a trigger- and pawl-spring, as had been done with Model 1883 revolvers; it became internationally popular, and is shown at Figure 19, in a form used in Scandinavian service revolvers.

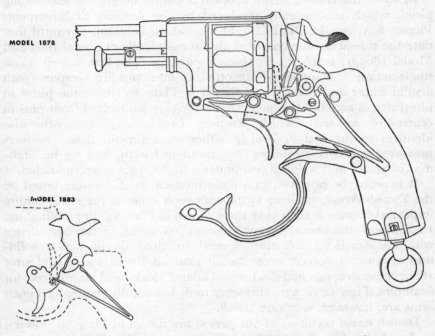

MODEL 1878

MODEL 1883

FIG. 14. M/1878 and M/1883 lock-mechanisms, for Belgian service revolvers.

In addition to providing the above-mentioned arms for issue to Belgian troops, Liège also manufactured a Nagant "gas-seal" design (described in Chapter IV), which was taken up by the Russian armed forces, and from time to time supplied more conventional weapons to Argentina, Brazil, Denmark, Norway, Portugal, Romania, Serbia, and Sweden. Inquiry of South American military museums failed to elicit any information about the Argentinian or Brazilian arms; however, these are known to have been a ·44 calibre centre-fire Nagant design, which this writer assumes to have been almost identical to the Belgian Model 1878–86 revolver (or with those Norwegian M/1893-Swedish M/1887 arms shown at Plates 17 and 21), and therefore to have had that lock-mechanism shown at Figure 19.

DANISH revolvers

Denmark appears to have had no native manufacturer of civilian revolvers, but (whilst eking out that capability with arms purchased from Liège) to have fostered a small production of service arms in at least one government arsenal.

In 1910, the Danish Army adopted a 9-mm. Bergmann self-loading pistol, which was actually produced by the Anciens Établissements Pieper, S.A. (see H. PIEPER), at Herstal, in Belgium, but until that date the side-arm issue consisted almost exclusively of Model 1865 and Model 1865/97 revolvers, in obsolete patterns. The first-named was a single-action "Lefaucheux-Francotte" 11-mm. pin-fire weapon (with a solid frame and rod-ejector) shown in Plate 10 (top); the pistol so illustrated is actually the later Model 1865/97 (converted from pin- to centre-fire at the Danish *Kronborg Gevaerfabrik*), but otherwise identical to the first design. In either embodiment, these revolvers measured just over 10 inches (255 mm.) in length, had $5\frac{1}{10}$-in. (128-mm.) barrels, and weighed just under 2 lb. (870 g.) when unloaded.

It is probable, however, that more modern revolvers were tested by the Danish Army, prior to 1910, with such arms as the small-calibre improved Nagant designs (like those shown in Plate 17) predominating. In addition (the Danish Army Museum has stated, in correspondence with an American collector) several hundred double-action solid-framed 9-mm. revolvers were actually made at Kronborg, in and after 1880; these weapons had "Schmidt-Galand" lock-mechanisms (see, for examples, Figs. 12 or 33), and were most beautifully made. Specimen arms are, however, very rare today.

Danish naval revolvers of our period are shown at Plate 10 (lower), as the Model 1871–81 and Model 1891 revolvers. The first of these may be seen to have both the lock-mechanism and appearance of a Gasser-Kropatschek revolver shown at Plate 7 (lower), but began life as a pin-fire revolver, and was subsequently converted, at the Copenhagen dockyard, to that 11-mm. centre-fire model shown; issue arms were marked upon the barrel "A. Francotte à Liège" (in recognition of their source), measured about 10 inches (257 mm.) in length, had $5\frac{1}{10}$-in. (128-mm.) barrels, and weighed fractionally over 2 lb. (970 g.) unloaded. The M/1891 revolver (which the *Tøjhusmuseet* credits also to Francotte, but which Dr. Arne Hoff ascribes to J. B. Ronge fils, another Liège house) was a double-action, hinged-frame, self-ejecting revolver, of 9-mm. centre-fire calibre, based upon a Belgian commercial weapon that is known to modern collectors as the "Le Vaux" arm, in recognition of a name frequently found upon specimens; the half-round and

half-octagonal barrel, and lever-safety, of Model 1891 Danish naval
arms are not features of the Le Vaux version, and were presumably specified by the purchasing authority. M/1891 pistols measure about 10
inches (260 mm.) overall, have 5½-in. (137-mm.) barrels, and weigh
under 2 lb. (900 g.) unloaded.

DUTCH revolvers

Civilian revolvers with Dutch markings are uncommon in British
collections, and those few observed by this writer appeared (from
proof-marks) to be of Belgian origin; indeed, the first service revolvers
issued to any Dutch forces had been imported from Liège, but this
practice was later abandoned, and weapons relevant to our own period
were of native manufacture, namely, "Model 1873" revolvers (produced in five versions, at the de Beaumont factory, in Maastricht) and
the less common "KNIL Model 1891" pistol.

Model 1873 revolvers were used by both army and navy, and are
called "Chamelot-Delvigne type" revolvers in Holland; such a practice
underlines that risk implicit in use of unofficial names for service weapons, since (apart from being also solid-framed, double-action, gate-
loaded, centre-fire arms) Dutch Model 1873 pistols have nothing in
common with, for example, French service revolvers to which a
"Chamelot Delvigne" name is commonly applied. Thus the Dutch
weapon is in 9·4 mm. calibre, has no attached rod-ejector, and uses a
Nagant M/1878 lock-mechanism shown at Figure 14, whilst French
M/1873 and M/1874 arms are in 11-mm. calibre, embody attached
rod-ejectors, and have that lock-mechanism sketched at Figure 15; the
dissimilar appearance of these Dutch and French arms may also be
noted, by reference to Plate 11 and Plate 12 (lower), respectively.

Plate 11 illustrates the original "OM" (Old Model) Dutch M/1873
revolver below, together with three variants later issued and being,
in order of ascent, the "NM" (New Model), the "Kl.M." ("Klein", or
Small Model), and an arm "voor traangaspatronen", using tear-gas
cartridges; the "OM", "NM" and Kl.M." weapons (all in 9·4-mm.
centre-fire calibre) were distinct patterns, but a "K.S.O." ("Kamer
schietoefening" or Indoor Shooting Model, in 6-mm. Flobert rim-fire
calibre) and tear-gas pistols may have been produced by modification to
standard arms available, by breakage or otherwise, for use in such a
manner. The "OM" revolver weighed about 2⅘ lb. (1300 g.) unloaded,
had a 6⅖-in. (161-mm.) barrel, and measured 11 inches (280 mm.)
overall; although having a lock-mechanism similar to one used, in due
course, for Belgian M/1878 arms, not even the latest Model 1873
revolvers embodied that ingenious Nagant take-down system adopted

by the Belgians (and shown in Figure 14) so that a large detachable side-plate gave access to their lock-components. In all versions relevant here, the Dutch revolver depended upon use of a separate rod, carried on the holster, for removal of cartridge-cases from their chambers.

The "KNIL Model 1891" revolver is shown at Plate 11, and was issued only to the Netherlands Colonial Army. It was also in 9·4-mm. centre-fire calibre, weighed 1·8 lb. (825 g.) unloaded, had a 4½-in. (113-mm.) barrel rifled with four grooves, and measured 8⅘ inches (222 mm.) overall; as may be seen from Plate 11 and Figure 12, the double-action lock-mechanism was of that "Schmidt-Galand" pattern, mentioned in earlier remarks upon Austrian M/1898 revolvers, and an attached rod-ejector and improved take-down system were other features of a weapon greatly superior to that issued for Dutch home forces. It would appear that defects in the Model 1873 design were recognized, since Nagant revolvers (probably of a pattern similar to Norwegian and Swedish arms shown at Plates 17 and 21) were tested by a Netherlands ordnance commission, but not adopted.

Both basic patterns of Dutch service revolver were over-large for police-issue, and a lighter weapon (of similar appearance to P1493 on Plate 9) was developed for that purpose. Chambering a 9·4-mm. centre-fire cartridge, such pistols are practically indistinguishable in appearance from a number of "Bull Dog" or "Constabulary" revolvers produced by the Belgian gun-trade, and were probably manufactured at Liège. Occasionally, this pattern of Dutch police arm will be found to have the 1-in. barrel designed for use with tear-gas cartridges.

FRENCH revolvers

During our period, French military thinking appears to have been against issue of handguns to its officers and troops, save in cases where (by the nature of their duties) personnel would otherwise have been quite unarmed without such a weapon; the sabre was as a cavalryman's primary arm (use of which required any user's full attention), whilst officers should concentrate upon directing their men, rather than trying to fight beside them. Even the Navy (which had, in 1854, pioneered the issue of service revolvers to French "other ranks") had to retain in service, after 1889, designs then several decades old, and could only augment such supplies with those models from time to time issued by the Army.

By 1889, such Army revolvers were of 11-mm. centre-fire calibre, and issued in solid-framed, rod-ejecting double-action six-shot Model 1873 and Model 1874 versions, the former to troops and the latter for officers only; both models are popularly described as "Chamelot Delvigne" revolvers but, for reasons indicated with remarks upon Dutch service revolvers also called "Chamelot Delvigne", use of that title should be avoided.

Since it is less commonly seen, a Model 1874 revolver is illustrated at Plate 12 (lower), but differs from the Model 1873 pistol only in minor detail; thus the Model 1874 cylinder was fluted (where a shorter Model 1873 component had a plain forward circumference), the metal was chemically-coloured (where troopers' arms were left "in the white"), and rather more care was taken over the finish and fitting of parts for the officers' version. In both cases, however, the lock-mechanism was that shown at Figure 15, and was both well-made and reliable.

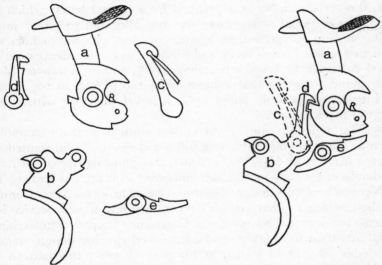

FIG. 15. *Double-action lock-mechanism for French M/1873 and M/1874 service revolvers.*

In Figure 15, "a" is the hammer (which has a projecting tooth on its breast), "b" the trigger, carrying on a common pivot both the pawl "c" and the lifter "d" (which latter engages the toothed hammer-breast, as shown, when "at rest"), and "e" is the sear. During self-cocking fire, pressure on "b" raises "a" by engagement of "d" with the hammer-breast (and causes "c" to rotate the cylinder), until "a" escapes from the lifter and falls on to a cartridge; at that moment when "a" escapes from the lifter "d", the sear "e" is rocked clear of bents on the bottom of the hammer, by a surface at the rear of the trigger. In single-action fire, "a" drags "b" to the rear (by its engagement with the lifter "d"), thus causing "c" to rotate the cylinder, until "e" engages bents on the

G

under side of "a", to hold it at half- or full-cock, as desired. Pressure on "b", at full-cock, then disengages "e" from the hammer-bents, and "a" falls, as before. In either case, a trigger-spring restores the trigger to its forward position after firing, which movement drags down "d", to re-engage the hammer-breast.

Model 1873 revolvers measured some $9\frac{2}{3}$ inches (242 mm.) overall and weighed about $2\frac{3}{5}$ lb. (1,195 g.) unloaded; Model 1874 revolvers measured just over 9 inches (239 mm.) overall, but weighed substantially less, at around $1\frac{9}{10}$ lb. (900 g.) when unloaded. In either version, barrel length was about $4\frac{1}{2}$ inches (say 113 mm.), and specimen arms observed by this writer were marked "Mre d'Armes St. Etienne", on their frames, and serially-numbered; in a high proportion of observed cases, this serial-number was prefixed by a capital letter, which suggested that a global serial-range was not allocated to either model. During most of our period, such arms (marked with an anchor) were also issued to the French Navy and marines, as earlier mentioned. The oiginal cartridge had a low muzzle-velocity, and an improved Model 73–90 round (boosting that velocity from 140 m./sec. to 190 m./sec.) was introduced, possibly based upon a naval cartridge with heavier charge of black powder.

In 1885, a new 11-mm. revolver was studied, and an example is shown as Plate 13 (top); this was still a rod-ejecting solid-framed arm (like the M/1873 or M/1874 weapons), though of lighter construction, and details of the lock-mechanism embodied in it are not known. This revolver was probably designed to the wishes of an *ad hoc* Army Committee, then belatedly charged with recommending a new service-issue sidearm, but was not adopted, the Committee instead transferring its official attention to another solid-framed rod-ejecting design, namely, the Model 1887 pistol shown at Plate 13 (lower); this pattern was issued for field tests, in limited numbers, and, in line with some military thinking of those days, was in much smaller calibre (8 mm. centre-fire) than any predecessor. Save for its ejector-rod, pierced trigger-guard, lever safety-catch (on the left of the action-body), and frame-mounted firing-pin (visible in Plate 13), this Model 1887 pistol was externally a quite close copy of that Swiss Model 1882 revolver shown at Plate 20 (top), although it is not known whether the lock-mechanism used in it was actually that design embodied in the Swiss arm. It was not adopted, the Committee eventually approving a Model 1892 pistol.

This French Model 1892 service revolver is shown at Plate 14 (top), and is today sometimes mistakenly called a "Lebel" revolver; Nicholas Lebel (b. 1838; d. 1891) was a noted small-arms authority of the French Army, and actually did have a military rifle (the Model 1886) named in honour of his chairmanship of that Rifle Test Board which introduced it, but he had resigned his commission before the Model 1892 revolver was adopted, and there is real doubt if he contributed to such adoption.

As may be noted from Plate 14, the Model 1892 revolver was a six-chambered double-action revolver (which chambered 8-mm. centre-fire cartridges, propelling 120-grain copper-jacketed bullets at around 625 f.p.s.), but although solid-framed, was a swing-out cylinder design of that type mentioned in earlier remarks upon Colt or Smith & Wesson arms. However, its crane-mounted cylinder swung out to the right of the frame, for loading or cartridge ejection, and not (as in the American manner) to the left. It weighed about 1 lb. 14 oz. (840 g.) unloaded, had a 4-in. (100-mm.) barrel, rifled with four grooves, and measured about 8½ inches (239 mm.) overall.

The cylinder was unlatched by means of a rearward-swinging lever on the right of the frame, which disconnected hammer from trigger when turned back (in that fashion later described for Portuguese "Abadie" revolvers), and the whole left-hand side-plate could be opened, on a forward pivot, to give access to the lock-components for cleaning or repair. The double-action lock-mechanism (which is sketched as Figure 16) was very similar to that Model 1889 Italian service revolver lock-mechanism shown in Plate 16 (lower); however, although of considerably better execution, this French design did lack an important safety-feature noticed in relation to the Italian arm.

In Figure 16, "a" is the hammer, "d" the trigger, "g" the pawl, and "k" the mainspring; there are no separate pawl- or trigger-springs, since "k" (by engaging a slot at the inner side of "g", which is itself pivoted on "d") serves both functions, in addition to that of mainspring; in either "at rest" or fully-retracted positions, "d" bolts the cylinder, by engagement with those protuberances and notches visible in Plate 14. The sequence of events in both self-cocking and single-action fire is virtually identical to that described for the "Schmidt-Galand" lock-mechanism in Figure 4, but with the mainspring here functioning exactly as if it were a "mainspring auxiliary" shown in that Figure.

Most observed specimens of the Model 1892 revolver shared with their predecessors the use of a letter-prefixed serial number, making it difficult to estimate those quantities likely to have been produced; M. Josserand has, however, established that 176,103 revolvers of this pattern were made from 1892 to 1900, inclusive. They are noted as issued to officers, by Bornecque, and were also apparently used by naval or marine personnel. In addition to the service version, a model "de Saint-Etienne" was also studied, and is shown at Plate 14 (lower); this rare version is sometimes called the model "à pompe", and used a cylinder-latching system similar to that described in relation to the Br. Pat. 6184/1894 of D. B. WESSON (*q.v.*), where the ejector-rod was pulled forward to free the cylinder for swinging out of the frame.

The French small-arms industry was a large one, with Tulle (a town in the Corréze Department), for example, almost economically dependent upon one factory there, and substantial manufacturing centres at

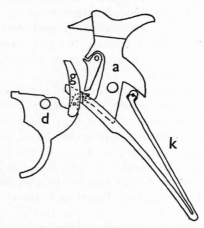

FIG. 16. *Double-action lock-mechanism of the French Modele d'Ordonnance 1892 service revolver.*

St. Etienne and Chatellerault, in the Loire and Vienne Departments, respectively, where both State and private production were carried on. However, revolvers of certain French manufacture are quite rare in both British and American collections, and it is very difficult to judge the extent to which such arms were commercially produced in France. Many weapons with the name of a French retailer prove, upon examination, to have been made in Belgium, and foreign-made copies of the Model 1892 service revolver were available, from Belgian or Spanish manufacturers, to such an extent that it is difficult to regard any appreciable part of the French small-arms manufacturing potential as occupied in this field.

GERMAN revolvers

As Appendix II entries will show (with reference to W. DECKER, K. DOBSLAW and P. SCHMIDT, the GRUSONWERK A. G., M. HASSELMANN, H. LANGENHAN, P. P. MAUSER, E. PAUL,

R. TARGAN and the W. T. G. "WESPI", and G. TRESENREU-
TER), German applicants for British patents relevant to this Chapter
form an appreciable part of the total, but their own country actually
contributed nothing of real value to revolver design, during our period.
The best German hand-gun designers (and there were none better)
concentrated instead upon self-loading pistols during most of that
period, and a large small-arms industry seems to have left us nothing
relevant (and made between 1889 and 1914), save one pattern of service
revolver, some pin-fire arms, a variety of sound hinged-frame self-
ejecting copies of Smith & Wesson designs, and quantities of cheap
solid-framed, rod-ejecting, pocket revolvers, similar to weapons shown
at Plate 6 (lower) and 9.

The German Model 1884 service revolver, for officers, shown in
Plate 15 (top) was a single-action, solid-framed weapon (chambering
six 10·6-mm. centre-fire cartridges), with an overall length of 10$\frac{1}{4}$
inches (260 mm.), an unloaded weight of just over 2 lb. (960 g.), and a
4$\frac{1}{2}$-in. (118-mm.) barrel, rifled with four grooves twisted to the right;
the Model 1880 pistol, for troopers, was similar (see Plate 15; lower),
although larger and of coarser workmanship, with an overall length of
13$\frac{3}{5}$ inches (340 mm.) an unloaded weight of almost 3 lb. (1320 g.), and
a 7$\frac{1}{5}$-in. (180-mm.) barrel with heavy muzzle-ring. Neither Model 1880
nor 1884 arms were fitted with an attached ejector (the arbor serving that
function, when removed from its seat), but both had a lever safety-catch
(on the left) which bolted the hammer "at rest", or in the half-cock
position.

The names of several makers appear upon both models, and it is
believed that all were manufactured between the Erfurt Arsenal, on the
one hand, and the commercial makers F. Dreyse (at Sommerda), Gebr.
Mauser & Co. (at Oberndorf), or Sauer & Son, V. Chas. Schilling, &
C. G. Haenel, at Suhl. Serial-numbers appear to be uniformly low on
Model 1880 weapons (no such number seen by this writer has exceeded
10000), suggesting that a global serial-range was never allocated to
them, but a Model 1884 pistol has been noted with a number as high as
45915. Commonly, both models are dated and several specimens marked
"Erfurt" were dated as late as 1894. However, the German armed forces
began to adopt Borchardt-Luger self-loading pistols, in and after 1900,
when these revolvers were withdrawn to police and reserve service.

The lock-mechanism used in both Model 1880 and 1884 arms was
simple and reliable; flat springs served the hammer and trigger, and
the vulnerable pawl-spring (working against a flat surface formed on the
pawl-pivot) was buried in the slotted hammer-breast. As may be seen
in Figure 17, a rocking cylinder-bolt was operated by the trigger, which

moved forward, at half-cock, sufficiently to tilt that bolt from engagement with the cylinder locking-notches.

ITALIAN revolvers

The Italian armed forces were issued with two basic patterns of solid-framed double-action rod-ejecting revolver, during most of those years between 1889 and 1914; both were six-chambered weapons, in 10·35-mm. centre-fire calibre, and respectively named the "Model 1874, Chamelot Delvigne" (a pistol very similar in appearance to the French arm on Plate 12; lower), and the "Model 1889, system Bodeo" shown in Plate 16.

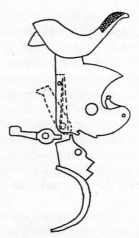

FIG. 17. *Single-action lock-mechanism for German M/1880 and M/1884 service revolvers.*
N.B. Main-, trigger-, and cylinder-bolt springs have been omitted.

As its name suggests, the Model 1874 weapon had a prior history in Italian hands, having been manufactured in no less than three slightly different versions (the "Glisenti", the "Pirlot", and the "Brescian"), prior to August, 1888; at that time, a somewhat lighter pattern was formally substituted for the earlier ones, but it seems probable that this merely saw service alongside its predecessors, which were in the hands of cavalry officers, N.C.O.s, certain transport personnel, and with the Carabinieri. Since most military text-books give dimensions apparently correct only for pre-1888 models, it is difficult to be certain, but this writer believes that even the improved Model 1874 revolver was a heavy pistol, weighing 2½ lb. (1,134 g.) unloaded, and measuring 11 inches (279 mm.) overall, with a 6¼-in. (156-mm.) octagonal barrel, rifled with four grooves twisted to the right; in all cases, however, the double-action lock-mechanism was identical to a French version shown at Figure 15, and was sufficiently well executed to ensure that reliability implicit in its design.

The Model 1889 revolver shown at Plate 16 (top) was originally issued (on 3rd June, 1891) to officers in the medical services, Army, and Carabinieri; in 1906, however, Carabinieri officers received instead a Model 1905 (Haensler-Roch) self-loading pistol and, in 1911, all Army officers were issued similar Glisenti arms. As a result, the Model 1889 revolver was, by 1914, in the hands of load-bearing "Other Ranks" in the Italian armies, such as tripod- or ammunition-carriers in machine-gun sections, and sanitary orderlies or stretcher-bearers. It was a less substantial arm than any Model 1874 pistol, weighing just over 2 lb. (910 g.), measuring just over $9\frac{1}{4}$ inches (235 mm.) in length, and with a $4\frac{3}{8}$-in. (114-mm.) octagonal barrel rifled by four grooves twisted to the right. Although coarsely executed in a version shown at Plate 16 (lower), the lock-mechanism was so thoroughly satisfactory in use that it was virtually copied for the French Model 1892 service revolver (in relation to which the cycle of its operation is indicated), but was apparently of quite elderly parentage. The point may never be finally settled but, save that it used a hammer-catch (i.e. that component hinged to the hammer-breast, for use in self-cocking fire), the Model 1889 Italian service revolver lock-mechanism appears to this writer as having been anticipated, in every material detail, by a design from Belgium (patented there, by Jean Warnant, in 1875), which is the principal subject of later notes upon O. JONES (q.v.) and A. T. DE MOUNCIE (q.v.), and which was the basis for a mechanism used in Swiss M/1878 arms.

However, although the Model 1889 weapon also embodied one safety-device copied from another earlier pistol (where the loading-gate pivot served as a hammer-disconnector, in that fashion shown in Figure 18, for Portuguese "Abadie" revolvers), it was not wholly derivative, and had another safety-feature unique in European service revolvers of this period, namely, a hammer-block. This component (visible in Plate 16; lower), might be mistaken for a pawl-spring, on casual inspection, since it is jointed to the rear of the pawl; however, the purpose which it actually serves is to ride between hammer and frame (preventing the former from reaching the cartridges) until the trigger has been pressed as far to the rear as it can possibly go. When this position is reached, the rising pawl has carried the hammer-block sufficiently high for it to face a relieving notch in the left side of the hammer (see Plate 16; lower), so that when the hammer falls it can now reach a cartridge. Accidental blows upon the hammer, or mishaps in cocking, will no more discharge this revolver than such accidents with a Colt revolver of that type shown at Figure 5.

Model 1889 revolvers were made at several factories, normally had a letter-prefixed serial number, and may be dated; the better-known factory-markings are those of "Castelli" (at Brescia), the "Fabbrica d'Armi Brescia", the "Metallurgica, Bresciana", the "Siderurgica Glisenti" (at Turin), and the "Royal Fabrica d'Armi Glisenti", at Brescia. An improved "Glisenti Model 1894" version of the Model 1889 pistol is listed by several authorities, and believed (by this writer) to be a version with trigger-guard; however, revolvers with the distinctive folding-trigger of the 1889 design will be found bearing dates decades later than 1914, so that the variant arm clearly did not supersede the original.

JAPANESE revolvers

Individual private possession was on a scale sufficient for each Japanese prefecture to maintain an official register of firearms within its borders, and hand-guns may be assumed to have formed an appreciable part of any total, but the Imperial armed forces took no precipitate action to adopt and issue such weapons. True, the Navy had purchased more than six hundred Smith & Wesson "No. 3, New Model" revolvers (see Chapter I) in 1879 and 1887, but a naval pistol of native manufacture or design was not issued during our period; in 1893, the Army did adopt a revolver produced in its own arsenals, but that weapon was superseded (by a Nambu self-loading pistol) in 1914, and it would appear that no general commercial manufacture of revolvers occurred in Japan, as a result of such adoption.

The Japanese Army revolver is shown at Plate 19 (lower), and was known as the "26th Year" Model, in recognition that 1893 (the year of its adoption) was the twenty-sixth year of that Meiji era then current by the Japanese calendar. It was a six-shot, hinged-frame, self-ejecting weapon, in 9-mm. centre-fire calibre, derived from a study of desirable features in sundry Western arms. Thus, the self-cocking lock-mechanism was based upon a Continental "Schmidt-Galand" double-action design then used in British, Austrian, and Dutch service revolvers, take-down details had been pioneered by Emile Nagant, a Belgian, in 1879, and both barrel-latch and cylinder-retainer designs were culled from Smith & Wesson devices (patented during 1877) used in the Imperial Navy's "No. 3, New Model" pistols.

Save that its large hinged side-plate did make it easier to service than any other hinged-frame self-ejecting service revolver, the "26th Year" pistol was a poor weapon, badly manufactured. As issued, it measured about $8\frac{1}{2}$ inches (212·5 mm.) overall, had a $4\frac{7}{10}$-inch (117-mm.) barrel, yet weighed 2 lb. 4 oz. (1,020 g.) unloaded. Although the cartridge had a fairly authoritative muzzle-velocity (at 750 f.p.s.), accurate shooting was difficult with the self-cocking lock-mechanism, particularly in the hands of cavalry, to whom it was largely issued. It is noticeable that Bornecque (writing in 1905) listed an 8-mm. "Carabine Mourata", Model 1894 long-arm as the Japanese service weapon of self-defence, and mentioned this revolver not at all.

NORWEGIAN revolvers

As was the case with Denmark, Norway depended heavily upon imported revolvers to arm troops issued with such weapons, but also maintained a small State manufacturing-capability within its own borders; it is believed, however, that no civilian manufacture of any significance occurred during our period.

Norwegian service revolvers in issue by 1914 (when they were augmented by purchase, and subsequent manufacture, of the Colt M/1911 self-loading pistol) consisted largely of "Model 1893" solid-frame, double-action, rod-ejecting arms, chambering six 7·5-mm. centre-fire cartridges; however, it is probable that earlier issues were represented by surviving specimens of "Model 1883", "Model 1864/1898", or even "Model 1864" arms.

Model 1864 revolvers were 11-mm. pin-fire weapons, largely purchased from France during 1864 (in both single- and double-action versions), but also manufactured on a small scale, during 1867, at the *Kongsberg Våpenfabrikk*; Model 1864–1898 pistols were modified survivors of the earlier model, in which their open frames had been bridged, with top-strap reinforcements, giving them a similar external appearance to that Swedish "Lefaucheux-Francotte" model shown at Plate 21 (top).

Model 1883 weapons were substantial, solid-frame, rod-ejecting revolvers (in 9-mm. centre-fire calibre), of which nearly 800 had been purchased from the Liège factory of Emile Nagant (see L. NAGANT), in both double- and single-action versions; save that their cylinders were dimpled, rather than fluted, these weapons were merely Belgian M/1878 and M/1883 service revolvers earlier described.

Norwegian Model 1893 service revolvers (shown at Plate 17) had that double-action lock-mechanism shown as Figure 19, and 12,964 of them were purchased from the factory of L. NAGANT (*q.v.*), in 1893; a small quantity were also produced at the Kongsberg Våpenfabrikk, and 350 more were purchased from the Swedish Husqvarna factory, during 1897. In Sweden (as may be seen, by comparing Plates 17 and 21) this particular Nagant model had already been in issue for some years, as the "Model 1887" revolver later mentioned, and the 7·5-mm. centre-fire arms supplied to Norway are almost indistinguishable from Swedish issue sidearms; they may be identified, however, by the acceptance stamps of Norwegian inspectors (Jacob Maximillian Gran Paaske, and Ole Adolf Julsrud) impressed upon them with the factory name, or by a pattern of foresight used. Both features are shown at Plate 17 (lower).

PORTUGUESE revolvers

Portugal had two "Abadie" service revolvers in issue at 1889, namely, the Model 1878 (for officers), and the Model 1886 (for troopers), both of which were Belgian-made, solid-framed, rod-ejecting weapons, chambering six 9·1-mm. centre-fire cartridges; issue of the officer's model ceased entirely in 1908 (when a 9-mm. Borchardt-Luger self-loading pistol was adopted as the service sidearm), but troopers pistols were then relegated to the *Guarda Fiscal*, and not finally discarded until many years later. A definite reason for the model-name lies in the legend "Systeme Abadie Brevete" stamped upon each frame, but the marking "L. Soleil, Liège" is also present.

In dimension, these two models were similar only in calibre, and in relation to that four-groove rifling, twisted to the left, which was used in their barrels. The Model 1878 pistol (shown at Plate 18; top) measured $8\frac{7}{10}$ inches (218 mm.) overall, had a $4\frac{1}{2}$-in. (113-mm.) octagonal barrel, and weighed 1·63 lb. (752 g.) unloaded; the Model 1886 revolver (shown at Plate 18; lower) measured about 10 inches (249 mm.) overall, had a $5\frac{2}{3}$-in. (142 mm.) octagonal barrel, and weighed 1·83 lb. (835 g.) unloaded. The frames were of different weights also, but other more noticeable differences of detail can be seen in the rod-ejector and arbor of these two models, and (internally) in the method used for mounting their lock-mechanism; the latter was, incidentally, of that Model 1878 double-action Nagant design, shown in Figure 14.

An important feature common to both Model 1878 and Model 1886 "Abadie" revolvers, was a loading-gate safety-device, elsewhere noticed in remarks upon Austrian (M/1898), French (M/1892), Italian (M/1889), and Swiss M/1882 service revolvers. The practical effect of the "Abadie" version (operation of which is shown at Figure 18) was that when the rearward-opening loading-gate was swung back, this action first half-cocked the hammer, and then permitted the trigger to be pressed repeatedly without further cocking the hammer. It was not therefore possible to fire the weapon whilst loading or unloading it, and

the chambers were rapidly and automatically aligned (without fumb-
ling) for loading, or use of the rod-ejector to clear any cartridges in
them.

In Figure 18 it will be seen that the inner end of the loading-gate
pivot extends across the plane of that hinged hammer-catch (on the
hammer-breast) against which the trigger-nose thrusts to raise the
hammer in self-cocking fire. When the loading-gate is open, a cylindrical
surface on the pivot forces back the hammer-catch, and pressure on the
trigger merely raises the pawl, to rotate the cylinder, without cocking

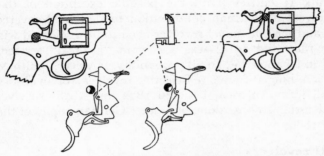

FIG. 18. *Portuguese "Abadie" loading-gate safety device.*
(Drawn by Senhor João de Figueiredo.)

the hammer; when the gate is closed, however, that side of the pivot
then opposite the hammer-catch is so shaped that the latter may be
reached by the trigger-nose, in normal fashion.

ROMANIAN revolvers

The *Muzeul Militar Central* has no information upon the scale of
issue (if any) to Romanian forces of that native revolver which is
described in relation to H. DIMANCEA (*q.v.*), and illustrated as
Figure 39. It is clear, however, that three different service revolvers
(together with a M/1912 Steyr 8·8-mm. self-loading pistol) were in the
hands of certain Romanian officers and troops, during our period.

The most elderly design is shown as Plate 20 (lower), and was known
as "Captain Buescu's revolver, Model 1876"; this gate-loaded, solid-
framed, rod-ejecting, double-action weapon had originally been issued
as the "system Galant Lebeau, Model 1874" (probably after purchase
from Liège), and subsequently modified to Captain Buescu's recom-
mendations. Both Model 1874 and Model 1876 weapons were superseded by issue of the Steyr pistol, Model 1912, mentioned above.

In addition, more modern revolvers (of 8-mm. centre-fire calibre) were issued under the model-names "system Nagant, Model 1895" and "system Saint-Etienne, Model 1896". The writer has not secured pictures of these Romanian models, but believes them respectively to have been copies of a widely-circulated Nagant arm (see, for example, Plate 17; top) and of that French Model 1892 service revolver shown at Plate 14; the first was presumably supplied from Liège, but the Model 1892 arms could have been of either French or Belgian origin.

RUSSIAN revolvers

Appendix II entries (with the possible exception of that for B. BEHR) reveal no Russian contribution to that field covered by this Chapter, and the only novel revolver even to be associated with Russia (between 1889 and 1914) was a Nagant "gas-seal" service weapon described in Chapter IV. In all probability, however, Smith & Wesson single-action, hinged-frame, self-ejecting revolvers (of an obsolete model purchased, from America, between 1872 and 1878) survived in the hands of Russian troops, along with later German copies of them, until well after 1889.

SPANISH revolvers

Writing in 1881, Barado & Génova had mentioned only one Spanish service revolver of that period, which was a large hinged-frame, self-ejecting, single-action Smith & Wesson pistol, with a detachable carbine-stock and, in view of the Spanish firearms industry then existing, it is tempting to suggest that this weapon was of native manufacture, perhaps by Orbea Hermanos, of Eibar, who were noted copiers of Smith & Wesson designs. In fact, however, the Springfield firm had supplied such arms for Spanish service, during the 1870s, and Parsons records both a shipment of the so-called "New Model Russian" revolver to Cuba, around 1875, and delivery of 1,000 modified "New Model No. 3" pistols (sold as the "Russian Model of 1877") to Spain itself. Since those markings reported upon the revolver illustrated by Barado & Génova are markings found upon the earliest version of "Russian Model" Smith & Wesson revolver (and not upon either "New Model No. 3" or "New Model Russian" pistols), it is clear that work remains to be done upon the source from and extent to which Spanish forces were armed with revolvers manufactured abroad, at the opening of our period.

In one case, at least, there was no doubt when (by Royal Decree, dated 6th October, 1884) a double-action "Smith revolver", manufactured by the Orbea Hermanos, was specifically approved for adoption, and became the Spanish officer's Model 1885 sidearm at 18th November, 1885; according to "un Officier Superieur" (whose remarks were published in 1894), the trooper's revolver then was a "Lefaucheux, Model 1883", but the details of both weapon and source are wanting.

As to civilian revolvers of Spanish manufacture, the chosen anonymity of makers in our period, and lack of material published in English, makes it difficult to establish the identity of manufacturers active between 1889 and 1914. Mathews certainly notices weapons from Barcelona, Eibar, Elgoeibar, Ermua, Guernica, Madrid and Zumorraga, but largely in patterns unaltered for whole decades, which could have been produced at almost any time between 1885 and 1935. The Orbea Hermanos earlier noticed, and Esprin Hermanos (using the variously-spelled "Euskaro" trade-name, at Eibar), are certainly producers relevant to these pages, but other identities remain to be verified.

Like their counterparts at Liège, Spanish makers could produce almost any pattern of revolver, and so inexpensively as to compete with the Belgian producers even at their cheapest levels of production. The Spaniards appear to have used rather more hand-work than the larger Liège manufacturers of our period, and to have had a smaller annual output; total figures are difficult to find, but *Artifex & Opifex* have provided annual-production figures for Eibar only, as 56,370 revolvers made in 1889, 67,664 in 1890, 65,434 in 1891, 66,101 in 1892, and 69,395 in 1893.

As a generality, it is true to say that most Spanish commercial revolvers of our period were not of the best quality, and that extensive use of cast-iron components (in association with obsolete proof rules) made some of the cheapest weapons actually dangerous to their owners. However, prompted by some undoubtedly vile pistols supplied to meet the First World War demands, criticism of Spanish hand-gun workmanship has undoubtedly been carried to extremes. Since the French officer class never hesitated to carry Spanish sidearms, even under the most severe conditions, since considerable markets for them long existed in Africa or South America, and since so many specimens have survived to this day, it must be accepted that (in all save the cheapest grades) Spanish revolvers were at least as safe in use as their Belgian or American equivalents, though sometimes not as reliable.

For a more specific and justified criticism, however, it can be said that all models relevant to our period were copied from the designs of other countries, and that Spanish manufacturers appear to have restricted their experiments to those for adapting the mechanisms of others into forms acceptable to an industry using a high proportion of hand-work.

Double-action solid-framed revolvers, with swing-out cylinders and manual ejectors, did not appear in substantial quantities until after 1914, but a few lines externally almost identical in appearance to Smith & Wesson arms of this type were produced; internally, however, these 8-mm. weapons did not normally follow the American lock-mechanism shown at Figure 11, but instead used a design adapted from that (shown at Plate 16; lower) used in Italian M/1889 and French M/1892 service arms.

Double-action or self-cocking hinged-frame self-ejecting arms were similarly based upon the Smith & Wesson "Double Action" (see Plate 5; lower), "New Navy", or "New Departure" models described in Chapter I; these were available in all the principal centre-fire calibres, and in poor qualities. An unattractive sales ploy, practised by certain makers, was the use upon these arms of a barrel-legend calculated to make the gullible (or illiterate) buyer believe that he was in fact purchasing an American pistol; "Smith & Wesson cartridges are those that are best for the Euscharo Revolver", "S. & W. Cartridges to be used for this Revolver", or (upon a self-styled "Model 1909" copy of the Smith & Wesson Safety Hammerless arm) "Smith & Wesson's Cartridges are Those Best Suite the Euskara Revolver", are examples.

As to solid-framed, rod-ejecting revolvers, the principal types produced were of either double-action "Bull Dog" and "Constabulary" patterns, similar to that shown as Plate 22 (top), or smaller self-cocking, concealed hammer "Velo Dog" models, with folding triggers, like that in Plate 6 (lower); the former were made in a variety of chamberings, the latter commonly in that 5·5-mm. centre-fire calibre peculiar to them, but occasionally for other small cartridges. In addition, pin-fire revolvers, of obsolete types, were made for certain South American countries where such arms remained fashionable.

SWEDISH revolvers

During 1871, Sweden had adopted the single-action, 11-mm. centre-fire, "Lefaucheux-Francotte" service revolver shown at Plate 21 (top), and this weapon remained in issue, with selected personnel, for a considerable period of time; thus, the *Kungl. Armémuseum* reports, it was still carried by sergeants and dismounted gunners, signallers, and medical or ambulance men, in 1897, and was not finally superseded until 1907. In that year, a Browning self-loading pistol was introduced by the Swedish Army, and a Model 1887 service revolver (next described) was passed over to men issued with Model 1871 arms, in substitution for that elderly design.

As early as 1885, shortcomings in the Model 1871 design had led a Swedish Army commission to seek more suitable revolvers for officers or senior N.C.O.s and, after trials with Gasser-Kropatschek (see Plate 7; lower), Nagant (Belgian), Schmidt (Swiss), native, and Warnant (Belgian) weapons, a field-testing of thirty Nagant and a like number of Schmidt arms, had resulted in adoption of a Model 1887 revolver shown at Plate 21 (lower); this weapon was later to be adopted also by the Norwegians (in a version shown at Plate 17; top), as their Model 1893 service sidearm, and was a six-shot, double-action, solid-framed, rod-ejecting pistol, in 7·5-mm. centre-fire calibre, with a 4½-in. (112-mm.) barrel.

The lock-mechanism used in Swedish M/1887 revolvers (as with Argentinian, Belgian M/1878–86, Brazilian, Norwegian M/1893, Romanian M/1895, and Serbian equivalents) is shown at Figure 19,

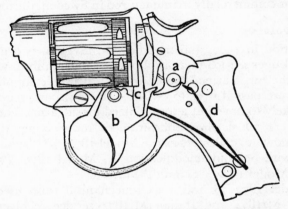

FIG. 19. *Swedish (Nagant) double-action lock-mechanism for M/1887 revolver.*

where "a" is the hammer, "b" the trigger, "c" the pawl, and "d" the mainspring, which also serves as both pawl- and trigger-spring; the cycle of operation, in single- or double-action fire, will be obvious, by reference to earlier descriptions of lock-mechanisms using a hammer-catch (for example, that relating to Figure 13), but it should be noted that here the mainspring tilts the pawl by engaging a flat on the pawl-axis, that this engagement of the mainspring also acts as a trigger-spring, and that trigger, mainspring and hammer positions "at rest" coincide to rebound the latter.

Although the first Swedish M/1887 service revolvers had been purchased from E. Nagant's factory, at Liège (see L. NAGANT), their later supply was from the Husqvarna Arsenal, in Sweden, whose present Director has confirmed those quantities actually manufactured. Under a Norwegian ministerial authorization (of 25th March, 1897) an order for 350 revolvers was first filled, but thereafter manufacture for the Swedish forces proceeded steadily, with production-runs in 1898 (5,400), 1899 (3,252), 1900 (690), 1901 (353), 1902 (377), 1903 (3,133), 1904 (144), and 1905 (383), during our period, to total 13,732 Swedish service revolvers of native manufacture; all were supplied to the Army Council complete with holster, spare cylinder, cleaning-rod, and turnscrew.

The Model 1887 design proved satisfactory enough to be also commercially available from Husqvarna, whose catalogue *Husqvarna Skjutvapen* (of 1st April, 1904) listed this weapon priced at 35kr., and there is no evidence that T. F. TÖRNELL's quite valid improvement to it was ever seriously developed. Indeed, it is this writer's belief that (*pace* the inventions of G. ENVALL and W. T. UNGE, *q.v.*) no other revolver was commercially manufactured in Sweden, during our period.

SWISS revolvers

By adoption in 1900, and modification in 1906, two models of the Borchardt-Luger self-loading pistol (in 7·65 mm. calibre) were issued to officers of the Swiss armed forces, so that available supplies of service revolvers were passed over to N.C.O.s (in transport, service corps, or artillery) likely to have but a formal need for sidearms. The revolvers in question were all six-shot, solid-framed, rod-ejecting, double-action weapons, known to collectors as the Model 1872–78 ("system Chamelot Delvigne, with Schmidt modifications"), Model 1878 ("system Warnant"), or Model 1882 ("Schmidt") arms.

The Model 1872–78 had a lock-mechanism (also used in French M/1873 or M/1874 and Italian M/1874 service revolvers) which is shown at Figure 15, and must have been quite scarce by 1900, since it had originally been issued (in 1872) as a 10·4-mm. rim-fire revolver, but was later converted to centre-fire when the then new Model 1878 revolver was introduced for mounted officers. This weapon measured about 11 inches (275 mm.) overall, had a 6-in. (150-mm.) octagonal barrel, and weighed over 2 lb. (1,000 g.) unloaded.

The 10·4-mm. centre-fire Model 1878 Swiss service revolver offers identification problems to anyone interested in establishing the sources from which its design was drawn. The Eidg. Waffenfabrik, Berne, where it was made, has described the arm to this writer simply as having been "after the system Scholberg and Cadet with lock-system Warnant", whilst Rudolf Schmidt (writing in 1889) described it as a "system

Schmidt" weapon, with his only acknowledgement to Warnant made in relation to the rod-ejector. However, Schmidt's own drawing of this lock-mechanism indicates that, whilst closely modelled upon an 1875 design of Jean Warnant, mentioned in Appendix II entries upon O. JONES and A. T. DE MOUNCIE, it was actually of a type midway between those mechanisms shown as Plate 16 (lower) and Figure 4. Thus it had the rebound lever or "mainspring auxiliary" (shown as "n", in Figure 4) of the "Schmidt-Galand" lock-mechanism, but lacked any "hammer catch" pivoted to the breast of the hammer, as in Plate 16. The weapon measured 9 inches (235 mm.) overall, had a $4\frac{1}{2}$-in. (116-mm.) octagonal barrel rifled with four grooves, and weighed over $1\frac{1}{2}$ lb. (750 g.) unloaded.

The Swiss Model 1882 service revolver shown in Plate 20 (top) was also called a "Schmidt" revolver (in honour of Rudolf Schmidt, a noted Swiss small-arms authority, and Director of the Eidg. Waffenfabrik), and had that "Schmidt-Galand" lock-mechanism, shown in Figures 4, 12 and 33, which was so extensively used by late nineteenth-century revolver-makers. These were beautifully-made arms, with the hammer-rebound and (after 1887) loading-gate safety-device described in relation to Colt and Portuguese weapons respectively embodying such features; they measured $9\frac{2}{5}$ inches (235 mm.) overall, had $4\frac{1}{2}$-in. (116-mm.) octagonal barrels rifled with four grooves, and weighed over $1\frac{1}{2}$ lb. (750 g.) unloaded. The original cartridge had a paper-patched bullet, but (from 1887) this was replaced by a copper-jacketed Rubin bullet.

TURKISH revolvers

Purchases of rim- and centre-fire Smith & Wesson single-action, hinged-frame, self-ejecting revolvers (and German copies of them) had been made for the Turkish armed forces, between 1874 and 1883. However, it seems likely that such weapons were bought for issue to cavalry-men, and not carried on the person. Until around 1908, indeed, a sword appears to have been the only approved sidearm for personnel and officers on foot; thereafter, pistols (with knives and bayonets) were carried by Turkish soldiers and officers, but no revolver or self-loading pistol seems to have been formally issued, even by 1914.

CHAPTER III

BRITISH ARMS

AS the Introduction has shown, our period was not one generally prosperous for the whole British gun-trade. There were, of course, exceptional cases amongst manufacturers of military rifles, machine-guns, and ammunition (G. Kynoch & Co., for example, grew from a single-factory concern, with twenty-three clerks, five travellers, and a year's trading-loss of £19,000, in 1888, to be the nine-factory Kynoch Limited, employing 235 clerks, forty-five travellers, and with a trading profit of £100,000, by 1904), but the overall picture was one of declining British commercial small-arms production, yet of expanding output in Belgium, France or Spain. Even those later wars and disturbances noticed with the Introduction failed, for example, to boost the total of proofs at the Birmingham Proof House back to that modest plateau (of slightly over half a million proofs) annually enjoyed between 1889 and 1891.

Admittedly, a fair proportion of entries in Appendix II relates to patentees of stated British domicile (though not necessarily of nationality), which might be taken at least to indicate a potential United Kingdom market for native ideas, but even the most casual examination of that listing demolishes any such assumption. Thus twelve names in the total are those of Patent Agents, acting for overseas applicants more interested in blocking British manufacture of their designs than in promoting the same, and only twenty-one patentees (marked with an asterisk in the list) actually achieved even modest commercial production of their inventions here.

Ignoring those devices dealt with in Chapter IV (but including the invention of I. WHEELDON, an Australian) we have the following Appendix II entries in point for this chapter, namely; J. G. ACCLES and H. H. GRENFELL* (revolver); A. ARBENZ (revolver safety-device); A. C. ARGLES (pepperbox revolver); L. ARMANNI (magazine pistol); B. R. BANKS (air-rifle magazine); A. J. BOULT (Patent

Agent); E. G. BREWER (Patent Agent); L. W. BROADWELL and M. H. DURST (rifle magazines); A. H. BUTLER and F. G. CLARK (air-rifle magazine); J. CARTER* (revolver improvements); F. CASHMORE, C. O. ELLIS and E. W. WILKINSON (revolver ejector); W. CHAINE (magazine pistol); A. CHAPMAN (rifle magazine; A. M. CLARK (Patent Agent); J. H. COX (air-rifle magazine); H. DIMANCEA* (revolver); G. C. DYMOND (Patent Agent); J. EASTWICK (rifle magazine); W. FLETCHER and H. A. SILVER* (revolver ejector); G. V. FOSBERY* (revolvers); H. W. GABBETT-FAIRFAX (self-loading pistol); R. GORDON-SMITH* (butt-cap for revolver); E. C. GREEN* (revolver); O. IMRAY (Patent Agent); P. JENSEN (Patent Agent); J. H. JOHNSON (Patent Agent); D. T. LAING (revolver lance); H. H. LAKE (Patent Agent); W. R. LAKE (Patent Agent); H. W. and J. F. LATHAM* (revolver adaptor and improvements to revolvers); A. LINES (revolvers); J. A. G. MARSHALL (wrist-support); F. MARTIN, R. C. ROMANEL and A. H. WILLIAMS (magazine-rifle); R. MORRIS* (adaptors for firearms); A. T. DE MOUNCIE* (revolver lock-mechanism); J. T. MUSGRAVE* (improved revolver adaptor); H. E. NEWTON (Patent Agent); R. PAULSON (gas-operated revolver); W. DE C. PRIDEAUX* (revolver-charger); C. RICCI (self-loading rifle); H. SCHLUND* (revolver); G. SHEPHEARD (automatic radial rifle); W. E. STEERS (revolver sight); L. F. TAVERNIER (magazine pistol); W. P. THOMPSON (Patent Agent); B. T. L. THOMSON and J. S. WALLACE (magazine for pneumatic small-arm); G. E. VAUGHAN (Patent Agent); A. J. WATSON* (revolver-charger); H. and T. W. WEBLEY* (improvements to revolvers); THE WEBLEY & SCOTT REVOLVER & ARMS CO. LTD. and W. J. WHITING* (improvements to revolvers); I. WHEELDON (wire-cutters); C. C. B. WHYTE (revolver carrier); and L. and S. S YOUNGHUSBAND (rifle). It should be noted, as significant of the situation within the British firearms industry, that out of twenty-one patentees marked in the above list as known to have produced their inventions commercially, nine of those cases related to protection secured before 1889.

The purpose of this Chapter being to deal (as in Chapters I and II) with those revolvers used or made in a particular country, the reader's attention is directed to Appendix II for details of any other type of invention noticed in the listing above, which was patented in the United Kingdom between 1889 and 1914.

As to revolvers (and bearing in mind that almost all commercial arms described in Chapters I and II were available to British buyers), the following is an alphabetical listing and commentary upon known United Kingdom manufacturers and suppliers of the period.

ADAMS revolvers

The Adams's Patent Small Arms Manufacturing Co. traded at No. 391 Strand, London, until 1894, when it moved briefly to Nos. 40 and 42 Crampton Street, S.E. (at Newington Butts), but went out of business in 1895; with it, passed the firm of Adams & Co., at No. 32 Finsbury Pavement, London, E.C., whose name is sometimes to be found upon both solid-framed and hinged-frame self-ejecting revolvers (similar to those shown at Plate 24; lower) which, the firm's advertisements notwithstanding, it almost certainly did not make.

In 1881, the Adams's Patent Small Arms Manufacturing Co. had been successors to a limited liability company of similar name (established in 1864) which had supplied a large solid-framed, double-action rod-ejecting revolver, patented by John Adams, to H.M. Government, as an official service side-arm of ·450 centre-fire calibre; although superseded by the "ENFIELD" revolver (q.v.) in 1880, this Adams weapon remained in police and gaol service over the earlier part of our period and the Adams's Patent Small Arms Manufacturing Co. certainly advertised itself as a revolver manufacturer and supplier of ". . . revolvers of every description" for so long as it traded.

ACCLES and GRENFELL revolvers

See Appendix II, i.e. "J. G. ACCLES" and "H. H. GRENFELL".

ARBENZ revolvers

See Appendix II, i.e. "A. ARBENZ" and "PIRLOT & TRESART".

ARGLES revolvers

See Appendix II, i.e. "A. C. ARGLES".

BOURNE revolvers

Joseph Bourne & Son (at 100/101 Bath Street, and 89–92 Lower Loveday Street, Birmingham) sold a full range of Birmingham-made small-arms and accessories to the British gun-trade, during our period. The firm's catalogues embraced revolvers, but these were poor weapons, consisting largely of Belgian types shown at Plate 9, with the addition of a cheap hinged-frame self-ejecting arm, significantly advertised as '. . . plain foreign make, not guaranteed".

CARTER revolvers

See Appendix II, re "J. CARTER", "H. WEBLEY", "THE

WEBLEY & SCOTT REVOLVER & ARMS CO., LTD.", and "W. J. WHITING"; see also "WEBLEY" and "WILKINSON" revolvers below, with Plate 24 (lower).

DIMANCEA revolvers

See Appendix II, re "H. DIMANCEA", with Figure 39.

DYKE revolvers

Frank Dyke & Co. were merchants and "manufacturers" of small-arms and ammunition during the latter part of our period with premises at 10 Union Street, London Bridge. The firm sold both American and Continental revolvers of standard patterns (including Velo Dog arms of the type shown in Plate 6, lower), but ranged no closer to British products than the description "English Finish and Proof", applied to certain solid-framed Continental arms.

ENFIELD revolvers

See Appendix II, re "O. JONES" and "A. T. DE MOUNCIE", with Plate 19 (top), and Figure 34.

FLETCHER and SILVER revolvers

See Appendix II, re "W. FLETCHER" and "H. A. SILVER", with Plate 30 (lower).

FOSBERY revolvers

See Appendix II, re "G. V. FOSBERY", with Plate 31 and Figures 40, 41 and 42.

GREEN revolvers

See Appendix II, re "E. C. GREEN", with Plate 32.

HENRY revolvers

See "Webley" revolvers (Mark IV), below.

JONES revolvers

See "Enfield" revolvers, above.

KAUFMANN revolvers

During the 1880s, P. WEBLEY & SON (*q.v.*) had manufactured two models of a heavy-calibre double-action hinged-frame self-ejecting "Army" revolver, designed by that Michael Kaufmann noticed in later Appendix II remarks upon O. JONES and A. T. DE MOUNCIE;

Kaufmann held British Patents Nos. 4302 of 21st October, 1880 (for the lock-mechanism shown at Figure 29, in comparison with a later version improved by J. G. ACCLES and H. H. GRENFELL), and 3313 of 29th July, 1881 (covering a barrel-latch used in the first "Webley-Kaufmann" model), whilst T. W. and H. WEBLEY held British Patent No. 5143 of 24th November, 1881, for the ejector-mechanism, and H. WEBLEY held British Patent No. 542 of 1st February, 1883, covering an improved barrel-latch used in the second or "Improved Government" model of this design.

By 1889, however, only the ejector patent remained in force (see Table I), for P. WEBLEY & SON had turned its attention to other hinged-frame designs, later described in remarks upon "WEBLEY" revolvers. Therefore, although it may be assumed that "Webley-Kaufmann" and "Improved Government" pistols (which were finely made) must have remained in use during our period, manufacture seems to have ceased before 1889, and such arms can only be dismissed here as of an obsolete pattern.

KERR or LONDON ARMOURY CO. revolvers

The firm of James Kerr & Co. (at 114 Queen Victoria Street, E.C.) also styled itself "The London Armoury Company" until, in 1894, a limited liability company was registered as The London Armoury Co., Ltd., and took over that firm's business; the new company traded until long after 1914.

Although described as "small arms and ammunition manufacturers and agents", it was in the latter field that both the original firm and the successor company shone, with such important agencies as those for Colt, Merwin Hulbert, or Winchester arms amongst their activities in this field. However, inexpensive solid-framed or self-ejecting revolvers (of those types shown in Plates 22 and 24; lower) will be encountered bearing the firm or the company name, and it is clear that a perfectly conventional retail business, selling arms from Birmingham and Liège, was carried on.

KYNOCH revolvers

See Appendix II, re "H. or H. A. SCHLUND".

LINES revolvers

See Appendix II, re "A. LINES", and Figure 50.

MORRIS revolvers

See Appendix II, re "R. MORRIS".

DE MOUNCIE revolvers

See "Enfield" revolvers, above.

OSBORNE revolvers

As mentioned in Appendix II (see "F. CASHMORE", "C. O. ELLIS", and "E. W. WILKINSON"), the Birmingham firm of Charles Osborne & Co., Ltd. sold a wide variety of small arms at its Whittall Street premises but, although advertised as "Manufacturers of Guns, Rifles, Revolvers and Pistols", it seems certain that most of the revolvers which it catalogued were actually imported, and not made in Birmingham at all.

The "Osborne" weapons shown at Plate 9 were all of Belgian origin (albeit some may have been finished at Birmingham, from Liège components), and the same catalogue also featured Colt, Harrington & Richardson, Iver Johnson, and Smith & Wesson revolvers, of patterns noticed in Chapter I. The firm had an agency for the first—and last—named American revolvers, and it is noticeable that no named Webley pistol of any kind appears in the "Osborne" catalogue. Since Cashmore, Ellis & Wilkinson troubled to secure that Br. Pat. 5151/1896 described in Appendix II, it must be assumed that their "Osborne" firm then had access to revolver-manufacturing facilities in the United Kingdom, but nothing illustrated in post-1896 catalogues seen by this writer can be definitely identified as of British manufacture, with the possible exception of a revolver (offered in ·320, ·380, ·450, ·455 or ·476 centre-fire calibres) closely resembling the weapon shown as Plate 24 (lower). Certainly, no revolver embodying the improvements of Br. Pat. 5151/1896 has been observed, either in fact or catalogue.

ROSSON revolvers

Charles Rosson (at No. 4 Market Head, Derby) catalogued shotguns, rifles, revolvers and accessories, of good quality, during the 1890s amongst them being Colt, Smith & Wesson, or Webley revolvers in models elsewhere described, and including that shown as Plate 24 (lower). He also listed "Rosson's Revolvers" (in "Constabulary", "Bull Dog", and "New Revolver" lines), which he did not illustrate, but which were probably of the general type illustrated at Plate 9. The source of supply for such arms is unknown but (since he also specifically listed Webley "R.I.C." weapons described below) was probably Liège.

SCHLUND revolvers

See Appendix II, re "H. or H. A. SCHLUND".

TRANTER revolvers

William Tranter had been an important Birmingham revolver-maker, in years prior to 1885 (when he retired), and it is reasonable to assume that many of his well-made arms remained in use after 1889. The Tranter factory (at Aston Cross) was also briefly involved in manufacture of SCHLUND revolvers, but Tranter-designed pistols were conventional double-action hinged-frame self-ejecting or solid-framed arms.

WEBLEY revolvers

The firm (and subsequent limited liability company) described in Appendix II entries relating to P. WEBLEY & SON or THE WEBLEY & SCOTT REVOLVER & ARMS CO. LTD., never depended upon revolver-manufacture to stay in business, although choosing to manufacture and sell a surprising range of such arms during our period, latterly even in competition with its own self-loading pistols. It was at various times contractor to the Admiralty and H.M. War Department of Great Britain (together with the London, Metropolitan and Dublin Police, and the Royal Irish Constabulary), as to India, the British Colonies, the French Government, the Imperial Chinese, Imperial Japanese, and Argentine navies, and to the Cape Mounted, Lisbon and Egyptian Police, and had (for almost the whole of our period) a monopoly in the supply of new issue service revolvers to the British armed forces. However, in relation to British civilians or British officers (the latter being free to buy any revolver chambering service ammunition), competition from American or Belgian suppliers was keen, and there being no preferential tariffs to favour British arms imported into the various countries of the British Empire, such competition had to be faced almost everywhere.

Webley revolvers of our period fall into two main categories, namely, solid-framed, gate-loading, rod-ejecting and (the firm having examined and rejected the swing-out cylinder, hand-ejector alternative) hinged-frame, self-ejecting arms.

As to the first category, by 1914 Webley solid-framed revolvers were offered in two basic double-action lines, being the "R.I.C." and "No. 2 Pattern" models, both of which were available in a variety of calibres, and both of which used a lock-mechanism similar to that shown at Figure 32, though lacking the patented cylinder-bolt of J. CARTER (*q.v.*) shown therein.

Webley's "R.I.C." line comprised:

(1) The "R.I.C. No. 1, ·450/·455" model, a six-shot weapon, chambering either ·450, ·455, or ·476 centre-fire cartridges, which was normally offered as a 30-oz. revolver with the $4\frac{1}{2}$-in. barrel shown upon a non-standard weapon in Plate 30 (lower), but could be supplied with 6-in. barrel (and weighing 33 oz.) for a few extra shillings. In this long-barrelled version, weapons were sometimes made up with a spring-loaded rod-ejector (housed in Colt style, against the barrel), apparently to simulate a "New Model Army Express" pistol briefly popularized by P. WEBLEY & SON during the early 1880s; specimens of this weapon are as rare as the arm which they imitated, and appear to be numbered into that global serial-range reserved for all heavy-calibre "R.I.C." revolvers although, to date, this writer has only observed such specimens in the series 77000–87000 therein. As shown at Plate 30 (lower) the short-barrelled model was used as a vehicle for the improvements of W. FLETCHER and H. A. SILVER (*q.v.*).

(2) The "R.I.C. 83/·450", "R.I.C. 83/·455" and "M.P. ·450" models, respectively a five-shot, 18-oz. revolver with 3-in. barrel; a five-shot 20-oz. revolver, also with 3-in. barrel, but having cylinder and frame lengthened to accommodate the more potent cartridge; and a six-shot 27-oz. weapon (with $2\frac{1}{2}$-in. barrel) adopted by both the London Metropolitan Police and by various shipping companies. Like all Webley "R.I.C." revolvers, these models were rifled with seven grooves, twisted to the right.

(3) The "R.I.C. No. 2, ·320" model, a 12-oz. revolver, with 2-in. barrel, which could be supplied in ·320 or ·32 S & W centre-fire chamberings.

(4) The "Webley No. 5 ·360 Express" (see Plate 22, top), which could be had in barrel lengths of 3 inches (weighing 19 oz.) or $4\frac{1}{2}$ inches (weighing 20 oz.), and which chambered either the No. 5 ·360 Rook Rifle cartridge, or standard ·38 revolver rounds. This model in the "R.I.C." line may have been introduced well after versions described at (2) and (3) above since, although specimens appear to be numbered into the same serial-range as those other arms, this writer has not yet seen a "Webley No. 5 ·360 Express" numbered below 61000.

As Major Dowell has demonstrated, this model was also available in a ·380 chambering only, and with long barrel or with self-cocking lock-mechanism and hinged-bar trigger; the latter variant may have been a late one, two specimens so far observed by this writer being serially-numbered 88844 and 100330. Finally, as can be noticed in Plate 22 (top), the cylinder-fluting and ejector-rod heads on early revolvers are in shapes later discarded for those patterns shown at Plate 30 (lower).

All of the "R.I.C." models listed above could be bought in blued or nickel-plated finishes, and gold- or silver-plated weapons (with exotic butts) can be encountered. The names of retailers appear upon these revolvers more commonly than that of their maker, but it was standard practice for their model-name (and the Webley "winged bullet" trade-mark) to be impressed upon the forward side of each frame.

The range of Webley "No. 2 Pattern" revolvers is shown at Plate 22 (lower), all had 3-in. barrels, and the weight or calibre of each model can be read in that Plate. Essentially, these were merely a slightly cheaper version of the Webley "R.I.C." line (though fitted with a "parrot beak" or "bird's-head" butt, less bulky than that fitted to their running-mates), and it is possible that some of their components were imported from Liège, for finishing in Birmingham, although their lock-mechanism was identical to that used in the "R.I.C." series.

It is worth recording that the "No. 2 Pattern" line shown in Plate 22 had been preceded by a similar series of Webley revolvers, which were also sold under, and marked with the name "British Bull Dog"; these earlier models closely resembled that revolver shown as P. 1493 on Plate 9, and were (unfortunately for the collector) matched by similar American and Belgian solid-frame revolvers, also marked "British Bull Dog" and only to be readily distinguished by their use of a prawled butt. The point is raised here in warning to the reader that not every revolver catalogued as a "British Bull Dog" arm will necessarily match another in a collector's possession.

As with those "R.I.C." models described above, "No. 2 Pattern" arms were available in a choice of finishes, including presentation, will be found to carry Webley's model-marking and trade-mark, and were sold by retailers whose names and addresses may appear upon them.

Webley hinged-frame self-ejecting revolvers of our period may conveniently be listed here in the following basic varieties, namely Webley-Fosbery; service issue; commercial "Target" and so-called "Army"; and "Police" or "Pocket" models, the first of which is sufficiently covered in Appendix II (see G. V. FOSBERY).

Although P. WEBLEY & SON had secured its first War Department contract to supply hinged-frame self-ejecting revolvers in July 1887 (that order being for 10,000 pistols), the model purchased did not formally supersede earlier "Enfield" or "Adams" pistols, still in issue, until very late in 1892. At that time, however, such competing arms began to be withdrawn and replaced by "Mark I" Webley revolvers and the latter model was itself then followed by the sealing of further patterns, namely,

the "Mark II" (in 1894), "Mark III" (in 1897), "Mark IV" (in 1899)
and "Mark V" (in 1913), to the exclusion of any other revolver as an
official issue to H.M. armed forces.

The "Pistol, Webley, Mark I, B. L. Revolver" is shown at Plate 23
(top), and was a six-chambered, double-action, hinged-frame, self-
ejecting weapon, originally issued in ·442 centre-fire calibre, but subsequently made in ·455 and ·476 centre-fire versions also. The majority
of examples encountered will be issue service arms, but this model was
also sold commercially, and can be found in plated finishes, with retailers' names engraved upon it. Ignoring "Corps numbers", later mentioned, or numbers used by shipping companies and other industrial
organizations, the basic Webley Mark I serial numbers appear to be
consecutive, from Major Dowell's observed 679 up to late weapons
(including several cut-away demonstration models) in the 39000 serial
range. All examined specimens measured 9¼ inches overall, had a 4
in. barrel (Metford-rifled, as for all Marks, with seven grooves twisted to
the right), and weighed about 35 oz. when unloaded.

Originally this weapon had a solid standing-breech, but later models
(officially designated "Mk I*") had a separate steel shield dove-tailed
into the standing-breech, which could be replaced whenever the firing-
pin hole in it wore to unacceptable dimensions. As was the case with all
Marks of issue Webley revolver, this first example had the famous
thumb-operated "stirrup" barrel-latch, which was pivoted upon a
screw passed transversely through the standing-breech, and locked
down the rear end of the barrel-strap when "at rest"; the latch was
protected by Br. Pat. 4070/1881 (of J. CARTER and H. WEBLEY,
q.v.), but claimed as an invention of E. C. GREEN (q.v.).

Cylinder and cylinder axis were removable, as a complete unit
embodying the ejector (or "extractor", as it was officially termed for all
Webley service revolvers), ejector spindle, and ejector spring, by
removing an external screw visible on the left of the barrel lug, at Plate
23 (top); the cylinder axis was tubular, but slotted to permit bearing of
the ejector lever against the ejector spindle (sliding inside that axis) to
expel the ejector when the barrel was depressed upon its hinge. The
cylinder was, of course, rotatably mounted upon the cylinder axis, and
only to be detached from that axis by turning out the ejector spindle
screw inside the axis, removing the ejector (with spindle and spring)
and then turning out an anti-friction nut, normally concealed by the
ejector upon which, bearing against the rear end of the cylinder axis,
the cylinder actually rotated.

Whilst this may sound a complex assembly, it was protected by Br.
Pat. 5143/1881 of T. W. & H. WEBLEY (q.v.), and it is hoped that

Figure 20 will make the above description clear, together with operation of the rotatable lever which (held by the joint axis screw, *in situ*)
expelled the ejector when the barrel was depressed upon its hinge. As
may be seen, that lever ("a" in Figure 20) had a tooth upon its lower
periphery, which bore against the front of the frame as soon as the barrel
began to be tilted and therefore caused "a" to revolve upon the joint
axis screw; since the curved upper arm of "a" bore against the front

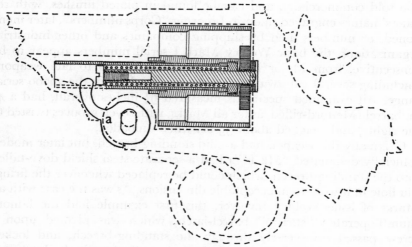

FIG. 20. *Cylinder-assembly and ejector detail of Mark I Webley service revolver.*
(After Br. Pat. 5143/1881.)

end of the ejector spindle, this rotation of "a" forced that spindle upwards (carrying with it the ejector to expel the cartridges) and compressed a spring around the spindle. Eventually, the tilting barrel over-
rode the tooth on "a" and (since "a" turned upon an oval aperture)
forced it upwards into the barrel-lug, clear of the frame, permitting the
ejector spring (working against a screw on the front end of the ejector
spindle) both to retract the ejector back into the cylinder and to tilt "a"
forward into engagement with the frame, when the barrel was tilted
back and latched. One minute spring-steel lever, embedded in a slot in
the wall of "a", sprang out that component from the frame-hinge (with
its tooth projecting to engage the frame again), when the barrel was
latched shut.

"Mark I" Webley revolvers embodied a double-action lock-mechanism of "Schmidt-Galand" design, the basic operation of which has
already been described in relation to Figure 4, and which was used in

certain Austrian (see Fig. 12) and Dutch service revolvers also; the
Webley version followed that form shown at Figure 33 (inclusive of the
improvement, sketched therein, protected by the Br. Pat. 16638/1888
of J. CARTER, *q.v.*), but also had a cylinder-bolt developed by this
firm, through use of which the cylinder was firmly bolted, whether the
pistol was cocked or the hammer was down and rebounded.

This cylinder-bolt is shown at Figure 21, where "A" is the trigger,
"b" is the cylinder-bolt (pivoted about the axis of the trigger-screw),
"c" the cylinder-bolt spring, secured by a screw, and "d" a fixed
cylinder-stop formed integrally with "A"; the parts are shown as they
would be when at rest, and it should be noted that "b" has two minute
bents (cut on the upper side of its pivot) with one or other of which,
dependent upon whether "b" is tilted up or down, the spring "c" can
engage.

At rest, "d" is not engaged with the cylinder, but "b" is lodged in
one of the forward cylinder locking-notches visible in Plate 23 (top),
and held there by engagement of "c" with the lower bent upon "b".
Rearward movement of "A" (whether by finger-pressure when self-
cocking, or *via* the trigger-toe in single-action fire) eventually takes "d"
upwards into engagement with one of the rearward cylinder locking-
notches visible in Plate 23, but initially disengages "b" from the
cylinder, and thus leaves the cylinder free for rotation by the pawl;
during this trigger-movement, however, "b" strikes the edge of that
frame-aperture through which it reaches the cylinder, and this engagement tilts "b" upon its pivot, and then causes "c" to flick "b" upwards
into engagement with one of the forward cylinder locking-notches, this
time by engagement of "c" with the upper bent on "b". The cylinder
is thus double-bolted at discharge. When the trigger is released, it is
restored to the "at rest" position by the mainspring auxiliary, and this
movement (since "b" is trapped against the cylinder) overrides "c",
and causes that component to engage once more in the lower bent of
"b". This system worked well, and was protected by Br. Pat. 5778/1888
of J. CARTER and W. J. WHITING (*q.v.*), although shown in the
Specification as applied to a solid-framed self-cocking revolver which
P. WEBLEY & SON never commercially developed.

As can be seen, by comparing Plate 23 (top) and (lower), those
"Mark II" Webley service pistols approved in 1894 differed only
slightly in appearance, from "Mark I" arms, notably in the absence of
any prawl to the butt, and in a bulkier hammer; internally, use of a
separate shield was maintained, and two mechanical changes occurred,
one to the ejector lever ("a" in Figure 20), which now had a separate
auxiliary lever and coiled spring, in place of a single spring-steel

component), and another by use of a coiled spring for the hammer-catch, to replace the "Mark I" V-spring. This new weapon officially chambered ·455 or ·476 centre-fire cartridges, and was dimensionally almost the same as a "Mark I" revolver, although an alteration to the shapes of trigger-guard and barrel latch boosted its weight by ¼ oz.; serial numbers ran on from those applied to "Mark I" arms, and have been noted by this writer as falling into a serial-range 44000–61000 approximately.

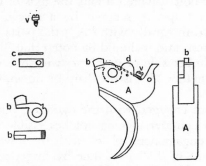

FIG. 21. *Cylinder-bolt detail from Mark I Webley Service Revolver.*
(After Br. Pat. 5778/1888.)

Although fractionally longer (at $9\frac{1}{2}$ inches) and heavier (at 37 oz.) than "Mark II" revolvers, "Mark III" weapons had the same general external appearance as their predecessors. Trigger-guard, barrel-latch, and lock-mechanism components (other than trigger and hammer) were interchangeable with "Mark I", "Mark I*" or "Mark II" equivalents; all "Mark III" parts interchanged with later "Mark IV" components. However, the cylinder assembly of "Mark III" or "IV" weapons would not interchange with that of earlier Marks, and constituted the only major improvement introduced by "Mark III" arms. Dowell records that early issues of the "Mark III" service revolver embodied a sear and spring, which permitted the hammer to be half-cocked; this writer has not observed a weapon modified in that fashion, but assumes the modification broadly to have followed equivalent Continental practice as (for example) in component "e" of Figure 15.

As to the "Mark III" Webley cylinder assembly, its axis was now permanently fixed to the barrel-lug, and the cylinder (complete with ejector, ejector spring, and spindle) could be readily removed from that axis, by use of a simple catch shown in Figure 22; this system was protected by Br. Pat. 17291/1896 of W. J. WHITING (*q.v.*), as a patent of improvement to his earlier Br. Pat. 3427/1891, and was used in all subsequent Marks of Webley service revolver.

In Figure 22, "x" is called the "cylinder cam", and is engaged (at the part-arcuate surface visible on its left underside) by fingers protruding from "y" (the so-called "cam lever") and from the head of the joint-axis pin beneath "y". The cylinder cam "x" is a stirrup, having its cross-member coming between the front end of the revolver cylinder "z", and the barrel-lug hinging barrel to frame; "x" is carried on that barrel-lug, by embracing it with arms pivoted to a screw passing transversely through the lug, and "x" may be tilted up or down (on that pivot) for its cross-member to engage or disengage an annular collar or groove on the front of "z". Such engagement must obviously keep the cylinder fast upon its axis, and is effected *via* the cam-lever "y" and by so dimensioning the knuckles of the barrel/frame hinge that the cross-member of "x" is sustained by wiping across the circumference of those knuckles, as the barrel is tilted to-and-fro upon its hinge.

Since, however, it is necessary, both that the cylinder revolves unhampered and that "x" be capable of releasing "z" for removal, the knuckles of the frame-joint are relieved by transverse grooves ("b" and "c" in Figure 22), and the cam lever "y" is provided for releasing "x". Thus the cross-member of "x" rests in shallow relieving groove "b" when the barrel is latched, and is thereby clear of any friction against the walls of the annular retaining collar on "z"; when the barrel is tilted down for removal of the cylinder, however, the cross-member of "x" is aligned with the deeper relieving groove "c", and may be depressed into that groove (clearing the annular collar altogether) by use of the cam lever "y". The latter has first to be released (by removal of a retaining screw visible in Figure 22), but lifting of its tail thereafter will turn the cam lever about its pivot, and cause the finger at its upper end to strike a pendant forward arm of "x"; this pressure raises the forward end of "x", and (since the component is pivoted) lowers the cross-member at its rear from engagement with the collar on "z".

Use of a flat nut (instead of a screw), to secure its joint-axis pin, distinguishes the "Mark III" weapon *as issued* from later "Mark IV" arms, but instructions to unit armourers that "Mark IV" components be used to repair "Mark III" pistols can (where markings are corroded or hardened grease covers them) make ready identification of the earlier model sometimes quite difficult. However, the "Mark III" does appear to have its own serial-range, in which Dowell notes a pistol numbered as low as 101, and this writer has seen one numbered above 10000. Revolvers reported with serial-numbers in the 70000 range have so far been found, upon examination, to be Mark IV weapons.

"Mark IV" Webley revolvers were extensively carried during the

South African war (but it is doubtful if they saw much combat use), had a lighter hammer than the "Mark III" pistol, and that screw-mounted cylinder cam actually shown in Figure 22. The service version had a 4-in. barrel, measured $9\frac{1}{4}$ inches overall, and weighed 36 oz., but specimens with barrels 3, 5 or 6 inches in length are also reported by Dowell, as sold commercially, together with modified arms either

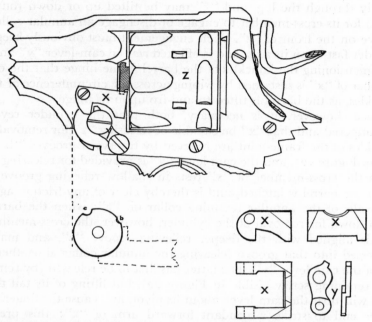

FIG. 22. *Cylinder-release mechanism of Mark III and Mark IV Webley service revolvers.*
(After Br. Pat. 17291/1896.)

chambering ·297/·230 small-bore centre-fire cartridges (in place of the ·455 service round), or embodying adaptors of a type mentioned in remarks upon J. F. and H. W. LATHAM, R. MORRIS or J. T. MUSGRAVE (*q.v.*); Dowell also notices a special target version (in service calibre), supplied for sale by an Edinburgh gun-maker, Alexander Henry, and having a brazed-in replacement barrel rifled to his specification. The serial-numbering of "Mark IV" service arms remains to be clarified, for although the bulk of observed specimens fell into a range 76000–127000, serial numbers well outside those limits have been reported to the writer.

In full-bore versions, the "Mark V" service revolver and the "Mark

IV" issue arm appear identical, though a cylinder dimensioned for smokeless powders boosted the unloaded weight by an ounce, and this new weapon was also sold commercially with a 6-in. barrel. The bulk of serial numbers upon issue arms were observed in a range 130000–170000, but higher serial-numbers (notably upon civilian arms, with 6-in. barrels) have been reliably reported.

In concluding these necessarily brief remarks upon Webley issue service revolvers, it may be useful to record that (by 1912) these were officially to be stamped, on the upper part of the butt-strap, both with the number and the month of their year of issue ("Ordnance marks") and with "Corps marks" embodying consecutive numbers, i.e. "R.S." for The Royal Scots (Lothian Regiment), "R.B." for The Rifle Brigade (The Prince Consort's Own), and so on. It was standard practice also for the factory to stamp each service pistol with Webley's own three-line frame legend as, for example, "Webley—Mark IV—Patents".

By the close of our period, three hinged-frame, self-ejecting commercial Webley revolvers were available in both target and regular versions, two being in "WG" and "WS" models (chambering centre-fire cartridges of ·450 ·455, or ·476 calibre) which are shown in Plate 25, and one a pistol available in ·38 or ·32 centre-fire calibres, later considered (with pocket arms) in that category to which it then properly belonged; additionally, the revolver shown at Plate 24 (lower) had been produced as a commercial "Army" weapon only, for part of that period, and some pistols of the "Mark IV" service pattern (in full-bore or sub-calibre versions) could also be classified as arms primarily intended for target shooting.

The "WG" revolvers are sometimes called "Webley-Green" arms (although their debt to E. C. GREEN has never been formally acknowledged) and were in production from 1885 until about 1912, when they were dropped from Webley catalogues, presumably as superseded by that "WS" series introduced around 1904. In "Target" get-up, both "WG" and "WS" arms commonly had $7\frac{1}{2}$-in. barrels, with special adjustable sights, but a shorter (6-in.) barrel was occasionally fitted to either pattern; in both commercial "Army" versions, the 6-in. barrel was normal, but 4-in. barrels have been reported, and were definitely catalogued for the "WS" line. However, in "Target" or commercial "Army" versions alike, the "WG" and "WS" lock-mechanisms differed radically in design, and other more detailed differences must be noted.

Since "WG" revolvers embodied both the famous stirrup barrel-latch and the double-action lock-mechanism claimed by J. CARTER and H. WEBLEY's Br. Pat. 4070/1885, it is unlikely that this model had been marketed prior to the date of such protection, namely, 31st March,

I

1885, and indeed there would have been little advantage to prior introduction since (apart from the risk of prejudicing any intended patent
application) the Webley house was then selling weapons of a very
similar type, as mentioned above in remarks upon "KAUFMANN
revolvers". However, Michael Kaufmann's patents were allowed to
lapse around 1888 and, whatever the scale of production achieved up
to that time, the "WG" Model certainly received its first real publicity
at Wimbledon N.R.A. meetings in 1889.

A Webley "WG" Target (Bisley Model) revolver at Plate 25 (top),
may be regarded as a typical example of its type; the Webley "WG"
(Army Model) pistol had a "parrot beak" butt similar to the "Mark I"
Webley service weapon shown at Plate 23 (top), in place of the flared
butt of the target model, but both had large removable side-plates on
the left of their frame (giving access to the lock-mechanism) and were
rifled with seven grooves, twisted to the right.

The patented lock-mechanism of the "WG" revolver is shown at
Figure 23, and its cycle of operation explained in the caption to that
Figure; the cylinder assembly, ejector-mechanism and cylinder-retainer
were originally of a kind described in relation to "Mark I" service
arms but, as may be noted from Plate 25 (top), the latter device was
shortly replaced by an improved retainer, at which time the cylinder-
assembly itself was changed along lines indicated in notes upon the
"Mark III" Webley service revolver. This new cylinder-retainer
(visible in Plate 25; top) was protected by W. J. WHITING's Br. Pat.
3427/1891, which gives some guide to dating of its introduction, and
worked in a manner generally similar to the "Mark III" device,
although not locked in its closed position by any screw. It will be
recalled that W. J. WHITING's Br. Pat. 17291/1896 (which protected
the "Mark III" retainer) was admitted to be a patent of improvement
to his Br. Pat. 3427/1891, but the pattern 1896 retainer was never
applied to "WG" revolvers.

A "WG" Army model revolver weighed 40 oz. unloaded (with 6-in.
barrel), chambered ·450, ·455 and ·476 centre-fire cartridges, and
could be supplied with a flared wooden butt, similar in shape to that
target stock shown in Plate 25 (top), mounted over the "parrot beak"
handle. Target Model "WG" revolvers weighed 42 oz. unloaded (with
7½-in. barrel) and, although they would chamber all three cartridges,
were sold as regulated to shoot that round actually specified by the
buyer.

In either model, a "WG" revolver could be bought with blued or
nickel-plated finish, and the "Army" version was also supplied in full
presentation engraving, plated, and with ivory or mother-of-pearl

grips. Cased weapons are not uncommon (some including sub-calibre single-shot or barrel and cylinder adaptors), and the names of a number of well-known retailers and gun-makers will be encountered upon the barrels of either model; Webley house-markings consisted of the words "Webley Patents" (with the winged bullet trade-mark) on the left frame, and "WG Army Model" or "WG Target Model", as appropriate, on the left of the barrel-strap, although a few early pistols were marked with model-year designations for 1889, 1892 and 1893.

Serial numbers between 1485 and 22099 have been noted by (or reported to) this writer upon "WG" arms, but it is not clear if a common serial-range existed, or whether "Target" and "Army" weapons were separately numbered. Since both patterns embodied features covered by British patents earlier noticed, this writer is inclined to the view that one serial-range served for calculating any royalties due from P. WEBLEY & SON to the patentees, but that opinion remains to be substantiated.

Webley "WS" revolvers were introduced around 1904, commercially to market improvements tested in "Mark IV" issue arms, and were almost identical to the latter in appearance, save for their use of a flared butt instead of the "parrot beak" profile; see Plate 25. As a result of this parentage, the "WS" lock-mechanism has already been described in relation to Webley service arms, all "Mark IV" service components would operate in "WS" weapons, ·450 or ·455 cartridges would chamber in them, and the pattern 1896 cylinder assembly and retainer (see Fig. 22) were present.

It is probable that a "WS" (New Army Model) revolver was actually the first version to appear, as a 37-oz. pistol, with 6-in. barrel and service sights, but a 36-oz. weapon with 4-in. barrel was certainly available by 1914, alongside "WS" Bisley Target arms, with 7½-in. barrels, and special sights; "WS" (New Army Model) revolvers could be supplied in blued or nickel-plated finishes, but the target weapon was always originally blued.

"WS" serial-numbers strictly related to our period are difficult to establish, because the model continued in production for many years after those of concern here, but they also appear to march within serial-ranges appropriate to Webley service revolvers Marks IV and V; one low "WS" serial number (on a "WS" Bisley Target weapon formerly in Major Dowell's Collection) was noted as No. 98980 and it seems likely that a level around No. 135000 had been reached by 1914.

In turning to consider a commercial Webley hinged-frame self-ejecting "Army" revolver of that type illustrated as Plate 24 (lower), the reader is reminded that this pattern of weapon was also extensively manufactured in Belgium and that, although some Liège versions (like hinged-frame "Montenegrin" pistols, for example) can never be mistaken for anything else, there are others which are very difficult indeed to distinguish from the Webley model, unless they are available for detailed examination.

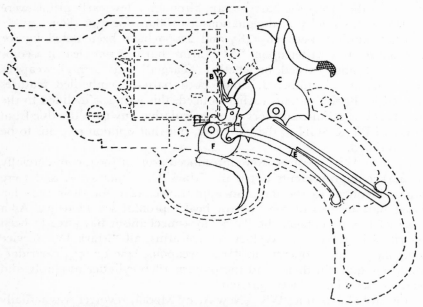

FIG. 23. *Double-action lock-mechanism for Webley "WG" revolvers.*
(After Br. Pat. 4070/1885.)

In single-action fire, a conventional trigger-nose/hammer-toe engagement is used. For self-cocking operation, however, a "hammer-lifter" (A) is provided, pivoted upon the same axis as the pawl (B), and pushes back the hammer (C) by engagement of a claw at the upper end of (A) with the breast of (C); at discharge the claw on (A) levers the hammer-lifter from engagement with (C), and the latter falls. The pawl-spring on (B) presses against (A), thus keeping (B) forward against the rotating ratchet, and (A) in contact with (C).

The mainspring bears upon a pivoted lever (E), which has a hammer-rebound surface; (E) acts also as a trigger-return, being engaged with a pivoted link on the underside of the trigger (F). An integral cylinder-bolting lump on top of (F) is complemented by a see-saw cylinder-bolt, as shown.

As can be seen in Plate 24 (lower), Webley sold their revolver as the "No. 4" Model (and permitted it to be advertised as "Webley's Army and Navy Extractor"), but the pattern is probably best known to collectors, in all its various forms, as the "Pryse" weapon. The name was that of Charles Pryse the Younger, a Birmingham gun-maker, who secured British Patent No. 4421 (of 15th November, 1876) for a cylinder-bolt used in early weapons of this type, but it has now become firmly associated with the distinctive barrel-latch, to the design of which Pryse's patent contributed nothing at all.

Webley "No. 4" Model revolvers of our period had the double-action lock-mechanism actually shown in Figure 32, and were sold in ·455 or ·476 centre-fire versions (either of which would chamber ·450 cartridges), with $5\frac{3}{4}$-in. barrels; during the early 1880s a Webley "No. $4\frac{1}{2}$" Model had also been sold, with a shorter barrel, but may no longer have been available by 1889. The barrel-latch was of the well-known "tong" pattern so firmly associated with so-called "Pryse" arms, where a vertical lever was pivoted (under spring-tension) at each side of the standing breech. At the upper end of each lever was a bolt, sliding transversely in the lump (on top of the standing breech) with which the barrel-strap engaged when the barrel was latched home, and these bolts also engaged a transverse hole in that barrel-strap, when latching barrel and frame together; pressure on the lower ends of the twin levers (by thumb and forefinger) withdrew the transverse bolts, and permitted the barrel to be tilted on its hinge, for cartridge-ejection or loading. The "Webley's Patent Automatic Safety Bolt" mentioned in Plate 24 (lower), was covered by the Br. Pat. 1820/1884 of J. CARTER (*q.v.*), whose patented cylinder-bolt (under Br. Pat. 2555/1884) was also embodied; the safety-bolt consisted of a pin attached to or operated by the left-hand barrel-latch lever, which pin projected into the lock-mechanism cavity (through a hole in the frame wall) to bolt the trigger, if the lower end of that lever was depressed. Such depression occurred automatically, of course, when unlatching the barrel, but also occurred if the transverse bolts failed to seat because the barrel was not fully latched.

The cylinder assembly on a slightly more expensive version of this Webley "No. 4" Model was similar to that used in "Mark I" Webley issue service revolvers but (instead of securing cylinder-axis to barrel lug by a transverse screw) the more complex turnover-button device visible in Plate 24 (lower) was used, which took into a notch on the underside of the axis, to hold that axis into the lug.

Due to the ease with which Webley "No. 4" or "No. $4\frac{1}{2}$" revolvers may be confused with other weapons of "Pryse-type", their serial-numbers can only be safely compiled by reference to examined specimens; however, it is tentatively suggested that they commenced at No. 1, and ran consecutively up to something over No. 12000. Blued or nickel-plated finishes were available, use of the Webley "winged bullet" trademark and Webley model-name frame markings was common, and the names of retailers appear upon the barrels of many specimens. Due to the construction of the barrel-latch, target sights were not readily attached to "Pryse-type" revolvers, and it is unlikely that a target version of the "No. 4" Model Webley revolver was ever produced.

As to that final "Police or Pocket Model" category in the classification chosen here for hinged-frame self-ejecting Webley revolvers, the reader should be warned, at the outset, that relevant model-names are confusing, since commercial weapons were here given "Mark" model-names similar to those used on issue full-bore service arms (see Plate 26).

So far as it is possible to judge, the first Webley pocket-sized hinged-frame self-ejecting weapon was a six-shot ·38 calibre "Mark II" revolver, which looked rather like a miniature "WG" (Army Model) pistol; this had a "parrot beak" butt, the same thumb-operated stirrup barrel-latch, and a cylinder-assembly and simple cylinder-retainer earlier described (for "WG" arms) in relation to the relevant Br. Pat. 3427/1891 of W. J. WHITING (q.v.). These arms (some of which had frame-mounted firing-pins and flat-bottomed butts, as in Plate 26 "D") are quite rare, and their serial-range appears to run only from No. 1 to just over No. 1000; they could be purchased in blued or plated finishes, but apparently only with 4-in. barrels (rifled with seven grooves, twisted to the right) and only in ·38 centre-fire calibre.

Around 1896, the "Mark II" pocket revolver design was slightly varied, and a "New ·380 Pocket Revolver" introduced as a replacement; the latter name was not used for very long, and the relevant weapon was briefly catalogued as the "New Improved, Mark III ·38" or "New ·38 Cal. Pocket Revolver", and ultimately became listed simply as the "Mark III" (Pocket, Target, or Police and Military Model, as the case might be), when memories of the Mark II had faded. In the concluding years of our period, a ·32 centre-fire calibre "Mark III" Pocket Model was also produced but (the superior "WP" revolver, later described, being available too) was not particularly popular, and seems to have been dropped from the line around 1912.

As Plate 26 "A" will show, these "Mark III" pocket revolvers differed from the common version of the "Mark II" in having a flat-bottomed, slightly flared butt, and in using a domed screw (over the cylinder-retainer) on the joint-axis, in place of a flat nut; the lock-mechanism of "Mark II" and "Mark III" arms was a miniature version of that (used in Webley issue service revolvers) shown in Figure 33.

The "Mark III" ·38 (Pocket Model) was eventually offered with 3-, 4- and 6-in. barrels (in versions respectively weighing 19 oz., 20 oz., and 21 oz., unloaded) rifled with seven grooves, twisted to the right. This writer has only observed the ·32 calibre "Mark III" Pocket Model as catalogued with 3-in. barrel, but it seems a safe assumption that the other barrel lengths were available, on special order.

For a brief period (probably between 1900 and 1912) a special "Mark III, Target Model" was catalogued by the Webley firm, with 6-in. barrel, adjustable front and rear sights, and a frame-mounted firing-pin; this revolver could be had in ·38 or ·32 calibres, at an unloaded weight of 21 oz., and had a special frame (found in no other "Mark III" pistols of our period) adapted to mount a particularly large and comfortable chequered one-piece wooden butt.

By 1914, a "Mark III ·38 (Police and Military Model)" revolver was being offered, in barrel lengths of 3, 4, 5 and 6 inches (for unloaded weights of 21, 22, 22½ and 23 oz. respectively), and that version with 6-in. barrel and special sights became the "Mark III" Target Model pistol; in all versions, this weapon had a large oversized two-piece butt. However, the special frame mentioned above was not retained for use in it.

The "Mark III" series embraced presentation pocket arms (fully engraved, plated, and with mother-of-pearl grips), and also a few weapons sold to commercial organizations, which were appropriately marked by their owners. Serial numbers (apart from those upon the intermediate "Target Model", mentioned above) appear common to ·38 and ·32 pistols, and to have started at No. 1; since production was merely interrupted by the Second World War, it is difficult to assess the break-off point for our period, but this seems likely to have occurred during the 25,000 serial numbers.

To conclude these notes upon Webley hinged-frame self-ejecting Pocket, Police, or Target revolvers, the "WP" arms must be noticed (although their production continued for some two decades after 1914), and are shown in Plate 26.

"Webley's New Hammerless Pocket Revolver" was introduced in 1898, as a six-shot self-cocking weapon, in ·32 centre-fire calibre; the shrouded lock-mechanism was merely a modified version of that basic "Schmidt-Galand" double-action design used in Webley issue service revolvers (see Fig. 33), but with a cylinder-bolt and cylinder-retainer used in no other models. The bolt appears to have been that envisaged in Michael Kaufmann's Br. Pat. No. 189 of 1st January, 1884 (which had expired in 1888), and the retainer to have been a device (envisaged in the Specification to W. J. WHITING's Br. Pat. 17291/1896) which worked transversely to the retaining collar on the front of the cylinder, instead of vertically, as in that version adopted for Webley service arms of "Mark III" and subsequent vintage. In addition, this revolver had a thumb-operated safety-catch (sliding on top of the hammer-shroud), which bolted the hammer when pushed forward, and a removable side-plate, on the left of the frame, giving access to the lock-mechanism (see Plate 26 "B").

At an uncertain date (possibly as late as 1905, a year when that noted retailer of Webley arms, the Army & Navy Co-operative Society, still did not catalogue any variant), a ·32 "New W.P. Hammer Revolver (Pocket Model)" was introduced, to sell alongside the hammerless arm. This model had a double-action version of the hammerless lock-mechanism, a detachable side-plate, and the same cylinder-retainer; however, it lacked a safety-catch, and the barrel-latch (unlike that for the self-cocking weapon) had no thumb-piece, but was operated by thumb-pressure against a notched surface on the cross-piece (see Plate 26 "C").

"WP" revolvers could be supplied in blued or nickel-plated finishes and (by 1914) in a choice of ·32 chamberings, but only with 3-in barrels and at an unloaded weight of 17 oz.; engraved plated arms, with mother-of-pearl grips, are known. Serial numbers do not suggest that total production was large, but it has not proved possible to estimate that serial-range relevant to our period.

WILKINSON revolvers

Appendix II entries relating to H. W. and J. F. LATHAM must suffice for indicating both background and patents activity of The Wilkinson Sword Company Limited, of London, and it is enough to begin here by stating that this Company does not appear to have manufactured any revolvers at all, but merely to have retailed weapons made by others.

Broadly speaking, Wilkinson-retailed revolvers of our period fell into two main categories, namely, standard models ordinarily sold by any maker, and Webley weapons embodying detailed improvements specified by the Wilkinson company to its supplier.

The first category is wide, for it embraced civilian versions of Webley issue service revolvers, Webley "WG" (Target and commercial "Army" models), Webley-Fosbery revolvers, and other hinged-frame self-ejecting weapons imported from Liège, including weapons similar to that shown as Plate 24 (lower), and also some Colt or Smith & Wesson arms of solid-frame swingout-cylinder type.

In our second category, it would appear, only P. WEBLEY & SON (or the successor limited liability company) were involved, those weapons within it comprising slightly modified Webley "No. 4" and "WS" revolvers only, known to modern collectors as (i)) the Webley-

Wilkinson-Pryse, (ii) the Wilkinson-Webley, Model 1892, and (iii) the Wilkinson-Webley Models of 1905, 1910, and 1911.

The Webley-Wilkinson-Pryse revolver (first identified by Major W. C. Dowell) was a version, in ·455/·476 centre-fire calibre, of that Webley "No. 4" pistol shown at Plate 24 (lower), with enlarged knuckles at the frame-hinge, its cylinder-assembly held to the barrel-lug (by a screw) in that fashion adopted for "Mark I" Webley service arms, and with a bigger butt; the automatic safety-bolt covered by **Br. Pat.** 1820/1884 of J. CARTER (*q.v.*) was also present, preventing a cocked revolver from being broken open, or a weapon with improperly-latched barrel from being cocked. Wilkinson's marking upon the Dowell specimen suggest that it was introduced prior to appearance of The Wilkinson Sword Co., Ltd., in 1887.

The Webley-Wilkinson-Pryse design was comparatively short-lived, and superseded by a weapon shown as Plate 27 (top), which was both marked and sold as the "Wilkinson Model 1892" revolver; this six-shot double-action hinged-frame self-ejecting pistol was in the same ·455/·476 calibre as its predecessor, used barrel, frame, cylinder, and lock-mechanism components from the Webley-Wilkinson-Pryse line, but had an improved barrel-latch and cylinder-retainer. The latch was now that Webley "stirrup" design protected by J. CARTER and H. WEBLEY's Br. Pat. 4070/1885 (a modification necessarily eliminating the safety-bolt of J. CARTER above-mentioned), whilst the cylinder retainer was a variant upon that used in Webley "WG" arms, under W. J. WHITING's Br. Pat 3427/1891; here a chequered spring-steel thumb-button (visible in Plate 27) was used to release the retainer, by pressing that button inwards, then turning it towards the muzzle, with the barrel tilted down, instead of the lower, tear-shaped, lever visible on "WG" arms.

Wilkinson-Webley revolvers, Models of 1905, 1910 and 1911 were ·450/·455 calibre Webley "WS" arms earlier described, but with the Model 1892 Wilkinson cylinder-retainer (in place of the Model 1896 Webley device), no holster-guides, and a six-groove right twisted rifling for the two later models, in place of the standard Webley seven-groove pattern. The Model 1905 (see Plate 27) was a 37-oz. "WS" New Army Model" revolver, with 6-in. barrel, rear sight dovetailed to the top of the barrel-latch, and both Wilkinson and Webley markings; Model 1910 and Model 1911 pistols seem to have been available in either of those "WS" target and standard versions mentioned earlier. All three models were marked "Wilkinson, Gunmakers, Pall Mall, London, S.W." on top of the barrel-strap, but the situation and scope of their model-markings could vary; thus Model 1905 and other "New Army" weapons have "Wilkinson-Webley '05" (or as appropriate) on the left side of the barrel-strap, where Target arms have "Wilkinson-Webley, Model 1910" (or "1911") engraved upon the left-hand barrel flat.

As Major-Dowell has recorded, it was the practice for Wilkinson-Webley revolvers to carry a Wilkinson serial-number, as well as that basic Webley serial-number appropriate to the Webley model on which the variant was based; thus a Model 1892 is numbered 9464/783 (the first being the Webley number and the second being Wilkinson's), a Model 1905 is numbered 127026/2977 (on the same basis), and so on. Unfortunately, the practice was not consistent (so that some Wilkinson-Webley arms have no Wilkinson serial-number), and it is not clear if the Wilkinson serial-range was common to every type of handgun, or to every type of revolver, or was actually applied in separate series to each model of revolver sold by the firm. Against this background uncertainty, it has not proved possible to suggest serial-ranges or production-figures for Wilkinson-Webley arms.

CHAPTER IV

"GAS-SEAL" ARMS

IN a conventional revolver (of that type, for example, shown at Plate 9) there is inevitably a leakage of combustion gases, between cylinder-face and barrel, when the weapon is fired; in theory, this escape must reduce that muzzle-velocity of which the chosen cartridge is capable, although the actual effect is small in barrels of a length normal for hand-guns, and a number of designers active in our period attempted to close the offending joint.

Taken in order of date, Appendix II entries relevant to this Chapter are only those for H. PIEPER (1886), the GRUSONWERK A.G. (1892), L. NAGANT (1894), C. RICCI (1894), H. M. KIPP and M. C. LISLE (1909), G. V. HAEGHEN (1909), and I. H. RODE-HAVER (1912); Leleu also commended the efforts of a Belgian named Gilthay but, as with certain other Continental designers (mentioned in Appendix II remarks upon the OESTERREICHISCHE WAFFEN-FABRIKS-GESELLSCHAFT; (*q.v.*), the dating and content of Gilthay's contribution to this art remains unknown.

H. PIEPER's Br. Pat. 2167/1886 aimed at preventing any escape of gas between revolver-cylinder and barrel, on discharge, by using the cartridge-case to bridge the gap, and his Specification mentioned the attainment of that end either (i) by use of a sliding barrel, or (ii) by means of a sliding cylinder, or (iii) by a breech-piece moving the cart-ridge-case forward and backwards in its chamber; however the basis for the first two of his routes had been anticipated decades earlier (see, for example, W. Greener's Br. Pat. No. 2693, of 21st December, 1854, and E. H. Collier's English Patent No. 4315, of 24th November, 1818, respectively), and Pieper therefore restricted the claims of his own Specification, firstly to the idea of using the cartridge-case as an obtura-tor or "gas-seal" of the joint between barrel and chamber and, secondly, to a specific combination of parts for effecting such a seal in a revolving gun, as shown at Figure 24.

In Figure 24, "a" is the barrel (sliding in the frame), "b" the cylinder, "c" the hammer, "d" the lever trigger-guard (pivoted at "e", in Winchester-rifle style), "f" a sliding bar linked to "d", and "g" a link between "a" and "d"; the cartridges are of a length to protrude from the front

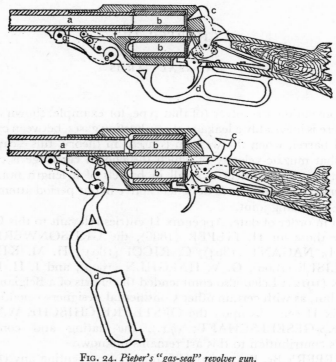

FIG. 24. *Pieper's "gas-seal" revolver gun.*
(After Br. Pat. 2167/1886.)

of their chambers, so that they bridge and seal the joint between barrel and cylinder, when "a" and "b" are in contact. The seal is, of course, made positive by expansion of the cartridge-case mouth on firing.

At the upper drawing in Figure 24, Pieper's rifle is shown after discharge, with the hammer down, the barrel resting against the face of the cylinder, and the cartridge projecting between chamber and barrel; in the lower drawing, however, use of "d" has levered "a" forward (clearing the breech from engagement with a fired case), cocked "c" through the medium of "d", thus rotating and bolting "b" conventionally, and return of that lever will, *via* those linkages shown, restore the gas-seal above-described.

Pieper's guns and rifles of this pattern are not common (although rumoured to have been marketed successfully in Mexico), and were only made in fairly small calibres. However, their design certainly constituted one answer to the problem studied here, and it must remain for surmise why the patentee allowed his Br. Pat. 2167/1886 to lapse so early in its potential life (see Table II), when that principle of cartridge-case obturation claimed therein was so fundamental to any effective suppression of the gas-leak in revolvers.

Pieper's next venture into this field appears to have been with a revolver of that type shown at Plate 28 (top), being a design for which he never troubled to secure British patent protection, but for which he eventually held French Patent No. 208174 of 11th September 1890; in Plate 28, the upper weapon (though actually made by the OESTER-REICHISCHE WAFFENFABRIKS-GESELLSCHAFT, *q.v.*) appears closely to follow the design of Pieper's M/1890 revolver, whilst the lower pistol is an improved Austrian version of that arm. Both examples are seven-chambered revolvers, in 7·62-mm. centre-fire calibre, with double-action lock-mechanisms, and crane-mounted cylinders (swinging out to the left) with manually-operated collective ejectors embodied in them. The upper specimen has its cylinder-latch forward of the cylinder (as Pieper himself envisaged it), where the lower has a rear-mounted sliding latch, similar to that used in Colt arms of the type shown at Plate 1.

As with his design of 1886, Pieper used a long cartridge-case to effect the gas-seal (on its insertion into the barrel), but now imparted the necessary reciprocating movement by sliding cylinder on to barrel, and not barrel towards cylinder, as in Figure 24.

To achieve this junction, a mechanism shown at Figure 25 was used, where "a" is the hammer, "b" the trigger, "c" a hinged cartridge support or abutment, and "d" the cylinder, which carries within it two coiled springs, the inner being an ejector spring and the outer a spring constantly urging the cylinder rearwards off the breech-end of the barrel. Both chamber-mouths and rear-end of barrel are shaped for a male/female union when pressed together, and the cylinder-retracting spring above-mentioned is assisted by the stud "e" (mounted on the trigger, rearward of the cylinder-bolting lump "f"), which also thrusts rearwards against the cylinder, when "b" is fully forward. In the Austrian versions shown at Plate 28 (top), it seems likely that "e" was omitted, since the notches on the circumference of both cylinders appear consonant only with the objective of bolting by the trigger in either its "at rest" or rearmost positions, and not with cylinder-retraction.

Basically (as a comparison of Figures 16 and 25 will show), Pieper's double-action lock-mechanism was quite similar to that design shown in Plate 16 (lower) or Figure 16, although it lacked a hammer-catch hinged to the breast of "a", and instead used a component "g", mounted on the left side of "b", to pick up the hammer in self-cocking action.

Assuming self-cocking fire, from the "at rest" position shown at Figure 25, the cycle of operations was as follows:

(i) Pressure on "b" raised "a" (by the medium of "g") against the thrust of the mainspring, and removed "e" and "f" from engagement with the cylinder, which was therefore conventionally rotated by the pawl "x", and thrust forward on its axis by the lump "h" (on top of the trigger) striking the metal of the cylinder between its two lowermost chambers.

(ii) When chamber and barrel were aligned, the cylinder had been thrust forward on its axis sufficiently for the mouth of the cartridge-case in the chamber to enter the barrel and, at that point, the hammer escaped from the trigger and fell under power from the upper limb of the mainspring.

(iii) In falling, the hammer-face struck the swinging abutment "c", which was hinged to the top of the frame (at a point visible in Plate 28) and thrust this forward to bear against and back-up the cartridge being fired. A tooth "i" on the hammer also took into a notch on "c" to bolt the abutment home, and the locking of "c" was further assisted by the inertia of a hinged component "j" (lodged in a cavity on the left of the hammer), also engaging the abutment.

(iv) Release of the trigger after discharge, permitted "b" to be restored by the lower limb of the mainspring (lodged, as shown, in the pawl pivoted on the trigger), which limb also struck the hammer-heel, and rebounded the hammer. Once free of hammer-pressure, the cylinder "d" was thrust back by its internal coiled spring (and by "e"), and could push back the now unsupported abutment "c".

Pieper revolvers were sold in blued or nickel-plated finishes, measured 264 mm. ($10\frac{2}{5}$ inches) overall, had a 117-mm. ($4\frac{3}{5}$-in.) barrel rifled with four grooves twisted to the right, and weighed 800 g. ($1\frac{3}{4}$ lb.) unloaded; they were chambered to accommodate either the Russian 7·62-mm. centre-fire service revolver cartridge (for that "Nagant" M/1895 pistol described below) with 7-g. bullet, or a cartridge loaded with a 5-g. bullet, or a variant cartridge containing three spherical lead balls of 7·62 mm. calibre. Both black powder or smokeless cartridges were available (the latter giving a muzzle-velocity of 370 m./sec. to the 5-g.

bullet, or of 275 m./sec. to the heavier), and either could be loaded
from chargers of a type similar to that patented by A. J. WATSON
(q.v.).

A weapon patented by the ACTIENGESELLSCHAFT GRUSON-
WERK (in 1892) is shown as Figure 26, and this writer has not succeeded in tracing any specimen arm. As may be seen from Figure 26,

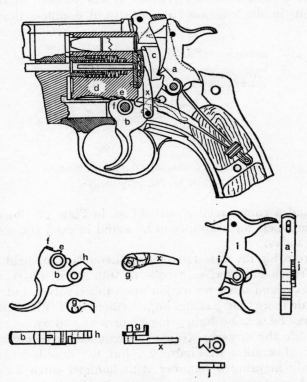

FIG. 25. *Mechanism of Pieper "gas-seal" revolver; M/1890.*

the design was an ingenious improvement upon the 1886 patent of
H. PIEPER (q.v.), applied to double-action revolvers, fitted with that
lock-mechanism described in relation to Figure 15. Here, the sliding
barrel was attached to the cylinder-axis which was, in turn, attached to
the hammer by a hook; when the hammer was cocked, therefore, the
barrel was pulled rearwards to mate with female cones machined at each
chamber-mouth, and the cartridge-case entered the barrel as a gas-seal.
After discharge, the barrel was pulled forward again, by a coiled spring,
and cylinder-rotation was effected by a bell-crank bearing on a ratchet

cut at the front of the cylinder. As might be expected (since H. PIE-
PER's Br. Pat. 2167/1886 still ran), the claims of the GRUSONWERK
A.G.'s Br. Pat. 7787/1892 were devoted to a method for moving the
barrel, and asserted no right in the principle of it.

In turning now to the gas-seal revolver of L. NAGANT (*q.v.*), that
arm may be accepted as the only weapon relevant to this Chapter
which proved commercially successful; it was adopted by the Russian
government, in single-action (trooper's) and double-action (officer's)

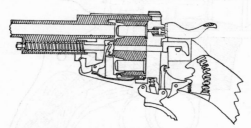

FIG. 26. *The Grusonwerk A.G. "gas-seal" revolver.*
(After Br. Pat. 7787/1892.)

versions, and a commercial model shown in Plate 28 (lower) sold in
sufficient numbers for examples to be found in even the most modest
collections today.

Apart from his Br. Pat. 14010/1894, Leon Nagant held an earlier
relevant French Patent (No. 220988 of 16th April, 1892), with equivalent Belgian and other protection upon this revolver, but the design
remains little more than a skilful improvement to H. PIEPER's ideas of
1890, as may be seen by comparing Figures 24 and 27.

To simplify the drawing, Nagant's single-action revolver has been
chosen for illustration in Figure 27, but the double-action version
differed only in using a hammer with hammer-catch hinged to its
breast, and in necessary modification to the sliding wedge-block "q"
for accommodating such a hammer; single-action weapons could be
converted to double-action, and *vice versa,* by mere substitution of
those two parts. Thus, in Figure 27, "m" is the hammer, "n" the
trigger, "a" the pawl, "p" the abutment, "q" the wedge-block, and
"r" a coiled spring constantly urging the cylinder rearwards along its
axis. The revolver in question (like that in Plate 28, lower) was seven-
chambered, solid-framed, gate-loaded, and with external rod-ejector
for expelling cartridges individually; it was loaded with rimmed cartridges of 7·62-mm. centre-fire calibre, which entirely encompassed the
bullet and the mouths of which protruded about 1·5 mm. from the

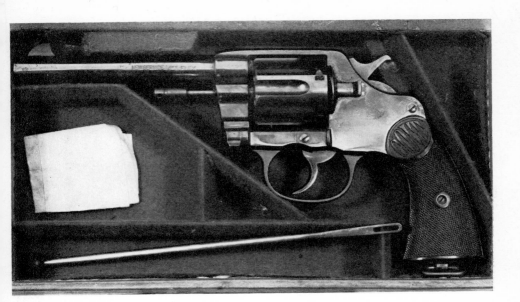

PLATE 2   COLT REVOLVERS

Top: Colt "New Service" double-action revolver, in ·455 centre-fire calibre, with swing-out cylinder and manual simultaneous cartridge-ejection. 5½-inch barrel. Serial number 3177. *Photograph by Wallis & Wallis, Lewes.*

Lower: Colt "Bisley" single-action revolver, in ·38 WCF calibre, with rod-ejection. Serial number 223765. Manufactured in 1902. *Photograph by Rolf H. Müller.*

PLATE 3   HARRINGTON & RICHARDSON REVOLVERS
Top: Five-chambered "Premier" double-action hinged-frame self-ejecting revolver, in ·32 centre-fire calibre, with 3-inch barrel. Serial number 269628.

Lower: Five-chambered "Model 1904" double-action solid-frame revolver, in ·38 centre-fire calibre, with 2½-inch barrel. Serial number 102210. *J. Darwent Collection.*

PLATE 4   IVER JOHNSON REVOLVERS

Top: Five-chambered "Safety Hammerless" self-cocking (concealed hammer) hinged-frame self-ejecting revolver in ·32 centre-fire calibre, with 3-inch barrel. Patent dates only to 1893, but embodying A. Fyrberg's safety-lock mechanism (*see text*). Serial number 33984.

Lower: Five-chambered "Safety Hammer" double-action hinged-frame self-ejecting revolver in ·32 centre-fire calibre, with 2-inch barrel. Patent dates to 1896 (*see text*). Serial number 20949. *J. Darwent Collection.*

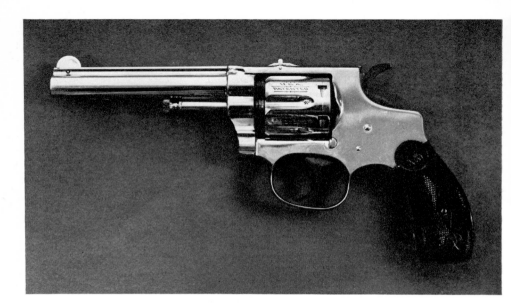

PLATE 5 SMITH & WESSON REVOLVERS

Top: Six-shot double-action solid-frame swing-out cylinder Smith & Wesson Model 1896 Hand Ejector revolver, in ·32 centre-fire calibre. Nickel-plated, and with black hard-rubber grips. Serial number 11351. Weapon has the lock-mechanism shown at Figure 10, and the cylinder latch mentioned in remarks upon the Br. Pat. 6184/1894 of *D. B. WESSON (Q.V.). A. G. Briggs Collection.*

Lower: Cased five-shot double-action hinged-frame self-ejecting Smith & Wesson revolver, in ·38 centre-fire calibre, with gold- and silver-plating of its engraved components, and mother-of-pearl grips. Overall length 7½ inches, with a 3¼-inch barrel. Serial number 334149. This specimen has a lock-mechanism shown at Figure 9, and the shape of the trigger-guard suggests that it was made prior to 1909. *Photograph by Messrs Wallis & Wallis, Lewes.*

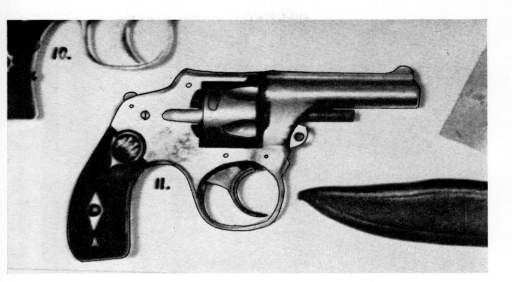

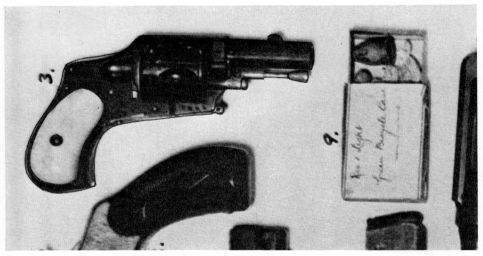

PLATE 6   CHEAP SOLID-FRAMED REVOLVERS

Top: Five-shot self-cocking solid-framed "Hammerless Model 1892" pocket revolver, in ·32 centre-fire calibre, by Maltby, Henley & Co., of New York. Serial number 36001. Made under the U.S. patents of John T. Smith (see also "Columbian" and "Smith" arms), the weapon illustrated was once in the collection of the late Sir Edward Marshall Hall, K.C., and was an exhibit in the case of *R. v Packham,* during 1900.

Lower: Five-shot self-cocking solid-framed "Velo Dog" pocket revolver, in 5·5 m/m centre-fire calibre, by an unknown Continental maker. Serial number 5424. This type of revolver was manufactured in large quantities at Liège, and the specimen shown (which has ivory grips) was formerly in the collection of Sir Edward Marshall Hall, K.C., It featured in the case of *R. v. Dyer,* during 1899. *Photograph by Wallis & Wallis, Lewes.*

Page 149

PLATE 7 AUSTRIAN SERVICE REVOLVERS

Top: Six-shot double-action Gasser Model 1870–74 Austrian service revolver, in 11 m/m centre-fire calibre. Serial number 12671. Note use of a wedge (partly concealed by the rod-ejector mount), which passes transversely from left to right through barrel-lug and arbor, to assist in securing the barrel. This feature was not used in the Austrian army version of this pistol, nor in the officer's version shown below.

Lower: Six-shot double-action Gasser-Kropatschek Austrian infantry officer's revolver, in 9 m/m centre-fire calibre. Serial number 123318. *Heeresgeschichtliches Museum Collection.*

PLATE 8   GROTESQUE REVOLVERS

Top: Six-shot, double-action, solid-framed "Montenegrino" revolver, in ·44 centre-fire calibre, with 9¼-inch barrel. Specimen has been refinished, erasing the frame and barrel markings, but has Belgian proof-marks. Similar arms were made in Austria, and see Plate 7 (*top*) for the weapon upon which this design is based.

Lower: Six-shot, self-cocking, solid-framed Kolb pocket revolver, Model 1910, in ·22 rimfire calibre. A penny demonstrates the small size of this revolver. Arbor-latch protected by H. M. Kolb's U.S. Pat. 954,191/1910. Mother-of-pearl grips. *Tower Collection.*

Revolvers

P 1489

P 1489—7m/m Pin Fire Revolver,
Blue or Nickel, **7/6**
If Chequered Stock, **1**/- extra.
P 1490—5m/m ditto - Blue or Nickel, **10**/-

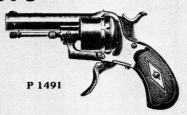

P 1491

P 1491—"**The Guardian,**" 7m/m Pin
Fire Revolver, Solid Body, with Top
Strap, Blue or Nickel - - - **11**/-

P 1492

P 1492—·320 Central Fire Revolver,
Blue or Nickel, **10**/-
If Chequered Stock, **1**/- extra.

P 1493

P 1493—·320, ·380, or ·450 Bull Dog Revolver,
Blue or Nickel - - - - **11**/-
P 1494—·320 Bull Dog, Superior, Black all
over, Chequered Ebony Stock and Jointed
Trigger - - - - - - **17**/-
P 1495—·320 ditto, Better Finish, with Guard
and Chequered Ebony Stock - - **21**/-

P 1496

P 1496—·320, ·380, or ·450 Constabulary
Revolver, Blue or Nickel - - **12**/-
P 1497—·320 ditto, Black all over - - **12**/-
P 1498—·320 ditto, Nickel, Chequered
Walnut Stock, Superior - - - **22**/-

P 1499

P 1499—·320 Central Fire Pocket Revolver,
Ivory Handle, Nickel - - - **25**/-
P 1500—·320 ditto ditto Pearl Handle **37**/-
P 1501—·320 ditto ditto Ivory Handle,
Hammerless - - - - - **45**/-
P 1502—·320 ditto ditto Ring Trigger,
Engraved, Cycle Revolver - - **30**/-

All sizes of Cartridges suitable for above kept in stock

Cleaning Rods for Revolvers

P 1513 Ring Handle Rods - - **3** - doz.
P 1514 Bristle and Wire Rods - **6** -
P 1515 Steel Rod and Brush - **18** -

PLATE 9   CHEAP CONTINENTAL REVOLVERS
Pocket pin- and centre-fire revolvers, made at Liège but listed by a Birmingham supplier to the British
gun-trade. Price List of Charles Osborne & Co. Ltd. (see C. O. ELLIS, F. CASHMORE, and E. W.
WILKINSON), at Whittall Street, Birmingham. Season 1907–8.

PLATE 10   DANISH SERVICE REVOLVERS

Top: Six-shot solid-framed single-action Model 1865–97 Danish army revolver, now in 11 m/m centre-fire calibre, but originally made as a pin-fire arm of "Lefaucheux-Francotte" design; compare with similar Swedish arm in Plate 21, and note pin-fire cuts still present in the cylinder walls of this Danish pistol.

Middle: Six-shot double-action Model 1871–81 Danish naval revolver, made by A. Francotte of Liège. Originally in 11·2 m/m pin-fire calibre, but later converted to centre-fire. Note similarity to the Austrian Gasser-Kropatschek revolver, on Plate 7.

Lower: Five-shot hinged-frame self-ejecting double-action Danish naval revolver, Model 1891, of Liège manufacture. Calibre 9 m/m centre-fire. *Tøjhusmuseet Collection.*

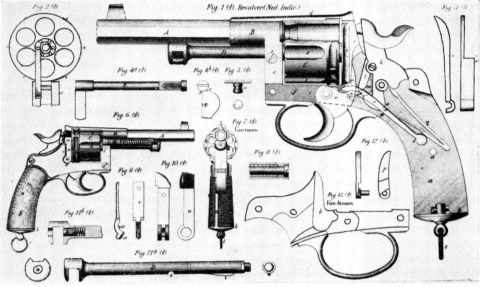

PLATE 11   DUTCH SERVICE REVOLVERS

Top: Double-action solid-framed Dutch Model 1873 service revolvers, called "Chamelot Delvigne", in 9·4 m/m centre-fire calibre; in descending order, (*A*) model for tear-gas cartridges, (*B*) Kl.M. or "small" model, (*C*) N.M. or "New Model", and (*D*) O.M. or "Old Model". The Kl.M. version has five chambers only, the others six.

Lower: Double-action solid-framed Dutch "KNIL Model 1891" service revolver, in 9·4 m/m centre-fire calibre, with "Schmidt-Galand" lock-mechanism (similar to that shown at Figure 12) quite unlike the Nagant lock-mechanism used in Model 1873 arms. *Collection of the Nederlands Leger en Wapenmuseum "General Hoefer".*

PLATE 12   SERVICE REVOLVERS

Top: Eight-shot double-action solid-framed Austrian Model 1898 service revolver, in 8 m/m centre-fire calibre. Serial number 188920. Made by "Rast & Gasser". *Tower Collection.*

Lower: Six-shot double-action solid-framed French Model 1874 officer's service revolver, in 11 m/m centre-fire calibre. Serial number N11694. Note the fluted cylinder, which is not used in the very similar trooper's revolver, Model 1873. *Rolf H. Müller Collection.*

PLATE 13   FRENCH EXPERIMENTAL SERVICE REVOLVERS
Top: Six-shot double-action solid-framed French Model 1885 revolver, in 11 m/m centre-fire calibre.
Never issued.

Lower: Six-shot double-action solid-framed French Model 1887 revolver, in 8 m/m centre-fire calibre.
This weapon had a frame-mounted firing-pin, and a safety-catch on the left of the frame; it was field-
tested and issued experimentally, in some numbers, but never adopted. *Collection of the Musée de la
Manufacture Nationale d'Armes de Saint-Etienne.*

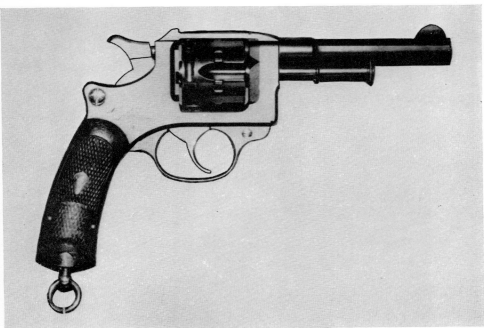

PLATE 14   FRENCH HAND EJECTOR REVOLVERS

Top: Six-shot double-action Model 1892 French issue service revolver (the so-called "Modele d'Ordonnance"), in 8 m/m centre-fire calibre, with swing-out cylinder and manually-operated simultaneous ejector.

Lower: A variant Model 1892 French revolver (the so-called model "de Saint-Etiènne" or "apompe"), which was never issued to the French armed forces. Here, the cylinder is unlatched by pulling forward the ejector-rod beneath the barrel. *Collection of the Musee de la Manufacture Nationale d'Armes de Saint-Etienne.*

PLATE 15 GERMAN SERVICE REVOLVERS
Top: Six-shot single-action solid-framed Model 1884 (Officer's) German service revolver, in 10·6 m/m centre-fire calibre. Serial number 3375C. Marked "Erfurt, 1893". *Collection of the Loyal North Lancashire Regimental Museum.*

Lower: Six-shot single-action, solid-framed Model 1880 (Trooper's) German service revolver, in 10·6 m/m centre-fire calibre. Serial number 1748. Made at Suhl, by Sauer und Sohm, V. Chas. Schilling and C. G. Haenel, whose mark is engraved upon the frame. *Rolf H. Müller Collection.*

PLATE 16   ITALIAN SERVICE REVOLVER

Top: Six-shot double-action solid-framed Italian Model 1889 service revolver, in 10·35 m/m centre-fire calibre, with folding trigger. Serial number AD 5966.

Lower: Lock-mechanism of Italian Model 1889 service revolver. The hammer-block is partly visible (attached to the rear of the pawl), together with a cut in the left hammer-face, in which the hammer-block rests at discharge. Compare this version of Warnant's lock-mechanism with that in Figure 16, as later used in French Model 1892 service revolvers of a type shown in Plate 14 (*top*). *Photographs by Messrs Wallis & Wallis, Lewes.*

PLATE 17 NORWEGIAN SERVICE
REVOLVER
Top: Double-action solid-framed Norwegian
Model 1893 Nagant service revolver, in 7·5 m/m
centre-fire calibre. Serial number 5072. Specimen illustrated is of Swedish manufacture; compare with Plate 21 *(lower)*.

Middle: Detail of foresight on Norwegian Model
1893 service revolver.

Lower: Detail of Swedish manufacturer's mark
and Norwegian's inspector's stamp (that of
O. A. Julsrud) upon revolver shown above.
Photographs from the Huskvarna Arsenal, Sweden.

PLATE 18   PORTUGUESE SERVICE REVOLVERS

Top: Double-action solid-framed Portuguese Model 1878 (Officer's) service revolver, in 9·1 m/m centre-fire calibre. Manufactured in Liège, and so marked. For details of a loading-gate safety-feature, see Figure 18.

Lower: Double-action solid-framed Portuguese Model 1886 (Trooper's) service revolver, in 9·1 m/m centre-fire calibre. Manufactured in Liège, and so marked. For details of a loading-gate safety-feature, see Figure 18. *Photographs by Senhor João G. L. de Figueiredo.*

PLATE 19   SERVICE REVOLVERS

Top: Six-shot double-action hinged-frame *self-extracting* British "Enfield" Mark II service revolver, in
·476 centre-fire calibre. Dated 1882. Serial number 3983. (For lock-mechanism, see Figure 34; see also
remarks upon O. JONES and A. T. DE MOUNCIE). *Tower Collection.*

Lower: Six-shot self-cocking hinged-frame self-ejecting Japanese Model 26 service revolver, in 9 m/m
centre-fire calibre. Serial number 51895. The lock-mechanism was a modified version of that shown in
Figure 12; barrel-latch and ejector features were based upon Smith & Wesson designs. *Rolf H. Müller
Collection.*

PLATE 20   SERVICE REVOLVERS

Top: Six-shot double-action solid-framed rod-ejecting Swiss Model 1882 (Officer's) issue service revolver, in 7·5 m/m centre-fire calibre. Serial number P.3344. Specimen has the gate-loading safety improvement introduced in 1887, which operated in a similar fashion to the device (sketched at Figure 18) used in Portuguese service sidearms. *Tower Collection.*

Lower: Six-shot double-action solid-framed rod-ejecting Romanian Buescu Model 1876 issue service revolver, of uncertain calibre. *Muzeul Militar Collection.*

PLATE 21 SWEDISH SERVICE REVOLVERS

Top: Single-action solid-framed Swedish Model 1871 Lefaucheux-Francotte service revolver, in 11 m/m centre-fire calibre. Serial number 6092.

Lower: Double-action solid-framed Swedish Model 1887 Nagant service revolver, in 7·5 m/m centre fire calibre. Compare with the Norwegian M/1893 version on Plate 17, which differed from this Swedish arm only in respect of its foresight. *Kungl. Armémuseum Collection.*

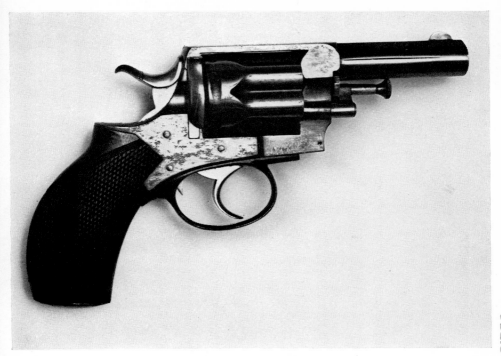

PLATE 22   WEBLEY SOLID-FRAMED COMMERCIAL REVOLVERS
Top: Six-shot Webley "No. 5   ·360 Centre-fire" double-action solid-framed pocket revolver, retailed by "Yorkhouse, Regent St., London". Serial number 65279. *I. McW. Davidson Collection.*

Lower: Page from Webley catalogue (undated, but *circa* 1910) featuring the line of "No. 2 Pattern (Double Action)" or "British Bull Dog" pocket revolvers.

PLATE 23   WEBLEY HINGED-FRAME SERVICE REVOLVERS

Top: Hinged-frame self-ejecting double-action Webley "Mark 1" service revolver, in ·450/·455 centre-fire calibre. Serial number 34336.

Lower: Hinged-frame self-ejecting double-action Webley "Mark II" service revolver, in ·455/·476 centre-fire calibre. Serial number 153. This model differed externally, from its predecessor, primarily by the more sturdy hammer and absence of any pawl on top of the butt. Later "Marks" of Webley service revolver in our period closely resembled this weapon in appearance. *J. Darwent Collection.*

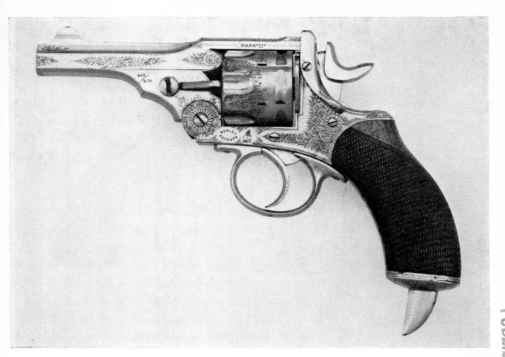

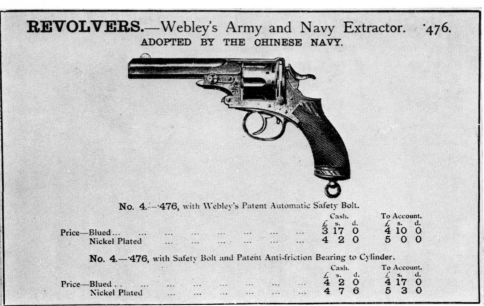

REVOLVERS.—Webley's Army and Navy Extractor. ·476.

ADOPTED BY THE CHINESE NAVY.

No. 4.—·476, with Webley's Patent Automatic Safety Bolt.

								Cash.			To Account.		
								£	s.	d.	£	s.	d.
Price—Blued...	...	...	...	...	...	...	...	3	17	0	4	10	0
Nickel Plated	...	...	...	...	...	...	...	4	2	0	5	0	0

No. 4.—·476, with Safety Bolt and Patent Anti-friction Bearing to Cylinder.

								Cash.			To Account.		
								£	s.	d.	£	s.	d.
Price—Blued ..	...	...	...	...	...	...	...	4	2	0	4	17	0
Nickel Plated	...	...	...	...	...	...	...	4	7	6	5	3	0

PLATE 24   WEBLEY HINGED-FRAME SELF-EJECTING COMMERCIAL REVOLVERS
Top: Plated and engraved commercial Webley "Mark II" revolver, in ·455/·476 centre-fire calibre. Specimen is mechanically identical to the service version in Plate 23 (lower), but has a butt modified to carry the device protected by Br. Pat. 3771/1897 of R. GORDON-SMITH (*q.v.*). Serial number 28771. *Tower Collection.*

Lower: A late cataloguing (by C. Rosson, Derby, 1896) of a revolver also known as the "Webley No. 4" model. Note references to a trigger-bolt (working off the tong barrel-latch, and covered by the Br. Pat. 1820/1884 of J. CARTER; *q.v.*), and to an anti-friction bearing for the cylinder (covered by the Br. Pat. 5143/1881 of H. WEBLEY; *q.v.*), but not to the cylinder-bolt covered by the Br. Pat. 2555/1884 of J. CARTER (see Figure 32), which the catalogue drawing shows as fitted. This type of revolver was also manufactured at Liège, but with the lock-mechanism shown at Figure 12.

PLATE 25   WEBLEY COMMERCIAL HINGED-FRAME SELF-EJECTING REVOLVERS
Top: Six-shot double-action Webley "WG" Target revolver, in ·455/·476 centre-fire calibre, with 7½-inch barrel. Serial number 16311. Barrel-latch and lock-mechanism after Br. Pat. 4070/1885 of J. CARTER and H. WEBLEY (*q.v.*); cylinder-retainer after Br. Pat. 3427/1891 of W. J. WHITING (*q.v.*). Weapon has been re-proofed, for smokeless powders. *J. Darwent Collection.*

Lower: Six-shot double-action Webley "WS" Target revolver, in ·450/·455 centre-fire calibre, with 7½-inch barrel. Serial number 450500. Barrel-latch patented as mentioned above, cylinder-retainer after Br. Pat. 17,291/1896 of W. J. WHITING (*q.v.*), lock-mechanism as in Figures 21 and 33. Compare with Plate 27 (*lower*). *Tower Collection.*

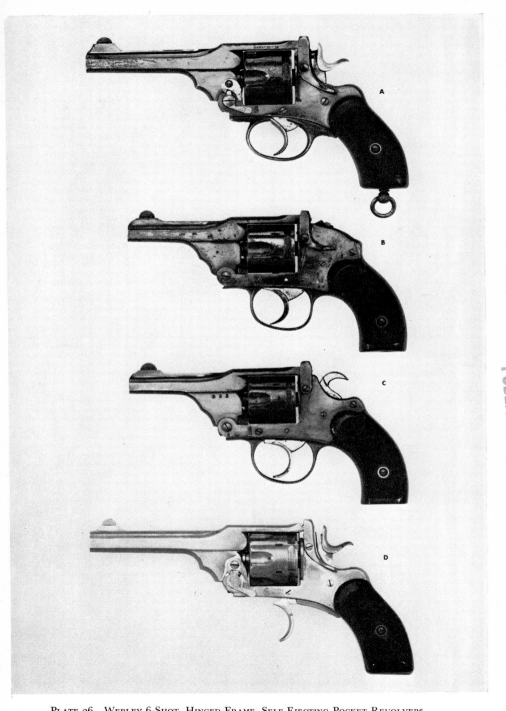

PLATE 26   WEBLEY 6-SHOT, HINGED-FRAME, SELF-EJECTING POCKET REVOLVERS

A. Double-action Webley "Mark III" pocket revolver, in ·38 centre-fire calibre, with 4-inch barrel.
Serial number 12594. Barrel-latch after Br. Pat. 4070/1885 of J. CARTER and H. WEBLEY (*q.v.*);
cylinder-retainer as Br. Pat. 3427/1891 of W. J. WHITING (*q.v.*).
B. Self-cocking Webley "WP" Hammerless pocket revolver, in ·32 centre-fire calibre, with 3-inch
barrel. Serial number 400. Note use of transversely mounted cylinder-retainer on these "WP" arms.
C. Double-action Webley "WP" revolver, in ·32 centre-fire calibre, with 3-inch barrel. Serial number
6114. Note that barrel-latch varies from that used on "B" above.
D. Double-action Webley "Mark II" pocket revolver, in ·38 centre-fire calibre, with 4-inch barrel.
Serial number 649. Frame-mounted firing-pin, squared butt, and unusual folding trigger. *Tower
Collection.*

PLATE 27   WEBLEY-WILKINSON REVOLVERS

Top: Six-shot double-action hinged-frame self-ejecting Webley-Wilkinson "Army" revolver, Model 1892, in ·455/·476 centre-fire calibre. Serial number 11468. Lock-mechanism as in Figure 32, and barrel-latch protected by Br. Pat. 4070/1885 of J. CARTER and H. WEBLEY (*q.v.*). Cylinder-retainer to the specification of H. Wilkinson & Son, but based upon Br. Pat. 3427/1891 of W. J. WHITING (*q.v.*).
J. Darwent Collection.

Lower: Six-shot double-action hinged-frame self-ejecting Webley-Wilkinson "Army" revolver, Model 1905, in ·450/·455 centre-fire calibre. Serial number 122427. Compare with the Webley "WS" revolver (Plate 25; *lower*), upon which this variant was based. See above, for remarks upon the cylinder-retainer.
Tower Collection.

PLATE 28 "GAS-SEAL" REVOLVERS

Top: Seven-shot double-action "gas-seal" revolvers, in 7·62 m/m centre-fire calibre, with crane-mounted swing-out cylinders, after H. PIEPER's (*q.v.*) design of 1890; although the lower specimen (serial number 5) is unsigned, it is believed to be of Austrian manufacture, like its companion (serial number 59), which is signed with the "Waffenfabrik Steyr" mark of the *OESTERREICHISCHE WAFFENFABRIKS-GESELLSCHAFT* (*q.v.*). At an overall length of 10½ inches (with 5¾-inch barrels), these pistols are slightly longer than the version made in Belgium. *Photograph by Wallis & Wallis, Lewes.*
Lower: Seven-shot double-action solid-framed "gas-seal" Nagant revolver, Model 1895, in 7·62 m/m centre-fire calibre. Serial number E. 22423. Dated 1898. Specimen is of Liège manufacture (see L. NAGANT), but almost identical to a version made in Russia, for the Imperial armies. *Private Collection.*

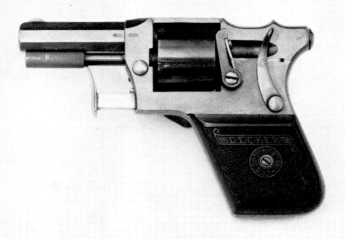

PLATE 29   DECKER'S REVOLVER
A self-cocking pocket revolver, made under Decker's German Patent No. 253148, and covered by the claims of his Br. Pat. 26,086/1912. 6·35 m/m Browning calibre. No serial number. *Rolf H. Müller Collection.*

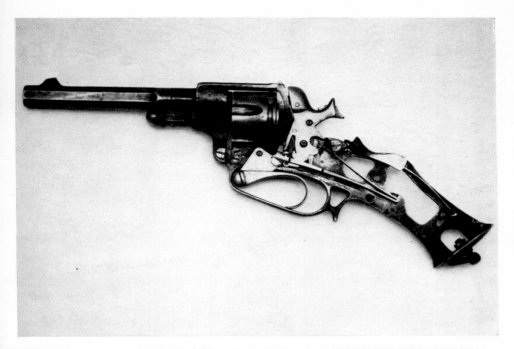

PLATE 30   SOLID-FRAME REVOLVERS OF ABERRANT FORM
Top: G. Envall's revolver, after Br. Pat. 5972/1885 and equivalent Swedish protection. Side-plate removed to show lock-mechanism. *Kungl. Armémuseum Collection, Stockholm.*

Lower: Silver & Fletcher's revolver, "The Expert", embodying automatic ejector and safety-hammer after Br. Pat. 16,078/1884. Basic weapon is P. WEBLEY & SON'S "RIC No. 1" revolver No. 36398, in ·450 centre-fire calibre. Retailed by S. W. Silver & Co., Cornhill, London, with their serial-number 316 added to the weapon. *Photograph by Wallis & Wallis, Lewes.*

PLATE 31   "AUTOMATIC" REVOLVERS

Model 1902 "Webley-Fosbery" recoil-operated revolver, after Br. Pats. 15,453/1895; 12,470/1896; 24,155/1896; and 4924/1901. Six-inch barrel, ·455 centre-fire calibre. Serial number 1692. *F. Peel Collection.*

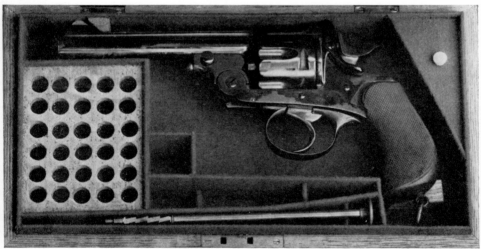

Top: Six-chambered ·450 centre-fire double-action revolver, marked "E. C. Green, High Street, Cheltenham". Serial number 1472. Turnover barrel-latch. Lock-mechanism as in Figure 32, but lacking Carter's patented cylinder-bolt.

Lower: Six-chambered ·455 centre-fire double-action revolver, after Br. Pat. 20,321/1889. Marked "E. C. Green & Son, Cheltenham & Gloucester". Serial number 5757.

PLATE 33   LANDSTAD'S RECOIL-OPERATED REVOLVER
Top: Breech-block is at full-recoil and ejection position. Side-plate legend reads "System Landstad".
Model No. 1. 1900.

Lower: Weapon cocked, but with magazine removed. The knurled rod beneath the barrel is used to
retract the breech-block, and thus to cock the firing-pin, for the first shot. *N.R.A. Collection.*

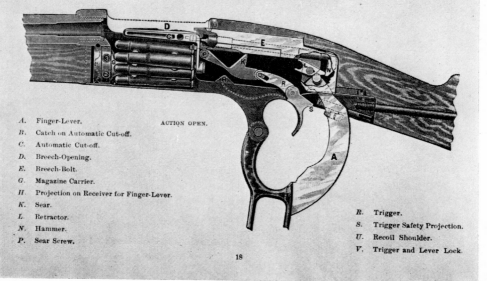

DESCRIPTION OF SYSTEM. Model 1899.

ACTION OPEN.

A. Finger-Lever.
B. Catch on Automatic Cut-off.
C. Automatic Cut-off.
D. Breech-Opening.
E. Breech-Bolt.
G. Magazine Carrier.
H. Projection on Receiver for Finger-Lever.
K. Sear.
L. Retractor.
N. Hammer.
P. Sear Screw.

R. Trigger.
S. Trigger Safety Projection.
U. Recoil Shoulder.
V. Trigger and Lever Lock.

18

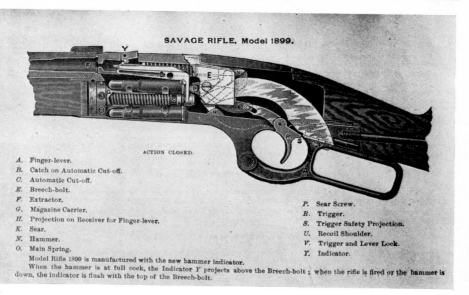

SAVAGE RIFLE, Model 1899.

ACTION CLOSED.

A. Finger-lever.
B. Catch on Automatic Cut-off.
C. Automatic Cut-off.
E. Breech-bolt.
F. Extractor.
G. Magazine Carrier.
H. Projection on Receiver for Finger-lever.
K. Sear.
N. Hammer.
O. Main Spring.

P. Sear Screw.
R. Trigger.
S. Trigger Safety Projection.
U. Recoil Shoulder.
V. Trigger and Lever Lock.
Y. Indicator.

Model Rifle 1899 is manufactured with the new hammer indicator.
When the hammer is at full cock, the Indicator Y projects above the Breech-bolt; when the rifle is fired or the hammer is down, the indicator is flush with the top of the Breech-bolt.

PLATE 34 SAVAGE ARMS COMPANY, MODEL 1899 RIFLE
Top: Action open, and see text for description of operation.

Lower: Action closed, and see text for description of operation. *Photograph courtesy Ray Riling*

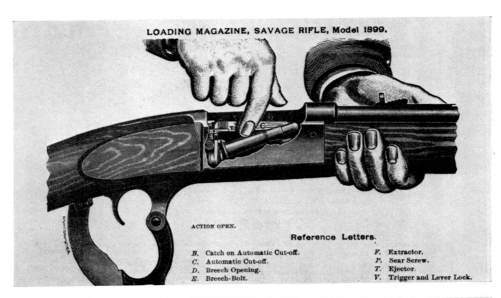

LOADING MAGAZINE, SAVAGE RIFLE, Model 1899.

ACTION OPEN.

Reference Letters.

B. Catch on Automatic Cut-off.
C. Automatic Cut-off.
D. Breech Opening.
E. Breech-Bolt.

F. Extractor.
P. Sear Screw.
T. Ejector.
V. Trigger and Lever Lock.

ANGULAR BAYONET.   SWORD BAYONET.

SAVAGE REPEATING HAMMERLESS MILITARY RIFLE.
Prices on application.

Length of Barrel,   28 inches.
Weight,   8¼ lbs.
Number of Cartridges,   6.
Caliber,   .303.

SAVAGE CARBINE, Model 1899.
Price, $20.00.

Length of Barrel,   20 inches.
Weight,   7¼ lbs.
Number of Cartridges,   6.
Caliber,   .303.

SAVAGE rifles can also be furnished to take the 30-30 smokeless cartridges, if so ordered.

PLATE 35   THE SAVAGE MODEL 1899 RIFLE
Top: Loading the rotary magazine of a Savage M/1899 rifle or carbine.
Lower: Military rifle and carbine versions of the Savage M/1899 design, illustrated in
the Company's catalogue of 1901.

PLATE 36 SMITH & WESSON REVOLVERS

Top: Seven-shot double-action swing-out cylinder Smith & Wesson Model (M) Hand Ejector revolver, in ·22 rimfire calibre. with 6-inch barrel. Serial number 17159. This was the last version, introduced in 1911.

Lower: Five-shot self-cocking hinged-frame self-ejecting Smith & Wesson "Safety Hammerless" or "New Departure" revolver, in ·32 centre-fire calibre, with 3-inch barrel. Serial number 86247. *Tower Collection.*

PLATE 37 A. W. SAVAGE

Picture of A. W. SAVAGE (*q.v.*), from a *Savage Arms Co.* catalogue of 1901, demonstrating the safety implicit in his design, by discharging a model 1899 rifle with most of its components removed. *Photograph courtesy of Ray Riling.*

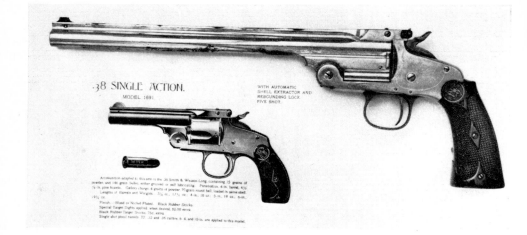

PLATE 38   SMITH & WESSON REVOLVERS

Top: Smith & Wesson Model 1893 single-shot ·22 rimfire target pistol, with 8-inch barrel and over-size target grips. Serially-numbered 17,090. An early model, capable of conversion to that ·38 Single Action Model 1891 revolver shown on the catalogue page below it. *Private Collection.*

Lower: Six-shot, double-action Smith & Wesson "New Century" or "Triple Lock" revolver, with swingout cylinder and manual simultaneous cartridge-ejection. Serial number 2523 and here in ·455 centre-fire calibre. Cylinder-latch after Br. Pat. 24588/1901 of D. B. Wesson (*q.v.*); see Figure 70. *J. Darwent Collection.*

front of the chambers, when *in situ*. As the cylinder was thrust forward, a male cone on the rear end of the barrel seated in a female cone in the chamber-mouth, and the protruding cartridge-case bridged the joint between barrel and chamber to make a gas-seal.

Forward movement of the cylinder (along its axis) was imparted by the pawl "a", which began to rotate the cylinder conventionally as soon as the trigger "n" turned rearward on its axis, caught at the nose by the rising toe of the thumb-cocked hammer "m"; such trigger-movement

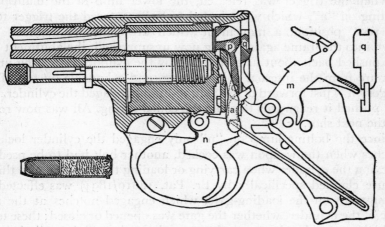

FIG. 27. *L. Nagant's single-action "gas-seal" revolver.*
(After Br. Pat. 14010/1894.)

eventually raised a cylinder-bolting lump (on top of "n") into engagement with locking-notches in the cylinder circumference, but only after the rising pawl "a" had rotated the cylinder *via* a conventional ratchet on the latter.

After the cylinder had been rotated one-seventh of a revolution, and bolted, in this manner, the pawl "a" escaped from the ratchet, but now (due to an inclined surface at the top of the frame-slot in which "a" was riding) it tilted to press against the rear of the cylinder and so pushed the latter forward along its axis, instead of rotating it, as cocking continued. This forward movement consummated the gas-seal, compressed the coiled spring within the cylinder, and was actually completed as trigger-nose and hammer-toe engaged conventionally at full-cock.

Meantime, during this cocking sequence, the trigger had been sliding the vertically-moving wedge-block "q" upwards in its own groove in the frame, by engagement of the trigger-nose with a mortise formed at

M

the lower end of "q"; at full-cock, the wedge-block "q" was jammed between the rear wall of the standing-breech and the abutment "p". This latter was pivoted as shown in Figure 27, and the pressure of "q" upon it therefore swung its head forward against the base of any cartridge in front of it, and thus backed up both the round and the cylinder on discharge, to prevent any movement which might break the gas-seal. The abutment "p" was, of course, pierced to permit the hammer-nose to reach and fire each cartridge.

When the trigger was released, the lower limb of the mainspring (resting on "a", which was pivoted to "n") restored the trigger to its "at rest" position, a movement which drew the wedge-block "q" down into the frame again; being now unsupported, the abutment "p" was pushed back about its own pivot, by the cylinder retreating under pressure from the internal coiled spring, and a knuckle on top of the trigger "n" (just forward of the bolting-lump) engaged the cylinder also, and pushed it rearwards to assist the coiled spring. All was now ready for the next shot.

Since the bolting-lump on "n" only engaged the cylinder locking-notches when the weapon was cocked, another bolt had to be used for indexing the cylinder when carrying or loading the weapon, and this (a feature claimed specifically by Br. Pat. 14010/1894) was effected by spring-teeth on the loading-gate, which engaged notches at the rear edge of the cylinder, whether the gate was opened or closed; these teeth could be overriden by manual- or pawl-rotation of the cylinder, but engaged adequately for the purpose stated. As in conventional post-1878 Nagant revolver lock-mechanisms (see Figs. 14 and 19), a hammer-rebound was embodied in Nagant gas-seal revolvers, in the form of an extension to the upper limb of the mainspring, which bore against the base of the hammer, when the latter was "at rest", to tilt it back off the cartridges.

Russian governmental adoption of these 7·62-mm. calibre Nagant gas-seal revolvers appears to have occurred in 1895, and both single- and double-action models are commonly described as "Model 1895" pistols; an alternative contemporary name for them was the "revolver de 3 lignes", in reference to their calibre of about ·30 inches. Initially, the arms were made in Liège and shipped to Russia but, subsequently, manufacture in the Imperial arms factory at Tula (125 miles to the south of Moscow) either supplemented or replaced Belgian production. For reasons unexplained, but presumably due to use of smokeless powder in the other weapon, Leleu noted the 7-g. jacketed bullet as having a higher velocity (300 m./sec. against 275 m./sec.) in Nagant's revolver than in that of H. PIEPER, and he also reported it as capable of penetrating 20 cm. of white pine, at 20 metres distance from the 114·5-mm. (4⅝-in.) Nagant barrel.

In addition to this service version, the house of Nagant also sold such gas-seal revolvers in barrel lengths of 140 mm. (5½ in.) or 300 mm. (12 in.) which yielded muzzle-velocities for the 7-g. bullet of 330 m./sec. or 425 m./sec., respectively, and prompted some contemporary speculation upon the value of high-velocity revolvers in general, and gas-seal arms in particular.

On the first point, some writers seem to have preferred American or British sidearms, firing a heavy slow-moving bullet, with high knock-down value against any assailant, rather than weapons of Nagant or Pieper characteristics, with fast-moving bullets completely penetrating their targets, whether human or equine.

As to the second matter, Leleu pointed out that the actual effect of the gas-leak was small in an ordinary revolver, elimination of the ·25-mm. gap between cylinder and 100-mm. (4-in.) barrel of a French M/1892 service sidearm (see Plate 14; top) improving the service cartridge muzzle-velocity by only 26 m./sec., whilst increasing that gap to 1 mm. decreased the velocity by only 30 m./sec.; on the other hand, a 300-mm. (12-in.) barrel, with ·25-mm. gap, added 10 m./sec. to the velocity.

In Leleu's view, consequently, there was little point (with regard to muzzle-velocities) either in a revolver barrel exceeding 120 mm. (4⅘ in.) in length, or in gas-seal features for short-barrelled black-powder weapons of this type, since the small 25 m./sec. advantage of the service Nagant M/1895 revolver's muzzle-velocity over that of the ordinary M/1892 French service pistol owed as much to the former's lighter bullet and powerful powder-charge, as to its gas-seal feature. He conceded the advantage of really long barrels for use in arms of the Nagant or Pieper gas-seal variety, but did not comment upon the practical difficulties of carrying such weapons in the field.

Leleu (writing in 1901) further recorded that the Russian government had by then taken assignment of Leon Nagant's patent rights in the M/1895 gas-seal revolver, rather than a mere licence under them, but that writer did not give details of the arrangements, unfortunately. Examination of available specimens yields some authority for suggesting that such arrangements may thereafter have prevented any manufacture of these revolvers in Belgium, save as expressly approved by the Russian government; thus commercial revolvers marked "L. Nagant Brevete Liège 1898" are quite common, and others with datings up to 1900 are known, whilst Russian service revolvers appear to be dated only in and after 1901, with no such Nagant commercial dating observed (by this writer) at all. Subsequent Romanian issue of a "Nagant, Model 1895" revolver mentioned in Chapter III would seem contrary to this idea of Russian exclusivity but, it must be emphasized, the Romanian pistol has not been positively identified as of gas-seal pattern, and may actually have been a conventional weapon, similar to that shown at Plate 17.

As might be expected, improvements to the solid-framed Nagant arm were studied, and Leleu's remarks can be read as authority for the view that a hinged-frame, self-ejecting design was developed; in more concrete terms, Mathews actually illustrates (as No. 1526) a "Model 1910 Special" revolver, as made by the Fab. d'Armes et Automobiles Nagant Frères, with crane-mounted swing-out cylinder, and manually-operated collective ejector. This rare double-action arm had a cylinder-latch of that pivoted, rearward-swinging, type used upon French M/1892 service revolvers, and was in that same 7·62-mm. centre-fire calibre as its predecessors.

To conclude these remarks upon the Nagant gas-seal revolver, it is in order to repeat that this weapon (see Plate 28; lower) quite closely resembled conventional Nagant service revolvers (see Plate 17) in appearance, and that those arms were not infrequently marked "Brevet Nagant". Further, both H. PIEPER (*q.v.*) and L. NAGANT (*q.v.*) made conventional solid-framed revolvers expressly chambered for the 7·62-mm. gas seal cartridge, although (being cheap weapons) they lacked either reciprocating cylinder or any other form of gas-seal. It is, as a result, quite common for the gas-seal weapon to be confused with others, on casual inspection or report.

As to the inventions of C. RICCI (*q.v.*), the weapon sketched as Figure 28 may be accepted as representative of various gas-seal revolvers claimed in his Br. Pat. 16272/1894, not one of which used either barrel- or cylinder-movement to secure its seal. Instead (and in accordance with one of those paths earlier-mentioned as listed in Br. Pat. 2167/1886, by H. PIEPER, *q.v.*), Ricci arranged that each cartridge be successively driven forward from its chamber in the cylinder, to mate in the rear-end of the barrel. After discharge, each cartridge-case was withdrawn into its chamber again, and the cylinder thus freed to rotate for the next shot.

The weapon shown in Figure 28 could be operated manually or (after reversing the change-lever "a", on its back strap) would function semi-automatically, under recoil from each fired cartridge; however, manual-operation alone was specifically envisaged for two other Ricci models (one having a thumb-operated trigger), and another worked only by recoil.

In all cases, however, a hinged-frame revolver chambered, tapered, rimless cartridges with concealed bullets, which were driven forward into the end of the barrel, in turn, by a sliding plunger; the latter carried firing-pin and extractor, to fire the round aligned with it, and subsequently to withdraw it into the chamber again, so freeing the cylinder for further rotation. In a version shown at Figure 28, this plunger was first thumb-cocked via "b", either initially for recoil-operated fire, or after each shot, in manual operation. Springs and linkages within this weapon both maintained the plunger against the recoil of discharge, and rotated the cylinder automatically as the plunger began passing forward to seat a fresh cartridge.

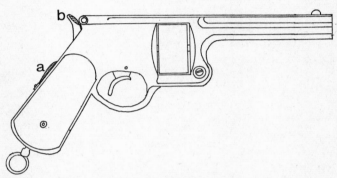

FIG. 28. *Ricci's "gas-seal" revolver.*
(After Br. Pat. 16272/1894.)

M. C. LISLE and H. M. KIPP's gas-seal revolver (under Br. Pat. 15753/1909) was a self-cocking weapon, with shrouded hammer and swing-out cylinder; the latter component was wedged forward, *via* a rise-and-fall linkage in the lock-mechanism, to mate male and female surfaces on barrel and chamber-mouth. The hammer could be full-cocked, by trigger-pressure, and held for release by a second pull at the trigger; since the unconventional lock-mechanism had no hammer-rebound, a manually-operated "retractor" (on the left frame) had to be turned to withdraw the hammer slightly from its discharged position, before the cylinder could be swung out of the frame. It seems clear that this weapon was never commercially produced.

G. V. HAEGHEN's Br. Pat. 18495/1909 envisaged a recoil-operated revolver, in which cylinder and barrel mated in a gas-seal when "at rest", but in which the cylinder recoiled along its axis (in a long frame-aperture) after firing, to permit cylinder-rotation. Only a coiled spring (with the inertia of comparatively heavy components) held cylinder to barrel, and it is therefore doubtful if any gas-seal still existed by the time that the bullet had left the muzzle.

Our last relevant design was that of I. H. RODEHAVER (*q.v.*), whose U.S. Patent No. 1042145 of 22nd October, 1912, proposed a reciprocating gas-seal cylinder for use in double-barrelled revolver firearms of that general type described (in Appendix II) in relation to Br. Pat. 6937/1911; no specimen arm is known.

CHAPTER V

PATENTS

THROUGHOUT that period relevant here, a British patent was a grant from the Crown (for a period not exceeding fourteen years) to the true and first inventor, of the sole right to make, use and sell an invention in the United Kingdom. This grant was made after application, suitable inquiry as to whether or not the invention was actually patentable under British law, and payment of statutory fees; preservation of the monopoly for its full potential term, however, required payment of renewal fees for the fifth and subsequent years of its duration. Parliamentary recognition of power vested in the Crown to grant such rights lay in the Statute of Monopolies (21 Jas. 1, c. 3), but the mechanics of grant and enforcement were actually governed (from 1889 to 1907) by the Patents, Design and Trade Marks Act, 1883, or (after 1907) by the Patents and Designs Act, 1907; remarks which follow are couched in terms of the 1907 Act, but are broadly true of the position prior to that year.

An application for British "letters patent" could be made to the Patent Office by any person who claimed to be the true and first inventor of an "invention", namely, any manner of new manufacture within the United Kingdom which others than the inventor did not use. An invention could therefore relate either to something entirely new (which was a rare event in the field here, but might perhaps be claimed to have occurred in the matter of Br. Pat. 19839/1901, secured by C. KRNKA and G. ROTH; q.v.), or some new method for carrying out a known objective (as, for example, in the case of Br. Pat. 8045/1900 from I. WHEELDON; q.v.), which was that category into which most inventions covered by this book will be seen to fall; in either case, however, novelty was absolutely essential and if, therefore, the invention had become known in the U.K., by prior use or publicity, then (save as noticed later, in remarks upon "Convention Date" patents) no protection could be granted in respect of it.

The inventor's application for a British patent had to be accompanied by either a provisional or a complete "Specification"; the first was a mere written description of the nature of his invention, whilst the latter also described how the invention was to operate, and both types of Specification were normally accompanied by drawings. In the former case, however, an inventor had subsequently to file a complete Specification (within six months of filing the provisional description), and every complete Specification had to end with a definite claim, or series of claims, as to exactly what constituted the invention.

If the Patent Office was satisfied that the complete Specification revealed an "invention" within that definition mentioned above, and that the Specification was correctly drafted, then (within twelve months of application) it would be "accepted" and publicly advertised. If the advertisement aroused no public opposition (as by bringing forward someone already using the "invention", whose rights would thus be prejudiced by grant of monopoly rights to the applicant) within two months, the patent was then granted and sealed by the Patent Office, on payment of fees.

It should be noted that "acceptance" of a complete Specification gave the applicant full privilege from its date, until sealing; the effect of grant and sealing was to establish the patentee's monopoly, against all comers, from date of original application, for a term of fourteen years thereafter, but subject to payment of the annual renewal fees mentioned above.

Every complete Specification (whether to current or patent long-expired) was filed at the Patent Office, and available, as today, for study by the public. Since the document had, by definition, to describe operation of the subject invention, these Patent Office records formed an invaluable store of data by which prospective patentees might establish whether their ideas had been anticipated, but this was not the primary object of the requirement that each patentee filed such a description of his invention.

The basis of reasoning, from earliest days, had been that the Crown gave benefit to its subjects by encouraging inventors to practise in the United Kingdom, and should therefore be permitted to strike a bargain with them. In return for a limited period of monopoly, the inventor had to reveal the secret of his invention so that all in the Kingdom might enjoy the benefits of his ingenuity, once that monopoly ended. The existence of complete Specifications, on public file at the Patent Office, ensured that right to the Crown's other subjects.

Although it should be clear from the foregoing that each patentee owned a potentially valuable property, in the rights of monopoly

granted to him by the British Crown, it will be seen from Appendix II
that not all patentees were free to develop those financial possibilities
inherent in their protection. Some patentees (see, for example, J.
CARTER or W. J. WHITING) were acting for, or with, principals
who really owned the relevant invention and patent, because they had
employed the patentee when he invented the device; others (see, for
example, A. J. BOULT or H. E. NEWTON) were professional Patent
Agents to whom inventors had communicated the subjects of the patent.
In the case of these "communicated" patents (where the Agent handled
all technicalities, to save his principal the trouble), an Agent was
merely a bare trustee of the patent, unable to deal with it in any way
contrary to his client's wishes, and he normally assigned, i.e. transferred
the patent to his principal, after grant and sealing.

In the majority of cases mentioned in Appendix II, however, the
patentee was free to exploit the patent himself, or to license others to
use it, as he saw fit.

Such men as D. B. WESSON (q.v.) or H. WEBLEY (q.v.), for
example, were members of or owned unincorporated firms manufacturing arms, and simply manufactured their patented devices through the
organization thus available to them. F. VON MANNLICHER (q.v.)
or G. V. FOSBERY (q.v.), on the other hand, were patentees without
private ways to manufacture their inventions, and therefore licensed
manufacture and sale by others, equipped to work their patents, subject
to payment of a suitable consideration, be it lump-sum, or royalty on
each article made. In many cases, of course, the expense of securing the
patent proved a purely speculative investment, for the inventor never
found a manufacturer willing to take a licence to work the patent, and
(upon this lack of interest becoming clear) the protection was duly
abandoned, by failure to pay renewal fees; C. RICCI (q.v.) or B. F.,
F. L. and A. B. PERRY may be cited as obvious examples here.

To conclude these brief remarks upon that protection invoked by the
inventors listed in Table I or II, the matter of a "Convention Date"
safeguard available to certain overseas inventors should be noticed and
the patents of M. V. B. ALLEN (q.v.) and O. HAGEN (q.v.) cited as
instances of its use.

In 1883, an International Convention for the Protection of Industrial
Property had been signed at Paris, and this treaty was modified in 1900;
Great Britain had acceded as early as 1884, and by 1907 twenty-two
other nations were also signatories, constituting a Union for the protection of industrial property. They agreed, amongst various matters, that
any applicant for a patent in one member State should enjoy a right of
priority to request similar patent protection from other member States.

In those cases cited above, therefore, M. V. B. ALLEN (*q.v.*) applied for his British patents in 1905, but (since the United States and Great Britain were signatories to the International Convention) those patents carried a "Convention Date" priority as if granted from the date in November or December of 1904 when equivalent U.S. patents had been secured by Allen; for O. HAGEN (*q.v.*), his Br. Pat. 409/1912 had priority in the U.K. from 7th January, 1911, as it had in any other member State where the patentee also secured protection in terms of his original Norwegian patent of that date.

Appendices

Appendix I sets out, in tabular form, notes of the applicant(s), date, number, field of invention, and duration of privilege for all relevant British patents; Table I relating to protection surviving from years prior to 1889, and Table II dealing with patents secured between 1889 and 1914.

Appendix II, or "Who's Who", catalogues alphabetically the background of each patentee listed in Appendix I, and describes the nature of the relevant invention.

Appendix III is an Annotated Bibliography.

APPENDIX I

TABLE I

Expiry (E) or voidance (V) dates of certain British patents (granted prior to 1st January, 1889), which survived into the period of this book and are relevant to it.

Voidance or Expiry Date	Patentee	Patent Number and Year	Field of Invention
1889			
Feb. 17th (V)	G. Shepheard	2214/1885	A radial rifle
July 28th (V)	H. Schlund	9084/1885	A revolver
Sept. 9th (V)	R. Paulson	10664/1885	Gas-operated firearms
1890			
Feb. 15th (V)	H. Pieper	2167/1886	"Gas-seal" gun
Mar. 3rd (V)	L. & S. S. Younghusband	3047/1886	A magazine rifle
June 10th (V)	E. G. Brewer (Patent Agent) *A communication from J. E. Turbiaux*	2731/1882	A radial revolver
July 1st (V)	G. E. Vaughan (Patent Agent) *A communication from the Austrian Small Arms Mfg. Co.*	7989/1885	A rifle magazine
July 7th (E)	W. R. Lake (Patent Agent) *A communication from O. Jones*	2777/1876	A revolver cartridge-extractor
Aug. 14th (E)	T. de Mouncie	3206/1876	A revolver
Aug. 18th (V)	L. Armanni	10587/1886	Self-loading pistols
Sept. 18th (V)	H. A. Schlund	11900/1886	Improvements to 9084/1885
Oct. 5th (V)	E. A. Salvator	12686/1886	A magazine rifle
Nov. 3rd (V)	R. Paulson	14130/1886	Gas-operated firearms
1891			
Mar. 30th (V)	A. M. Clark (Patent Agent) *A communication from the Osterreichische Waffenfabriks-Gesellschaft*	1272/1878	A rifle magazine

TABLE I (continued)

Voidance or Expiry Date	Patentee	Patent Number and Year	Field of Invention
1891			
Apr. 1st (V)	G. E. Vaughan (Patent Agent) *A communication from O. Schoenauer*	5793/1884	A rifle magazine
May 15th (V)	G. Envall	5972/1885	A revolver
July 16th (V)	F. Martin, R. C. Romanel, and A. H. Williams	9998/1887	A magazine rifle
Aug. 11th (V)	A. Arbenz *A communication from Messrs. Pirlot & Tresart*	10974/1887	A safety-device for revolvers
1892			
Jan. 14th (V)	F. Mannlicher	632/1888	A rifle magazine
Feb. 13th (V)	H. Pieper	2166/1888	A magazine rifle
Mar. 7th (E)	J. H. Johnson (Patent Agent) *A communication from P. P. Mauser*	922/1878	A revolver
Apr. 16th (V)	G. H. Schnee	5607/1888	Magazine firearms
May 10th (V)	F. Martin, R. C. Romanel and A. H. Williams	6994/1888	A rifle magazine
June 7th (V)	T. F. Törnell	8331/1888	Improved revolver
July 12th (V)	J. Schulhof	9066/1886	A magazine rifle
July 16th (V)	J. Schulhof	10286/1888	A rifle magazine
July 23rd (V)	C. C. B. Whyte	10651/1888	A weapon-carrier
July 26th (V)	J. Schulhof	10423/1887	A rifle magazine
Aug. 22nd (V)	H. Dimancea	9973/1885	A revolver
Nov. 1st (V)	E. Fabre & A. Tronche	15771/1888	A magazine pistol
Nov. 26th (V)	A. Lindner	17159/1888	A magazine rifle
1893			
Oct. 1st (V)	K. Krnka	14088/1888	A magazine pistol

1894
No patent protection relevant to Table I terminated in this year

1895			
Apr. 25th (E)	R. Morris	1773/1881	Firearm converters
Nov. 24th (E)	T. W. & H. Webley	5143/1881	Improvements to revolvers
Dec. 6th (V)	H. A. Silver & W. Fletcher	16078/1884	Ejector and safety-device for revolvers

1896 and 1897
No patent protection relevant to Table I terminated in these years

TABLE I (continued)

Voidance or Expiry Date	Patentee	Patent Number and Year	Field of Invention
1898			
Jan. 21st (E)	J. Carter	1820/1884	Trigger-bolt for revolvers
Feb. 1st (E)	J. Carter	2555/1884	Cylinder-bolt for revolvers
1899			
Feb. 10th (V)	W. J. Whiting	1923/1886	Anti-fouling device for revolvers
Mar. 31st (E)	H. Webley & J. Carter	4070/1885	Barrel-latch for revolvers
1900			
Nov. 16th (V)	J. Carter	16638/1888	Safety-lock for revolvers

1901
No patent protection relevant to Table I terminated in this year

1902

Apr. 18th (E)	J. Carter & W. J. Whiting	5778/1888	A lock-mechanism for revolvers

1903–14
No patent protection relevant to Table I terminated in these years

TABLE II

British letters patent (covering revolving arms or rotary ammunition-feed devices) for period 1/1/1889–31/12/1914, with dates of their voidance.

Date of Patent	Patent No.	Patentee	Voidance Date	Field of Invention
1889				
Apr. 11th	6216	B. Kreith	11/4/1893 (V)	Combination of lance and revolver
Apr. 13th	6360	E. Reiger	13/4/1893 (V)	Magazine pistol
Apr. 30th	7200	H. E. Newton *A communication from the Colt's Patent F. A. Mfg. Co. (Inc.)*	30/4/1893 (V)	A revolver charger
Apr. 30th	7201	H. E. Newton *A communication from the Colt's Patent F. A. Mfg. Co. (Inc.)*	30/4/1895 (V)	Lock-mechanisms for revolvers

TABLE II (*continued*)

Date of Patent	Patent No.	Patentee	Voidance Date	Field of Invention
1889				
May 4th	7490	A. J. Boult *A communication from J. Schulhof*	4/5/1893 (V)	A rifle magazine and charger
Oct. 15th	16216	C. A. Davis & W. W. Herron	15/10/1893 (V)	Improvements in revolver handles
Nov. 18th	18430	P. Jensen *A communication from O. H. J. Krag & E. Jörgensen*	18/11/1903 (V)	A magazine rifle
Dec. 18th	20321	E. C. Green	18/12/1895 (V)	Improvements in revolvers
1890				
Sept. 16th	14639	W. T. Unge	16/9/1894 (V)	Gas-operated firearms
Oct. 14th	16350	L. F. Tavernier	14/10/1895 (V)	A radial magazine pistol
1891				
Feb. 25th	3427	W. J. Whiting	25/2/1896 (V)	Revolver cylinder-retainer
Mar. 9th	4205	J. S. Wallace & B. T. L. Thomson	9/3/1895 (V)	Pneumatic small-arms
Mar. 31st	5552	P. Monnerat	31/3/1895 (V)	A fire-sword
Apr. 23rd	7037	L. W. Broadwell & M. H. Durst	23/4/1895 (V)	A rifle magazine
Sept. 2nd	14853	L. W. Broadwell & M. H. Durst	2/9/1895 (V)	A rifle magazine cut-off
Oct. 14th	17532	A. C. Argles	14/10/1896 (V)	A walking-stick firearm
Oct. 20th	17993	H. H. Grenfell & J. G. Accles	20/10/1896 (V)	A revolver
Oct. 27th	18516	M. H. Durst	27/10/1896 (V)	A magazine rifle
1892				
Jan. 14th	792	M. H. Durst	14/1/1896 (V)	A magazine rifle
Feb. 24th	17082	O. H. J. Krag & E. Jörgensen	24/2/1905 (V)	A magazine rifle
Apr. 7th	6683	S. N. McLean	7/4/1906 (E)	Magazine firearms
Apr. 25th	7787	H. H. Lake *A communication from Die Actien Gesellschaft Grusonwerk*	25/4/1896 (V)	A "gas-seal" revolver
May 9th	8760	M. H. Durst	9/5/1896 (V)	Magazine improvements to 18516/1891 and 792/1892
Nov. 9th	20215	A. Chapman	9/11/1897 (V)	Belt feed for rifles

TABLE II (continued)

Date of Patent	Patent No.	Patentee	Voidance Date	Field of Invention
1892				
Dec. 13th	22901	A. W. Savage	13/12/1897 (V)	A magazine rifle
1893				
Jan. 3rd	120	A. G. Nolcken	3/1/1897 (V)	A magazine rifle
Jan. 11th	646	M. H. Durst	11/1/1897 (V)	A magazine rifle
Feb. 17th	3560	W. de C. Prideaux	17/2/1903 (V)	Revolver chargers
Mar. 13th	5420	A. J. Watson	13/3/1901 (V)	Revolver chargers
Mar. 28th	6541	W. P. Thompson *A communication from D. E. Grant*	28/3/1897 (V)	A magazine rifle
Apr. 5th	7003	C. Ricci	5/4/1899 (V)	A magazine rifle
Aug. 21st	15833	A. J. Boult *A communication from Clair Frères*	21/8/1899 (V)	Gas-operated firearms
Sept. 12th	17104	M. Hasselmann	12/9/1897 (V)	An improved revolver
Sept. 21st	17790	J. F. Latham	21/9/1898 (V)	A revolver adaptor
Oct. 17th	19544	P. H. Finnegan	17/10/1899 (V)	An improved radial revolver
Oct. 21st	19861	J. F. Latham	21/10/1899 (V)	A revolver converter
Dec. 20th	24502	J. T. Musgrave	20/12/1898 (V)	An improved ejector
1894				
Mar. 27th	6184	D. B. Wesson	27/3/1907 (V)	Improvements to revolvers
July 20th	14010	L. Nagant	20/7/1901 (V)	"Gas-seal" revolvers
Aug. 27th	16272	C. Ricci	27/8/1898 (V)	Revolvers
Aug. 27th	16308	E. Paul	27/8/1898 (V)	Combination of dagger and revolver
Oct. 8th	19083	J. Courrier	8/10/1899 (V)	A rifle magazine
Nov. 23rd	22719	J. F. & H. W. Latham	23/11/1899 (V)	Latching revolver barrels
Nov. 27th	22930	B. R. Banks	27/11/1899 (V)	An air-rifle charger
1895				
Jan. 26th	1905	W. Chaine	26/1/1899 (V)	A magazine pistol
Aug. 16th	15453	G. V. Fosbery	16/8/1908 (V)	A magazine pistol
Oct. 5th	18686	H. W. Gabbett-Fairfax	5/10/1900 (V)	An automatic pistol

N

TABLE II (continued)

Date of Patent	Patent No.	Patentee	Voidance Date	Field of Invention
1896				
Mar. 7th	5151	C. O. Ellis, E. W. Wilkinson & F. Cashmore	7/3/1900 (V)	Ejectors for revolvers
June 6th	12470	G. V. Fosbery	6/6/1908 (V)	A recoil-operated revolver
Aug. 5th	17291	W. J. Whiting	5/8/1908 (V)	Improvements to 3427/1891
Aug. 11th	17808	H. W. Gabbett-Fairfax	11/8/1900 (V)	Feed-mechanisms for automatic firearms
Oct. 29th	24155	G. V. Fosbery	29/10/1908 (V)	Improvements to 15453/1895 and 12470/1896
Nov. 13th	25561	F. Praunegger & L. P. Schmidt	13/11/1901 (V)	An automatic ejector for revolvers
Dec. 12th	28484	H. Pieper	12/12/1903 (V)	A magazine rifle
1897				
Jan. 18th	1328	A. Lines	18/1/1902 (V)	Revolvers
Feb. 12th	3771	R. Gordon-Smith	12/2/1905 (V)	Combination of revolver and axe
July 12th	16432	D. T. Laing	12/7/1901 (V)	Combination of lance and revolver
1898				
May 3rd	10145	A. Lines	3/5/1902 (V)	Improvements to 1328/1897
May 26th	11998	B. Behr	26/5/1905 (V)	A double-barrelled pistol
June 2nd	12367	A. Lines	2/6/1903 (V)	Improvements to 1328/1897
1899				
Apr. 26th	8761	B. Reyes	26/4/1903 (V)	A revolver-sword
Aug. 17th	16734	F. von Mannlicher	17/8/1906 (V)	A magazine rifle
Aug. 29th	17520	J. Rupertus	29/8/1903 (V)	A revolver lock-mechanism
Oct. 3rd	19848	A. W. Savage	3/10/1906 (V)	Improvements to a magazine rifle
Nov. 10th	22479	G. C. Dymond *A communication from H. F. Landstad*	18/11/1904 (V)	An automatic revolver
1900				
Jan. 24th	1567	F. von Mannlicher & O. Schoenauer	24/1/1904 (V)	A rifle magazine
May 1st	8045	I. Wheeldon	1/5/1904 (V)	Wire cutters
Aug. 4th	14576	O. H. J. Krag	4/8/1904 (V)	A rifle magazine

TABLE II (continued)

Date of Patent	Patent No.	Patentee	Voidance Date	Field of Invention
1900				
Oct. 13th	18225	The Webley & Scott R. & A. Co., Ltd. & W. J. Whiting	13/10/1909 (V)	Revolver cylinder-alignment device
Oct. 29th	19320	J. A. Schwarz & T. A. Fidjeland	29/10/1904 (V)	A magazine rifle
1901				
Mar. 8th	4924	W. J. Whiting	8/3/1909 (V)	Improvements to automatic revolvers
Mar. 11th	5169	F. von Mannlicher	11/3/1906 (V)	A magazine rifle
Sept. 13th	18294	The Webley & Scott R. & A. Co., Ltd. & W. J. Whiting	13/9/1905 (V)	Revolver chargers
Oct. 4th	19839	G. Roth & C. Krnka	4/10/1915 (V)	An automatic rifle
Nov. 9th	22653	W. P. Thompson *A communication from the Ideal Holster Co.*	9/11/1906 (V)	Detachable stock connection
Nov. 9th	22654	W. P. Thompson *A communication from the Ideal Holster Co.*	9/11/1906 (V)	An improved revolver
Nov. 9th	22657	J. Tambour	9/11/1910 (V)	Safety-devices for firearms
Dec. 3rd	24588	D. B. Wesson	3/12/1908 (V)	Cylinder-latch for revolvers
Dec. 3rd	24597	D. B. Wesson	3/12/1908 (V)	Cylinder-latch for revolvers
1902				
Jan. 13th	921	G. Tresenreuter	13/1/1906 (V)	Combination of revolver and walking-stick
Feb. 18th	4148	H. H. Lake *A communication from T. Thorsen*	18/2/1906 (V)	Recoil-operated rifle
Sept. 2nd	19265	W. J. Turnbull & W. H. Bofinger	2/9/1906 (V)	A magazine pistol
Sept. 17th	20307	J. Tambour	17/9/1912 (V)	Safety-devices for firearms
Sept. 19th	20430	The Webley & Scott R. & A. Co., Ltd. & W. J. Whiting	19/9/1906 (V)	A lock-mechanism for revolvers
Sept. 30th	21276	V. C. Tasker	30/9/1911 (V)	A firing-mechanism
Oct. 30th	23739	M. Dozin	30/10/1907 (V)	Ejectors for revolvers

TABLE II (continued)

Date of Patent	Patent No.	Patentee	Voidance Date	Field of Invention
1903 Jan. 13th	859	B. F., F. L. & A. B. Perry	13/1/1907 (V)	A magazine rifle
June 23rd	14026	O. Imray *A communication from the Colt's Patent F. A. Mfg. Co. (Inc.)*	23/6/1908 (V)	A revolver sight
1904 Feb. 8th	3127	C. von Mannlicher	8/2/1915 (V)	Improvements to 26270/1902
1905 May 13th	10072	W. J. Whiting	13/5/1909 (V)	A revolver lock-mechanism
July 3rd	13680	O. Imray *A communication from the Colt's Patent F. A. Mfg. Co. (Inc.)*	3/7/1917 (V)	Safety-device for a revolver lock-mechanism
July 10th	14223	J. Lauber	10/7/1909 (V)	A magazine rifle
Oct. 30th	22131	H. Danner	30/10/1910 (V)	A magazine rifle
Oct. 30th	22135	M. V. B. Allen	30/10/1909 (V)	Safety-device for revolvers
Oct. 30th	22136	M. V. B. Allen	30/10/1909 (V)	Safety-device for revolvers
1906 Jan. 2nd	177	P. A. Phillippides	2/1/1910 (V)	A rifle magazine
Feb. 26th	4622	A. H. Butler & F. G. Clark	26/2/1911 (V)	An air-rifle magazine
May 9th	10882	H. Langenhan	9/5/1910 (V)	Combination of revolver and umbrella
Nov. 23rd	26611	H. Renfors	23/11/1911 (V)	Firearm clamp
1907 Feb. 27th	4824	J. H. Cox	27/2/1918 (V)	An air-rifle magazine
1908 Feb. 12th	3154	A. Mund	12/2/1912 (V)	A burglar alarm
1909 Feb. 2nd	2462	B. Kreith	2/2/1913 (V)	Combination of knuckledusters and revolver
July 6th	15753	M. C. Lisle & H. M. Kipp	6/7/1913 (V)	A "gas-seal" revolver
Aug. 11th	18495	G. V. Haeghen	11/8/1912 (V)	An automatic revolver
1910 Jan. 25th	1926	T. Montmeny & J. T. Momnie	25/1/1914 (V)	A magazine rifle
Jan. 25th	1927	J. Sabo	25/1/1914 (V)	A rifle magazine
Feb. 22nd	4395	H. Sunngärd	22/2/1914 (V)	A magazine

TABLE II (continued)

Date of Patent	Patent No.	Patentee	Voidance Date	Field of Invention
1910				
July 9th	16425	J. A. G. Marshall	9/7/1915 (V)	A rest or support for firearms
Aug. 20th	19566	J. B. A. Guindon & I. Belair	20/8/1914 (V)	A rifle magazine and loader
Oct. 12th	23659	B. R. Reid	12/10/1913 (V)	A lock-mechanism
1911				
Jan. 25th	1928	E. Tatarek & J. Benkö	25/1/1915 (V)	A magazine
Mar. 20th	6937	I. H. Rodehaver & C. W. Randall	20/3/1915 (V)	A double-barrelled firearm
Apr. 10th	8910	W. E. Steers	10/4/1915 (V)	A sight for pistols
1912				
Jan. 5th	409	O. Hagen	5/1/1916 (V)	A support for firearms
Apr. 11th	8623	C. A. Lewis	11/4/1916 (V)	A light projector for firearms
Aug. 12th	18486	V. de Marais & G. E. Gardner	12/8/1916 (V)	A light projector for firearms
Nov. 13th	26086	W. Decker	13/11/1916 (V)	A revolver
Dec. 16th	28924	Waffen-Technische Gesellschaft "Wespi" & R. Targan	16/12/1916 (V)	Improvement to luminous sight tube
1913				
Aug. 26th	19324	M. Ferguson & J. O. Fitzgerald	26/8/1917 (V)	A light projector for firearms
1914				
Apr. 2nd	8353	P. Schmidt & K. Dobslaw	2/4/1917 (V)	A light projector for firearms
May 20th	12459	J. Eastwick	20/5/1921 (V)	A rifle magazine
Nov. 17th	22653	W. de C. Prideaux	17/11/1924 (V)	A revolver charger

APPENDIX II

"WHO'S WHO"

ACCLES, J. G. James George Accles (from Holford House, Perry Bar, Birmingham) secured Br. Pat. 17993/1891, jointly with H. H. GRENFELL (*q.v.*); Haseltine, Lake & Co., a firm of London Patent Agents then located at 45 Southampton Buildings, W.C., acted for the two applicants.

Br. Pat. 17993/1891 protected a double-action revolver with an old-fashioned cartridge-ejection system more popular in preceding decades; see, for example, remarks upon H. DIMANCEA. To eject cartridges in revolvers of this type, the barrel was first unlatched from the pistol-frame, and then barrel and cylinder were tilted sideways, as a unit, upon a pivot projecting from the front of the weapon; once Accles & Grenfell's cylinder had cleared the standing-breech, a rod protruding beneath the barrel was then pressed rearwards, manually, to expel all cartridges simultaneously by means of a star-shaped ejector (mounted at the rear-end of that rod) embedded in the rear of the cylinder.

The Specification filed with Br. Pat. 17993/1891 contained eight detailed claims of novelty for various features of such a revolver, but the basis for that lock-mechanism shown in the drawings was (like the ejection-system) derivative being in fact a modified version of an earlier design by Michael Kaufmann (a designer working with the Birmingham firm of P. WEBLEY & SON (*q.v.*), in the 1880s), which had been used most successfully in Webley "Improved Government Pattern" revolvers that were barely obsolete in 1891. Kaufmann had secured

(in curious circumstances, later explored with remarks upon O. JONES and A. T. DE MOUNCIE) the relevant British Patent No. 4302 of 21st October, 1880, for a revolver lock-mechanism which contained only five components, but he had abandoned that protection in 1888.

Accles and Grenfell's lock-mechanism is shown at left in Figure 29, beside Kaufmann's design, where "a" is the hammer, "b" the trigger, "c" the mainspring, "d" the pawl, and "e" the hammer-lever transmitting thrust (from the lower limb of "c") to pawl and trigger. Accles and Grenfell's refinements to Kaufmann's design were only the separate firing-pin "f" and pivoted cylinder-bolt "g".

However, J. G. Accles (whose business relationship with H. H. GRENFELL is also explored under remarks upon that patentee) was in fact a project and ordnance engineer whose livelihood and place in history never rested upon the fortunes of Br. Pat. 17993/1891.

Born at Bendigo, Australia, in 1850, his parents moved (via Northern Ireland, from whence they had originally come) to the United States, in 1861. At seventeen, their boy was apprenticed at the factory of the COLT'S PATENT FIRE ARMS MANUFACTURING CO. (*q.v.*) in Hartford, Conn., and by 1871 he was involved with the Russian government negotiators (headed by General Gorloff) purchasing American "Berdan" rifles and ammunition for the Imperial armies.

In 1872, Accles came to England, and worked at Ward End, Birmingham (whether on his own account, or for others, is not clear) at the production of caps for Russian "Berdan" ammunition.

A year later, he was in China, as a project engineer for Richard Jordan Gatling, establishing Gatling machine-gun and ammunition factories at Canton and Shanghai. Between 1876 and 1886, he laid out and commissioned twelve such plants, in various countries, and these activities culminated (in 1887) with the construction and equipping of cart-ridge factories, near Foochow and on Formosa, for the Chinese government.

tainly inherited from its predecessors, and actually manufactured under a patent of H. DIMANCEA (*q.v.*). No specimen arm made under Grenfell and Accles' own Br. Pat. 17993/1891 can be seen any-where in the photograph.

It is probable that Accles (who had designed the "Accles Positive Feed" drums used on Model 1883 Gatling machine-guns) continued to assemble and sell such guns, through Grenfell & Accles Ltd., for as long as his inherited stocks of components lasted, but the

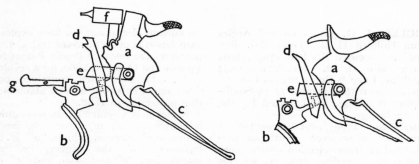

FIG. 29. *Grenfell & Accles's and Kaufmann's lock-mechanisms.*
(Grenfell & Accles's after Br. Pat. 17993/1891.)

In 1888, Accles left his employment with the Gatling organization in America, and became involved in a venture at Holford Works, Perry Bar, Birmingham, where an American named F. C. Penfield attempted (through a company called The Gatling Arms & Ammunition Co. Ltd.) to develop European and Eastern Hemisphere mar-kets for Gatling guns, and to all comers.

This venture was under-capitalized, and went into liquidation in 1890. Accles (who had an investment of £8,600 in the company) then joined with H. H. GRENFELL (*q.v.*) to form Grenfell & Accles Ltd., a company which took over the Holford Works, and seems also to have bought the stock-in-trade of the moribund Penfield venture. Grenfell & Accles Ltd. was an exhibitor at the Royal Naval Exhibition, Chelsea, in 1891, but a surviving photograph of the stand shows (amongst artillery, machine-gun and ammunition exhibits) a case of revolvers and components almost cer-

Company also introduced its own machine-gun and sold this with notice-able (if short-lived) success, under Accles' British Patent No. 9455 of 28th June, 1888. This was a crew-served, crank-operated, rotating-barrel design (similar to the Gatling), and was chiefly remarkable for a capability of use with the Pattern 1888/89 disposable maga-zines noticed in later remarks upon H. H. GRENFELL (*q.v.*).

Following that collapse of Grenfell & Accles Ltd., described in relation to H. H. GRENFELL (*q.v.*), J. G. Accles briefly operated a company called the Accles Arms, Ammunition & Manufacturing Co., Ltd. (or Accles Ltd.) to produce bicycles and sporting ammunition at the Holford Works, and also secured one British patent for cooling machine-gun barrels (No. 18858 of 3rd September, 1899), which may have indicated an in-tention to work again in that particular field. However, 1899 was that year in which the bicycle "bubble" busts, and this new company failed as its predecessor had done. In 1901, J. G. Accles was briefly associated with yet another company, called Accles & Pollock Ltd. (which continues today, at Oldbury), but shortly severed his connection with it.

He then worked alone, as a consultant upon small-arms and ammunition, and was for three years retained by the Birmingham Small-Arms Co., Ltd., securing jointly with that Company (and Mr. G. Norman) six British patents, relating to bolt-action rifles, in the years 1910 and 1911.

In 1913, however, he joined with Mr. G. E. Shelvoke to form Accles & Shelvoke Ltd., at Aston: it was in this year that his first patent for a humane cattle-killer was secured (jointly with C. Cash), and he took out further patents for this type of weapon, in years after those of concern here. Accles survived the period of this book by many years, and in 1914 still occupied his consultant's offices at the Accles & Shelvoke Ltd., Talford Street engineering premises, in Aston.

ALLEN, M. V. B. Martin Van Buren Allen, from 232 West 144th Street, New York, secured Br. Pats. 22135/1905 and 22136/1905 (through London Patent Agents Wheatley & Mackenzie, of 40 Chancery Lane, W.C.), and described himself simply as a "Manufacturer", in his patent Specifications; however, contemporary New York directories list him as a lock-maker at 23 Union Square West, as well as of the address mentioned above.

He filed Complete Specifications with both applications, and also claimed "Convention Date" priority of invention from 28th November, 1904 (for Br. Pat. 22136/1905) and 16th December, 1904 (for Br. Pat. 22135/1905), which were presumably those dates at which he had filed application for what became the equivalent U.S. Patents, Nos. 792381 and 792382 (both dated 13th June, 1905), which he also secured. As to "Convention Date" priority, see Appendix I.

In addition to these two U.S. Patents, Allen held another brace covering similar types of safety-device for use in revolvers; the first (U.S. Patent No. 741754 of 20th October, 1903) was partly assigned to W. N. Thayer and Theodore Allen, of New York, and may indicate passing interest by someone in these ideas. There is, however, no evidence that any one of those four devices was ever commercially developed.

Both British patents were for improvements to concealed-hammer, self-cocking revolvers, of the cheaper kind, by provision of distinctive safety-devices for such arms. In the case of Br. Pat. 22135/1905, a rotatable hammer-lock was concealed within the butt, and operated by moving what appeared externally to be one of the butt-cheek retaining-screws. In Br. Pat. 22136/1905, two small sliding and interlocking pins in the top butt-strap (which must have required a watch-maker's dexterity to operate them) could be used to bolt the hammer.

It was Allen's view that the practical difficulty in finding (to say nothing of unbolting) these safety-devices constituted their principal advantage, since children were unlikely to discover how to free a weapon kept handy for household defence, and a policeman (if suddenly disarmed by a suspect) could not readily be shot with his own pistol.

ARBENZ, A. Adolphe Arbenz (of 107/108 Great Charles St., Birmingham) secured Br. Pat. 10974/1887 with the assistance of Patent Agent A. W. Turner, of Cobden Buildings, Corporation St., Birmingham, and it survived into years of concern here (see Table I); the subject of that protection is discussed in remarks upon PIRLOT & TRESART (q.v.), a Belgian firm which communicated the design to be patented by Arbenz. As to "communicated" British patents see, generally, Appendix I.

Arbenz (who described himself as a "Gun Manufacturer" in the Complete Specification to Br. Pat. 10974/1887) was actually an import merchant, who took out British patent protection on some of the lines which he imported here from the Continent; in 1887, for example, Messrs. Flurscheim & Bergmann, of Gaggenau, communicated to Arbenz an air-rifle design (without revolving features) upon which the merchant also secured a British patent. Despite this Teutonic surname, Arbenz apparently maintained his business (then at 33 Ludgate Hill, Birmingham) on the outbreak of the First World War.

ARGLES, A. C. Augustus Charles Argles secured Br. Pat. 17532/1891, through his Patent Agent, H. Gardner, of 166 Fleet Street, London, and described himself (in the Specification) as a "Manufacturer", with his address as that of The Arms and Ammunition Co., at 143

ARMANNI, L. Luigi Armanni was an Engineer, who secured a number of British patents relating to firearms (or to unrelated mechanical devices) in the two decades after 1883; his Br. Pat. No. 8131 of 18th June, 1886, was for a machine-gun with an interesting rotary magazine, but only his Br. Pat. 10587/1886 (which survived until 1890, see Table I) is of concern here.

In the Specification to Br. Pat. 10587/1886, Armanni mentioned addresses at 46 Langdon Park Road,

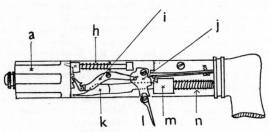

FIG. 30. *Argles's revolver.*
(After Br. Pat. 17531/1891.)

"a" = cylinder; "h" = cylinder-bolt and spring; "i" = pawl-lever, with pawl pivoted at forward end; "j" = tumbler; "k/m" and "n" = composite firing-pin and firing-pin spring.

Pressure on "l" depresses one end of "i", raising the pawl to rotate the cylinder "a"; at the limit of trigger-travel, "h" is pressed forward (by an angle on "j") to bolt "a", but is retracted by its spring when "l" is released. There is no conventional sear, the firing-pin "k/m" being pressed back on its spring "n" by a lighter spring (hidden in the Figure, but on the far side of "j") which ultimately is over-ridden by "n", which then drives "k/m" forward on to the rim-fire cartridge. A safety-spring is visible above "m", and normally holds "k/m" off the chambers, but is lifted out of its notch in "m", by a shoulder on "j", when "l" is pressed.

Queen Victoria Street, London. Br. Pat. 17532/1891 related to a self-cocking, rim-fire "pepperbox" revolver (with three or more barrels), which was to be detachably mounted at the handle-end of a walking-stick, and pulled off the stick for use (see Fig. 30).

The weapon falls specifically into that category exemplified in these pages by the revolver of G. TRESENREUTER (*q.v.*), and generally into the class of combination firearms later described in remarks upon R. G. GORDON-SMITH; B. KREITH; D. T. LAING; P. MONNERAT; E. PAUL; and B. REYES.

Highgate, or Richmond Road, Dalston, and he was assisted to secure his protection by the London Patent Agents, Day, Davies & Hunt, of 321 High Holborn; the Specification set out thirty detailed claims for improvements to firearms, amongst which were designs for a gas-operated self-loading pistol in which the barrel was blown forward to operate the loading-cycle, another (recoil-operated) self-loading pistol in which the breech-block tilted upwards to expel cartridge-case on discharge, and various tubular magazines revolving around or beneath the barrels of Armanni's pistols. No specimen arms are known to have survived.

Certain features of Armanni's lock- and magazine-rotation systems were claimed as applicable to conventional revolvers, one of the latter using a zigzag cylinder race of the type discussed in remarks upon G. V. FOSBERY (*q.v.*) and P. MAUSER (*q.v.*).

AUSTRIAN SMALL-ARMS MANUFACTURING CO.
This firm communicated Br. Pat. 7989/1885 to London Patent Agent G. E. VAUGHAN (*q.v.*), and it survived into our period, as shown in Table I; the Specification mentioned domicile of the communicant at Steyr, Austria. It is not clear whether the subjects were actually communicated by a company of this name, or if the title of the OESTERREICHISCHE WAFFEN-FABRIKS-GESELLSCHAFT (*q.v.*) was anglicized for the application, but the invention was probably that of Anton Spitalsky, and to be associated with those Austrian service-rifle trials later mentioned in remarks upon F. VON MANNLICHER (*q.v.*), O. SCHOENAUER (*q.v.*), J. SCHULHOF (*q.v.*), and the OESTER-REICHISCHE WAFFENFABRIKS-GESELLSCHAFT (*q.v.*).

Br. Pat. 7989/1885 was abandoned early in the period, because a revolving rifle magazine which it protected proved unsatisfactory under test. In this design, a truncated conical magazine-case was to be mounted just forward of the trigger-guard, and to contain a fluted rotary cartridge-feeder, powered by a spiral spring. Loading cartridges into this feeder, from the top, put the spring into tension, and an escapement (linked to the rifle-bolt) then allowed the feeder to turn cartridges, successively, up into the rifle-breech.

BANKS, B. R.
Bernard Rodwell Banks (of 22 Elgin Road, Croydon, Surrey) was an Engineer, who secured Br. Pat. 22930/1894 without professional assistance; one claim under this patent was for a detached, rotatable pellet-magazine, which embodied a tube and plunger for pressing each round into the breech of an air-rifle.

BEHR, B.
Burkard Behr (of Bendlikon, near Zurich, Switzerland) described himself as a "citizen of the Russian Empire", and as an "Inventor", when filing application for Br. Pat. 11998/1898; he was assisted to secure his protection by W. P. Thompson & Co. (see W. P. THOMPSON), a well-known firm of Patent Agents, and his patent protected design-features of a famous pocket-firearm, the so-called "Bar" Pistol. This was a self-cocking weapon, with double (over-and-under) barrels about 2 inches in length, from which four shots could be fired at one loading.

The cartridges (normally 6·35-mm. rimless rounds) were carried in four chambers bored one above the other through a flat magazine-block, which was pivoted on a central arbor, and locked into position by a spring-catch on top of the butt. Two cartridges aligned with the barrels would be successively discharged (by twice pulling the folding trigger) *via* an automatically rotated firing-head on the face of the concealed hammer, when the magazine-block could be unlocked, and manually rotated to bring two more cartridges into alignment with the barrels. Ejection of fired cases was effected by use of a separate rod, normally screwed into the butt.

Behr held Belgian, German, Russian and United States patents covering this weapon (in addition to Br. Pat. 11998/1898), and it apparently remained popular until the introduction of small self-loading pistols, to Europe, in the early 1900s. The inventor was an active patentee in various fields unconnected with firearms, but he also secured (between 1903 and 1906) other patents relating to cattle-killers, breech-actions and recoil-absorbers, in the realm of small-arms design.

BELAIR, I.
Isai Belair, a Canadian "Manufacturer" (of St. Eustache, County of Two Mountains, Quebec) joined with J. B. A. GUINDON (*q.v.*) to secure Br. Pat. 19566/1910, under advice from London Patent Agents Boult, Wade and Tennant, of 111/112 Hatton Garden.

Br. Pat. 19566/1910 laid eight claims of novelty to a peculiar rotary magazine (and its loader), specially intended for use with lever-action rifles of the general type shown in Plate 35; this magazine was formed in two halves (hinged at one side, latched at the other) and literally wrapped around the receiver of the rifle. Step-by-step rotation of the magazine occurred (*via* a suitable ratchet mechanism) as the lever-action of the rifle was operated, so that the uppermost cartridge dropped by gravity in front of the breech-bolt.

There seems no obvious reason to doubt that Belair and Guindon's magazine could be made to work, but today's lack of surviving specimens suggests that few Canadian riflemen of the period were prepared to share such an opinion.

VON BENKÖ, J. Johann von Benkö (of Debrecen, Hungary) was an army Captain, and joint-applicant with E. TATAREK (*q.v.*) for Br. Pat. 1928/1911. A Patent Agent, named F. H. Rogers (of Broad Sanctuary Chambers, London, S.W.), acted for the two applicants.

Protection was secured for a spiral cartridge magazine, for self-loading firearms "of the Browning type", which could also be used as an aiming rest. Br. Pat. 1928/1911 was not renewed in 1915, and it remains for conjecture whether the First World War prevented payment of the necessary fee, or whether the applicants would, in any event, have then abandoned their protection.

Convoluted "snail" magazines of this type had been envisaged, by a British engineer, some forty-five years before Br. Pat. 1928/1911 (see W. J. Curtis's Br. Pat. 1810 of 10th July 1866) but, as can be seen from Figure 31, von Benkö and Tatarek's magazine bears a striking resemblance to another magazine used (by Germany) during the First World War, with both the Parabellum self-loading Pistole o8, and the Bergmann Machine Pistol 18-1. In this later magazine, the spiral part of the device was raked at an angle to the straight part, but an acknowledgement to these Hungarian patentees appears due, as to parentage of the basic idea.

BOFINGER, W. H. William Henry Bofinger was joint-applicant with W. J. TURNBULL (*q.v.*) for Br. Pat. 19265/1902. The Specification described Bofinger as

a "Merchant" (at 1531 Camp Street, New Orleans, Louisiana), and contained seven detailed claims for the magazine pistol shown in Figure 69, and described in the remarks upon Bofinger's co-patentee. The latter was an engineer, who probably invented the weapon, and

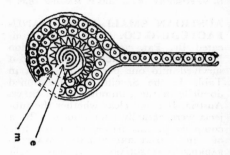

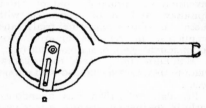

FIG. 31. *Von Benkö & Tatarek's Magazine.*
(After Br. Pat. 1928/1911.)

A crank "a" on the outer casing puts a coiled spring "e" into tension within the magazine. The thrust of "e" is transmitted to the cartridges *via* a spiral spring "m", and its follower.

Bofinger's contribution to the project is assumed to have been purely financial.

BOULT, A. J. Alfred Julius Boult was a British Chartered Patent Agent, to whom CLAIR FRÈRES (*q.v.*) communicated Br. Pat. 15833/1893, and to whom J. SCHULHOF (*q.v.*) communicated Br. Pat. 7490/1889; as to the matter of "communicated" British patents, generally (see Appendix I).

Boult handled a considerable number of applications for British patent protection, over the three decades prior to 1914, but the majority did not relate to firearms at all.

In the two cases cited about, Boult

gave as his address premises at 323 High Holborn, London, and it is probable that he then worked for W. P. THOMPSON (*q.v.*), whose practice was at that address.

In 1893, a partnership was apparently formed as W. P. Thompson & Boult, then Boult & Wade was formed, and endured until around 1902, when the firm of Boult, Wade & Kilburn appeared. Finally, from about 1909, Boult either set up or joined to form the well-known firm of Boult, Wade & Tennant, at 111/112 Hatton Garden, London, and stayed with it until his death or retirement.

BREWER, E. G. Edward Griffith Brewer was a London Patent Agent (at 33 Chancery Lane) to whom J. E. TURBIAUX (*q.v.*) communicated the subjects of Br. Pat. 2731/1882. He does not appear to have handled many patent applications for firearms, and the claims of Br. Pat. 2731/1882 are discussed in later remarks upon Monsieur Turbiaux.

BROADWELL, L. W. Lewis Wells Broadwell was joint-applicant with M. H. DURST (*q.v.*) for Br. Pats. 7037/1891 and 14853/1891, covering a rifle magazine and an application therefor.

Both men are described as of the same address, in the Specifications to these patents, but their respective contributions to the inventions are not indicated.

Since the patents were so short-lived (see Table II), and it was Durst who pressed on, alone, with improvements to the original idea, both patents are described in later remarks upon that patentee.

BUTLER, A. H. Arthur Harry Butler (a Clerk, resident at 51 Witton Road, Birmingham) was joint-applicant for Br. Pat. 4622/1906, with F. G. CLARK (*q.v.*). The invention protected was an air-rifle magazine, described under remarks upon the latter patentee.

CARTER, J. John Carter was joint-applicant for Br. Pat. 4070/1885, with H. WEBLEY (*q.v.*), and for Br. Pat. 5778/1888, with W. J. WHITING (*q.v.*); he also secured Br. Pats. 1820/1884,

2555/1844 and 16638/1888 in his own name. All five patents survived into the period of concern here, and all were handled, for these various applicants, by W. E. Gedge, a Patent Agent at 11 Wellington Street, Strand, London.

In the Specifications to these patents, Carter was described either as an "Action Filer" or as a "Pistol Action Filer", and addresses at 33 Ford Street, and Mona Terrace, Bracebridge St., Aston juxta Birmingham, were mentioned.

It is obvious, both from the identity of those other applicants for Br. Pats. 4070/1885 or 5778/1888, and from its use of all five patented devices, that Carter was then closely associated with the Birmingham firm of P. WEBLEY & SON (*q.v.*), which preceded THE WEBLEY & SCOTT REVOLVER AND ARMS CO., LTD. (*q.v.*)

In later years (between 1904 and 1907), Carter was sole or joint patentee in a number of British sporting-gun and self-loading pistol patents, which were developed by the above-named Webley successor company, in which Carter was a departmental foreman.

It is not entirely clear, however, if he was a Webley employee at the time that the patents of concern here were secured. He could, by the pattern of the Birmingham gun-trade in the 1880s, have been an outworker craftsman, who filed-up the lock-mechanisms of Webley revolvers, working as an independent contractor and on a piece-work basis.

Plainly, however, all five of the first-mentioned patents were regarded as valuable, since only one of them (Br. Pat 16638/1888) was abandoned, and even in that case the protection had only one year to run when it was allowed to become void.

Carter's Br. Pats. 1820/1884 and 2555/1884 related to trigger- and cylinder-bolting improvements for that weapon shown in the advertisement on Plate 24; this pistol (now more commonly known, in England, as the "Webley-Pryse" or the "Webley No. 4" revolver, than by the title used in the advertisement shown in Plate 24) was a popular arm, in the medium price-range, from around 1876 until 1914. At least three lock-mechanisms were used in it, by various British and Continental manufacturers, including M. HASSELMANN (*q.v.*), but the version shown in Figure 32 (and in the Specifications to both of Carter's patents) was obsolete by about 1900, and was thereafter largely replaced, in such arms, by the Schmidt-Galand lock-mechanism shown in Figure 33.

The improvements covered by Br. Pats. 4070/1885 and 5778/1888 were respectively dealt with in Chapter III and related to the famous "stirrup"

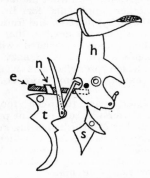

FIG. 32. *Carter's cylinder-bolt.*
(After Br. Pat. 2555/1884.)

barrel-latch visible in Plate 23 (for example), to a lock-mechanism shown at Figure 23, and to the cylinder bolt sketched at Figure 21.

In Br. Pat. 16638/1888 (the last of his patents to concern us here), Carter claimed improvements in respect of the two British service revolvers then current, by modifying their lock-mechanisms to prevent discharge by the hammer being accidentally knocked down on to a cartridge, from its rebounded position.

For the "Pistol, Webley, Mark I", shown in Plate 23, Carter proposed to form a lump, projecting upon the inside of the pawl, over the front end of the mainspring auxiliary shown in Figure 33. If the hammer were knocked forward hard enough, in a revolver not fitted with Carter's improvement, its heel could lift the mainspring auxiliary (which was the hammer-rebounding component) and permit the hammer to reach any cartridge before it. If Carter's improvement was present, however, the mainspring

auxiliary hit this lump on the inside of the pawl, as the hammer-heel began to lift the auxiliary, and prevented any further movement of the hammer. All Webley service revolvers, in the period of concern here, embodied Carter's improvement.

For the semi-obsolete "Pistol, Revolver, ·476 Mk II Enfield" shown as Plate 19 (top) Carter envisaged a "sear block" pivoted in the rear of the trigger-guard; this device (see Fig. 34) engaged a bent under the hammer, when the latter had rebounded after firing, and only deliberate full pressure on the trigger would disengage it from this bent. The sear block was a very stout component, and no merely accidental blow was likely to be heavy enough to drive the hammer forward, off its bent, and on to a cartridge.

CASHMORE, F. Frank Cashmore, a "Pistol Action Maker", at 44 Moseley Road, Birmingham, was joint-applicant for Br. Pat. 5151/1896, with C. O. ELLIS and E. W. WILKINSON (*q.v.*). Messrs. Marks & Clerk (of 18 Southampton Buildings, London, and 13 Temple Street, Birmingham), a well-known and still active firm of Patent Agents, handled the application for these patentees.

It is assumed that Cashmore (by reason of his trade) contributed markedly to the subject of this patent, but there is no evidence that the contribution of the other patentees was purely financial.

However, it is true that the name of Cashmore had been well-known throughout the British gun-trade, since 1855. In that year, Paul Cashmore (a West Bromwich pistol manufacturer) joined with the Birmingham gun-maker Charles Pryse, to secure Br. Pat. 2018 of 6th September, protecting a successful percussion revolver, and by the period of concern here Frank Cashmore already held (with Thomas Bland, the London gun-maker) one British patent for a self-cocking lock-mechanism used in multi-barrelled "man-stopper" pistols fashionable at that time, whilst an E. J. Cashmore had secured similar protection for a hammerless rifle design. By the close of the period, one William Cashmore was an established gun-, rifle-, and

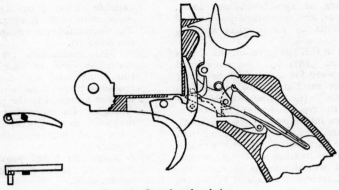

FIG. 33. *Carter's safety devices.*
(After Br. Pat. 16638/1888.)
Version for "Pistol, Webley, Mk. I".

In the Figure, Carter's improvement, as described in the text, consists in the small (black) diamond-shaped lump formed on the inner side of the pawl, immediately over the shelf upon which the tip of the rebound-lever rests in this Schmidt-Galand lock-mechanism.

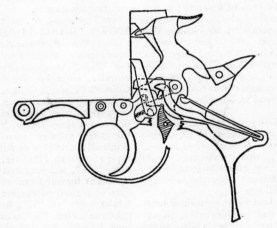

FIG. 34. *Carter's safety devices.*
(After Br. Pat. 16638/1888.)
Version for "Pistol, Revolver, ·476 Mk. II Enfield".

In this Figure, part of the trigger-guard and frame has been cut away to reveal Carter's (shaded) safety-sear, as claimed for use in "Enfield" revolvers, by his Br. Pat. 16638/1888; as the hammer rebounds it is caught (on a safety-notch) by this sear, which itself can only be moved by pressure from the trigger at the extreme rearward point in its travel.

(For parentage of the lock-mechanism see, generally, remarks upon O. JONES and A. T. DE MOUNCIE.)

pistol-maker at 130 Steelhouse Lane, Birmingham, and three-time patentee of improvements to hammerless sporting guns.

In view of this background, the claims of Br. Pat. 5151/1896 are considered here, and were for a cartridge extractor and ejector mechanism, to be used in "drop-down" (i.e. hinged-barrel) revolvers of the type shown on Plate 25.

As shown in Figure 20, it was normal, in such arms, for an ejector-lever (pivoted around the barrel-hinge) steadily to expel the ejector, by bearing against its stem as the barrel was depressed to open the weapon. Cashmore, Ellis and Wilkinson improved upon this simple system, by causing their ejector to spring suddenly clear of the cylinder, and thus eject the cartridges completely, instead of merely easing them from their chambers.

In a preferred method, as described in the Specification to this patent, two ejector-levers were mounted side-by-side and, on opening the revolver, one lever moved out the ejector in a conventional manner, until the second lever tripped a spring-loaded rod (which had been "cocked", automatically, by closing the weapon) to strike the ejector stem, sharply, and so eject the cartridges into the air. An alternative mechanism, also claimed in Br. Pat. 5151/1896, used a single ejector-lever and combined ejector-stem and ejector-rod in one component.

CHAINE, W. William Chaine described himself as "Retired Colonel, of Kensington Palace", in the Specification to Br. Pat. 1905/1895; this protection was secured for him by Haseltine, Lake & Co., London Patent Agents, at 45 Southampton Buildings.

This patentee had been commissioned Cornet, 4th Hussars, in December, 1856, and he had retired about 1881, after service also in the 10th Hussars. On his retirement, Colonel Chaine received both the post of "Assistant Master of Ceremonies to the Queen", and the imposing address stated in his Specification.

Broadly, the six claims of Br. Pat. 1905/1895 were as follows:

(i) A magazine pistol with a detachable tube for containing the cartridges, and a loading/ejecting mechanism capable of being operated by the movements of the trigger.

(ii) The detachable tube magazine mentioned in (i).

(iii) A feed mechanism for expelling cartridges, one by one from the tube magazine, and a device for retaining them in the tube when this was not attached to the pistol.

(iv) A socket for attaching the tube magazine to the pistol, and a cartridge feed-lever operated by the trigger.

(v) A magazine pistol provided with either of two claimed loading mechanisms.

(vi) A magazine pistol provided with either of two claimed cartridge-ejecting mechanisms.

However, an examination of Figure 35 (showing one of the weapons illustrated in Chaine's Specification) will reveal that the "magazine pistol" was in fact created by ingeniously adapting well-established solid-frame revolvers, of a species nearly thirty years old when Colonel Chaine secured his patent.

In Figure 35, a weapon similar to the Webley "R.I.C., Model 1883" pistol is shown, but other drawings in the patent Specification showed a "Webley No. 5" (or "New Army Express") revolver as equally suitable for modification to Colonel Chaine's design.

As can be seen from Figure 35, the trigger-guard of such a revolver was sawn off, and a ring-trigger, "D" (which gave the user greater purchase than that originally fitted) was substituted for the type shown in Plate 22. A heavy metal plate, "A", was screwed to the pistol, at the right forward end of the frame, and carried a pivoted cartridge ejector, "B", whilst a socket, "C", for attachment of tube magazine, "E", was mounted at the rear left of the cylinder. An external cylinder-bolt, "F", was also used, to ensure correct alignment of chambers (in the conventional revolver-cylinder "G") with cartridges in the tube-magazine "E".

This long tube magazine, when attached to the pistol, could lie against a user's shoulder (as an aid to aiming, or to reduce recoil, on firing) but, as an alternative, a bundle of shorter tube magazines might be carried around the user's forearm, and successively used as cartridges in the pistol were exhausted.

The detailed claims in Chaine's patent envisaged alternative loading and ejecting mechanisms, but his basic idea is shown in Figure 35, where a spring-follower in "E" urges cartridges towards the cylinder "G", and these rounds are successively admitted to the chambers of "G", by a lever linked to the trigger "D". The cylinder "G" (conventionally

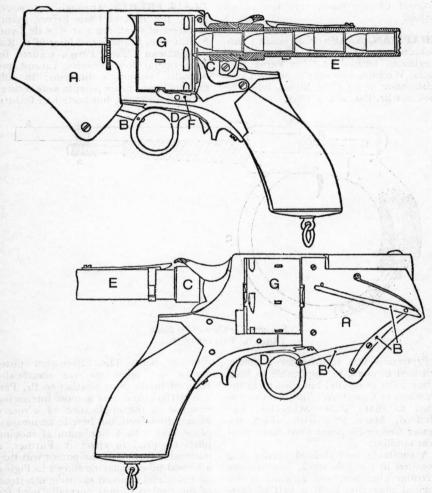

FIG. 35. *Chaine's magazine pistol.*
(After Br. Pat. 1905/1895.)

Effect of the linkage between the three levers which constitute the ejector "B" is to thrust the topmost lever into the "five o'clock" chamber of the cylinder "G", when the trigger "D" is pulled, thus expelling any cartridge in that chamber.

o

revolved by a pawl within the weapon) carries fired cases round until they are expelled rearwards, from the weapon, by the trigger-operated ejector "B".

It seems clear from the short life of his patent (see Table II), and the fact that specimen arms are unknown today, that Colonel Chaine made very few of his pistols.

CHAPMAN, A. Alfred Chapman ("late Colour-Sergeant of the Leicestershire Regiment, located at Glen Parva Barracks, Wigston, Leicester"), was a Commissionaire at 54 Fleet Street, when he took out Br. Pat. 20215/1892.

posited on a pivoted carrier in the old magazine well; when the bolt was fully retracted, this carrier was raised, by a spring, to place the cartridge in the path of the bolt, for loading as the bolt was thrust forward.

CLAIR FRÈRES. Through A. J. BOULT (*q.v.*), the firm of Clair Frères, manufacturers of small-arms at Rue de Lyon, St. Etienne, France (and later of 10 Rue de Château d'Eau, Paris), secured Br. Pat. 15833/1893, covering various gas-operated automatic firearms; in subsequent years, other patents were secured for such weapons, but none had features

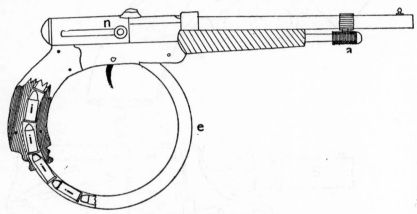

FIG. 36. *The Clair Frères pistol.*
(After Br. Pat. 15833/1893.)

Protection was secured for a rotary belt-feed mechanism, applicable to bolt-action rifles generally, but shown (in the drawings to Chapman's Specification) as fitted to that "Rifle, Magazine, Lee Metford, Mark I*", with which the former Colour-Sergeant must have been most familiar.

A rotatable and skeletal carrier was mounted in the rifle stock, beneath the cartridge chamber, and forward of the original magazine well; a belt of cartridges was fed up and over the carrier, from below, and given step-by-step feed rotation by a vertically-mounted rod, operated by the rifle bolt. On pulling back the sliding bolt, a cartridge was extracted from the belt, and then de-

relevant here. The fifteen-shot pistol shown as Figure 36 was specifically claimed in the Specification to Br. Pat. 15833/1893, and was a most interesting example of the application of a rotary ammunition-feed, but here in an unusual plane and with a minimum of moving parts required to effect it. Further, a noticeable feature of the patent was that a helical tube-magazine shown in Figure 36 contained rimmed cartridges, instead of the rimless rounds normally used for self-loading or automatic arms, and it is clear (from Leleu's remarks upon trials with a specimen) that the weapon both was intended to operate with normal commercial 8-mm. French Mlle 1892 service revolver cartridges and that it actually did so. Leleu's tabulated details yield little information about the weapon, referred to as the "Clair Model 1805" (which may have been a misprint of "1895"), but it would seem that the Clair brothers did achieve tests of a pistol within the claims of their Br. Pat. 15833/1893, although Leleu's description of a *five-round* magazine suggests that (unless another misprint occurred) the helical tube-design visible in Figure 36 was not fitted to the test-weapon. The pistol tested apparently measured 440 mm. in length, weighed 1362·5 g. loaded, and was 25 mm. in thickness; a pull of 7·5 kg. was required to cock the recoil spring, and an actual calibre of 7·7 mm. was used for the barrel.

Although the firm had been working upon gas-operated firearms since 1888, the Specification to Br. Pat. 15833/1893 makes it endearingly plain that an empiric approach still governed the efforts of Benoit, Jean Baptiste and Victor Clair, in this field. "From experiments [the Specification stated] it has been found that a barrel measuring ·30 cm. from the gas chamber's admission orifice to the mouth of the barrel answers very well and opens the breech only after the bullet has left the barrel." It was then remarked that the breech would no longer open unless the charges were increased, if the distance from gas-chamber orifice to muzzle was ·08 cm. and that the patentees could not account for this at all. The Specification roundly concluded that ". . . these theoretical reasonings however have really nothing to do with the action of the rifle", and we may assume that the same was true of the Clair pistol.

CLARK, A. M. The name of Patent Agent Alexander Melville Clark appeared upon a number of British patents secured between 1868 and 1898, but is only of concern here as that of the applicant for Br. Pat. 1272/1878. The subject of this protection was communicated to him (at 53 Chancery Lane) by the OESTERREICHISCHE WAFFENFABRIKS-GESELLSCHAFT (*q.v.*), to whom it was an important patent, and it was maintained into the period of concern here. The

invention is dealt with in later remarks upon this Austrian company.

CLARK, F. G. Frederick George Clark (of 64 Tennyson Road, Small Heath, Birmingham) was joint patentee with A. H. BUTLER (*q.v.*) for Br. Pat. 4622/1906.

Clark is described (in the Specification) as a "Mechanic", and it is probable that he actually made some examples of the patented device. This was a revolving magazine for use in fixed-barrel under-lever air-rifles, of that type known today as the "B.S.A." rifle. When Butler and Clark secured Br. Pat. 4622/1906, however, this type of single-shot weapon was both a novelty and the subject of several current British patents secured by a maker named Lincoln Jeffries (of Steelhouse Lane, Birmingham); the design was certainly open to improvement by the addition of a pellet magazine.

Butler and Clark proposed to mount a revolving cylindrical magazine (with radial pellet-chambers) transversely across the breech of the air-rifle, more or less in the position of that transverse roller or "tap" actually used in loading single-shot weapons of the Jeffries type. A pawl on the under- or cocking-lever acted against ratchet teeth (cut about the left-hand end of the magazine) to rotate pellets successively into alignment with the barrel, each time that the rifle was cocked. Their magazine should be compared with that of J. H. COX (*q.v.*).

COLT'S PATENT FIRE ARMS MANUFACTURING CO. (INC.).
Although this world-famous arms-manufacturing Company was better known for its revolvers and self-loading pistols, various shot-guns, rifles and machine-guns were also produced (at a factory in Hartford, Conn., U.S.A.) during the years of concern here; they did not, however, embody rotating ammunition-feed systems, and are ignored in these pages.

Apart from a corporate reorganization in 1901, the affairs of the Colt company seem to have prospered smoothly enough over the whole period, and only five corporation Presidents headed its management between 1889 and 1916;

they were Richard W. H. Jarvis (until 1901), John H. Hall (1901–2), Lewis C. Grover (1902–9), William C. Skinner (1909–11), and Charles L. F. Robinson (1911–16).

In the field of concern here (see, for example, Plates 1 and 2), this Company concentrated upon one major design-feature, namely the one-piece frame, with or without a swing-out cylinder, used for all its revolvers. Unlike Smith & Wesson (the Colt Company's chief American competitor) and THE WEBLEY & SCOTT REVOLVER AND ARMS CO., LTD. (*q.v.*) of England, the Hartford factory never offered a hinged-frame self-extracting revolver to customers.

As John E. Parsons has convincingly demonstrated, the Company's U.S. sales were primarily to wholesalers (or to jobbers and dealers) up and down the country, although domestic sales agencies were also granted to firms in New York and San Francisco. It seems probable, too, that orders for less than fifty pistols were not readily accepted at Hartford until after about 1900, the Company choosing to refer would-be purchasers on this sort of scale to one of its larger dealers or wholesalers. However, it was always Colt policy to handle orders direct from the public if it chose to do so, and Mr. Parsons cites some interesting correspondence and small orders (even for single pistols) where the fame of the customer, or the degree of ornamentation required, was sufficient to arouse interest at Hartford.

Abroad, a Sales Office was maintained in London for most of the period, and this apparently had referred to it also all inquiries for business to be fulfilled in Europe and the Near East; two London addresses (at 26 Glasshouse Street and 14 Pall Mall) appear in contemporary Colt advertisements, and on case-lid labels, but the dates of their respective occupations have yet to be firmly established. Clearly, too, a number of British wholesalers and retailers carried fair stocks of Colt arms, and devoted space to these revolvers in their catalogues. Amongst the better-known were Messrs. Holland & Holland, and The Army & Navy Co-operative Society Ltd. (in London), with Charles Rosson (of Derby) and

Charles Osborne & Co. (of Birmingham) to serve the provinces.

Between 1897 and 1902, Colt's London manager was James J. Lawrence (whose service with the Company dated back to its ill-fated Pimlico factory, in the 1850s), and he was succeeded by Mr. P. H. Bailey. Eventually, a Mr. Goodbody secured the London agency (when the Sales Office was finally abandoned), and at the close of our period this was in the hands of a London Armoury Co. Ltd., owned by the Kerr family. This company (incorporated in 1894) was the second of that name and, interestingly enough, the first London Armoury Co., Ltd. had been chiefly instrumental, by its vigorous promotion of the British Beaumont-Adams percussion revolver, in driving Colonel Samuel Colt's London manufactory out of business, by 1857.

In America, the Company were always active patentees of improvements to revolvers (as demonstrated in Chapter I), but British patent protection was only sought in four cases.

Reasons for this policy must remain a matter for conjecture, but probably lay in the fact that no British manufacturers offered a solid-frame, swing-out cylinder, simultaneous-ejecting revolver like that with which the Colt Company excelled, and it was obviously unlikely that any would introduce one. Accordingly, it was only necessary for Colt to patent, in Britain, such devices as might be applicable to any type of self-or simultaneous-ejecting revolver, and consideration of those patents described below would seem to support this reasoning; in the field of self-loading pistols, on the other hand, where the Webley Company was a more direct competitor, it is noticeable that Colt filed a higher number of British patent applications.

The first Colt Company revolver patents of the period were communicated patents, secured by H. E. NEWTON (*q.v.*) on 30th April, 1889. Br. Pat. 7200/1889 was for the revolver-charger shown in Figure 37, which corresponded to C. T. Ehbet's U.S. Patent No. 402423 of 30th April, 1889, and may be compared with the devices of W. C. PRIDEAUX (*q.v.*) and A. J. WATSON (*q.v.*); Br. Pat. 7201/ 1889 was for a self-cocking revolver lock-mechanism shown in Figure 58. This lock-mechanism was based loosely upon that used in Colt double-action revolvers of the type shown in Figure 2, but apparently was never put into production.

At 23rd June, 1903, O. IMRAY (q.v.) secured Br. Pat. 14026/1903, on a communication from the Colt Company; this protected a stout adjustable rear-sight, for use in military revolvers, comprising a cylindrical sight-bar mounted (on

"Colt Positive Safety Lock" already described in respect of Figure 5.

COURRIER, J. Joseph Courrier, "Gentleman" of No. 5 Rue Yoon-Villarceau, Paris, secured Br. Pat. 19083/1894 for an improved rifle; Messrs. Haseltine, Lake & Co. (of 45 Southampton Buildings, London) were his Patent Agents.

Courrier's Specification contained three claims for an unusual bolt-action

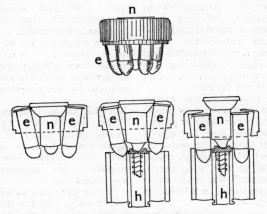

FIG. 37. *Colt's revolver charger.*
(After Br. Pat. 7200/1889.)

Six cartridges "e" are held in the charger, by a wooden wedge "n". When presented to a revolver-cylinder "h", pressure on the tip of "n" (against the ejector-head and ratchet of "h") displaces it upwards, and the cartridges "e" are then free to drop into the chambers of "h".

trunnions) transversely and rotatably across the axis of the barrel, at the rear of the barrel strap. Accidental rotation of this sight-bar was inhibited by a spring detent, embedded below it in the pistol frame, and (by means of knurling at its ends) the bar could be thumb-turned to align one of four sighting-notches with the foresight. The device therefore permitted range-alterations (since these sighting-notches were of various depths), but was not apparently intended to be adjustable for transverse windage settings.

Finally, O. IMRAY (q.v.) secured for the Company (on a communication from it) Br. Pat. 13680/1905, which protected a

magazine rifle, with thumb-operated trigger on the stock-wrist, and interrupted-screw bolt-head. An eight-round cylindrical magazine was rotated by a bell-crank lever, each time the bolt was drawn back, and a cut-off mechanism was provided so that the rifle might be used as a single-loader.

COX, J. H. In the Specification to his Br. Pat. 4824/1907, Joseph Henry Cox described himself as an "Air Gun Requisites Manufacturer", of 137A Guildford Street, Lozells, Aston juxta Birmingham. George T. Fuery (of 11 Burlington Chambers, New Street, Birmingham) was the Patent Agent who handled Cox's application for protection.

The subject of Br. Pat. 4824/1907 was a pellet magazine for fixed-barrel under-lever air-rifles. However, unlike the contemporary device of A. H. BUTLER and F. G. CLARK (*q.v.*), Cox proposed to use a flat drum magazine, mounted on top of the air-rifle (at right angles to the barrel axis), and operated by the loading-plug used with conventional single-shot rifles of this "Lincoln Jeffries" type, rather than by employing the movement of the cocking-lever, as Butler & Clark had proposed. Cox's Specification set out six claims of novelty, detailing those methods by which a ratchet-and-pawl mechanism should rotate the drum magazine (to effect a gravity pellet-feed each time that the loading-plug was turned), and also envisaging a manually-operated version of the device.

Destruction of records in the British Patent Office has probably now made identification of the other party or parties impossible to establish, but *The Official Journal of the Patent Office* still records that (between 12th and 17th August, 1912) one entry relating to an "assignment, transmission or licence" was made upon the Patent Office registers, in relation to Br. Pat. 4824/1907.

It is possible that Cox interested a British company in using his magazine, but those air-rifles most likely to be found with a mechanically-rotated drum device, of this Cox type, were made by the German firm of Haenel; this company sold a Model IV E weapon in the United Kingdom and many other countries, with such a magazine, and continued such sales (with an improved model) in the years between 1918 and 1939. It is possible, therefore, that it was to the Haenel firm that Cox either assigned Br. Pat. 4824/1907, or to which he gave rights (under licence) to sell arms in Great Britain with a magazine *prima facie* infringing his design.

DANNER, H. Heinrich Danner, a Merchant at 4 Hauptstrasse, Neufelden-an-der-Mühlkreisbahn (in Austria), secured Br. Pat. 22131/1905 through the assistance of Messrs. Herbert Haddan & Co., a firm of Patent Agents at 31/32 Bedford Street, Strand.

Since Danner filed a Complete Specification with his application for British patent protection, and that Specification embodied seven detailed claims for his invention, it can be assumed that the design was viable, and that at least some specimen arms had been produced.

Danner proposed to perform all the actions of loading, firing, extraction and ejection of cartridge cases, in a rifle with a rotary magazine, by successive pulls on its four-armed rotating trigger; a safety-catch prevented accidental discharge, and permitted ejection of loaded cartridges. The "paddle-wheel" trigger-operation was similar in principle to that earlier employed by W. H. BOFINGER and W. J. TURNBULL (*q.v.*) in a magazine pistol. Danner's degree of success with his design was probably comparable to that enjoyed by the Americans.

DAVIS, C. A. Charles A. Davis was a Physician, at No. 1310 16th Street, Washington D.C., U.S.A., and joint applicant with W. W. HERRON (*q.v.*) for Br. 16216/1889. The Patent Agent handling this application was W. P. THOMPSON (*q.v.*).

There were only two claims to Br. Pat. 16216/1889, and the invention consisted in adapting handles of guns, pistols or tools to fit the hand by forming them of, or providing them with, a body of material capable of being rendered plastic, softening the material, grasping the same firmly in the manner of grasping it in use, and finally causing or permitting the material so shaped to harden. Dental vulcanite was a recommended material, but other compositions having a softening point of about 212°F were deemed as desirable.

The conception of Br. Pat. 16216/1889 was adopted by shooters in more modern times, and Major J. S. Hatcher recorded (in 1927) that "Dr. Bastey, of Boston, a well-known shot, altered the grip of his gun with the material that is used in dental work for making plates—a sort of red rubber compound".

DECKER, W. Walter Decker (of 22 Grosse Bahnhofstrasse, Zella St. Bl. in Thuringia, Germany) describing himself as a "Manufacturer" in the Specification to his Br. Pat. 26086/1912. This protection was secured for him by London Patent Agents Boult, Wade & Tennant, of 111/112 Hatton Garden, and it consolidated into one Specification those ideas earlier stated in Decker's German Patents Nos. 253148 and 262583.

Three claims for the lock-mechanism of a solid-framed revolver shown in Figure 38 were set out in the Specification to Br. Pat. 26086/1912, and

this trigger-bar was the vertical sear, which carried back a firing-pin (against the tension of a coiled spring) as the trigger was pressed rearward; at the ultimate point in the trigger-bar travel, a lump inside the rear butt-strap struck the bottom end of the sear, tilted it backwards, and so released the firing-pin. Cylinder rotation was effected by a conventional ratchet (cut at the rear end of the cylinder) engaged by a pawl driven

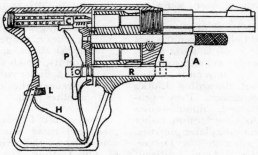

FIG. 38. *Decker's revolver.*
(After Br. Pat. 26086/1912.)

Pressure on the trigger "A" slides to the rear a trigger-bar "R" and the cylinder-bolt "E"; since "R" carries a pivoted sear "P" which is, in turn, engaged with the bent of the firing-pin "C", pressure on "A" must cock "C" against its coiled spring. At the limit of travel, the tail of "P" strikes the frame-lump "L", causing the sear to pivot and release "C" against a cartridge, by which time "E" has engaged a cylinder-locking notch, and bolted the cylinder with its top chamber aligned with the barrel. The spring "H" is the trigger- and sear-spring combined.

Cylinder rotation occurs by means of a pawl (hidden by "P", and not shown in the Figure), which engages conventional ratchet-teeth at the rear of the cylinder and is mounted on a lever pivoted to the frame; the rear end of "P" strikes that lever, as "P" travels to the rear, raising the pawl to rotate the cylinder.

(although specimens are rare today) a small quantity of these weapons were made in Germany; a five-shot specimen illustrated in Plate 29 (from the Rolf H. Müller Collection) is in 6·35-mm. Browning calibre, has a 2-in. barrel, measures 4⅝ inches in overall length, and weighs about 9 oz. when unloaded.

The Decker revolver was self-cocking and hammerless, with a straight-pull sliding trigger (similar in appearance to that used in small self-loading pistols) connected to a long trigger-bar mounted fore-and-aft inside the frame. Pivoted to

upwards by the rearward motion of the trigger-bar, and a cylinder-bolt (formed at the top forward-end of the trigger-bar) engaged long locking-notches, cut rearward from the front circumference of the cylinder, to index chamber and barrel for firing. A light buffer-spring at the forward-end of the firing-pin rebounded that component off each fired cartridge (to ensure an uninterrupted cylinder rotation), and the cartridge cases were expelled singly, *via* the loading-gate, on withdrawing the arbor and using it as an ejector-rod.

It will be observed, by Plate 29, that the cylinder of Decker's revolver was both longitudinally grooved (to permit passage of the sliding cylinder-bolt) and partially shrouded on the right side; the shroud, apparently, served to retain cartridges in their chambers on that side. The escutcheon of each butt-cheek was surrounded by an acknowledgement to German Patent No. 253148.

Decker's revolver, although self-cocking and with a conventional system for cylinder rotation, bore some resemblance to a pocket weapon designed by J. H. Dery, a Belgian, in 1909. Dery himself can be said to have taken the best features from patents of A. LINES (*q.v.*), by using a zigzag cylinder-rotation system, working off a lump on top of the sliding trigger, but discarding Lines's complex lock-mechanism. Dery produced a solid-framed, double-action revolver, with a lock-mechanism rather close in conception to that later proposed (in self-cocking form only) by Decker, and the latter's debt to Dery is difficult to assess. However, if it did exist at all, it was quite long-lived. Decker was briefly active as a patentee of self-loading pistols after the First World War, and two such patented arms had self-cocking lock-mechanisms (or "slip locks", as Decker termed them) which owed something of their parentage to the claims of Br. Pat. 26086/1912, and to the prior work of Dery.

DIMANCEA, H. Haralamb Dimancea (then described as a "Captain of Roumanian Artillery") secured Br. Pat. 9973/1885, whilst resident at 299 Aston Lane, Witton, Birmingham; a Patent Agent named W. T. Whiteman assisted him to secure such protection, and (see Table I) it survived into the period of concern here.

Br. Pat. 9973/1885 related to a revolver shown in Figure 39, and the Specification contained five claims of novelty, as to:

(1) Constructing the revolver with barrel and cylinder capable of being swung over (as a single unit) to lie parallel with one side of the arm.
(2) Constructing the weapon so that all cartridges were simultaneously ejected (once the barrel and cylinder had been swung out) by merely pulling forward the barrel.
(3) Methods for locking together barrel and action-body by the hammer-like component visible, at the rear of the latter, in Figure 39.
(4) Discharging the weapon by means of a sliding firing-pin, which was cocked and released by an internal six-limbed "paddle-wheel", turned by the trigger; only self-cocking fire was possible.
(5) Rotating the cylinder by a wheel (similar in shape to that mentioned at (4) above, and mounted alongside it), which struck a ratchet on the cylinder with one arm, and retracted the cylinder-bolt with another limb.

Specimens of Dimancea's revolvers are rare, and those which have been encountered by this writer bore the name of The Gatling Arms & Ammunition Co., Ltd. (see J. G. ACCLES), whose Holford Works, at Perry Bar, Birmingham, was subsequently taken over by Messrs. Grenfell & Accles Ltd. It may be recalled that Dimancea's revolvers were exhibited by the latter company, at a Royal Naval Exhibition of 1891, although the firm also attempted to introduce its own revolver (of similar frame-construction to Dimancea's), under Br. Pat. 17993/1891.

Subsequently, the Continental arms authority Gerhard Bock has stated (in a second edition of his work), Dimancea's revolvers were made by Messrs. Kynoch Ltd., for the Romanians, during the First World War, but this remark seems open to question.

It is true that (to prevent periodic drains upon its works staff, to short-lived ammunition-manufacturing companies operating there) the Kynoch company bought Holford Works in 1901, and may thus have secured Dimancea revolvers, or gauges and equipment for making them, abandoned by the departing Accles Ltd. However, it seems improbable that any Kynoch manufacture of Dimancea's arms can have occurred in the First World War. On taking over Holford Works,

Kynoch Ltd. put the machine-shop to small-bore rifle-cartridge manufacture, and the bicycle-shop to production of cycle-fittings; it seems past belief that (more than thirteen years later, and during the First World War) the firm should turn aside from its most important function, to manufacture this complex revolver, even for an ally of Great Britain.

Army Pyrotechnics, in the years 1884–90.

DOBSLAW, K. In the years immediately prior to 1914 a number of attempts were made to introduce light-projecting sights for night use with hand firearms. Karl Dobslaw and P. SCHMIDT (*q.v.*) secured jointly Br. Pat. 8353/1914 for such a device, and the inventions of such patentees as C. A. LEWIS (*q.v.*) DE MARAIS &

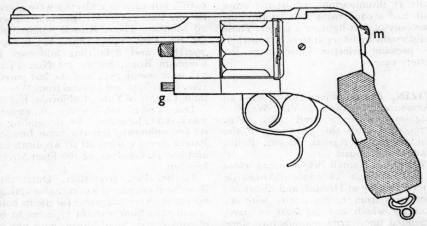

FIG. 39. *Dimancea's revolver.*
(After Br. Pat. 9973/1885.)

Barrel and cylinder are swung over laterally to the left (i.e. towards the reader) upon the pivot "g", for loading or unloading the cylinder, after depressing the latch "m".

Colonel Victor Militaru (of the *Muzeul Militar Central*, Bucharest) has most courteously advised that Haralamb Dimancea was born on 1st October, 1855, as the son of a Romanian Army officer, and that he went to a military artillery school in 1874. On concluding his studies he became a Second Lieutenant, Romanian Artillery, in 1876.

Awarded the medal "Virtutea militără de aur", for bravery in action during Romania's War of Independence (1877–78), Dimancea became a Lieutenant, on 8th April, 1879, then Captain, on 8th April, 1883, and died in 1890, with the rank of Major. During his service in the Romanian Army, he fulfilled various functions in the matter of armaments, amongst them that of Sub-Director,

GARDNER (*q.v.*), W. T. G. "WESPI" (*q.v.*), and FERGUSON & FITZGERALD (*q.v.*) are in point.

Karl Dobslaw was a German policeman (of Kottbuserufer 25, Berlin S.O. 36), and Br. Pat. 8353/1914 was secured for the two patentees through Messrs. Abel & Imray, London Patent Agents at Bank Chambers, Southampton Buildings. The patent had a "Convention Date" priority from 28th April, 1913 (as to which see, generally, Appendix I), but became void, through failure to pay renewal fees, in 1917. Existence of the "Convention Date" priority, and of a Complete Specification filed with the patent application, indicates that an equivalent German patent existed.

There were nine detailed claims to

Dobslaw & Schmidt's Specification, which actually showed the invention fitted to a Dreyse self-loading pistol, but their essential idea was that (unlike other contrivances cited above) the device clamped to a pistol or revolver should actually serve two purposes.

Accordingly, an electric pocket lamp was to be clamped beneath the barrel, which had two bulbs; one was fitted with a dispersing lens (to cast light around for ordinary illumination), whilst the other bulb had a condensing lens for the purpose only of spot-lighting a target. These bulbs could be lit separately or together, by pressing selector buttons on the battery case.

DOZIN, M. Mathieu Dozin was an "Armourer", of Route de Visé, Wandre, Belgium, who secured Br. Pat. 23739/1902 with the assistance of the London Patent Agents, Messrs. Boult, Wade and Kilburn.

Wandre is a small Belgian town, close to the Fabrique Nationale d'Armes de Guerre factory at Herstal, and about ten kilometres from Liège, a city with an economy which has (at least in part) depended upon arms-manufacture since the sixteenth century. Whether M. Dozin carried on a gun-making business at Wandre, or whether the address above was his private residence is not known; it is assumed, however, that his activities fitted generally into the Liège manufacturing-framework mentioned in Chapter II.

The Specification to Br. Pat. 23739/1902 set out five claims of novelty for two basically similar cartridge-ejection systems to be used in revolvers. Unlike the mechanism of CASHMORE, ELLIS & WILKINSON (*q.v.*), Dozin's Specification drawings showed his invention applied to small hinged-frame, concealed-hammer pocket revolvers (with folding triggers) quite similar in external appearance to the arm illustrated in Plate 6 (lower).

A useful refinement in the Dozin design was that high ejection could be suppressed, at will. The user could therefore gently expel the cartridges into his hand, from an unfired pistol, or eject fired cases completely from their chambers.

DURST, M. H. Murray Durst was joint-applicant with L. W. BROADWELL (*q.v.*) for Br. Pats. 7037/1891 and 14853/1891; he secured in his sole name Br. Pats. 18516/1891, 792/1892, 8760/1892 and 646/1893.

In the Specifications to these patents, Durst described himself as a "Gentleman", but various addresses were given: for Br. Pat. 7037/1891, the address was 29 Montagu Place, Russell Square, but for Br. Pats. 14853/1891, 18516/1891, 792/1892 and 8760/1892 addresses in Clapham Road, Surrey (at Nos. 13 or 71) were mentioned, and the last patent (No. 646/1893) was secured from Wheatland, County of Yuba, California, U.S.A.

Durst's relationship with L. W. BROADWELL (and the reasons for the ending of it) are unknown, but the same London Patent Agent guided all six applications, and was H. Gardner, of 166 Fleet Street, London.

In Br. Pat. 7037/1891, Durst and Broadwell envisaged a detachable spring-operated rotary magazine for use in bolt-action rifles (one variant type might be of convoluted "snail" form, with two or three layers of cartridges), which had an ingenious blade on its feeder-plate, to lift the last cartridge into the rifle breech. Br. Pat. 14853/1891 was primarily concerned with a system for converting Martini (or similar single-shot tilting block rifles) into bolt-action magazine arms, but the Specification did claim a cut-off device for use in such arms, when fitted with the Broadwell-Durst magazine; this cut-off was effected by turning the magazine slightly, in its well, so as to bring a closed part of the casing to the top of the well.

Br. Pat. 18516/1891 dealt with a bolt-action rifle, in which another rotary magazine (on a principle established by Br. Pat. 7037/1891) was to be embodied. The magazine spring was put into tension by loading cartridges into the magazine (from the top), and a sliding plate acted both as a cut-off and to prevent the spring from ejecting the cartridges whilst the magazine was being charged.

Br. Pat 792/1892 was for yet another

bolt-action rifle, with rotary magazine. In this case, the end of a spiral spring (wound about the central stem of the magazine) bore against the last cartridge, and so rotated the cartridge carrier round, step-by-step, to the breech; this cartridge carrier could be held, out of alignment with the breech, to act as a cut-off. Br. Pat. 8760/1892 consisted merely of improvements to the bolt-mechanism and the magazine envisaged by Br. Pats. 18516/1891 and 792/1892.

The Specification to Br. Pat. 646/1893 was extremely long, and contained seven claims for a bolt-action rifle and its rotary magazine; in one or two of these claims, principles from the earlier patents appeared to be simply restated, but the British Patent Office was obviously satisfied that they were sufficiently novel to enjoy protection.

It might seem reasonable, at this distance in time, to dismiss Durst's ideas as too complex to warrant commercial or military adoption. There were, after all, a number of excellent clip- or charger-loaded vertical rifle magazines in existence by 1893, and rotary designs might seem a needlessly complicated alternative.

In fact, as remarks upon O. KRAG (q.v.), F. VON MANNLICHER (q.v.), the OESTER-REICHISCHE WAFFENFABRIKS-GESELLSCHAFT (q.v.), A. W. SAVAGE (q.v.) O. SCHOENAUER (q.v.), and J. SCHULHOF (q.v.) will show, there was considerable turn-of-the-century interest in rotary or semi-rotary magazines for rifles, and several bolt-action designs were adopted by the armed forces of certain countries.

Indeed, the American author E. S. Farrow (in a work published in 1904) specifically noticed a ten-shot commercial version of the Durst rotary-magazine bolt-action rifle, in company with several similar designs. One of these arms was an eight-shot "Blake" rifle, described in ·30 U.S. Army and ·400 calibres; the cartridges were carried in cylindrical reloadable packets of seven rounds, and the complete packet was loaded in the rifle magazine. Another bolt-action rifle described by Farrow was the "Boch" weapon, with a detachable wheel-operated twenty-round rotary magazine delivering cartridges to the receiver.

Farrow even marketed his own rifle, with packet-magazine loading; this he described as an "improved Blake", and the packet had a trunnion at each end, to permit its rotation in the magazine.

The point is capable of development, but enough has been said here to show that Durst (and other inventors of rotary rifle magazines, who are later mentioned) worked in a promising design-field, at the time when he secured his patents.

DYMOND, G. C. George Cecil Dymond was a Member of the Institution of Mechanical Engineers, and of the Firm of W. P. Thompson & Co. (see W. P. THOMPSON), to whom H. F. LANDSTAD communicated the subjects of Br. Pat. 22479/1899, which was secured in Dymond's name.

No entry was traced in *The Official Journal of the Patent Office*, to record that Dymond eventually assigned Br. Pat. 22479/1899 to Landstad, the true inventor, but it may be assumed that such an assignment in fact occurred. Dymond acted for several foreign designers of firearms, who communicated inventions to him in the midand late-1890s, as a London Patent Agent.

EASTWICK, J. James Eastwick was a Barrister-at-Law (of Fyning Wood, Rogate, Sussex), who secured Br. Pat. 12459/1914; his Patent Agents were the London firm of Carpmael & Co., at 24 Southampton Buildings, Chancery Lane.

Prior to 1914, Eastwick had been a fairly prolific patentee, notably of self-loading rifles with hydraulic or inertia breech-locking systems; see Br. Pats. 15928/1908; 2401/1910; 12227/1910; 16743/1910; 16158/1911; 28493/1911; 16175/1912, and 13808/1913 with A. L. Chevallier; 14016/1913 and 7004/1914. None of these patents had any revolving ammunition-feed details, but Eastwick's Br. Pat. 12459/1914 did propose application of a rotary magazine to the optional manual- or self-loading bolt-action rifle covered by his own Br. Pat. 14016/1913. The magazine was rotated (without use of spring pawls or catches) by bell-crank levers acting on ratchet wheels at the rear end of the revolving cartridge carrier, and these levers were moved solely by the longitudinal motion of the rifle bolt.

A disconnector and cut-off were fitted to Eastwick's magazine, together with indicators to show how many cartridges it contained, and whether or not a round was in the rifle-breech.

ELLIS, C. O. Charles Osborne Ellis was joint patentee with E. W. WILKINSON (*q.v.*) and F. CASHMORE (*q.v.*), in Br. Pat. 5151/1896; Ellis & Wilkinson also traded together as Charles Osborne & Co., at 12, 13 and 14 Whittall Street, Birmingham.

The subjects of Br. Pat. 5151/1896 have already been covered in remarks upon F. CASHMORE (*q.v.*), but it should be emphasized that there can be no certainty that Ellis & Wilkinson were not practical contributors to the inventions of that patent.

At the time of securing Br. Pat. 5151/1896, Ellis and E. W. WILKINSON (*q.v.*) were already joint-holders of several British patents (outside the scope of this work) relating to lock-mechanisms for double-barrelled shot-guns, ejectors for such arms, and to punt-guns; in 1898 and 1900, the two men secured further British patent protection for single-trigger mechanisms applicable to double-barrelled shot-guns. Clearly, they had the technical ability to tackle the subjects of their joint-patent with F. CASHMORE (*q.v.*), although their particular field of patenting endeavour without him had not been related to revolving arms.

The firm of Charles Osborne & Co. had been founded in the 1850s, and by the period of concern here was substantial. Catalogues issued for the Season 1899–1900 ran to 96 pages, and this total increased (for the Season 1907–8) to 106 pages. At these times, the firm also maintained London premises (at 2 Great Scotland Yard, S.W.), and acted as Sole Agency and Depot in the United Kingdom, for "Borchardt Automatic Quick-Firing Pistols", for the Union Metallic Cartridge Co., and for "Smith & Wesson Revolvers"; non-exclusive agencies were also held, from time to time, for the Marlin Fire Arms Co., the J. Stevens Arms & Tool Co., the Remington Arms Co., the COLT'S PATENT FIRE ARMS MFG

CO. (INC.) (*q.v.*), the Winchester Repeating Arms Co., H. M. Quackenbush, the Ideal Manufacturing Co., the Savage Arms Co., and the Lyman Gun Sight Corporation.

At the turn of the century, it was possible to purchase breech- or muzzle-loading ship's cannon and Gardner machine-guns from the firm, together with rifles or automatic pistols from major Continental manufacturers, whilst a very wide range of shot-guns, spare parts, and shooting- or loading-accessories (the bulk of it made in Birmingham's gun-trade) was also catalogued; the patented punt-gun and single-trigger devices of Ellis and Wilkinson were naturally included.

ENVALL, G. Gustav Envall, a Major in the Swedish Army, secured from Linnégatan No. 20, Stockholm, Sweden, Br. Pat 5972/1885 (which survived into years of concern here), with assistance from London Patent Agent W. L. Wise, of 46 Lincoln's Inn Fields. The Specification to this patent proposed six claims of novelty for a curious solid-framed revolver shown in Plate 30, which had a lock-mechanism in which the hammer was cocked by pulling straight to the rear a lever within the "trigger-guard", but released (after aiming the weapon) by pressing forward, with the thumb, a button-trigger on top of the action, just behind the hammer; pressure upon a lever visible in the thumb-piece of the hammer permitted the latter to be lowered from the cocked position, at will. Major Envall claimed his system as both safer and permitting greater accuracy of aim than was the case with ordinary lock-mechanisms, but he apparently based this design upon modifications to the work of others. The *Kungl. Armémuseum*, Stockholm, regards this revolver as based upon "A. Francotte's system", but the basic lock-mechanism does appear to owe something to that design of J. Warnant later used in the French Mlle 1892 service revolver shown in Plate 14. The specimen arm shown in Plate 30 may be used with a detachable carbine-stock, and appears to be of sturdy construction; it is not known whether (as was the case for T.

F. TÖRNELL; *q.v.*) any semi-official approval came to the service use of Envall's revolver in Sweden.

FABRE, E. Emile Fabre was joint-applicant with A. TRONCHE (*q.v.*) for Br. Pat. 15771/1888, which survived into the period of this book; the addresses and occupations of both applicants (as mentioned in the Specifications) were, respectively, at No. 1 Beaumont Crescent, West Kensington, and that of "Civil Engineer". These men were assisted with their patent application, by J. H. Johnson & Co.; see J. H. JOHNSON.

The subject of Br. Pat. 15771/1888 was not of great commercial significance, and the principle of it can be grasped by reference to Figure 67, showing a similar self-cocking magazine pistol by L. F. TAVERNIER (*q.v.*). Five claims were set out in the Specification to Br. Pat. 15771/1888, relating to (i) the endless chain of cartridge chambers travelling fore-and-aft along a firearm, (ii) combining the chain of chambers with a reciprocating barrel that mated with each chamber at its discharge, (iii) a folding butt for the weapon, (iv) a general claim for a firearm similar in appearance to that shown in Figure 67, and (v) an alternative configuration of parts, in which barrel and trigger were both mounted on one side of the action body.

It is clear, from the drawings in the Specification to this patent, that a very flat, compact, firearm could be made under it; the patentees mentioned a "waistcoat pocket" version loaded with 16 to 20 cartridges.

FERGUSON, M. Meade Ferguson and J. O. FITZGERALD (*q.v.*) jointly secured Br. Pat. 19324/1913, under guidance from Messrs. J. S. Withers & Spooner, London Patent Agents. The two applicants described themselves as of "Richmond, County of Henrico, Va., Gentlemen".

The invention of these two patentees was another light-projector sight, as to which remarks upon the patents of DOBSLAW & SCHMIDT (*q.v.*), C. A. LEWIS (*q.v.*), DE MARAIS & GARDNER (*q.v.*), and the W. T. G. "WESPI" (*q.v.*) are in point.

An unusual feature of Ferguson & Fitzgerald's device was that it was specifically designed for use on hinged-frame revolvers, or other small-arms with drop-down barrels, and had an ingenious "electric collector" at the barrel-hinge. Most of the other electric sights above mentioned were intended for solid-framed weapons, and could not be satisfactorily adapted to the other frame configuration.

Additionally, in Fitzgerald and Ferguson's sight, a parabolic reflector was mounted behind the bulb and a lens, with flattened front centre-surface, was before it; by these means, a large dot of light was projected on to the target, and made deliberate sighting (at least in theory) unnecessary. If the spot of light was cast upon an object, then the revolver should (on discharge) hit that object.

FIDJELAND, T. A. Terje Aakensen Fidjeland (of Iveland, Kristiassand, S., Norway) was a gun-maker, and joint-applicant with J. A. SCHWARZ (*q.v.*) for Br. 19320/1900; this patent application was secured under advice from London Patent Agents W. P. Thompson & Co. (see W. P. THOMPSON), and is one of a quartet of British patents for improvements to firearms secured by these men, either as individuals or as the Aktiesel-skabet *Schwarz-Fidjelands Gevaersyndicat*. However, T. A. Fidjeland was also active as a patentee of self-loading pistols (in his own name) or non-rotary rifle-magazine improvements (with O. A. Fidjeland), and therefore the subjects of Br. Pat. 19320/1900 are considered here, on the assumption that Captain Schwarz's contribution to the design may have been financial as much as technical.

The Specification to Br. Pat. 19320/1900 contained ten claims of novelty for a manually-operated bolt-action magazine rifle, fitted with a concealed sliding bayonet similar in principle to that claimed in the 1896 patent of H. PIEPER (*q.v.*); the bolt and magazine were later also protected in Norway (by Fidjeland and Schwarz), under Norwegian Patent No. 10626, of 18th January, 1901.

Fidjeland and Schwarz's rifle magazine was of eight-round capacity, a rotary "feeding-wing" (by which cartridges were borne round in the magazine) being put into tension, against an internal coiled-spring, by the action of opening the side-lid to that magazine, but this tensioning feature had been anticipated by others, as mentioned in remarks upon O. H. J. KRAG (*q.v.*). In addition to the magazine, this rifle carried clips of cartridges in a butt compartment, the door of which was so situated that, when opened, a correct number of rounds to reload the magazine fell out into the user's hands.

Although this weapon bore a glancing resemblance to Krag-Jörgensen rifles (see O. H. J. KRAG), the bolt claimed by Br. Pat. 19320/1900 was actually locked at four separate points (when closed), instead of using the single locking-lug of the earlier design.

It should be noted that the *Abridgement of Specifications, Class 119*, A.D. *1897–1900* credited Br. Pat. 19320/1900 to three patentees, the compiler of the *Abridgement* listing "S. Christiassand" as a surname, after anglicizing the name of Fidjeland and Schwarz's domicile.

FINNEGAN, P. H. Peter Henry Finnegan secured Br. Pat. 19544/1893 for a self-cocking radial revolver, which was sold under the trade-name "Protector"; his address was stated (in the patent Specification) as of Nos. 437 and 438 Monadnock Building, Chicago, County of Cook and State of Illinois, U.S.A., and his status as that of "Manufacturer". Messrs. Haseltine, Lake & Co., of 45 Southampton Buildings, were the London Patent Agents assisting Finnegan to secure this protection.

Essentially, the story of Finnegan's "Protector" revolver is an extension to that of J. E. TURBIAUX (*q.v.*), and the credit for unearthing it lies with an American arms authority, W. P. Smith.

Briefly, it appears that an American company called the Minneapolis Fire Arms Co. (of that town) was incorporated in 1890/91 to develop the U.S. patent of J. E. TURBIAUX (*q.v.*) for a radial revolver shown in Figure 68, and that such arms (made for the Company, in a seven-shot ·32 calibre version, by J. Duckworth, of Springfield, Mass.) were sold through agents, of whom Finnegan was one.

The Minneapolis Firearms Co. revolvers measured about 4½ inches in overall length, and were marked "The Protector. Minn. Fire Arms Co. Patented March 6, 1883"; after sale, many were subsequently returned as defective, by customers, and the selling-agents' commissions suffered as a result. Accordingly, in October 1892, Finnegan set up a company called the Chicago Fire Arms Co. (having the address mentioned above, in Finnegan's Br. Pat. Specification), and he purchased the U.S. patent of J. E. TURBIAUX (*q.v.*), and the necessary equipment for making "Protector" revolvers, from the Minneapolis company; almost on completion of these purchases, he also opened ambitious negotiations with the Ames Sword Co. (of Chicopee, Mass.), to make 25,000 arms for sale by his new company. Clearly Finnegan (and Corrigan, his fellow promoter) regarded any defects in Turbiaux's design as capable of correction.

The Ames Sword Co. accepted Finnegan's order, but employed Elbert M. Couch to design and build machinery for fulfilling it. Couch not only worked to his brief, but also suggested certain improvements to the design of the weapon, and upon these latter suggestions Finnegan himself secured U.S. Pat. 504154, of 29th August, 1893; it is believed that this U.S. patent prompted Finnegan (who then still had great hopes for the "Protector") to secure Br. Pat. 19544/1893. Thus both the U.S. and the British patent protection essentially related to a safety-device, an improved construction of case, barrel and breech-block, a remodelled grip, an improved cover-lock, and an ejector, all grafted upon the original Turbiaux arm.

Couch, meantime, had left the Ames Sword Co.'s direct employment but (in company with Oliver E. Smith) he now tackled the problem of making Finnegan's revolvers as a sub-contractor to the Ames company. In due course, Couch himself secured three U.S. patents relating to the arm; U.S. Pat. 516476 (of 13th March 1894) improved the cartridge carrier and its rotation system, whilst U.S. Pats. 530823 and 530824 (both of 11th December 1894) respectively protected machine-tools for counter-boring the barrels and the chambers, of these pistols.

Unfortunately, Couch and Smith found it quite impossible to approach that rate of production needed to meet Finnegan's contract with the Ames Sword Co. Those revolvers made by them were a little sturdier than the Minneapolis Fire Arms Co. version, and although still chambered for seven ·32 rim-fire cartridges now measured $5\frac{1}{2}$ inches in overall length, $2\frac{1}{4}$ inches in diameter, and had $1\frac{3}{4}$-in. barrels. The case was now marked "Chicago Fire Arms Co.—Chicago, Ill." on one side, and "The Protector, Pat. Mch. 6. 83. Aug. 29. 93" on the other; these arms, of course, embodied the improvements of Finnegan's U.S. patent.

Although serial-numbers higher than 10000 have been observed on these Chicago Fire Arms Co. "Protector" arms, Couch and Smith had only succeeded in delivering 1,500 weapons (of 25,000 that the Ames Sword Co. were under contract to supply) by August 1894. Since Finnegan had largely based his order upon hopes of huge sales at the Chicago World's Fair, and that event was (by the Fall of 1894) part of history, a certain irritation developed in the various relationships, and all parties sought their recourse at law.

The Chicago Fire Arms Co. sued the Ames Sword Co. for damages arising from breach of their contract to deliver 25,000 revolvers; the Ames company counter-claimed that Finnegan's failure to provide models, and his actions in changing designs, had led to the débâcle; Duckworth sued the Minneapolis Firearms Co. for failure to meet an agreement with him; the Chicago Fire Arms Co. sued Duckworth for payment for the revolver-machinery (retained by him), which they had bought from the Minneapolis company; and Couch and Smith alleged that Finnegan had appropriated Couch's inventions.

In regard to the first of these actions, the U.S. courts found for the Chicago Fire Arms Co. Early in 1897, therefore, the Ames Sword Co. directors reluctantly purchased all patent and other rights to the "Protector" revolver, from Finnegan's company, and began to promote

and manufacture it as an Ames Sword Co. product. In this endeavour, but without much success, they persevered until about 1910.

FITZGERALD, J. O. James Obediah Fitzgerald was joint-applicant for Br. Pat. 19324/1913, with M. FERGUSON (*q.v.*).

FLETCHER, W. Walter Fletcher was joint-applicant for Br. Pat. 16078/1884, with H. A. SILVER (*q.v.*); this application was handled for the pair by a London Patent Agent, H. Gardner, of 166 Fleet Street, and the patent survived into those years of concern here, as shown in Table I.

Br. Pat. 16078/1884 related to a cartridge-case ejection-system for solid-framed revolvers, and to a safety-hammer suitable for such arms; like the device of F. PRAUNEGGER (*q.v.*) and L. P. SCHMIDT (*q.v.*), this ejector was operated by the blow of the revolver hammer, as it fired a cartridge. In the case of Silver & Fletcher's design, however, the ejector lever was pivoted horizontally across the rear of the revolver frame. Their patented safety-hammer was never apparently developed as originally envisaged, and where the Specification to Br. Pat. 16078/1884 proposed a hammer-beak that could be hinged upwards, out of alignment with the cartridges, these patentees developed a more satisfactory device altogether. As eventually retailed, a grooved thumb-piece on the hammer (visible in Plate 30) was turned, through 180°, to retract the hammer-beak into the hammer; in this condition, the hammer could safely be used to eject loaded cartridges.

Silver and Fletcher's ejector and safety-hammer were normally fitted together, and on Webley "R.I.C. No. 1" ·450 calibre revolvers of the type shown in Plate 30; occasionally, however, they can be found upon solid-framed arms of other types, and there were cases in which only the safety-hammer was fitted. Fully-equipped Webley R.I.C. No. 1 revolvers (of the Model 1883 pattern shown in Plate 30) were normally marked "Silver & Fletcher's Patent", "The Expert", as well as "S. W. Silver & Co., Cornhill, London", and the safety-hammer of such arms often bore a special serial-number of its own, quite unrelated to the Webley serial-number on the pistol. Barrel length was normally 4½ inches (although 6-in. barrels can be found), and most of the Webley R.I.C. No. 1 revolvers thus embellished were found in a Webley serial-range of 33000–36000.

In 1904, Fletcher left his employment with H. A. SILVER (*q.v.*), and started his own business at 46 Wilson Street, Finsbury.

FOSBERY, G. V. George Vincent Fosbery, a clergyman's son, was born at Sturt (near Devizes) in Wiltshire, around 1834; after leaving Eton, he went into the service of the Honourable East India Company and was (in January 1852) commissioned Ensign in the 3rd Native Infantry Regiment of the Bengal Army. It is probable that he later served with the 35th Regiment also.

Fosbery's career during the Indian Mutiny (1857–8) is uncertain, but it is probable that his regiment mutinied (since it was raised in that area principally involved) and that it was accordingly disbanded. At all events, Fosbery was listed on the strength of the Bengal Staff Corps for some years after 1858, and this service was common to officers of disbanded regiments, who were then seconded to other regiments for duty.

As Lieutenant Fosbery, he was posted to the 4th Bengal European Regiment, and won a Victoria Cross for bravery (with the Umbeyla Expedition, on the N.W. Frontier of India) during a hill assault on 30th October, 1863.

After this incident, promotion followed to Captain (1864), to Major (1866), and to Lieutenant-Colonel (1876); in 1877, however, Colonel Fosbery sent in his papers and retired from the Army.

Even as a young man, G. V. Fosbery had been interested in firearms, and he had secured his first British firearms patents (for breech-loading rifles and cartridges) as Nos. 1417 of 19th May, 1866, and 2293 of 6th September, 1866; W. W. Greener (*Modern Breech-Loaders*, London, 1871) noticed Fosbery's rifle specifically, and it has been recorded that, on the occasion of winning his Victoria

Cross, Lieutenant Fosbery had under his charge a company of marksmen from the 71st and 101st Regiments, who were armed with rifles firing explosive bullets of his own invention.

This interest in firearms-design remained with Colonel Fosbery for the rest of his life (he died in 1907), and amongst his activities in this field, he also secured three British patents of direct concern here. All three patent applications were handled by London Patent Agents Haseltine, Lake & Co. (of 45 Southampton Buildings), and the applicant's address was given at 279 Vauxhall Bridge Road, London, in every case.

Br. Pat. 15453/1895 related to a recoil-operated "magazine firearm" (as the patentee termed it) which is shown in Figure 40. It will be clear from the Figure that Fosbery had designed a recoil-operated revolver, based upon components from a Colt Model 1873 pistol (described in Chapter I) upon which the "Bisley" weapon shown in Plate 2 (lower) was based. It can be seen from Figure 40, that Fosbery mounted barrel, cylinder and frame to slide to-and-fro (against a recoil-spring) in the butt component; on discharging this single-action weapon, a lump on the recoiling hammer-trunnion struck a cocking-cam (externally mounted on the left-hand end of the butt component) and so cocked the hammer. An ingenious disconnector (similar in principle to that used on the Luger (Parabellum) P /08 self-loading pistol) prevented more than one shot from being fired at each pressure on the trigger.

The weapon shown in Fig. 40 must have operated most harshly, and since the conventional pawl-and-ratchet system of the original Colt revolver was retained for cylinder rotation, the length of time for which those components stood the battering of use must have been brief. However, Br. Pat. 15453/1895 contained the germ of what was to become a commercially viable "automatic revolver", and *The Official Journal of the Patent Office* eventually recorded entry in the patent registers (between the 1st and 6th of October, 1906) of an assignment, transmission or licence in respect of this patent. No specific details of that entry have survived, but subsequent events make it fairly certain that the other party to the transaction was THE WEBLEY & SCOTT REVOLVER AND ARMS CO. LTD. (*q.v.*).

Fosbery's next relevant patent was Br. Pat. 12470/1896, and it is clear (from the Specification drawings) that a considerable amount of practical development-

although cylinder rotation was still by ratchet-and-pawl, considerable ingenuity was now devoted to a method for reducing the effects of recoil upon those two relatively fragile components.

Cartridge-ejection was now by the familiar Webley system, of tilting down the barrel on its hinge, but it was still

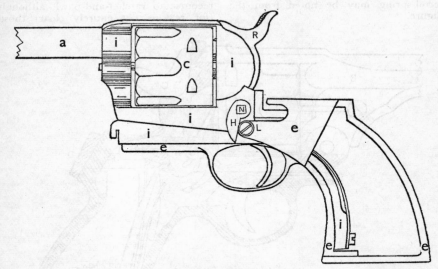

FIG. 40. Fosbery's "*magazine firearm*".
(After Br. Pat. 15453/1895.)

"a" = barrel; "i" = frame-components; "c" = cylinder; "e" = butt-components; "H" = cocking-lump; "L" = cocking-cam; "N" = hammer-trunnion; "R" = hammer.

On discharge, components "a", "c", "i", "H", "N", and "R" recoil together along "e" (with the impact of "H" on "L" cocking "R", through the medium of "N"), and are all then thrown forward again by a coiled spring concealed in "e". Rearward movement has rotated "c", and leaves "R" cocked for normal discharge by the trigger.

work had gone into improving the basic idea behind his Br. Pat. 15453/1895, during those ten months which had separated the dates of application for the two patents.

From Figure 41, it may be seen that, in this new patent, the original solid-framed Colt components had now been discarded, in favour of a hinged-frame design (retaining, however, the recoiling barrel-cylinder-frame configuration), of obvious Webley parentage; further,

necessary to thumb-cock the hammer for the first shot.

Thus, in Figure 41, the cylinder "A", barrel "B", and hammer "C" are mounted on a frame recoiling along the butt-component "D", when the weapon is fired; during this recoil, a projection "E" on the rear of hammer "C" bears against an incline "F" on the inside of the top butt-strap, and so cocks the pistol. A pawl "G" is pivoted to the lever "H", which latter is acted upon by a coiled-spring "I"; this spring first absorbs the shock of recoil by the cylinder-ratchet against "G", and then expands to force up "G" (against the ratchet) and so complete rotation of the cylinder. A trigger-disconnector is to be fitted to the single-action lock-mechanism (preventing full-automatic fire), and use of a "recoiling-lever" and coiled quadrant recoil-spring may be noted from the Figure.

the field. This patent Specification described use of a rear butt-strap formed as a separate component (hinged and pinned to the remainder of the butt), which permitted barrel, cylinder and frame to be more readily removed from the pistol.

This patent also claimed two methods for rotating a revolver cylinder without recourse to ratchet-and-pawl, although (for reasons not entirely clear) those

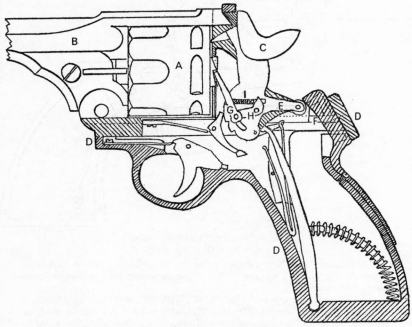

FIG. 41. *Fosbery's Automatic Revolver*
(After Br. Pat. 12470/1896.)

In all essentials save one (a method for cylinder rotation covered by that patent next to be described), the weapon shown in Figure 41, and claimed in Br. Pat. 12470/1896, was that arm manufactured by THE WEBLEY & SCOTT REVOLVER AND ARMS CO. LTD. (*q.v.*), and sold as "The Webley-Fosbery Automatic" revolver (see Plate 31).

Colonel Fosbery secured further patent protection for his revolver, as Br. Pat. 24155/1896, but it was his last patent in

components did appear in Specification drawings. The first rotation system was never commercially developed, and depended upon engagement by pins, protruding around the cylinder, with a cam surface assembled to the butt. The second design (visible in Plate 31, and used without supporting ratchet-and-pawl in those Webley-Fosbery revolvers likely to be encountered) had a spring-loaded, non-recoiling, vertical pin mounted in the trigger-guard assembly, which engaged zigzag grooves or races cut across the cylinder walls; as the barrel, cylinder and frame recoiled, this pin (protruding up into one leg of these V-shaped cylinder races) rotated the cylinder $\frac{1}{12}$th of a complete revolution, and then completed the $\frac{1}{6}$th of a turn needed for the cylinder of any six-chambered arm, by riding down the other leg of the "V", as cylinder and barrel were driven forward by the recoil-spring. In an eight-chambered arm later described, these rotation steps were, of course, by $\frac{1}{16}$th of a complete cylinder revolution.

The Official Journal of the Patent Office recorded filing of an assignment, transmission or licence of Br. Pat. 24155/1896, between 1st and 6th October, 1906; the other interested party can be assumed to have been THE WEBLEY & SCOTT REVOLVER AND ARMS CO., LTD. (*q.v.*), and it is noticeable that no such entry was recorded by the *Journal* in relation to Br. Pat. 12470/1896, a protection apparently of equal importance to the later patent.

On the basis of these two Fosbery patents of 1896, the patentee and THE WEBLEY & SCOTT REVOLVER AND ARMS CO., LTD. (*q.v.*) began to develop a weapon suitable for marketing, but it was not until 1900 (at the Bisley Meeting) that any serious attention appears to have been paid to their arm. In fact, this unveiling was not wholly successful because the sample revolver occasionally skipped a chamber in firing, but that defect was overcome in good time for the 1901 Bisley Meeting, and a number of complimentary articles appeared in summer issues of *The Country Gentleman*, *The Naval & Military Gazette*, *Country Life*, *The Sporting Goods Review*, or in other periodicals concerned with firearms.

As to details of the various models of Webley-Fosbery revolver sold thereafter, the interested reader is referred to Chapter IX of Major W. C. Dowell's definitive work upon Webley arms, and only a summary of them will be attempted here.

The earliest version was probably as shown in Major Dowell's Plate 54 (b) and (c), a specimen serially-numbered "1" which may actually have been the sample arm exhibited at Bisley in 1900. This particular weapon is made from as many components as possible of the standard Webley Mark IV hinged-frame service revolver, and therefore is in ·455 calibre with 6-in. barrel. Mechanically, this pistol follows closely the claims of Br. Pats. 12470/1896 (see Fig. 41) and 24155/1896, save that the cylinder-rotation stud is not spring-loaded and is mounted on the left side of the butt assembly, rather than centrally within that component, as was later practice. Dowell records this arm as marked "Fosbery Auto Revolver" and "Made by the Webley & Scott Revolver and Arms Co. Ltd." on the barrel, with Webley & Scott's trade-mark on the barrel-lug, and Birmingham proof marks. No other specimen of this model is known to this writer, although later serial-numbers suggest that a small production-run occurred.

Once production had properly commenced, Webley-Fosbery revolvers were offered in ·455 and ·38 calibres, with barrel lengths of 4, 6, or 7½ inches available at choice. The six-chambered ·455 arm (of which a specimen appears in Plate 31) was regulated to use the British service rimmed revolver cartridge, with 6½ grains of Cordite and a 265-grain bullet; moreover, in emergencies (and with some faltering in its "automatic" rôle) this weapon could also handle the earlier ·455 rimmed revolver round, with 18 grains of black-powder and 265-grain lead bullet, or even ·450 rimmed revolver cartridges with only 13 grains of black-powder and a 225-grain lead bullet. The eight-shot version of smaller calibre, however, was chambered and regulated to use only ·38 Automatic Colt Pistol cartridges, with 130-grain jacketed bullets; normally, all chambers were simultaneously loaded, with these semi-rimless cartridges, by use of the metal charger described in later remarks upon W. J. WHITING (*q.v.*) and Br. Pat. 18294/1901.

In describing these later production arms, Major Dowell recognizes Models of 1901 and 1902, as sufficiently distinctive to warrant separate attention, and in the main features of their mechanisms both such versions of the Webley-Fosbery revolver are as shown in Figure 42. However, a comparison of Figures 41 and 42 will show that some alterations were made to the weapon shown in

Specification drawings to Br. Pats. 12470/1896 and 24155/1896, notably in the hammer (which no longer had a long cocking-tail), in the later use of integral cylinder-rotation studs, and in adoption of V-shaped recoil-springs, to replace the original coiled design. Additionally, a safety-catch was fitted on the left side of the butt assembly.

As between Model 1901 and 1902 revolvers, therefore, a number of minor differences in construction are noticeable.

Thus the Model 1901 pistol used that separate, butt-strap assembly and coiled recoil-spring claimed in Br. Pat. 24155/1896, but had no detachable side-plates on its frame; the trigger-guard, trigger, trigger-spring and spring-loaded cylinder-rotation stud were formed as a complete but detachable unit, which was held in the butt assembly by a screw. Noticeable also, on these Model 1901 arms, is the use of a cam-lever cylinder-release (as used, for example, in a "WG" Webley revolver shown in Plate 25) and fitting of chequered wooden butt-cheeks to all non-presentation weapons.

Model 1902 revolvers (see Plate 31) dispensed with the hinged rear butt-strap, had detachable side-plates screwed on to their butt assembly, used a V-shaped recoil-spring, and had trigger, trigger-spring and integral cylinder-rotation stud all as part of the butt component, and no longer as a detachable unit to be mounted by means of a screw. Hard rubber or vulcanite butt-cheeks were fitted to this model, as an alternative to wooden cheeks, and a notable change occurred in that device used for releasing the cylinder from its arbor, when dismantling the weapon.

Neither the integral cylinder-rotation stud nor the new cylinder-dismount was the work of Colonel Fosbery, and both had been developed by his partner in the manufacture of these revolvers, namely, THE WEBLEY & SCOTT REVOLVER AND ARMS CO., LTD. (*q.v.*).

In 1900 the Webley company (with W. J. WHITING; *q.v.*) secured Br. Pat. 18225/1900 for a spring to be fitted into the top barrel-strap of Fosbery revolvers, for the purpose of locking their cylinders against accidental rotation when a weapon was opened. There is a tendency for the cylinder of any partly-emptied revolver to rotate (through the un-balancing weight of unfired cartridges) when the weapon is opened, and this can have the undesirable effect of bringing a fired cartridge up to the hammer, at a time when the user believes, after inspection, that one or more loaded rounds are still immediately in train to it.

The spring alignment device proposed in Br. Pat. 18225/1900 (which was also claimed as suitable for any hinged-frame revolver) was screwed to the underside of the top barrel-strap and had a stud projecting below it. When the revolver was opened, the spring forced this stud into one of the zigzag races on the Fosbery cylinder, and so locked the cylinder against accidental rotation. On closing the weapon, however, the spring engaged a shoulder on the standing breech of the pistol and the stud was accordingly lifted out of the cylinder race.

Entry of an assignment, transmission or licence relating to Br. Pat. 18225/1900 was recorded in *The Official Journal of the Patent Office*, as occurring between the 1st and 6th of October 1906, and this may have signalled the assignment of his interest in this patent, by W J. WHITING (*q.v.*) to THE WEBLEY & SCOTT REVOLVER AND ARMS CO., LTD. (*q.v.*).

Although the alignment-device of Br. Pat. 18225/1900 was not notably successful, it was fitted to a few Model 1901 arms, and obviously sired an improved version, which is (along with use of an integral cylinder-rotation stud) the hallmark of all Model 1902 arms. This new device was, yet again, the invention of W. J. WHITING (q.v.), to whom Br. Pat. 4924/1901 was granted in respect of it.

In Model 1902 arms, therefore, the old cam-lever cylinder-release was discarded, and a double-armed spring-catch (operated by a press-button visible in the top barrel-strap) performed instead both the service of retaining the cylinder upon its arbor, and that of preventing accidental rotation when the weapon was opened.

At rest, the two separate arms of this device point fore-and-aft along the top barrel-strap, and it is the forward component which carries a thumb-piece. The rear arm serves (in the same manner as that device described under Br. Pat. 18225/1900) to keep the cylinder aligned when the weapon is open; further, when the pistol is opened, the forward arm acts as a retainer to keep the cylinder upon its arbor. This is accomplished by forming a series of small depressions around the front circumference of the cylinder, into which a stud on the underside of the forward arm is depressed (by a spring) if the weapon is opened. Pressure on the thumb-piece (protruding upwards through the top barrel-strap) frees both arms from the cylinder, and permits that component to be pulled off its arbor.

In addition to claiming this cylinder alignment/dismount device as actually used, Br. Pat. 4924/1901 also claimed four variant forms (some of them applicable to ordinary revolvers) together with use of integral cylinder-rotation studs and uniform-depth cylinder races, as found on the Model 1902 Webley-Fosbery revolvers. It was thus an important part of the patent protection for these arms, but (oddly enough) no assignment or other interest in it was recorded by *The Official Journal of the Patent Office* when, in October 1906, such interests were noted in relation to Br. Pats. 15453/1895 and 24155/1896.

The reason for this apparent omission

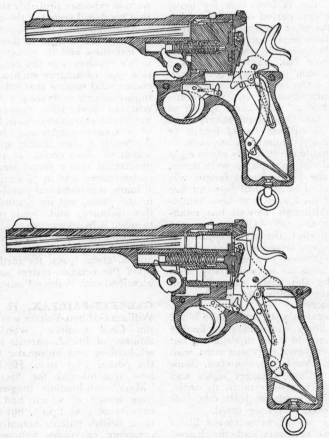

FIG. 42. *Production-version of M/1902. Webley-Fosbery lock-mechanism.*

is not known, but the recording of assignments or licences of British patents was not then mandatory. Since Colonel Fosbery died in 1907, it is possible that the 1906 transactions were arranged because he was too ill to take any further practical part in developing his designs, and therefore sold his interest in any patents to his partner THE WEBLEY & SCOTT REVOLVER AND ARMS CO., LTD. (*q.v.*), or WEBLEY & SCOTT LTD., as that firm became in the same year. At that time, as a matter of convenience, it would appear that w. J. WHITING also disposed of his interest in Br. Pat. 18225/1900 to his employers.

Webley-Fosbery revolvers were catalogued by the Webley firm for many years after that period of concern here, and it is therefore extremely difficult to suggest a likely serial-range for the period 1900–14. However, it was noticed that ·455 revolver No. 2431 was marked "C.S.F.W. 1909", and this does suggest that about 3,500 revolvers had probably been manufactured by 1914, since the serial-numbers of these arms appear to have been allocated consecutively (and regardless of calibre, barrel length or finish) from serial-number 1 onwards.

It is probable too that only about eight hundred Model 1901 pistols were made, and that the 7½-in. barrel length was not introduced at all until between five and six hundred arms had been manufactured. Although Dowell has established that the ·38 ACP version was available in 1901, the great majority of Webley-Fosbery arms are in ·455 calibre, and the eight-shot weapon is a rarity. Such ·38 arms as have actually been observed by the writer have been in 1000 or 1100 serial-ranges, and all had the 6-in. barrel.

As a general rule, all arms had a blued finish, so finely executed that further decoration would seem superfluous, but occasional engraved or plated arms, with ivory grips, can be encountered. Similarly, the fitting of target sights and special grips was undertaken to order, and Dowell records at least one case where a special barrel was fitted.

Markings on the arms varied little; Model 1901 revolvers had the legend "Webley Fosbery Automatic" on the left

side of the top barrel-strap, but this was shortened to "Webley Fosbery" on the Model 1902 arms. Both models had Webley's "flying bullet" trade-mark on the left side of the butt assembly, with the words "38 Automatic", "455 Cordite Only" (Model 1901) or "455 Cordite" (Model 1902), as appropriate, beside this mark. The names of various retailers can be found upon the top of the barrels on either Model, but "Army & Navy C.S.L." or "P. Webley & Son, London & Birmingham" markings were particularly common. Use of this old Webley trading-style, when THE WEBLEY & SCOTT REVOLVER AND ARMS CO., LTD. (*q.v.*) or WEBLEY & SCOTT LTD. companies were in existence probably stemmed from that good-will vested in the older name.

Although other recoil-operated revolving arms are noticed in these pages (see G. HAEGHEN and H. F. LANDSTAD), Fosbery's revolver was the only weapon of this type to achieve such a measure of commercial success that others patented improvements to it; see J. TAMBOUR, W. J. WHITING and THE WEBLEY & SCOTT REVOLVER AND ARMS CO LTD. In the hands of a steady marksman, this was undoubtedly a most deadly weapon, from which six shots could (at 12 paces) be discharged into a target smaller than a coffee-saucer, and in 7½ seconds; Walter Winans, a professional pistol-shot of note in the 1900s, put up a similar mark at this distance, and fired twelve shots through it in 20 seconds.

In conclusion, the reader's attention is directed to notes upon P. MAUSER (*q.v.*) and A. LINES (*q.v.*), for further remarks upon the rotation-system so commonly identified with Webley-Fosbery revolvers.

GABBETT-FAIRFAX, H. W. Hugh William Gabbett-Fairfax was a Leamington Civil Engineer, who secured a number of British patents for complex self-loading and automatic firearms, in the period 1895–1900. He is probably best remembered for his formidable "Mars" self-loading long-recoil pistol (one model of which had a muzzle-velocity of 1750 f.p.s.), but only two of these British patents actually embodied revolving or rotary ammunition feed-systems.

Br. Pat. 18686/1895 (in the Specification to which Gabbett-Fairfax mentioned addresses at 29A Gillingham Street and 107 Lambeth Palace Road, London) protected a fully automatic pistol with a six-shot rotary magazine; Br. Pat. 17808/1896 was for an improvement to that long-recoil pistol protected by the earlier patent, and contained seven claims for endless-chain, rotary, and annular magazines for it. In each case, the cartridges were to be pushed straight forward out of the magazine (and not withdrawn from it) for feeding to the breech. This second patent Specification mentioned Gabbett-Fairfax's Lambeth Palace Road address, and he was assisted in both patent applications by London Patent Agents, Messrs. Haseltine, Lake & Co., of 45 Southampton Buildings.

Bewley & Craig have recorded that Gabbett-Fairfax approached THE WEBLEY & SCOTT REVOLVER AND ARMS CO., LTD. (q.v.) in May 1898, and interested that company in developing his "Mars" pistol with a view to the Company manufacturing that weapon, by licence under his patents.

It seems probable that Gabbett-Fairfax was not wholly successful in this endeavour to make the Webley company his sole licensees, for a "Mars Automatic Firearms Syndicate" was later formed, and it was for sale by this syndicate that THE WEBLEY & SCOTT REVOLVER AND ARMS CO., LTD. (q.v.) apparently made "Mars" pistols.

It is not known if Gabbett-Fairfax managed to interest the members in his Br. Pats. 18686/1895 or 17808/1896, and the Syndicate was dissolved around November 1902. Mr. Gabbett-Fairfax was not again active as a firearm patentee until the close of the First World War.

GARDNER, G. E. George Ezra Gardner was joint-applicant with V. DE MARAIS (q.v.) for Br. Pat. 18486/1912; both were described as "Gentleman" in the patent Specification, and both were apparently resident at Oroville, County of Butte, California, U.S.A. They were assisted to secure their protection by London Patent Agents J. S. Withers & Spooner.

Although there were four claims to Br. Pat. 18486/1912, their scope was re-stricted to a minor improvement in light-projecting sights of the kind described in remarks upon K. DOBSLAW and P. SCHMIDT (q.v.), M. FERGUSON and J. O. FITZGERALD (q.v.), C. A. LEWIS (q.v.), and the W.T.G. "WESPI" (q.v.).

In a revolver carrying a light-projector under its barrel, Gardner and de Marais proposed to mount a slidable circuit closer, of rod shape, within the frame; operated by an external knob (just forward of the left butt-cheek, on the pistol), this circuit-closer switched the sight on or off, and was retained at its selected position by a spring detent engaging notches in the rod.

GORDON-SMITH, R. A Birmingham Patent Agent (Henry F. Talbot, of 7 Cherry Street) assisted Richard Gordon-Smith to secure Br. Pat. 3771/1897. The Specification describes this applicant as a "Gentleman", of 23 Clarence Parade, Southsea, Hants.

Mr. Gordon-Smith proposed to construct the butt-caps of revolvers with a double cutting-edge or "axe" embodied in them; preference for a shape similar to that at the very tip of a cavalry sword was expressed in this Specification.

The revolver shown in Plate 24 (from the Tower Collection) actually embodies one example of Gordon-Smith's idea, and the drawings to this Specification showed his device fitted to a hinged-frame revolver, of Webley type.

Modern thought is against striking anyone with the butt of a revolver, since the victim may catch the pistol and shoot his assailant, but it is fair to say that the Gordon-Smith heel-plate does appear to have been capable of causing a severe puncture-wound in use.

As to other devices intended for similar embodiment in revolver pistols, see B. KREITH; E. PAUL.

GRANT, D. E. Duncan Edmund Grant (of 14 St. Amable Street, Quebec, Canada, a "Manufacturer") communicated Br. Pat. 6541/1893 to W. P. THOMPSON (q.v.).

By a tedious Specification, which ended with thirty-four specific claims of novelty, Grant described a twin-trigger hammerless magazine rifle, in which loading and extraction of cartridges were to be effected by squeezing the weapon against the firer's shoulder.

A rotating magazine had its axis in line with the barrel, and cartridges in it received a step-by-step rotation from a receiver operating off the to-and-fro motion of the breech-bolt. On pulling this rifle against the user's shoulder, the receiver first ejected any fired case (*via* an ejection port) and then received a loaded round from an opening in the casing of the rotary magazine; further rearward pressure sent the breech-bolt into the receiver (picking up a cartridge, and chambering it in the barrel), compressed the firing-pin, and then locked the breech-mechanism for firing.

The second (rear) trigger could be used to lock the breech at its forward position and the magazine could be "thrown out of gear" to permit use of this rifle as a single-loader.

No specimen arms are known to this writer.

GREEN, E. C. Edwinson Charles Green was a well-known gun-maker over the period in point here, and (until 1913) an active patentee of lock- or trigger-mechanisms, cartridge-extractors, and safety-devices applicable to sporting-guns with drop-down barrels. He also secured Br. Pat. 20321/1889 (without the assistance of a Patent Agent) which is of concern here.

Br. Pat. 20321/1889 related to:

(*a*) forming the "stirrup" barrel-latch of a hinged-frame revolver with such projections to or recesses in its rear face that the barrel could not be unlatched whilst the hammer was down.

(*b*) A vertically-sliding barrel-latch, worked by a thumb-piece hinged on the right rear frame of hinged-frame revolvers.

(*c*) Forming a metal or leather "shell" over revolver cylinders, to prevent sand or dust from clogging them.

(*d*) A concealed-hammer self-cocking lock-mechanism for revolvers, in which the cylinder was rotated *via* a separate spindle within the lock-case; this spindle was conventionally rotated by the lock-mechanism of the weapon, and might impart rotation to the cylinder by means

of a ratchet on the latter, or by studs at the front-end of the spindle engaging sockets in the rear-end of the cylinder.

(*e*) Holes were to be drilled at the breech-end of a revolver barrel, to release gases which might otherwise foul the cylinder; the outside of revolver barrels was (for lightness) to be made of a polygroove shape; and, to provide a firm grip, revolver butts were to be covered with cork.

A specimen revolver made under Br. Pat. 20321/1889 is shown in Plate 32 (as a ·450 calibre, six-shot weapon, with 5½-in. barrel and double-action lock-mechanism), and it will be seen quite closely to resemble hinged-frame Webley arms, of the type shown in Plate 23. Fitted with Green's patented barrel-latch, under Claim (*a*) above, the weapon was retailed by "E. C. Green & Son, Cheltenham and Gloucester", and probably made-up by Green from imported Continental components, although it bears Birmingham proof-marks.

Major Dowell has published a bitter exchange of letters (in *The Field* of 22nd May and 29th June, 1889), by the first of which E. C. Green had laid claim to introducing, in 1883, that "stirrup" barrel-latch used in the new (at 1889) Webley "Mark I" service revolver, and had mentioned an improved barrel-latch which was presumably that shortly to be covered by the above-mentioned Claim (*b*) to his Br. Pat. 20321/1889. However, P. Webley & Son's letter firmly rebutted Green's suggestion that he had any founded claim to improvements used in their revolvers, and the correspondence appears to have been abandoned.

Green also retailed another revolver which is rather more commonly encountered than the weapon covered by his Br. Pat. 20321/1889, but (due to the considerable period for which he traded) it remains to be established whether or not this pistol should be regarded as antedating that period of concern here. The weapon is a six-chambered self-ejecting arm, in ·450 centre-fire calibre, which is shown above in Plate 32, and can be seen as of lighter construction than Green's other revolver, and as being fitted with a different type of barrel-latch.

These arms bear upon their 5½-in.

barrels the legend "E. C. Green, High Street, Cheltenham", and have unfluted cylinders stamped with the word "Steel". At first glance, they may be mistaken for the cheaper "Pryse" revolvers (similar to an arm shown on Plate 24), which were manufactured in Belgium, and either finished or simply retailed by a number of British gun-makers. On examination, however, the Green version is found to have a half-pin turnover barrel-latch, instead of the twin-lever or "tong" latch of the Pryse arm, and it seems probable that Green himself had unfinished Belgian revolver-components made up in this fashion, at his 87 High Street, Cheltenham premises. Establishing a date at which the firm's trading-style changed from E. C. Green to E. C. Green & Son will presumably settle the dating of these arms.

Although Green's revolvers are fairly rare in either form, they have a deserved place in any history of British revolving arms.

In 1907, "Artifex" and "Opifex" wrote it as worthy of mention that '. . . for years past there has been in the whole of the British Empire only one manufacturer of revolvers, and . . . for some years the Webley-Scott Co. have had the sole monopoly . . ." E. C. Green's revolvers cast doubt upon the accuracy of that statement.

GRENFELL, H. H. Captain Hubert Henry Grenfell, R.N. (of 18 Ashburn Place, London) was joint-applicant with J. G. ACCLES (q.v.) for Br. Pat. 17993/1891, and enough has been said about the subjects of that patent, under remarks upon Grenfell's fellow-applicant. It may be of interest here, however, briefly to trace the fortunes of that company formed by these two men.

Grenfell & Accles, Ltd. was incorporated on 23rd February, 1891, with a nominal capital of £100,000 in £1 shares; the Memorandum of Association stated the company's principal object as being the carrying on of business in "ordnance" of all kinds (with ammunition), and defined "ordnance" in terms sufficiently broad to cover all types of artillery, machine-guns and small-arms.

The Articles of Association provided for not less than two (nor more than five) directors, who must each hold not less than £1,000 nominal value of stock or shares, to qualify as directors. The Registered Offices of the company were at The Holford Works, Perry Bar, Birmingham, already mentioned in remarks upon J. G. ACCLES (q.v.).

At 13th July, 1891, shares to the value of £63,007 were already issued as fully paid-up, with only four shareholders of any consequence, although six other men held one share each, as subscribers to the Memorandum of Association. The principal shareholders were:

James George Accles (Holford Works, Engineer): 1,000 shares
John Alexander Ferguson (16 Earls Court Sq., E.C., Gentleman): 1000 shares
Hubert Henry Grenfell (7 Great St. Helen's, E.C., Military Engineer): 1,001 shares
New Oriental Bank Corporation Ltd. (40 Threadneedle St., E.C., Bankers): 60,000 shares

It was recorded in the Companies Registry file on Accles & Grenfell Ltd. that the New Oriental Bank Corporation Ltd. had transferred 1,000 shares to each of the other three shareholders, on 9th June, 1891. Presumably these shares were so transferred in consideration of services rendered (or to be rendered) to the new company, by these men.

On 10th October, 1891, two licences (made between J. G. ACCLES (q.v.) and Grenfell & Accles Ltd., on 2nd October, 1891) were filed at the Companies Registry in relation to the British and Foreign patents of J. G. ACCLES (q.v.). The British patents were:

(1) Gun Carriage
24/1/1885   No. 2517
(2) Cartridges
16/3/1888   No. 5625
(3) Machine-Guns
28/6/1888   No. 9455
(4) Cartridge Boxes or Cases
23/8/1888   No. 4487
(5) Double-Headed Cartridges:
12/8/1889   No. 12704

The Foreign patents were:

(i) Cartridges:

12/10/1888	Austria	38
		———
		2730

(ii) Cartridge Boxes or Cases, and Cartridges:

26/2/1889	Denmark	101188
23/6/1888	France	191401
23/6/1888	Belgium	82302
28/6/1888	Germany	46445
30/6/1889	Italy	46
		———
		449

(iii) Machine-Guns:

20/4/1889	France	197625
23/4/1889	Belgium	85942
7/9/1889	Austria	39
		———
		1926

In relation to both of these Licences, J. G. ACCLES (q.v.) and H. H. Grenfell signed for Grenfell & Accles Ltd., as Directors. It is clear from those terms of the Licences which were filed, however, that the contribution of J. G. ACCLES (q.v.) to the Company's success was anticipated to be considerable, and apparently outweighed that of Grenfell.

By the British Licence, Grenfell & Accles Ltd. became solely and exclusively entitled to manufacture, use and sell under the above-mentioned Accles patents in the United Kingdom for the life of the patents (and enjoyed similar rights in any improvements to them), subject only to an earlier agreement, dated 23rd June, 1888, which had been made between J. G. ACCLES (q.v.) and John Adams Norton. The latter was Director and General Agent of the Gardner Gun Co., which manufactured a non-rotary-barrelled manually-operated machine-gun, and the 1888 agreement apparently permitted this Gardner company to use cartridge boxes or cases made under Br. Pat. 4487/1888.

J. G. ACCLES received (under the British Licence) only £100 in cash and £2,500 in shares of Grenfell & Accles, Ltd., whilst that Company took over the duty of paying renewal and maintenance fees for the British patents, but could give the patentee one month's notice of intention not to renew or maintain them. In any event, this Licence was terminable by either the patentee or the Company, by three months prior notice given on or after 21st March, 1892.

The Foreign Licence was in similar terms to the British Licence, and was also subject to the 1888 Agreement with J. A. Norton. Grenfell & Accles Ltd. could develop the patents of their choice, and seek additional patent protection anywhere else in the world save the United States.

J. G. ACCLES (q.v.) received £50 cash and a further 2,500 shares for entering into the Foreign Licence, but in this case he was to share net profits equally with the Company, in respect of any additional patents secured by it for his inventions.

On 18th March, 1896, J. Jackman (Secretary of Grenfell & Accles Ltd.) wrote to the Registrar of Companies to say that negotiations had been in train for about twelve months to dispose of the Company's business, and that these negotiations would probably be completed in a "very few weeks". As a result no General Meeting of the Company had been held in 1895. Mr. Jackman concluded his letter by saying "I may state that the Company is still carrying on business, although in a very small way, and that negotiations for the disposal of the business have been entered into because the Company has insufficient Capital to carry it on successfully."

He wrote to the Registrar again, on 23rd November, 1897, to say that Grenfell & Accles Ltd. had not carried on business for more than twelve months, except to try to realize a few assets "remaining after sale of Holford Works to the Accles Arms, Ammunition & Manufacturing Co., Ltd.", but he did file Annual Returns for the Company's activities in 1896 and 1897, on 20th December, 1897.

These Annual Returns showed 75,007 shares of Grenfell & Accles Ltd. as then in issue:

J. G. Accles: 6,000 shares
J. A. Ferguson: 1,000 shares
H. H. Grenfell: 10,601 shares
New Oriental Bank Corporation Ltd.: 56,400 shares
Thomas Newton: 1,000 shares

On 20th December, 1899, the Registrar of Companies became impatient, and sent a Notice (under s. 7 (1) of the Companies Act, 1880) to Grenfell & Accles Ltd. at the Holford Works; his notice was returned, marked in red, "Delivered as addressed. Refused by 'Accles Ltd.' later 'Grenfell & Accles Ltd.'. 6.2.900. Can trace no officials at these Works. 2/2/1900."

On 26th October, 1900, a Notice in the *London Gazette* dissolved Grenfell & Accles Ltd., in accordance with s. 7 (4) of the Companies Act, 1880.

There can be no certainty now, as to reasons for the failure of this Company. However, lack of capital was presumably the prime cause of that failure, and hence responsible for the rarity of revolvers manufactured under Br. Pat. 17993/1891.

GRUSONWERK, A. G. Die Actien Gesellschaft Grusonwerk (of Magdeburg, Germany) communicated Br. Pat. 7787/1892 to the London Patent Agent H. H. LAKE (*q.v.*), in whose name it was granted; as to "communicated" British patents, generally, see Appendix I. Magdeburg, a substantial town in what was then Prussian Saxony, had in it several large iron foundries, and many manufacturers dependent upon metal supplies were established in it.

The subjects of Br. Pat. 7787/1892 were a "gas-seal" revolver more particularly described in Chapter IV, where such arms are considered together; the A. G. Grusonwerk also secured "communicated" Br. Pat. No. 8652 of 6th May, 1892, through H. H. LAKE (*q.v.*), which contained no claims of direct concern here, but is worth passing note; in a multi-barrelled pistol, that double-action revolver lock-mechanism shown in Figure 15 was adapted to rotate a separate firing-pin successively across the breeches of the barrels, to fire each cartridge in turn.

At some date subsequent to these patents, the A. G. Grusonwerk was apparently merged into the Krupp group of companies and (as the F. Krupp Akt.-Ges. Grusonwerk) secured four British patents relating to machine-guns, during 1905; no claims relevant to this study appeared in these latter patents, and the A. G. Grusonwerk does not appear again amongst the names of those holding British patents for small-arms.

GUINDON, J. B. A. Jean Baptiste Adrien Guindon (of 2040A Hutchinson Street, City of Montreal, Quebec, Canada) was joint-applicant for Br. Pat. 19566/1910, with I. BELAIR (*q.v.*). Guindon was described in this patent Specification as a "Watchmaker", and the rifle design claimed in Br. Pat. 19566/1910 is briefly discussed in those earlier remarks upon his fellow-applicant.

HAEGHEN, G. V. Georges Van der Haeghen was an engineer, resident at rue Saint Martin en Ile, Liège, Belgium. Assisted by H. D. Fitzpatrick (a Patent Agent in practice at 100 Wellington Street, Glasgow) Van der Haeghen secured Br. Pat. 18495/1909, with a "Convention Date" priority of 25th August, 1908; as to "Convention Date" patents see, generally, Appendix I.

Br. Pat. 18495/1909 protected a weapon which was a recoil-operated "automatic" revolver; although weapons of a superficial similarity are discussed elsewhere in these pages (see, for example, G. V. FOSBERY and H. LANDSTAD), Van der Haeghen's revolver had certain almost unique features.

In the first place, when this weapon was discharged, only the cylinder recoiled in its over-long frame-aperture, the barrel being a fixed component; to avoid malfunctions, of course, the cartridges had to be retained from jarring out of their chambers, and this was effected by use of a plate (or "abutment", as the patentee termed it) fixed to the rear of the cylinder. In one version of this arm, the firing-mechanism was to be mounted upon the abutment.

Rotation of the cylinder was by ratchet and pawl, placed at the *front* of this component, or "spiral grooves" on the cylinder might be used; in either case, rotation occurred on the forward passage of the cylinder, sped by the energy of a compressed recoil-spring. When at rest, cylinder mated with barrel to form a "gas-seal", but the nature of Van der Haeghen's design suggests that such a seal was too fleeting to have served much purpose.

In applying for Br. Pat. 18495/1909, Van der Haeghen's Specification also proposed a modified long-recoil version of his revolver in which, after firing each shot, the cylinder was held at its rearmost position, until the trigger was pressed again, when forward movement of the cylinder operated the firing-mechanism. For reasons now unknown, this modification had to be withdrawn before the Specification was accepted for publication.

Van der Haeghen (whose name can be found printed as "Vanderhaeghen") was patents adviser to the *Musée d'Armes*, at Liège, in the 1900s, and contributed a regular bulletin upon current patents to the magazine *L'Armurerie Liegeoise*. He held a number of British, and other, patents for improvements to self-loading pistols of a more conventional type than that covered by Br. Pat. 18495/1909.

HAGEN, O. Olaf (of 38 Waldemar Thranes Gate, Christiania, Norway) secured Br. Pat. 409/1912, with the assistance of London Patent Agents Mark & Clerk, at 57/58 Lincoln's Inn

Fields. He described himself as a "Mechanical Engineer", and the patent had a "Convention Date" priority (see Appendix I) from 7th January, 1911.

Hagen proposed to steady any pistol, whilst firing, by a system of cords coming from a point on the user's shoulder, chest or collar, and attached to the pistol in such a manner that the weapon was given its proper firing position when the arm was stretched out far enough to tighten those cords.

The cords could also be stiffened, at those ends attached to the pistol, by means of rods screwed into holes in the pistol butt, and although a Model 1905 Colt self-loading pistol was shown in Hagen's Specification, his idea was applicable to revolvers.

In recent years, devices similar to those claimed by Br. Pat. 409/1912 have reappeared in the United States, notably in alliance with high-velocity single-shot pistols like the Ruger ·256 Winchester Magnum weapon. However, current practice is to engage the end loop of a neck cord in the user's thumb, and not to attach it permanently to the pistol.

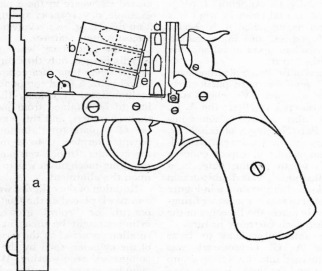

FIG. 43. *Hasselmann's revolver.*
(After Br. Pat. 17104/1893.)

"a" = barrel; "b" = replaceable cylinder; "d" = permanently-attached cylinder rotation-plate; "e" = cylinder-retainers.

HASSELMANN, M. Max Hasselmann secured Br. Pat. 17104/1893 with the assistance of Messrs. H. B. Barlow & Gillett, Patent Agents at 17 St. Ann's Square, Manchester; in the Complete Specification, filed with his patent application, Hasselmann described himself as an "Armourer", at Breite Gasse 52, Frankfort on the Main.

The principle of Br. Pat. 17104/1893 can be grasped (from Fig. 43) as one means for accomplishing the quick-loading of revolvers; an alternative idea is considered in remarks upon the COLT'S PATENT FIRE ARMS MFG CO. (INC.), A. J. WATSON, and W. C. PRIDEAUX (*q.v.*).

In the cheap Pryse-type revolver shown in Figure 43 (which is similar in appearance to a weapon described in earlier remarks upon J. CARTER; *q.v.*), Hasselmann proposed to dispense altogether with the cartridge-ejection mechanism, and to replace each discharged cylinder with a loaded one. This was accomplished by mounting a cylinder rotation-plate permanently on the standing-breech, and inserting successive cylinders to engage centres formed on the rotation-plate and the barrel-lug. It should be noted that the basic idea of Br. Pat. 17104/1893 had been anticipated by Captain Henry Spratt (of the Royal Marines) in his British Patent No. 1918 of 22nd August, 1859.

Specimens of Hasselmann's revolver are rare, but a few arms were made, chambering 10·8-mm. German service revolver cartridges.

HERRON, W. W. William W. Herron, of 1307 F. Street, Washington D.C., U.S.A., was joint-applicant with C. A. DAVIS (*q.v.*) for Br. Pat. 16216/1889. The Specification described Herron as a "Real Estate Dealer", and the patent itself is briefly discussed in earlier remarks upon C. A. DAVIS (q.v.).

IDEAL HOLSTER COMPANY. The Ideal Holster Co. (of 254 South Broadway, Los Angeles, California, U.S.A.) communicated Br. Pats. 22653/1901 and 22654/1901 to a London Patent Agent W. P. THOMPSON (*q.v.*), in whose name they were secured. The Specifications to both patents described this Company as "Manufacturers and Dealers in Attachments for Guns", but nothing is now known as to who promoted it, or the scale of its operations.

Br. Pat. 22653/1901 set out three claims for an absolutely rigid mechanical connection between a detachable stock and a revolver. The stock (preferably a leather holster, with tubular metal reinforcements) was furnished with one pair of fixed and one pair of movable jaws, for effecting union with the pistol. A shaped metal plate was first sandwiched between each butt-cheek of the revolver, and its central butt-straps, whereupon the jaws of the stock were inserted into suitable notches in the plates, and the movable (lower) jaws were locked or unlocked from engagement with these notches, by a sliding locking-device. A fairly explicit drawing of a Colt "Bisley" revolver (see Plate 2), adapted for the stock, is shown in the Specification drawings.

Br. Pat. 22654/1901 really covered only improvements to the Company's earlier patent, although the first claim was actually made for a complete firearm (with folding aperture sight) having a detachable, extensible and collapsible stock of the type shown in Figure 44; the extensible reinforcements were the only real modification to the basic idea of Br. Pat. 22653/1901 and enabled this stock (when used as a holster) to be reduced to reasonable size. It was still necessary to mount auxiliary metal plates under the butt-cheeks of a revolver using this stock.

Specimens of the Ideal holsters are extremely rare. Mr. J. Aplan (of Sturgis, S.D., U.S.A.) has one externally identical to that drawn in the Specification to Br. Pat. 22654/1901, but which is also extensible. Marked only "Patents Pending", this contrivance fastens to the user's belt by a quick-detachable spring-clip, and marks in the leather confirm that it once held a Colt "Bisley" revolver, with $5\frac{1}{2}$-in. barrel, as shown in the relevant Specification drawings. Inside this stock, two springs secure the pistol from accidental loss. Another stock was formerly in the collection of Mr. Carlos H. Mason (of Bristol, Conn., U.S.A.), complete with a Smith & Wesson Model 1899 (·38 Hand Ejector Military & Police) revolver, First

Model, adapted to use it. I am indebted to Mr. Mason for confirming that this specimen follows the claims of Br. Pat. 22654/1901 in almost every particular.

IMRAY, O. Oliver Imray was a Chartered Patent Agent (at Birbeck Bank Chambers, Southampton Buildings, London), to whom COLT'S PATENT FIRE ARMS MANUFACTURING CO. (INC.) (*q.v.*) communicated Br. Pats. 14026/1903 and 13680/1905; as to "communicated" patents see, generally, Appendix I. The first of these patents has been discussed in remarks upon the Colt Company, and the second (which related to Colt's well-

F. L. PERRY and for H. SUNNGÄRD (*q.v.*), amongst those patentees noticed in these pages, practising as P. Jensen & Son, at 77 Chancery Lane, London.

JOHNSON, J. H. John Henry Johnson was the name of a London Patent Agent in practice from the 1850s, to whom P. MAUSER (*q.v.*) communicated the subjects of Br. Pat. 922/1878, which survived into the period of this book; as to "communicated" patents see, generally, Appendix I. The date of Johnson's death is not known, but his practice was carried on as "J. H. Johnson & Co.", at 47 Lincoln's Inn Fields, and that firm

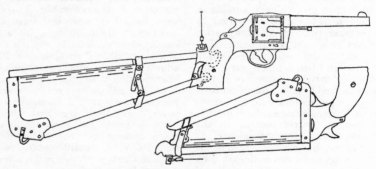

FIG. 44. *The Ideal Holster Co. stock.*
(After Br. Pat. 22654/1901.)

known "Positive Safety Lock") is dealt with at Chapter I, in relation to arms manufactured by the Company.

Imray's name appeared in a large number of applications for British patent protection, between 1898 and 1918, and he acted for the COLT'S PATENT FIRE ARMS MANUFACTURING CO. (INC.) (*q.v.*), over the years of concern here, in other applications beyond the scope of these pages.

JENSEN, P. Peter Jensen was a London Patent Agent, to whom O. H. J. KRAG and E. JÖRGENSEN (*q.v.*) communicated the subjects of Br. Pat. 18430/1889; he also handled their application for Br. Pat. 17082/1892, and acted for Krag in the matter of Br. Pat. 14576/1900. An active patentee of improvements to firearms (until 1907, in the period of concern here), he also acted for A. B., B. F., and

acted for E. FABRE (*q.v.*) and A. TRONCHE (*q.v.*) in the matter of another surviving British patent, No. 15771/1888.

JONES, O. Owen Jones had communicated to a London Patent Agent, W. R. LAKE (*q.v.*), the subjects of Br. Pat. 2777/1876, which had survived into years of concern here (see Table I), to protect the basic *extractor* mechanism for an "Enfield" British service revolver shown on Plate 19. To extract cartridges, by Jones's system, a barrel-latch was drawn back, and the barrel tilted down on its hinge, in a conventional manner; however, instead of expelling an ejector at the rear of the cylinder, this tilting movement drew the cylinder forward, on its arbor, leaving the cartridges caught (by their rims) on a star-shaped *extractor* fixed to the standing-breech.

British "Pistols, Revolver, B.L., Enfield" had a double-action lock-mechanism (see A. T. DE MOUNCIE, and Fig. 34) with an extractor-mechanism based upon Jones's Br. Pat. 2777/1876. They were made at the Royal Small-Arms Factory, Enfield Lock, Essex, as six-chambered weapons (with 6-in. Henry-rifled barrels for the Mark I and Mark II versions) of ·455- or ·476-in. calibre. Although in issue to British and Colonial armed forces or police for nearly twelve years (the weapon and its cartridges being declared officially obsolete only in September 1892), these "Enfield" revolvers had been effectively superseded in 1887, by the commercially-manufactured "Mark I" revolver of P. WEBLEY & SON (q.v.), the cartridges for which arm were latterly all catalogued as "Also Enfield".

Jones was actually an American firearms designer, from Philadelphia, who had secured, during the 1870s, a number of American, British and other patents for improvements to revolvers, travelled extensively to promote interest in them, and first aroused British War Office interest in his extractor, during 1878.

Although it has been stated, by the late J. N. George, that Jones was actually a staff-member of the Royal Small-Arms Factory when it began manufacturing "Enfield" revolvers, in fact contemporary records (P.R.O. SUPPLY/6/49) reveal him as still trying to establish even the existence of such manufacture, by the British government, as late as July, 1880. He then had to commence a lengthy correspondence, with the War Office, to seek an award for this use of his patented extractor, and had gone unrewarded until 9th May, 1882, when he had received an award of £750, for Crown operations in the field of his Br. Pat. 2777/1876.

Oddly enough, P.R.O.SUPPLY/6/49 reveals that Jones had also participated in the award made for use of that double-action lock-mechanism embodied in "Enfield" revolvers (see Fig. 34), though he accomplished this feat by exercise of commercial, rather than inventive acumen, since he had contributed nothing at all to that design.

In summarizing the events of this incident, it is enough to say that Jean Warnant (true inventor of the design upon which this "Enfield" revolver lock-mechanism was based) had contacted Jones, in 1879, and prevailed upon him to raise with the War Office (for reasons explained in remarks upon A. T. DE MOUNCIE; q.v.) the justice of a financial award to Warnant, as opposed to the holders of relevant British patents.

Jones had handled this situation most adroitly, for (whilst honestly pressing his protégée's claim with the War Office) he had secured a quarter-share in the relevant Br. Pat. 3206/1876 of A T. DE MOUNCIE (q.v.), and paid the £50 fee due for its maintenance, in August 1879. By this ploy, Jones had a position where (if any Crown award for the "Enfield" lock-mechanism be made at all) he stood to receive either something from a grateful Jean Warnant, or his (Jones's) entitlement as part-owner of Br. Pat. 3206/1876, or both.

Since, by 1880, Warnant had apparently relinquished entirely to Jones the conduct of this claim to Crown compensation, and had empowered Jones to state that Warnant had no interest in Br. Pat. 3206/1876 at all, the former had been able to put squarely to the War Office the question of whether the inventor of the lock-mechanism (i.e. Warnant) or the holders of a British patent covering the basis of it (i.e. Jones himself, and the man Kaufmann, described in remarks upon A. T. DE MOUNCIE; q.v.) were to receive any award made in respect of the use of Warnant's design, with modification, in "Enfield" revolvers. He had then wisely left the officials concerned, to reach their own decision (which is described in later remarks upon A. T. DE MOUNCIE; q.v.), and may be assumed to have benefited quite handsomely from the resultant award.

Apparently, Jones remained in England, and Major Dowell records his address as being of 17 Keppell Street, Russell Square, London, in 1893; it is therefore possible that it was after he had secured the awards described above, that Jones became formally associated with "Enfield" revolver manufacture at the Royal Small-Arms Factory, but such an association still remains conclusively to be established.

JÖRGENSEN, E. Erik Jörgensen joined with O. H. J. KRAG (*q.v.*) in Br. Pats. 18430/1889 and 17082/1892. Little seems to be known of him (save that he was Works Manager of the Royal Norwegian Gunfactory, at Kongsberg), but he may have been associated with Colonel Krag in a *Krag Jörgensens Gevaerkompagni*, which developed some non-rotary rifle magazines, in the years 1898–1900. Accordingly, the subjects of those two British patents above-mentioned are described in remarks upon Jörgensen's fellow-inventor.

KIPP, H. M. Herbert Melvin Kipp was a Druggist at 168 McCaul Street, Toronto, Province of Ontario, Canada, and joint-applicant with M. C. LISLE (*q.v.*) for Br. Pat. 15753/1909; the "gas-seal" revolver covered by the claims of that patent is briefly described in Chapter IV, with other arms of this *genre*.

KRAG, O. H. J. Ole Herman Johannes Krag (jointly with E. JÖRGENSEN; *q.v.*) communicated the subjects of Br. Pat. 18430/1889 to London Patent Agent P. JENSEN (*q.v.*), and was joint-applicant with Jörgensen (again under advice from Jensen) for Br. Pat. 17082/1892; he later secured Br. Pat. 14576/1900 (in his own name), again under the guidance of Peter Jensen.

Krag was born in Norway during 1837, and joined the Royal Norwegian Army, twenty years later, as an artillery officer. However, he exhibited great talent as a designer of small-arms, and served mainly at Kongsberg, in the *Kongsberg Våpenfabrikk*, or Royal Norwegian Gunfactory, rather than with the armed forces, and became Director of the Gunfactory in 1880. By 1895, he was the *Generalfelttøymerterens*, or Master of Ordnance, and the Specification to Br. Pat. 14576/1900 mentions an address at 23 Uranienborgveien, Christiania; he retired from the Royal Norwegian Army in 1902, and died in 1912.

During an energetic and successful professional career, Krag invented and patented a number of magazine rifle-designs, which enjoyed varying degrees of technical success, but one manually-operated bolt-action rifle (developed

with E. JÖRGENSEN; *q.v.*) came to be successively adopted by the armies of Denmark (Models 1889 and 1889–10), the United States of America (Model 1892) and Norway (Rifles M/1894 and

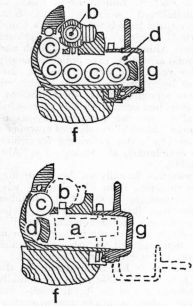

FIG. 45. *Krag & Jörgensen's rifle magazine.* (After Br. Pats. 18430/1889 and 17082/1892.)

At the top, the rifle-bolt "b" is closed, and the magazine is charged with five cartridges "c"; below, the bolt is open, and all but one of the cartridges has been discharged. The carrier "a" has passed the cartridges "c" across by pressure on the follower "d", lifting the last cartridge for the bolt to pick up on its forward stroke. "f" is the fore-end of the rifle; the gate "g" (through which the cartridges are loaded) is shown (dotted) open in the lower drawing.

M/1894–10; Carbines Model 94, 95, 04, 07 and 12); both the bolt-mechanism and the semi-rotary magazine of these Krag-Jörgensen rifles and carbines eventually covered by the claims of Br. Pats. 18430/1889 and 17082/1892, or their foreign equivalents. In the magazine of these arms, cartridges (urged sideways by a vertically-pivoted carrier and follower) traversed from right to left beneath the bolt-way, and were then deflected, up and over, into the receiver, by a curved side-plate (as shown in Fig. 45), to be collected and chambered, successively, by the bolt. Loading was effected through a hinged magazine lid (on the right) which hinged forward or sideways, according to the Model of rifle, for that purpose.

It should be noted of the above-mentioned British patents that the first was a "communicated" patent secured in the name of P. JENSEN (*q.v.*), whilst the second protected Krag and Jörgensen's improvements (to that basic design

a toothed segment on the side-mounted magazine-lid, so that the carrier was racked around (against its spring) as the lid was opened. This particular feature had been anticipated by the Br. Pat. 10423/1887 of J. SCHULHOF (*q.v.*), and appeared again in the Br. Pat. 19320/1900, of J. A. SCHWARZ (*q.v.*) and T. A. FIDJELAND (*q.v.*).

KREITH, B. Count Bela Kreith (of Theresiengasse No. 2, Währing, near Vienna, Austria) secured Br. Pat. 6216/1889, with the assistance of London Patent Agents Phillips & Leigh, of 22 Southampton Buildings, Chancery Lane.

FIG. 46. *Count Kreith's revolver.*
(After Br. Pat. No. 2462/1909.)

claimed under Br. Pat. 18430/1889) from a date earlier than that at which the two men actually applied for it. As to "communicated" British patents see, generally, Appendix I; the priority of date for the second patent (running from date of application for equivalent Norwegian protection, i.e. 24th February, 1892) was a concession secured under S.103 of the Patents &c. Act, 1883.

In Krag's own Br. 14576/1900, a true rotary rifle-magazine was claimed, where cartridges carried in a cylindrical magazine below the bolt-way, were borne to the receiver, by a centrally-mounted rotating wing or carrier; this latter was actuated by a coiled spring around its core, which was wound into tension (and thus withdrew the carrier to permit loading) when the side-lid of the magazine was opened. Withdrawal was actually effected by a pinion on the core engaging

Nearly twenty years later (but then from Nepszinhaz utcza 23, Budapest, Hungary) he secured Br. Pat. No. 2462/1909, with assistance from the London Patent Agents Boult, Wade & Tennant, of 111/112 Hatton Garden. In both Specifications, Kreith was described simply as "Gentleman", and the subjects of his British patents were combination weapons; as to such arms, see also remarks upon R. G. GORDON-SMITH, D. T. LAING, P. MONNERAT, E. PAUL: and B. REYES.

Br. Pat. 6216/1889 proposed detachably to combine lance, rifle and revolver; the hand-gun was to be hooked on to the lance (by suitable claws formed at butt-cap and trigger-guard), and retained by a spring-catch.

Br. Pat. 2462/1909 claimed two "knuckleduster" revolvers, of the type shown as Fig. 46; the weapon illustrated can be seen to have an integral knuckle-duster stock, but the second (and more unpleasant) arm had a detachable knuckleduster with a blade mounted in it.

KRNKA, C. Charles Krnka secured Br. Pat. 19839/1901, jointly with G. ROTH (q.v.); both men gave their address as at No. 50 Rennweg, Vienna, Austria, and they were assisted to secure that protection by London Patent Agents Marks & Clerk, of 18 Southampton Buildings, Chancery Lane.

Krnka was one of a trio of active designers with this unusual surname (see K. KRNKA), and he secured five British patents during the period of this book, covering rifling and projectiles, rifle magazines, a self-loading pistol, and (the patent in point here) an automatic rifle with a rotary cartridge magazine; G. ROTH (q.v.) was joint-applicant with Charles Krnka for all but one of these patents.

Br. Pat. 19839/1901 claimed improvements to a type of automatic rifle with fixed non-recoiling barrel, in which the breech-bolt was both unlocked and thrown back by gas-pressure acting on the firing-pin. Energy was transmitted to the latter component by use of special centre-fire ammunition, with an unusually deep primer-pocket in the cartridge-head. On discharge, the primer was blown backwards by combustion gases, and (in this set-back) struck the firing-pin, which was made in two parts; the front part of that pin could not move far enough back to permit any primer to be blown completely out of its cartridge-case, but was driven back so smartly that its impact against the rear part of the firing-pin both unlocked and withdrew the breech-block, and also put a combined recoil- and firing-pin spring into tension, to chamber another round as the spring drove the breech-block forward again. On that forward stroke, the front part of the two-piece firing-pin kicked any empty cartridge case off the extractor hook, before the breech-block picked up another round from the rotary magazine.

It is known that a few of these Roth-Krnka rifles were manufactured, and Br. Pat. 19839/1901 was maintained (see Table II) for a surprising length of time.

However, this breech-system then exhibited no marked advantage over less complex designs, and nothing more was heard of it in those years of concern here.

KRNKA, K. Karl Krnka was one of that trio of designers mentioned in remarks upon C. KRNKA (q.v.), and he secured eight British patents (relating to fire-arms) during the period of concern here, as well as securing other such patents both before 1889 and after 1914. Primarily, his field of endeavour lay in bolt-action magazine rifle-designs (some with straight-pull bolts), but he was also associated with G. ROTH (q.v.) in the manufacture of early self-loading pistols, at the turn of the century, and was active in developing automatic rifles with inertia-weight breech systems.

However, Karl Krnka appears here only by virtue of his Br. Pat. 14088/1888, which (see Table I) survived into the period of this book, and covered a manually-operated sliding-bolt pistol, with a removable rotary magazine embodied in it; externally, this weapon was not dissimilar in appearance to the magazine pistol of E. REIGER (q.v.) shown in Figure 63.

LAING, D. T. Major David Tyrie Laing secured Br. Pat. 16432/1897 (with the assistance of London Patent Agents Carpmael & Co.) from the Royal Colonial Institute, Northumberland Avenue, London, W.C.

Laing proposed a combination of lance and revolver along broadly similar lines to those proposed by B. KREITH (q.v.), but without means for detaching the smaller from the larger arm. A fourteen-shot revolver cylinder was to be mounted around the shaft of the lance, and fired (through a short pistol barrel) by a simple self-cocking straight-pull firing-mechanism behind it. All that was necessary in order to fire this weapon was for the user to pull rearwards on a hooked finger-piece projecting upwards at the point of grasp on the lance, and this movement (by means of a ratchet at the front of the cylinder) brought a cartridge-chamber into alignment with the barrel before the firing-pin was released.

In his Provisional Specification (see

Appendix I), Laing mentioned the idea of embodying a rifle in his lance, with a tube magazine buried in the lance shaft, and he also claimed (in his Complete Specification) that the revolver could be rotated and fired by mechanisms normally employed in conventional revolvers. However, there is no indication that he developed either of these ideas to the point of practical application.

In his Complete Specification to Br. Pat. 16432/1897, Major Laing described himself as "late Officer Commanding Belingwe Field Force", and the drawings to this Specification have a rough simplicity suggesting the work of a man amusing himself in circumstances where access to only the crudest of tools could be had. The Belingwe Relief Force consisted of forty men in all, and was one of several small troop-columns used (by the British South Africa Company) to subdue Matabele tribesmen, in Southern Rhodesia, during 1896/97.

Major G. Tylden (an authority upon these small irregular units) has expressed an opinion that Laing probably held his rank in the Militia, but that he may have been the Officer Commanding "Commander-in-Chief's Bodyguard" who was killed in action (during January 1901) at Lindley, during the second South African War.

LAKE, H. H. Henry Harris Lake was one member of a firm of London Patent Agents (Haseltine, Lake & Co., at 45 Southampton Buildings, W.C.) to whom DIE ACTIEN GESELLSCHAFT GRUSONWERK (q.v.) and T. THORSEN (q.v.) respectively communicated the subjects of their Br. Pats. 7787/1892 and 4148/1902; as to "communicated" British patents see, generally, Appendix I.

Lake appears to have been an extremely busy Patent Agent, active in the years between 1884 and 1904.

LAKE, W. R. William Robert Lake was a member of the same firm of London Patent Agents as H. H. LAKE (q.v.), and one founder of that firm, around 1868/69; to him, O. JONES (q.v.) communicated the subjects of Br. Pat. 2777/1876, which survived into the period of concern here. Lake had been an

active and successful Patent Agent, but he died or retired at about 1890, and was not involved in any other patents relevant to this study.

LANDSTAD, H. F. Halvard Folkestad Landstad was a Norwegian Mechanical Engineer (then of 2 Kort Aldersgade, Christiania) who communicated the subjects of Br. Pat. 22479/1899 to G. C. DYMOND (q.v.); as to "communicated" British patents see, generally, Appendix I.

Br. Pat. 22479/1899 protected a recoil-operated semi-automatic revolver of extraordinary design, similar in principle to the arms of G. V. FOSBERY (q.v.) and G. VAN DER HAEGHEN (q.v.), but having several unique features. Thus its "cylinder" has only two chambers, the lower one of which communicates with a magazine in the butt, as shown in Plate 33 (lower); the top cartridge is stripped from this butt-magazine, into the lower chamber of the "cylinder", by the impact of a projection formed on the underside of the breech-block, as that component (after recoiling, on discharge) is thrown forward again by recoil-springs. The firing-pin (or "hammer", as Landstad termed it) is cocked by the recoiling breech-block, and when the trigger is pulled a pawl linked to the trigger causes the lower (loaded) chamber of the cylinder to be rotated, clockwise, to align it with the barrel, after which the firing-pin is released. Extraction and ejection of fired cases are conventionally effected, during recoil of the breech-block, and the weapon is designed to handle rimmed 7·5-mm. centre-fire revolver cartridges, of a type used in that Norwegian Model 1893 Nagant service revolver discussed in Chapter II.

The specimen Landstad arm shown at Plate 33 (No. 580 in the National Rifle Association Collection, Bisley) weighs 2 lb. 4 oz. unloaded, and measures $9\frac{1}{4}$ inches in length; it has an unproved $4\frac{1}{2}$-in. barrel, rifled with five grooves, twisted to the right, and generally follows those design-features claimed in the Specification to Br. Pat. 22479/1899.

Landstad listed, in the Specification to his patent, those features which he personally regarded as desirable in any revolver, and although (with benefit of hindsight) it may be possible to cavil at some stated aims, it would be difficult to quarrel with this patentee's proposed methods for achieving them. In his list, which follows, all but the last Item were probably attained in that weapon shown as Plate 33, although wear in the mechanism makes it difficult to know if Items 3 and 6 were definitely present:

(1) The magazine arranged for quick-loading, so that the pistol may be

(6) The mechanism of the arm to lock automatically after the last shot from the magazine, to warn the user that reloading is necessary.
(7) Assembly and disassembly to be easy, and preferably without the aid of screws.
(8) Manufacture to be cheap.

LANGENHAN, H. Heinrich Langenhan secured Br. Pat. 10882/1906 with the assistance of Patent Agents W. P. Thomp-

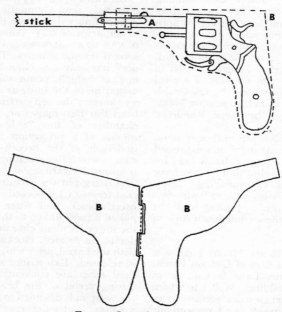

FIG. 47. *Langenhan's revolver.*
(After Br. Pat. 10882/1906.)

kept in the right hand, and loaded with the left.
(2) The hammer to be constantly (but safely) cocked, without being bolted.
(3) The pistol to be capable of use as a single-loader, with its magazine full.
(4) An empty cartridge case to be ejected at each shot.
(5) The trigger-pull easy and pleasant, but the hammer to be cocked automatically.

son & Co., of 322 High Holborn, London; in the Specification to his patent, Langenhan was described as a "Gunmaker", of the Waffenfabrik Mehlis, Thuringen, Germany. A namesake (F. Langenhan) secured three British patents for air-rifles, in years prior to 1906, and may also have been associated with the Waffenfabrik Mehlis.

Br. Pat. 10882/1906 proposed the combination of a revolver with a walking-stick or umbrella; similar ideas may be studied in remarks upon A. C. ARGLES (*q.v.*), H. RENFORS (*q.v.*), and G. TRESEN-REUTER (*q.v.*).

Langenhan put forward five claims of novelty, for the arm sketched as Figure 47:

(1) Combining a revolver with a stick or umbrella, so that the stick goes into the barrel of the weapon, and the two are united by a spring-catch "A" shown in Figure 47.

(2) Combining a revolver and a stick by means of a screwed sleeve.

(3) A removable cover for the revolver, which also serves as the handle of the stick; "B" in Figure 47.

(4) A soft foldable cover for the revolver, secured by buttons.

(5) Using an internally rifled stick (which could be closed by a ferrule) as an extension barrel for the revolver.

LATHAM, H. W. Henry Wilkinson Latham (1860–1904) was the brother of J. F. LATHAM (*q.v.*), and joined his father, John Latham, in the firm of Wilkinson & Son, during 1878. He acted as assistant to his brother until 1887, and then became a director of The Wilkinson Sword Co., Ltd.; in 1898 (on his brother's death) he became Chairman and Managing Director of the firm, until his own decease.

In 1894, he had been joint-applicant for Br. Pat. 22719/1894, with his brother, and they were assisted to secure this protection by London Patent Agents Boult & Wade at 323 High Holborn; the subjects of that patent are discussed in remarks upon J. F. LATHAM (*q.v.*).

H. W. Latham was described (in the Specification to Br. Pat. 22719/1894) as an "Engineer", at 30 Priory Road, Chiswick. He appears to have been interested in small-calibre adaptors for use in other full-bore arms, and later secured a British patent (of 1902) jointly with The Wilkinson Sword Co. Ltd., for such a device to be used in rifles.

LATHAM, J. F. John Francis Latham (1856–98) was the brother of H. W. LATHAM (*q.v.*) and son of John Latham, (1830–80); the latter had joined Henry Wilkinson, a famous sword- and bayonet-maker, in 1847, and had then taken over the business of Wilkinson & Son (at 27 Pall Mall, London) on Wilkinson's death, in 1861. J. F. Latham joined his father in 1871, took over the Company on the death of his parent, and converted it into The Wilkinson Sword Co., Ltd. (a joint stock company, of limited liability) in 1887. He was responsible for concentrating the Company's numerous small London workshops at one Chelsea factory (in which substantial contracts with the British Army were fulfilled), and was a nationally recognized authority upon sword manufacture and design, serving as a member of the War Office Committee of 1884 studying cavalry swords.

He secured Br. Pats. 17790/1893 and 19861/1893 with the assistance of London Patent Agents W. P. Thompson & Boult, and was joint-applicant with H. W. LATHAM (*q.v.*) for Br. Pat. 22719/1894; these patents are of concern here, and it is noteworthy that J. F. Latham described himself as "Gun-maker" in all three of these Specifications.

It is probable that Wilkinson & Son had first begun to retail firearms during the early 1850s (at the instance of officers purchasing swords from them), and by the 1880s that Company had established a firm association with the Birmingham house of P. WEBLEY & SON (*q.v.*) and was selling hinged-frame self-extracting Webley and Continental revolvers, which actually embodied some improvements specified by the sword-makers. Eventually, and during those years of concern here, the firm carried this interest one stage further, and secured patent protection upon three additional refinements to such arms.

Br. Pat. 17790/1893 protected a single-shot adaptor, which could be used to convert heavy-calibre hinged-frame self-extracting revolvers to use "miniature" ammunition, and the Webley "Mark I" service revolver (see Plate 23) was specifically mentioned as suitable for use with this adaptor. In such arms, the cylinder was to be removed completely, and that unit shown in Figure 48 (comprising sub-calibre barrel and single-shot breech-block) was inserted to replace it; the insert barrel rested in the original barrel by its end-supports, and the standard ejector-lever (remaining in the pistol) operated an ejector in the breech-block to eject each sub-calibre cartridge after discharge. The invention of J. T. MUSGRAVE (*q.v.*) was an improvement to this patent, and remarks upon R. MORRIS (*q.v.*) are also in point.

Br. Pat. 19861/1893 was (although technically ingenious) no more than a logical extension to that idea proposed in Br. Pat. 17790/1893; here, the small-bore barrel visible in Figure 48 had attached to it (instead of a single-shot breech-block) a revolving cylinder chambered for miniature cartridges, so that the owner might use his revolver as such.

For convenience, Br. Pat. 22719/1894

means mentioned in the Specification. Thus a stirrup-latch (as used in most Webley arms, and protected by H. WEBLEY'S (*q.v.*) and J. CARTER'S (*q.v.*) Br. Pat. 4070/1885) was actually illustrated. However, an alternative means was suggested as a hook-latch, pivoted on the side of the weapon, and engaging a lug protruding from the side of the top barrel-strap, which was a type of latch (once protected by British Patent No. 2855, of 14th July, 1879) which had been used by William Tranter, a famous Birmingham revolver manufacturer, who had retired from business nearly a decade earlier.

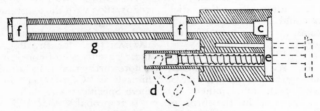

FIG. 48. *J. F. Latham's adaptor.*
(After Br. Pat. 17790/1893.)

"c" = sub-calibre rim-fire or centre-fire cartridge; "d" = ejector-lever in revolver; "e" = ejector; "f" = end-supports, keeping the surface of the sub-calibre barrel "g" clear of the rifling in the revolver barrel.

will be considered here, although there is no evidence that J. F. Latham contributed more or less to the subjects of invention than his brother and fellow-applicant, H. W. LATHAM (*q.v.*). The Specification to Br. Pat. 22719/1894 had five claims, which related either to means for locking shut the barrels of hinged-frame revolvers, or to a means for braking the cylinder against accidental rotation by the action of the ejector, when the pistol was opened.

As to the first of these matters, it was proposed to form the rear end of the top barrel-strap with a T-shaped extension, the narrow part of which passed between two lugs on top of the standing-breech, and the wide part of which passed behind those lugs to engage (when the pistol was shut) in contact with chamfered surfaces at their rear. This union of barrel with frame had to be suitably latched, which might be accomplished by one of two

The cylinder brake was merely a flat damper-spring, screwed to the underside of the top barrel-strap, which bore against the cylinder when the pistol was opened, and was lifted clear of it (by engagement with the standing-breech) when the pistol was shut.

Drawings to the Specification of Br. Pat. 22719/1894 show a revolver with features not so far found together in any actual weapon. At the date of application for this protection, it is probable that The Wilkinson Sword Co., Ltd. were retailing that revolver shown at Plate 27 (top), being the "Wilkinson-Webley 1892 Model", which was a six-chambered hinged-frame self-ejecting revolver in ·455/·476 calibre, with a frame-shape similar to that of the Webley No. 4 revolver, but embodying a stirrup barrel-latch, instead of the twin-lever "Pryse" latch of the No. 4 arm; however, the revolver actually drawn in the

Specification to Br. Pat. 22719/1894 has the frame of a Webley "WG" revolver (see Plate 25) allied with the oversized frame-hinge of a "Webley-Wilkinson-Pryse" weapon introduced in 1890, and a manual ejector-release (permitting examination of cartridges without ejecting them) used in an earlier "Pryse-type" revolver, of Continental manufacture, sold by Wilkinson and Son a decade before.

Since the design-features from Br. Pat. 22719/1894 were never apparently applied to production arms, it is difficult to make any confident assertion about the history of Br. Pat. 22719/1894, or the means by which J. F. and H. W. Latham had intended to manufacture (or have manufactured) the revolver-design protected by it.

As shown in Chapter III, the Wilkinson firm sold a number of revolvers designated as "Model 1905", "Model 1910" and "Model 1911" arms, but these weapons embodied no features from Br. Pat. 22719/1894 (which had been allowed to lapse in 1899), and were merely modified versions of "WS" and "WS Bisley Target" revolvers introduced by THE WEBLEY & SCOTT REVOLVER AND ARMS CO., LTD. (*q.v.*), at about 1904; see Plates 25 and 27.

In all the circumstances, it seems probable that J. F. Latham's death, in 1898, removed from the scene that person particularly desirous of manufacturing arms under Br. Pat. 22719/1894, and The Wilkinson Sword Co., Ltd. thereafter continued its existing satisfactory relationship with the Webley firm, and abandoned any idea of serious competition with it.

LAUBER, J. Joseph Lauber (of No. 15 Laxenburgerstrasser, Vienna, Austria) secured Br. Pat. 14223/1905, with assistance from Patent Agents Cruikshank & Fairweather, of 65/66 Chancery Lane, London, and 62 St. Vincent Street, Glasgow. The Specification to his patent described Lauber simply as a "Manager", and it contained five claims of novelty for a trigger-operated "self-cocking, self-loading and self-ejecting" magazine rifle. This curious weapon had a large annular magazine feeding cart-

ridges into the left side of the receiver, and a rise-and-fall breech-system which carried each round up into alignment with the barrel (for discharge) or downwards to a port, for ejection.

Although a Complete Specification was filed with Lauber's application for British patent protection, and this suggests that the design was regarded as fully-developed, no specimen arm is known to this writer.

LEWIS, C. A. Clifford Albert Lewis, of 381 East 12th Street, Portland, County of Multnomah, Oregon, U.S.A., secured Br. Pat. 8623/1912, with the assistance of London Patent Agents J. S. Withers & Spooner, of 323 High Holborn, London. The Specification to his patent described Lewis as a "Gentleman", and contained two claims of novelty for improvements to light-projecting sights of the kind noticed in remarks upon K. DOBSLAW and P. SCHMIDT (*q.v.*), M. FERGUSON and J. O. FITZGERALD (*q.v.*), V. DE MARAIS and G. E. GARDNER (*q.v.*), and the W.T.G. "WESPI" (*q.v.*).

Lewis's improvement is sketched as Figure 49, and really consisted in a detachable battery-container at the bottom of the pistol butt. This unit might be readily attached to or removed from the revolver, and when it was slipped into position, the battery was automatically (and without more attention than was necessary to insert the unit) connected with wiring embodied in the weapon.

This patentee had earlier been joint-applicant, with S. D. Adair, for Br. Pat. No. 8751 of 11th April, 1910; this patent covered a light-projecting gun-sight, beyond the scope of these pages.

LINDNER, A. Adolph Lindner, Gentleman, of No. 8 Jäger Strasse, Berlin, Germany secured Br. Pat. 17159/1888 which (see Table I) survived into the period of concern here. He was assisted to secure this protection by London Patent Agents Allison Bros., and filed a Complete Specification with his patent application, suggesting that his design had been finalized by the relevant date of 26th November, 1888.

Br. Pat. 17159/1888 set out eight claims of novelty for a bolt-action rifle, with a rotary magazine in which the carrier revolved under the action of a compressed spring and forced the cartridges, one by one, upon an elevator which aligned them with the breech for loading by the bolt. It is probable that the bolt-action claimed in this patent was regarded (by the patentee) as of primary value, since he secured Br. Pat. No.

Student". He was assisted to secure his first two patents by the London Patent Agents Haseltine, Lake & Co., of 45 Southampton Buildings, Chancery Lane.

In Br. Pat. 1328/1897, Lines proposed eight claims of novelty for a revolver quite similar in external appearance to the revolver of w. DECKER (q.v.) shown in Plate 29, being constructed with a

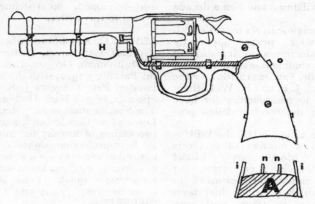

FIG. 49. *Lewis's light projector.*
(After Br. Pat. 8623/1912.)

The detachable electric-battery container "A" is secured to the butt by straps "i/i". The contacts "n/n" on "L" connect with a switch (operated by the external button "o") within the pistol, the switch being connected to the light-projector "H" by the externally-mounted leads at "j".

17160 of 26th November, 1888, for the use of it with a box magazine lacking rotary features.

Lindner secured several British patents for improvements to long-arms, in the years 1887 and 1888, but did not appear as a British firearms patentee during the period relevant here; his name is sometimes confused with that of Edward Lindner, a German-American designer of breech-loading conversion systems for muzzle-loading rifles, in the 1860s.

LINES, A. Alfred Lines secured Br. Pats. 1328/1897, 10145/1898 and 12367/1898 for an unusual revolver, and for certain improvements to it; in the Specifications to these patents, he mentioned addresses at 57 Victoria Road, Deal, Kent, and 17 Eyre Street, Chesterfield, Derby, and described himself as an "Engineering Student" or "Civil Engineering

butt more or less at right angles to the barrel, and with trigger sliding parallel to the axis of the cylinder; the patentee claimed for this configuration that the "throw-up" of the weapon, on discharge, was much reduced. Internally, however, Lines's revolver anticipated nothing in Decker's design, having a hinged breech-block which contained both a pivoted firing-lever (to be struck by a vertically sliding member, operating off the mainspring) and the pawl. Unlike Decker's weapon, Lines's design had a double-action lock-mechanism, and permitted simultaneous *extraction* of all cartridges; two versions of the arm were described in the Specification, one having an extractor worked automatically by the act of opening the breech-block, and another (which had a more complex breech-locking system) with a manually-operated extractor.

Br. Pat. 10145/1898 was for improvements to the earlier lock-mechanism, and embodied means for keeping the firing-lever clear of the cartridges (except at discharge), and for arresting cylinder-rotation before release of the firing-lever.

Br. Pat. 12367/1898 claimed the rotation of revolver cylinders (in arms of that type protected by Br. Pats. 1328/1897 and 10145/1898) *via* a stud on top of the sliding trigger, which engaged zigzag races cut across the forward circumference of the cylinder, and rotated that component as the trigger was first pulled back, and then released to move forward under the control of a trigger-spring (see Fig. 50).

It should be noticed that this general method for cylinder-rotation had been covered (prior to 1892) by a patent of

P. MAUSER (*q.v.*), and that it also had been claimed by G. V. FOSBERY'S (*q.v.*) Br. Pat. 24155/1896 as one method for rotating the cylinder of an automatic revolver. It must be assumed that Lines secured patent protection upon this well-known idea simply because of one feature proposed in his Specification, namely,

use of the cylinder races also as a cylinder-bolt; it is otherwise difficult to see that basic element of novelty required to permit grant of protection to the patentee.

LISLE, M. C. Myron Clark Lisle (of 284 Wilton Avenue, Toronto, County of York, Province of Ontario, Canada) was joint-applicant with H. M. KIPP (*q.v.*) for Br. Pat. 15753/1909; the "gas-seal' revolver covered by that patent is

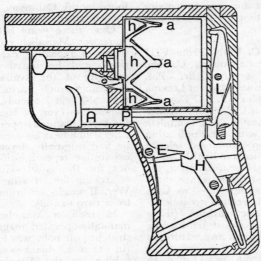

FIG. 50. *Lines's revolver.*
(After Br. Pat. 12367/1898.)

Pressure on the trigger moves trigger-bar "A" rearwards, and rotates the cylinder $\frac{1}{12}$th of a revolution, by engagement of a lump "p" thereon with one of the rotation-grooves "h". Part of the cylinder-rotation has occurred after the previous discharge, as the trigger moved forward again. Bolting of the cylinder, for firing, occurs when "p" reaches the notch "a", at the finish of its travel.

(The distinctive lock-mechanism was not claimed in this particular patent, but consisted of the bell-crank "E" (when engaged by the trigger-bar "A") depressing the hammer "H" against the mainspring, and then releasing it to strike the pivoted firing-pin "L".)

discussed, with other such arms, in Chapter IV.

The two applicants were assisted to secure their protection by Messrs. Haseltine, Lake & Co., of 7/8 Southampton Buildings, Chancery Lane, London, and 60 Wall Street, New York City. Mr. Lisle was described (in the Specification to Br. Pat. 15753/1909) as a "Gunsmith", and it is assumed that his was the major practical contribution to this revolver design.

MANNLICHER, C. VON. From VIII Floriangass 16, Vienna, Austria, Caecilie von Mannlicher secured Br. Pat. 3127/1904, with the assistance of London Patent Agent John P. O'Donnell, F.C.I.:PA, M.Inst.C.E., at Palace Chambers, Westminster. The Complete Specification filed with the application for this protection contained eleven claims for improvements to British Patent No. 26,270 of 28th November, 1902, the subjects of which F. VON MANNLICHER (*q.v.*) had earlier communicated to A. G. Bloxam, but which related to a long-recoil semi-automatic carbine (using bottle-necked high-velocity self-loading pistol cartridges) without any features of concern here.

F. VON MANNLICHER (*q.v.*) died in 1904, and it is believed that Caecilie (perhaps as his executor) secured Br. Pat. 3127/1904 in respect of improvements to Br. Pat. 26270/1902, already in hand at the time of his death; these improvements related to methods for easier assembly or disassembly of the weapon, to a safety-device for it, and to a rotary magazine which held open the breech-bolt when emptied. The carbine could be used as a single-loader, with this magazine.

Since Br. Pat. 3127/1904 was maintained until the First World War made further renewal impossible, it is assumed that some features of the patent were of commercial interest to the OESTER-REICHISCHE WAFFENFABRIKS-GESELLSCHAFT (*q.v.*) at Steyr, Austria, which company developed a number of the patents of F. VON MANNLICHER (*q.v.*).

MANNLICHER, F. VON. Ferdinand Mannlicher was born at Mainz (in Hesse) in 1848, but died at Vienna (as *Ritter* von Mannlicher) during 1904, and he spent most of his life in Austria, being both trained there as an engineer and later serving as Chief Engineer to the Austrian Northern Railway. He became associated with the OESTERREICHISCHE WAFFENFABRIKS-GESELLSCHAFT (*q.v.*), as a comparatively young man, and it was for his work upon magazine rifles developed by this Company, that Mannlicher was ennobled.

Over those years between 1875 and 1904, von Mannlicher designed literally scores of repeating carbines, pistols or rifles, and he tested or improved a majority of the available systems for operating such arms, whether by manual-, gas-, recoil-, or blow-back routes. However, he is best remembered for those manually-operated bolt-action rifles which bear his name, some of which he had originally developed for test in exhaustive repeating-rifle trials, carried out for the Austro-Hungarian armies (searching for an arm to replace their Werndl single-shot rifles) in the years from 1879 to 1885.

In 1886, a Mannlicher clip-loaded manually-operated magazine rifle, with straight-pull bolt, was formally adopted (in 11-mm. black-powder centre-fire calibre) as the Austrian service rifle. During 1888, however, the calibre of this weapon was reduced to 8 mm. (but still using black-powder), and it was finally developed (as the Model 1888/90) to use smokeless powders; the manufacturer, for all versions, was the OESTERREICHISCHE WAFFENFABRIKS - GESELLSCHAFT (*q.v.*). Later, von Mannlicher re-designed his straight-pull bolt (with an improved front-locking head), and the Austrian forces entered the First World War armed, in large measure, with 8-mm. Steyr-Mannlicher Model 1895 clip-loaded rifles and carbines, embodying the new bolt-head, although a number of earlier Mannlicher and other service arms were inevitably pressed into Austrian service also. It should be noted, too, that both the Netherlands (Model 1895) and Romania (Model 1893) adopted Mannlicher clip-loaded bolt-action rifles at about this time, and in 6·5 mm. calibres; unlike the Austrian weapons, however, these arms had conventional turning-bolts designed by von Mann-licher, and not the straight-pull action. In Italy, on the other hand, Mannlicher's clip-loading magazine system was merged with a native (Parraviccini-Carcano) bolt-action, to produce a Model 1891 service rifle in 6·5 mm. calibre.

During the 1880s there had been (see remarks upon the OESTERREICHISCHE WAFFENFABRIKS-GESELLSCHAFT) consider-able Continental interest in rotary magazines for bolt-action rifles, and von Mannlicher covered this field amongst his other activities, having secured his first relevant British Patent, as No. 2915 of 4th July, 1881 (by communication to the London Patent Agent C. D. Abel), well before years of concern here; this proposed a mechanically-operated revolving magazine in the butt-stock of a bolt-action rifle, but although it was examined by the Austrian army, it was neither adopted nor a commercially successful design.

Seven years later, von Mannlicher secured Br. Pat. 632/1888, which sur-vived into those years of concern here (see Table I) and protected a rotary magazine to be mounted immediately below the bolt-way and receiver of his rifles. Although not commercially success-ful, this magazine (which had a spring-operated star-wheel to carry cartridges) convinced the OESTERREICHISCHE WAF-FENFABRIKS-GESELLSCHAFT (q.v.) that such magazines warranted further develop-ment work, despite disappointing results to that date achieved in the market-place by over a decade of effort by the Com-pany, and by its employees (O. SCHOE-NAUER (q.v.) and J. Werndl) or consultants.

However, it was not until the Exposition Universelle de 1900 (in Paris) that any Mannlicher rifles embodying rotary magazines aroused serious attention. At the Exposition were exhibited the Mann-licher "Fusil Automatic Modele 1900" (a gas-operated semi-automatic weapon) and the Mannlicher-Schoenauer Model 1900 turning-bolt manually-operated rifle, both of which had rotary maga-zines; the first-mentioned arm was pro-tected in the United Kingdom by von Mannlicher's Br. Pat. 16734/1899, and the latter weapon (at least as to its rotary

magazine) by Br. Pat. 1567/1900, in the names of F. R. von Mannlicher and O. SCHOENAUER (q.v.). Oddly enough, the Specification to Br. Pat. 16734/1899 claimed only the mechanism and stock-construction of the "Fusil Automatic" (together with cartridge chargers suitable for loading it), and simply expressed a preference for the use of a rotary maga-zine, whilst conceding that other types of magazine were equally acceptable.

Mannlicher-Schoenauer rotary maga-zines exhibited at the Exposition Universelle de 1900 followed the claims of Br. Pat. 1567/1900 most faithfully, and the design is illustrated in Figures 51–53.

In Figure 51, the spindle "b" is sur-rounded by five cartridges (thumb-loaded through the top of the rifle receiver, from a charger) and contains a spiral spring "s", which is put into ten-sion by the act of stripping cartridges into the magazine; a spring lip "i" (on the right of the magazine) prevents "s" from ejecting all the cartridges, but permits forward movement of the bolt to carry the topmost round off into the breech. After discharge, the bolt is drawn back to extract and eject the empty case, where-upon "s" and "b" together rotate another cartridge to the top. Lip "i" has an overrider "p", which can be pressed to move "i" aside and eject all the cart-ridges from the magazine, if desired.

Figure 52 is a view of the magazine, looking rearwards, with five cartridges in it and, although the Figure cannot make this clear, it should be noted that the cartridges were only supported at front and rear, by suitable shaping of the magazine casing; elaborate carriers were unnecessary.

The whole magazine was removable from the rifle, as a unit; this was accom-plished in the manner shown in Plate 53, where the tray "p" carrying the maga-zine components had pivoted to the bottom of it a rotating plate "v", which engaged suitable recesses "x" and "y" undercut at front and rear of the maga-zine well in the rifle. To remove the magazine, it was only necessary to rotate "v" (after releasing a retainer-button "t") and pull the magazine unit down-wards out of the rifle.

It is noticeable (in studying the

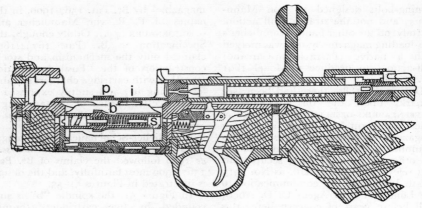

FIG. 51. *The Mannlicher-Schoenauer rifle magazine.*
(After Br. Pat. 1567/1900.)

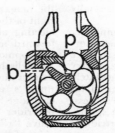

FIG. 52. *Front view of Mannlicher-Schoenauer magazine.*
(After Br. Pat. 1567/1900.)

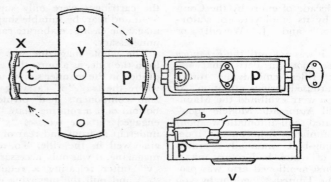

FIG. 53. *Removal of Mannlicher-Schoenauer magazine.*
(After Br. Pat. 1567/1900.)

Specification to Br. Pat. 1567/1900) that London Patent Agents Abel & Imray, who advised both applicants, drafted the claims of the relevant patent with great care. In fact, the claims relate solely to (i) constructing the breech casing with arc-shaped hollows to support tips and heads of the cartridges, (ii) forming the revolving carrier with a helical spring ("s" in Fig. 51) which serves as both an axis and a rotator, and (iii) the removable tray ("P" in Fig. 53) of the magazine.

O. SCHOENAUER (q.v.) and the OESTER-REICHISCHE WAFFENFABRIKS-GESELLSCHAFT (q.v.) developed this Model 1900 Mannlicher magazine with great commercial success. Having already interested the Greek government in purchasing 8-mm. straight-pull clip-loading Austrian Model 1895 service rifles and carbines, the Austrian firm ultimately secured adoption by the Greek Army of Model 03 and 03/14 rifles in 6·5 mm. calibre. These arms embodied Mannlicher charger-loading and turning-bolt features along with the Mannlicher-Schoenauer rotary magazine covered by Br. Pat. 1567/1900 (or its foreign equivalents), and were matched by a series of fine Mannlicher-Schoenauer sporting rifles (in various centre-fire calibres, but weighing between 7½ and 7¾ lb.) which were retailed as the Model 1903 (6·5-mm. or ·256-in. calibre); Model 1905 (8-mm. or ·315-in. calibre); Model 1905 (9-mm. or ·355-in. calibre); and Model 1910 (9·5-mm. or ·375-in. calibre). In later years, versions using the 7·62-mm.; ·30–06; 7-mm.; and 8-mm. high-velocity cartridges were added to this range.

F. von Mannlicher's last British Patent (secured from Getreidemarkt 10, Vienna) was 5169/1901, and the patentee was again assisted by the London Patent Agents Abel & Imray, of Southampton Buildings, Chancery Lane. In the five claims of this patent, von Mannlicher proposed certain improvements to rotary magazines for his rifles (notably in the use of a forward-hinged bottom-plate or tray for the magazine) and also a catch on the receiver which prevented both gravity-closing of the bolt whilst loading, and closure of the bolt if this had been accidentally assembled in the rifle without its loose head. It is believed that some of these improvements were used by the OESTERREICHISCHE WAFFENFABRIKS-GESELLSCHAFT (q.v.) in Mannlicher-Schoenauer sporting rifles made prior to 1914, but arms embodying the hinged magazine tray seem less common today, than those with magazines of the pattern shown in Figure 53.

In concluding these remarks upon F. von Mannlicher, the reader's attention is drawn to that patent mentioned against C. VON MANNLICHER (q.v.), which was probably under development at the time of F. von Mannlicher's death, in 1904.

DE MARAIS, V. Victor de Marais was joint-applicant with G. E. GARDNER (q.v.) for Br. Pat. 18486/1912; he was assisted to secure that protection by London Patent Agents J. S. Withers & Spooner (of 323 High Holborn), and the invention protected is discussed in remarks upon his fellow-applicant.

MARSHALL, J. A. G. James Aubrey Garth Marshall secured Br. Pat. 16425/1910, under guidance from London Patent Agent John Gray, at 83 Cannon Street. In the Specification to this patent, Marshall described himself as "Rifle Expert to the Maxim Silencer Co., Ltd., of 72 Victoria Street, London, S.W.", and put forward three claims of novelty for the wrist support shown in Figure 54. No specimen arm with Marshall's improvement is known to this writer.

MARTIN, F. Frederick Martin (of 43 Ossian Road, Stroud Green, Middlesex) was joint-applicant with R. C. ROMANEL (q.v.) and A. H. WILLIAMS (q.v.) for Br. Pats. 9998/1887 and 6994/1888. In both Specifications Martin is described simply as a "Gentleman", and it is believed that his contribution to the rifle design covered by these patents (which is discussed in remarks upon R. C. ROMANEL; q.v.) may have been largely financial.

MAUSER, P. P. Peter Paul Mauser was born at Oberndorf, in Wurttemberg, on 27th June, 1838, as one of the numerous children of a workman employed at the Royal Wurttemberg Arms Factory; the boy began working at that Factory in

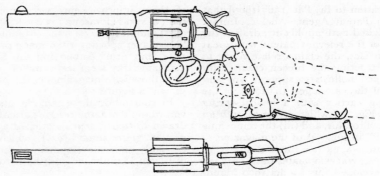

FIG. 54. *Marshall's wrist-support.*
(After Br. Pat. 16425/1910.)

1852, and had (with the assistance of Wilhelm Mauser, his brother) developed a reasonably sound improvement to the Dreyse bolt-action Prussian service needle-rifle, by 1865. The Mauser brothers moved to Liège, in an attempt to develop this invention commercially, and although they were unsuccessful in that attempt, the Prussian government were sufficiently impressed to bring both brothers back to Oberndorf, and (in 1871) to adopt a single-shot 11-mm. centre-fire bolt-action rifle designed by Peter Paul Mauser.

In 1873, the brothers somehow financed and commissioned their own rifle-manufactory at Oberndorf, and when this burned down, they not only re-equipped it, but also both purchased the Royal Wurttemberg Arms Factory and secured a State order for 100,000 Model 1871 rifles. By that time, a corporation had been formed (as Gebruder Mauser & Co.) which became increasingly successful as the years passed; until Wilhelm Mauser's death (in 1882), the brothers worked as a team, with Peter Paul designing the weapons and Wilhelm handling contract terms with customers. After 1882, Peter Paul headed the business alone, and it came to monopolize (by its own manufacture or through the efforts of licensees working under Mauser's patents) the supply of service rifles to the Imperial German armies and those of many of its allies. Around 1900, the firm became the Waffenfabrik Mauser (later Mauser Werke A-G) and it established

a remarkable commercial liaison with the OESTERREICHISCHE WAFFENFABRIKS-GESELLSCHAFT (*q.v.*) at Steyr, and the Fabrique National d'Armes de Guerre S.A., at Herstal, Belgium, to control both quality and interchangeability of parts for Mauser rifles made in any of the three plants.

An indefatigable patentee, Peter Paul Mauser designed both turning-bolt and semi-automatic rifles, along with several self-loading pistols, and some Mauser weapons (as, for example, the 7·63-mm. Military Model self-loading pistol or the 7·92-mm. *Gew.* and *Kar.* 98 turning-bolt long-arms) became known and adopted all over the world. However, Peter Paul so rarely ventured into the design-field of concern here that on his death, in May, 1914, it would have been fair to recall only one of his many patents as in point.

During 1878, Mauser had communicated Br. Pat. 922/1878 to the London Patent Agent J. H. JOHNSON (*q.v.*) which survived into our period (see Table I) and protected design-features used in two highly distinctive Mauser revolvers. Both of these arms were six-chambered single-action weapons (one a hinged-frame self-ejecting pistol, the other solid-framed) with a lock- and cylinder-rotation system common to both.

Mauser's lock-mechanism used a coiled mainspring, lying horizontally fore-and-aft within the frame, and the cylinder was rotated (*via* zigzag races cut around the circumference of the cylinder) by a hammer-operated stud sliding to-and-fro in a frame-slot beneath the cylinder, and engaging these races.

The basic idea of rotating a revolver-cylinder by such means was old at the date of Mauser's patent, for an American named Otis W. Whittier had secured U.S. Patent No. 216 of 30th May, 1837, for such a system, in the year before Mauser was born, and later U.S. Patents of E. K. Root (No. 13999 of 25th December, 1855) and W. H. Elliott (No. 28,461 of 29th May, 1860) had embroidered upon the same theme. Indeed (see remarks upon L. ARMANNI, G. V. FOSBERY, G. VAN DER HAEGHEN and A. LINES) variations upon the system remained patentable even after the grant of Mauser's Br. Pat. 922/1878, and it was again used by the Union Arms Co. (of Toledo, Ohio, U.S.A.), when manufacturing a recoil-operated "automatic revolver" under C. F. Lefever's U.S. Patent No. 944448 of 28th December, 1909. It is difficult to see how that degree of novelty essential to the securing of patent protection was ever established to the satisfaction of officers examining patent applications for either Mauser's or the later "zigzag" cylinder-rotation systems mentioned above, but it is noticeable (although this point was not invariably made in the Specifications) that the *patterns* of these various patented cylinder-races were rarely identical. It is possible, therefore, that although the basic idea was unpatentable after the 1860s, particular applications for or forms of cylinder-race could be claimed as novel.

As to the revolvers actually produced under Peter Paul Mauser's patents of 1878, specimens are rare; it is clear that no arms were made under the British patent, and only a small quantity under the equivalent German protection. Even in this latter case (having regard to the length of time for which the British patent was maintained, see Table I) it is difficult to establish that date at which the surviving arms were made.

A study of available serial-numbers suggests that something over 3,000 rifles and revolvers were produced at Oberndorf, with hinged-frame pistols predominating. The solid-framed rifle (with 17½-in. barrel) is rare, has normally a low serial-number, and can be assumed to have been made prior to 1888; the revolvers were all six-shot arms, normally in special 7·6-mm. centre-fire calibre (8 inches overall, with 3½-in. barrels) or 9-mm. centre-fire calibre (11 inches overall, with 5¼-in. barrels), although a few larger arms were made to chamber 10·6-mm. Mauser cartridges.

McLEAN, S. N. Samuel Neal McLean secured Br. Pat. 6683/1892, without the assistance of any Patent Agents; in the Specification to his patent, McLean gave his address as at 221 West Washington Street, Washington, Iowa, and mentioned that the magazine firearm for which this British protection had been secured was already the subject of United States Patent Applications, Cases 384944 and 409191.

S. N. McLean (who is sometimes confused with an earlier inventor of repeating firearms, Doctor James H. McLean) became interested in the design and improvement of manually-operated repeating magazine firearms as quite a young man, but transferred his attention to gas-operated self-loading or automatic arms around 1898. He formed the McLean Ordnance and Arms Co. (of Cleveland, Ohio) during 1903, and achieved U.S. Army tests of a 37-mm. gas-operated automatic cannon in 1904, although this weapon was not adopted.

Undismayed, McLean reorganized his company, and developed (with Lieut.-Col. O. M. Lissak, U.S.A.) a ·30-calibre gas-operated machine-gun, weighing about 19 lb., for which he had great hopes. When these expectations were not realized, McLean sold his relevant U.S. Patents to the Automatic Arms Co., of Buffalo, N.Y., and turned his attention to other matters. Commander Chinn records that Colonel I. N. Lewis, U.S.A., and the Automatic Arms Co., persevered with McLean's design and developed it (between 1911 and 1913) into the world-famous Lewis light machine-gun.

The subjects of S. N. McLean's Br. Pat. 6683/1892 related (as might be expected) to his first field of interest, being concerned with twenty-seven detailed claims for a manually-operated magazine firearm, of which a pistol-version (see Fig. 55) was illustrated in the Specification. In this arm, cartridges were held in a bundle of parallel tubes beneath the barrel, and fed rearwards (by a coiled spring in each tube) to a carrier which lifted the round for chambering by the breech-bolt, and discharge

separate firms of British Patent Agents; the Provisional Specification (see Appendix I) was filed by the London firm of Herbert & Co., at 18 Buckingham Street, Strand, whilst the Complete Specification was filed by a Manchester firm, F. Bosshardt & Co., of No. 4, Corporation Street.

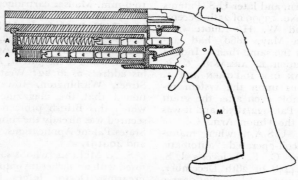

FIG. 55. *McLean's magazine pistol.*
(After Br. Pat. 6683/1892.)

The arm is discharged by a conventional hammer "H" and trigger "T", but the cycle is effected by squeezing the lever "M", in front of the butt. Cartridges "c" are carried in tubes "A" (rotatably mounted below the barrel) and are successively raised into alignment with the barrel and chambered by a sliding breech-block. As each tube "A" is emptied, a projection on the magazine-follower is struck by the vertically-sliding cartridge carrier, and a fresh tube "A" is thus rotated into alignment with that carrier.

by the hammer. When a tube was empty, this upward motion of the carrier caused the whole magazine-bundle to rotate and to bring a fresh tube of cartridges into alignment for use. The entire loading-, firing- and ejection-cycle was operated by squeezing the front butt-strap rearwards. Specimen arms are extremely rare.

MOMNIE, J. T. Joseph Tanislaus Momnie (of 228 Main Street, City of Chicopee, County of Hampden, Massachusetts, U.S.A., was joint-applicant with T. MONTMENY (*q.v.*) for Br. Pat. 1926/1910; the magazine rifle protected by this patent is briefly described in remarks upon the latter applicant.

MONNERAT, P. Pierre Monnerat (of Firming, Loire, France) secured Br. Pat. 5552/1891, with assistance from two

Br. Pat. 5552/1891 was for yet another combination firearm, as to which see also remarks upon R. G. GORDON-SMITH; B. KREITH; D. T. LAING; E. PAUL; and B. REYES. Protection was claimed for "a fire sword, characterized through the combination of any kind of sword with a revolver; the mechanism of the said revolver being enclosed in the handle of the sword . . ." Monnerat's drawing is shown in Figure 56, and may be contrasted with the revolver-sword of B. REYES (*q.v.*).

MONTMENY, T. Theodore Montmeny (of 52 Main Street, City of Chicopee, County of Hampden, Massachusetts, U.S.A.) was joint-applicant with J. T. MOMNIE (*q.v.*) for Br. Pat. 1926/1910. The two applicants were assisted by London Patent Agents Wheatley &

Mackenzie (of 40 Chancery Lane), and Montmeny was described in the Specification as a "Mechanic".

The four claims of Br. Pat. 1926/1910 related to a lever-operated concealed-hammer magazine rifle, with a hinged barrel and a revolving magazine; the latter was loaded from the front, after tipping down the barrel, and a bolt forced cartridges forward out of the magazine, and into the barrel for firing. The bolt operation and the magazine rotation were accomplished *via* a rack on the under-lever, and discharge (by a pin sliding longitudinally with the bolt)

on behalf of employers, and only the location of a signed specimen arm can really settle that question.

MORRIS, R. It would be inconceivable to compile this list of patentees without reference to Richard Morris, whose aiming-tubes and small-bore adaptors (in ·22 rim-fire and ·297/·230 or ·297/·250 centre-fire calibres) were used throughout the period, in hundreds of rifles, shot-guns, revolvers and cannon. In fact, however, Morris (unlike H. W. & J. F. LATHAM; *q.v.*) secured no British patent protection for any device claimed for use

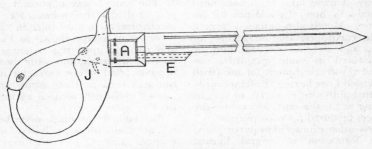

FIG. 56. *Monnerat's fire-sword.*
(After Br. Pat. 555/1891.)

The cylinder "A" of the revolver has its axis above that of the barrel "E". The trigger "J" is concealed within the sword-guard.

was accomplished by a hammer with self-cocking lock-mechanism.

The Specification drawings show a neat sturdy weapon, which cannot be dismissed as useless (albeit the length of magazine argues that very short cartridges were to be used in such rifles), but the purpose for such a design remains difficult to suggest, other than as a gallery rifle.

Chicopee (where both Montmeny and Momnie were apparently based) and Chicopee Falls were both small Massachusetts towns, but a number of famous American arms manufacturers were located in or near them at the relevant time. These two patentees (who do not appear again as applicants for any British patent protection in respect of firearms) may therefore have been developing an idea of their own, or acting

exclusively in revolving arms, and appear here only in relation to one of the numerous patents which he secured between 1880 and 1891.

Br. Pat. 1773/1881 was secured from an address at Cleopatra Grove, Lewisham (or Blackheath), and without acknowledged assistance from any Patent Agent. The Specification described Morris's invention as relating to "Improvements in the Method and Apparatus for Controlling the Accuracy of Sighting and Aim in Rifle Drill or Practice", and it proposed the use (in heavy-calibre service rifles) of removable small-calibre rim- or centre-fire barrels, with their own attached breech and extractor; these barrels were to be slipped into the service rifle barrel, and secured in position by a nut on the muzzle which was turned down onto a rimmed sleeve (which also

R

protected the rifling of the full-bore barrel from damage) until the adaptor was held rigidly in position between the muzzle-nut at one end, and the chamber of the rifle at the other. The normal extractor-mechanism of the service rifle (then a Martini-Henry single-shot tilting-block arm) operated the extractor of the converter, and the small-calibre cartridge was fired by the original firing-pin.

The patentee sought to improve his basic design, in a number of ways, over the years following 1881, but the basis of all Morris single-shot converters used in revolvers was laid down by the Specification to Br. Pat. 1773/1881, and the ingenuity of these later inventions need not detain us here. In addition to his converters, Morris also patented targets, reusable cartridges, rifle magazines or actions, and sighting devices, and he manufactured in some quantities unpatented revolver-cylinders for use (with his patented liner barrels) in temporarily converting full-bore revolvers to use, as repeating arms, the ·297/·230 centre-fire cartridges favoured for such purpose.

Morris either promoted or participated in the formation of several limited liability companies, which manufactured or sold his inventions, and these traded as The Morris Tube Co., Ltd. (from about 1883). The Morris Tube Ammunition and Safety Range Co., Ltd. (from 1888), or The Morris Aiming Tube & Ammunition Co. Ltd. (from 1900), through those years of concern here. Morris himself ceased any traceable activity as a patentee of improvements to firearms in 1891, but Major Dowell has recorded that although (in 1907) the British War Office began the use of arms permanently constructed to use small-calibre cartridges, in place of Morris's removable adaptors, yet a fourth company was trading in 1908 (as The Morris Tube & Rifle Clubs Accessories Co., Ltd.), in witness to the demand for this patentee's inventions.

Morris, of course, never had this field to himself, and faced competition from The Wilkinson Sword Co., Ltd. (see H. W. & J. F. LATHAM or J. T. MUSGRAVE), from THE WEBLEY & SCOTT REVOLVER AND ARMS CO., LTD. (q.v.) who manufactured unpatented single-shot adaptors for revolvers, in the early 1900s, and from other manufacturers (whose devices are strictly outside the scope of these pages) like the Belgian, H. PIEPER (q.v.), and a Briton, Staff Sergeant M. Mullineux, who was (in the years between 1892 and 1902) as active a patentee as Morris himself had earlier been.

DE MOUNCIE, A. T. or "Baron Thornton" Amedée Thornton de Mouncie (otherwise known as "Baron Thornton") had secured Br. Pat. 3206/1876 without assistance from a Patent Agent and his protection had survived into years of concern here, as shown in Table I. The patent was important (since it protected the design-basis for a lock-mechanism used, until 1892, in "Enfield" revolvers of a type shown in Plate 19), and remarks upon this patentee should be read in association with those upon O. JONES (q.v.), whose extractor mechanism was used in these arms, and who himself eventually secured an interest in Br. Pat. 3206/1876.

Although de Mouncie described himself, at various times, as "Baron" (of Paris, France, and Queen Victoria Street, London) or "Gentleman" (of Hill Street, Rutland Gate, London), his true background remains obscure, save that he was almost certainly a British subject and seems to have had connections with the Belgian gun-trade.

In October 1877, he had approached the British War Office for official reaction to six sample revolvers earlier submitted for test (on de Mouncie's behalf) by Walter Scott, a Birmingham gun-maker; these arms were six-chambered solid-framed centre-fire arms, with a four-component double-action lock-mechanism covered by the claims of de Mouncie's Br. Pat. 3706/1876. The Royal Small-Arms Factory, Enfield (to which these weapons had been passed for study) had found their design to be interesting, but their workmanship substandard, and requiring rectification, if tests were to be continued.

By means still unknown, de Mouncie had now become associated in this venture with Michael Kaufmann (a designer later associated with P. WEBLEY & SON (q.v.), during the 1880s), and in the course of negotiations for rectifying de Mouncie's sample arms, the Factory most unwisely revealed to this pair that the addition of a fifth lock-component did greatly improve the "pull-off" of the lock-mechanism, as originally submitted. De Mouncie had then first attempted to patent such an improvement as part of his Br. Pat. 2161 of 30th May, 1878, but abandoned that application, assigned his Br. Pat. 3206/1876 to Michael Kaufmann on 5th June, 1878 (overlooking, it would be charitable to believe, that he had already assigned one quarter-share in it to a Mr. Thomas Edwards), and vanished from the negotiations altogether.

Kaufmann had thereafter signed his letters to the War Office as "Proprietor of Thornton's Patent For Revolvers", and had shortly submitted an improved solid-framed revolver for test. This arm had embodied the fifth lock-component incautiously suggested by the Royal Small-Arms Factory, and Kaufmann had then (jointly with a Julien Warnant) also patented this new lock-mechanism, as British Patent No. 5031 of 9th December, 1878, for improvements to de Mouncie's patent.

In due course, the British War Office had adopted the hinged-frame self-extracting "Enfield" revolver shown in Plate 19, which embodied the extractor-system of O. JONES (q.v.) and also a five-component double-action lock-mechanism (see Fig. 34) strictly covered by the claims of those Br. Pats. 3206/1876 and 5031/1878 then controlled by Kaufmann, and it had been during the negotiation of Crown awards for such use that the rather unedifying scope of de Mouncie's original operations had been revealed.

It was certainly established, to the satisfaction of those officers charged with considering the merits of various claims for these awards, that the lock-mechanism used in "Enfield" revolvers was one specifically claimed by Michael Kaufmann and Julien Warnant's Br. Pat. 5031/1878, that this patent itself was one of stated improvement to de Mouncie's Br. Pat. 3206/1876 (now controlled by Kaufmann and O. JONES; q.v.), and that a *prima facie* case accordingly existed for Crown payment to the holders of these patents.

However, it also became clear, as inquiries progressed, that neither of these two patents had actually been secured by the true inventor of those improvements claimed in them.

The original four-component lock-mechanism claimed by de Mouncie's Br. Pat. 3706/1876 had actually been invented by Jean Warnant, a well-known arms-maker at Hognée, in Belgium, who had patented the design in Belgium on 27th November, 1875. He had then empowered de Mouncie to seek a British patent for that design, and on a profit-sharing basis, but the Baron had stolen any U.K. rights by filing application for Br. Pat. 3206/1876 in his own name only.

The case was no better in regard to Kaufmann and Julien Warnant (whose relationship to Jean Warnant remains to be established), with their Br. Pat. 5031/1878 for the five-component lock-mechanism actually used in the "Enfield" revolvers, for these patentees had simply adopted the idea of a fifth lock-component (as suggested to Kaufmann and de Mouncie, by Mr. Thomas Perry, General Manager of the R.S.A.F., in February, 1878), established that it did improve the original Jean Warnant design, and secured the above-mentioned Br. Pat. 5031/1878 for a lock-mechanism embodying it.

As indicated in earlier remarks upon O. JONES (q.v.), the task of these examining officers was unenviable, since some case could be argued (if any *ex gratia* Crown payment was to be made at all) for the legal claims of Kaufmann and O. JONES (q.v.), as holders of the basic Br. Pat. 3206/1876 of de Mouncie, or for the moral claims of Jean Warnant as a true inventor, and it could not be denied that another British patent (Kaufmann and Julien Warnant's Br. Pat. 5031/1878) covered the "Enfield" revolver lock-mechanism actually in use.

To their real credit, those officers charged with settlement of this confusion had eventually arrived at a reasonable compromise, by first awarding £650 "to the owners of Thornton's Patent" (i.e. the de Mouncie Br. Pat. 3206/1876), which description was specifically to include Jean Warnant for the purposes of that award, and then by denying altogether the payment of any award to the holders of Br. Pat. 5031/1878, namely, Michael Kaufmann and Julien Warnant, in respect of Crown operations in the field of that patent.

At that time, perhaps, the needs of commerce trod harder upon the heels of God and Country than they do today (so much harder indeed, to quote the late Thorne Smith, as occasionally to have left both God and Country a trifle winded), and therefore contemporary comment upon the conduct of those who had filched Jean Warnant's design does not appear to have survived. Certainly, the relevant War Office minutes and memoranda neither recorded views upon that conduct, nor stated officially that proportion of the Br. Pat. 3206/1876 award which should go to Jean Warnant. Unofficially, however, War Office deliberations had indicated that £500 seemed the latter's due, and it would be interesting to know how much he did eventually agree to accept from Kaufmann and Jones (the owners of Br. Pat. 3206/1876) as his share, when payment of the award was made, in December 1882.

As to "Baron Thornton", it seems fair to assume that (his overheads being probably light) he secured a better return on his initial investment, in sample arms and the filing fees for Br. Pat. 3206/1876, than was the case for those who purchased that protection from him.

MUND, A. August Mund, of 49 Auf den Häfen, Bremen, Germany secured Br. Pat. 3154/1908 with the assistance of London Patent Agent J. Hans, of 345 St. John Street, E.C.; Mund described himself (in his Specification) simply as a "Merchant".

Two claims of novelty were stated for an electrically-operated alarm-device, which successively discharged the cartridges in a spring-rotated drum, when the door or window to which it was connected was opened.

MUSGRAVE, J. T. John Tolhurst Musgrave secured Br. Pat. 24,502/1893 without assistance from a Patent Agent, and was described in the Specification as

an "Engineer"; his stated address was at 27 Pall Mall, London, where The Wilkinson Sword Co., Ltd. was established.

Musgrave had joined the firm of Wilkinson & Son in 1880, and when, in 1887 (see remarks upon J. F. LATHAM), that firm had become The Wilkinson Sword Co., Ltd., Musgrave was the new limited liability company's first Secretary; he was elected to the Board of Directors around 1910, and served on that Board for many years after those of concern here. In addition to Br. Pat. 24502/1893, he also held British Patent No. 22836 of 24th November, 1894 (jointly with J. F. LATHAM; q.v.) for a sub-calibre cartridge adaptor outside the scope of these pages, and was inventor of the "Musgrave Patent Sword Knot".

Musgrave's Br. Pat. 24502/1893 was for an ingenious improvement to the ejector-mechanisms of miniature ammunition adaptors for revolvers, of the type described in earlier remarks upon J. F. LATHAM (q.v.). As may be seen from Figure 57, the adaptor tube "b" had an ejector "c" which was provided with a small flat spring "d" on its underside. When the revolver was opening, the main (or original) ejector "e" of the revolver withdrew "c" to eject the miniature cartridge-case, whereupon "d" flipped down behind "e". Accordingly, when "e" snapped back into the revolver cylinder, in the normal fashion, "c" was also carried back into "b", by the bearing of "e" against "d".

NAGANT, L. Léon Nagant secured Br. Pat. 14010/1894 with the assistance of London Patent Agents, Gedge & Feeny, of 60 Queen Victoria Street, E.C.; in the Specification, Nagant was described as a "Manufacturer of Firearms" (at 49 Quai de l'Ourthe, Liège, Belgium), and his patent related to a famous "gas-seal" revolver which needs no attention here, since it is described (with other such arms) in Chapter IV.

Léon Nagant was related to the Belgian gun-maker Emile Nagant, who had (from 41 Quai de l'Ourthe) earlier secured Br. Pat. No. 4310 of 22nd October, 1879, for certain constructional and rod-ejecting improvements to solid-framed breech-loading revolvers, being features used both in those Belgian service revolvers, Models 1878, 1878/86 and 1883 described in Chapter II, and in similar Nagant models adopted by the armies of other countries. Emile was probably (with Colonel Sergei Mosin, of the Russian Imperial Army) the designer of the Nagant-Mosin 7·62-mm. bolt-action "pattern 1891" magazine rifle

it is significant upon the position of the Nagant house in Belgium's small-arms industry, that Leleu noticed the Fabrique d'Armes Léon Nagant amongst a bare handful of Liège small-arms manu-facturers (out of more than 130 firms then actually in business), when commenting upon the Belgian exhibitors at the *Paris Exposition Universelle* of 1900, namely:

Auguste Francotte et Cie. Established

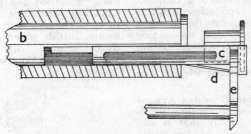

FIG. 57. *Musgrave's ejector.*
(After Br. Pat. 24502/1893.)

with which many Russian units were armed at the outbreak of the First World War, but his relationship to Léon remains to be established, as does his contribution to later models of Nagant revolver (described in Chapter II) like the Norwegian Model 1893 and Swedish Model 1887 service arms.

Upon the latter point, at any rate, Leleu appears to leave little room for doubt, by listing (in his remarks upon the Fabrique d'Armes Léon Nagant exhibits at the *Paris Exposition Universelle* of 1900) no less than eight countries, as mentioned in Chapter II, which were equipped with Nagant service revolvers of con-ventional type, in addition to the "gas-seal" weapon covered by Br. Pat. 14010/1894 and adopted by the Russians. Indeed, the firm was versatile, for Leleu credited it with manufacture of surveying instruments, machine tools and motor cars, in addition to small-arms, and it later became (around 1910) the Fabrique d'Armes et Automobiles Nagant Frères.

This type of diversification was by no means unusual amongst small-arms manufacturers of the period immediately prior to 1914, as earlier remarks upon J. G. ACCLES (*q.v.*) will have shown, but

in 1810, this was an important Liège firm, with an annual production-capacity in the order of 35,000 small-arms. A considerable range of qualities was offered in Francotte catalogues of the day, but (within that range) the firm concentrated mainly upon the manu-facture of shot-guns, Francotte-Martini rifles, and revolvers, to the virtual exclusion of other types of small-arm. The "Nimrod Gun Manufactory" was also highly mechanized by Belgian stand-ards of the time, and holder of numerous diplomas and medals, including a Grand Prix at the earlier Brussels Exhibition, of 1897; internal examination of many revolvers bearing the names of British and Continental retailers, in cheaper grades, will often reveal the modest "AF" trade-mark of this firm, and it must have been something of a thorn in the flesh to the house of Nagant.

Fabrique Nationale d'Armes d'Hers-tal. This firm is now better known as the Fabrique Nationale d'Armes de Guerre S.A., and was first established (in 1866) as the "société des fabricants d'armes de guerres réunis" at Liège. In 1889 it was transformed into a "Société Anonyme" having (with the financial participation of most of the principal Belgian gun-makers, of a number of German firms, and of the Belgian government) a capital of 11,000,000 francs. A factory was then established at Herstal (see remarks upon M. DOZIN) under the direction of Monsieur H. Frenay, and manufacture of Mauser rifles, for the Belgian government, began in October 1891. This firm was never apparently concerned in the manufacture of revolvers, but presented a different menace to Nagant (and other revolver-makers) by engaging in the licensed manufacture of competing self-loading pistols, under the patents of an American, John M. Browning.

S. A. des Établissement Pieper. See H. PIEPER.

S.A. pour la Fabrication des Armes à Buda-Pesth. Leleu gave little space to this firm, remarking only that it was under the directorship of M. Epperlein, and that (amongst other arms) it exhibited at the 1900 *Exposition* Gasser revolvers of an unidentified type. Leleu had a poor opinion of the Austrian M.1898 revolver shown in Plate 12, and this arm (which was principally manu-factured by Rast and Gasser, of Austria) may have been that shown by this firm.

MM. Francon and Gorget. About these exhibitors, Leleu remarked only that Francon showed a wide range of revolvers (including the French Mlle 1892 service revolver shown in Plate 14), and that a Browning self-loading pistol was included on his stand.

Gorget apparently showed only the old French single-action pin-fire naval revol-ver, as designed by Eugene Lefaucheux in 1854. The reason for such an exhibit in the 1900 *Exposition* escapes this writer, but it may simply have recorded past manufacturing glories by the house of Gorget. It is noteworthy that the *Musée Retrospectif de la Classe 51 à l'Exposition Universelle Internationale de 1900 à Paris* listed similar by-gones on the stand of the *Musée Municipal* of Saint Étienne, where the exhibits included a "Carbine-Revol-ver, Système Javelle; a Revolver, barillet horizontal; a Revolver Perwel, St. Étienne; a Revolver Devisme, Paris; and a Revolver Lefaucheux". Clearly, not all

of the exhibitors had their eyes fixed upon the twentieth century.

NEWTON, H. E. Henry Edward New-ton was a Civil Engineer, and member of a well-known family of London Patent Agents practising (at the time in point here) from No. 6 Breams Buildings, Chancery Lane; to him THE COLT'S PATENT FIRE ARMS MANUFACTURING CO. (INC.) communicated the subjects of Br. Pats. 7200/1889 and 7201/1889, as that Company had done in years prior to those of concern here, so that he might secure British patent protection upon these designs, with minimal incon-venience to the Company.

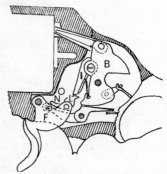

FIG. 58. *Newton's (Colt) lock-mechanism.* (After Br. Pat. 7201/1889.)

Something has been said earlier (see Fig. 37) upon the revolver-charger pro-tected by Br. Pat. 7200/1889, and one of the two self-cocking revolver lock-mechanisms claimed in Br. Pat. 7201/1889 is shown in Figure 58. Here the trigger "F" has a pivoted member "L" which bears against the strut or hammer-catch "I" to turn back the hammer "B" when the trigger is pulled. At full-cock, the tail "N" of "L" strikes the frame at "O" (causing a hesitation in the trigger-pull to warn the firer that discharge is imminent) and disengages "L" from the strut, so that the hammer may fall.

NOLCKEN, A. G. Axel Gustavus, Baron Nolcken (of Moisekatz, per Werro, Livonia, Russia) secured Br. Pat.

120/1893 with the assistance of London Patent Agents Abel & Imray, of 28 Southampton Buildings, Chancery Lane.

The Specification drawings illustrated a lever-action rifle, quite similar in appearance to the Savage rifle shown in Plate 35, but claim of novelty was laid only to three features of this design, namely, the laterally-fed revolving sheet-steel magazine (which retained fired cartridge cases), the rise-and-fall breech-block (in combination with a safety-lock automatically controlled by the block), and the automatic safety-lock itself, which bolted the firing-pin in the cocked position.

Unusually, the Baron claimed his improvements as applicable to double-barrelled arms which ". . . would offer the great advantage of being able first to fire two shots almost simultaneously in the usual manner, and then two or three more separate shots from the left-hand barrel".

OESTERREICHISCHE WAFFEN-FABRIKS-GESELLSCHAFT. Although the name of the Oesterreichische Waffen-fabriks-Gesellschaft ("OWG" hereafter) appears in this listing only by virtue of Br. Pat. 1272/1878, which was communicated by the Company to A. M. CLARK (*q.v.*) and survived into the years of concern here (see Table I), it would be quite impossible to limit remarks upon this famous arms manufacturer to a bare summary of improvements claimed in that patent. The OWG not only fostered European interest over the use of revolving magazines in long-arms for a decade before those years of concern here, but also developed all relevant patents of F. VON MANNLICHER (*q.v.*), O. SCHOENAUER (*q.v.*), J. SCHULHOF (*q.v.*) and J. Werndl, relating to such devices, over most of the quarter-century with which we are concerned. It is probable that Br. Pat. 7989/1885 (see the AUSTRIAN SMALL-ARMS MANUFACTURING CO.) was actually communicated to G. E. VAUGHAN (*q.v.*) by the OWG, and (see Plate 28) although better-known in the hand-gun field for those self-loading pistols that it manufactured, the OWG clearly did not ignore the potentialities of "gas-seal" revolvers, n its search for saleable products.

It should not, of course, be inferred from these remarks that the OWG enjoyed any sort of European monopoly either of interest or in the manufacture of long-arms embodying a revolving cartridge-feed, for (as was the case in America; see remarks upon DURST, M. H.) other Continental manufacturers and designers were also concerned. Thus Georg Koch (in 1891) specifically noticed the *Revolvergewehre* of von Langer (at Glogau), Goldammer (of Rupfermuhle) and H. PIEPER (*q.v.*), with those of von Raestner (of Magdeburg) or von Dreyse (of Sommerda), and a *Jagdmitrailleuse* of the *Grafen* Goronini, at Gorz; listed too, in these pages, will be found the inventions of J. COURRIER, H. DANNER, O. H. J. KRAG, J. LAUBER, A. G. NOLCKEN, P. A. PHILLIPPIDES, C. RICCI, G. ROTH & C. KRNKA, J. A. SCHWARZ & T. A. FIDJELAND, H. SUNNGÄRD and T. THORSEN to indicate a wider European interest in this field than one confined to the OWG, but the lead provided by that company remains manifest in literature of the period.

As one example of this fact, Ippolito Viglezzi wrote (in 1890) upon both past and then existent bolt-action service rifles, and noticed no less than eight such arms embodying rotary magazines; for Austria, he named the Spitalsky (Models 1879 and 1884); the Spitalsky-Kromar (Model 1882); the Mannlicher, second system (Model 1880–81), with rotating tubular magazines; the "Schoenauer" (of unstated Model); and the Werndl (Kropatschek Model) with a three-tube rotary magazine in the fore-end; together with the Clavarino (Model 1877) in relation to Italy, and the Schulhof (Model 1887) against the name of Belgium. Austrian arms, it will be observed, form the majority of those rifles listed by Viglezzi, and all were developed by the OWG.

The OWG itself had sprung from a small-arms manufactory at Steyr, in Northern Austria, which had been established by Leopold Werndl, in the mid-1830s, and which was rapidly developed by Werndl's son, Josef, after the outbreak of the American Civil War. Steyr was not the only Austro-Hungarian arms-making town (there were other centres of great importance at Ferlach,

Prague, Vienna and Weipert), but Werndl early developed the manufacture of small-arms by machinery, and MacLean records that the OWG factories employed more than 5,500 men (making 8,000 rifles each week) by 1893. The OWG plants were not only of great and obvious importance to Imperial Austro-Hungarian forces, but were also (until overtaken by aggressive German salesmanship, around the turn of the century) exclusive suppliers of rifles to countries all over the world; even Great Powers (of which France and Germany were examples) had bought Austrian rifles prior to 1889, and the armed forces of some smaller countries (like Greece, Holland, Mexico or Romania) were literally armed from Steyr.

In concluding these remarks, therefore,

rifle, noticed above in remarks upon Viglezzi.

PAUL, E. Ernst Paul, Gentleman, of Alwinenstrasse, Wiesbaden, Germany, secured Br. Pat. 16308/1894, with assistance from London Patent Agent T. R. Shillito, of 87 Chancery Lane. This was Herr Paul's only appearance as a patentee (under British law) of firearms, and his design is shown in Figure 59.

The Specification to Br. Pat 16308/1894 contained two claims of novelty for a combination firearm of that type discussed in remarks upon A. G. ARGLES, R. G. GORDON-SMITH, B. KREITH, D. T. LAING, P. MONNERAT, B. REYES and G. TRESENREUTER. As may be seen from Figure 59, Paul proposed to embody a dagger-blade in the butt of a particular

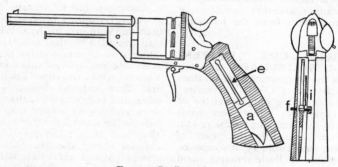

FIG. 59. *Paul's revolver.*
(After Br. Pat. 16308/1894.)

The blade "a" is normally retained in the butt, against the tension of a coiled spring "i", by the catch "f" which locks "a" in the open or closed positions by engaging in rounded apertures at either end of the slot "e" in the blade "a". When "f" is pressed inwards, it presents a smaller diameter to the slot "e", and permits "i" to expel the blade "a", or the user to press "a" back into the butt against a suitable hard surface.

with a brief reference to Br. Pat. 1272/1878 (which survived into our period, see Table I), enough has already been said to show that a most important contributor to the subject of these pages is masked by that modest reference. This patent protected a cylindrically-cased revolving cartridge magazine for bolt-action rifles and was probably (although that point remains to be established) the basis for Anton Spitalsky's Model 1879

type of popular cheap double-action centre-fire revolver, and he claimed novelty for (a) the idea of unsheathing such a blade mechanically, and (b) the mechanism for accomplishing that unsheathing.

PAULSON, R. Richard Paulson, an Engineer, of Boon Mills, Langwith, Nottinghamshire, secured Br. Pats. 10664/1885 and 14130/1886, which survived into the period of concern here (see Table I).

The first of these patents claimed certain methods for operating the firing- and loading-cycle of small-arms by bleeding gas (from the explosion of each cartridge) into a chamber beneath the barrel, and spending the expansive force of that gas against a spring-loaded operating arm. A Martini-Henry rifle was illustrated with a mechanism of this sort, which was also claimed as applicable to other rifles or guns with vertically- or longitudinally-sliding breech-blocks, and the principle was stated (though not shown) to be also suitable for revolvers. In the Specification to his Br. Pat. 14130/1886, however, Paulson both illus- trated and claimed as novel a simple gas-operated revolver, which (although no specimen arm is known to have sur- vived) probably did work.

During the period of concern here, Paulson can be said to have anticipated the work of L. ARMANNI (q.v.), the CLAIR FRÈRES (q.v.) and W. T. UNGE (q.v.); however, the principle of operating small-arms with rotary magazines by employing the expansive force of their combustion gases had been anticipated twenty years earlier, in W. J. Curtis's Br. Pat. No. 1810 of 10th July, 1866.

PERRY, A. B., B. F. and F. L. Asa Byron Perry, Benjamin Franklin Perry and Fidelia Lillie Perry secured Br. Pat. 859/1903, with the assistance of London Patent Agents Jensen & Son, of 77 Chancery Lane; in the Specification to this patent, the applicants described themselves, respectively, as "Farmer", "Shepherd" and "Canvassing Agent", of 447 White Street, Grand Junction, County of Mesa, State of Colorado, U.S.A.

The Specification to Br. Pat. 859/1903 set out eighteen claims for an automatic (clockwork) magazine rifle, in which cartridges were fed tangentially to a vertically-rotating carrier from a stock- magazine, and were successively offered up to the barrel, for discharge actually in the jaws of that carrier. This rifle could, at will, be operated single-shot.

Drawings filed with the Specification were almost child-like in execution, but fairly explicit as to how various com- ponents of the weapon were intended to function; however, these details impart no conviction (to the student) either that the design could have worked or that even a prototype weapon once existed. Apart from Br. Pat. No. 860, of 13th January, 1903 (for a type of bayonet presumably applicable to the Perry rifle), Br. Pat. 859/1903 was the sole appearance of these applicants in the field of British patents for firearms, and it is difficult now to suggest grounds for the necessary investment of their time, energy and money, in that project.

PHILLIPPIDES, P. A. Philipp Aposto- lou Phillippides, an Engineer, of 88 Rue de l'Acadamie, Athens, Greece, secured Br. Pat. 177/1906, with assistance from London Patent Agents Haseltine, Lake & Co., at 7/8 Southampton Buildings, Chancery Lane. A Complete Specifica- tion (see Appendix) was filed with Phil- lippides' application for the patent, an act suggesting that his design was fully developed when protection was sought and the applicant also secured Br. Pat. No. 178 of even date with Br. Pat. 177/1906, for a sliding breech-block rifle design, to which the rotary rifle magazine claimed in Br. Pat. 177/1906 was presumably applicable.

Five claims of novelty were made in the Specification to Br. Pat. 177/1906 for features of a rotary magazine for bolt-action rifles, in which the "drum" (i.e. the cartridge-follower) of the maga- zine could be inserted or removed from the top of the magazine casing, rather than from below, as was the case with the Model 1903 Mannlicher-Schoenauer rifles then recently introduced to some Greek Army units; see remarks to F. VON MANNLICHER. Phillippides accomplished his purpose by use of a drum-retaining plate, pivoting outwards horizontally from its forward end, through 90°, to permit the drum to be lifted upwards free of its well.

PIEPER, H. Henri Pieper ("Gun Manufacturer", at Rue des Bayards, Liège, Belgium) secured Br. Pats. 2167/1886 and 2166/1888, with the assistance of London Patent Agents J. H.

Johnson & Co. (see JOHNSON, J. H.) at 47 Lincoln's Inn Fields, which patents survived into the period of concern here, as shown in Table I. He also secured Br. Pat. 28484/1896, under guidance from London Patent Agents Gedge & Feeny, of 60 Queen Victoria Street, E.C.

The first of these patents related to a "gas-seal" revolver-gun, which is shown as Figure 24, and more particularly described in Chapter IV, with other arms on the "gas-seal" principle. In view of the number of "gas-seal" designs for revolving arms, attempted in the relevant period, it is curious that (see Table I) Br. Pat. 2167/1886 was maintained for such a short period of time, when the primary claim of that patent was "in firearms having cartridge-chambers separate from and movable in respect to the barrel, the employment of the cartridge-case as obturator of the joint between the barrel and the chamber, in combination with means for producing a clearance between the cartridge-case and the barrel . . .", so that had this patent been maintained for its full potential "life" (i.e. until 1900), it would have been extremely difficult for L. NAGANT (*q.v.*), and other designers of "gas-seal" revolvers in our period, to have patented their ideas at all either within the United Kingdom or in any other country where Pieper had equivalent protection.

Br. Pats. 2166/1888 and 28484/1896 covered bolt-action rifles with rotary magazines, the first being mechanically-rotated by retraction of the bolt, and the second being spring-rotated. Both arms were unusual in the patentee's preference for using a centre-hammer (behind the bolt), rather than a spring-operated firing-pin, as the means for discharge. Both patents contained substantial claims of novelty (over and above those for the rotary magazines) in relation to stocks and sights, magazine cut-offs and disconnectors, or (as to the later patent) a sliding bayonet mounted inside the stock. Pieper held an equivalent French patent (No. 261946 of 7th December, 1896) to Br. Pat. 28484/1896, and the "Société Anonyme des Établissements Pieper" exhibited a magazine-rifle made under that protection at the *Exposition Univer-*

selle, in Paris, during 1900; this weapon was chambered for a 7-mm. cartridge (similar to the Spanish Mauser rifle round) which was loaded into the rotary magazine by use of chargers protected under Pieper's French Patent No. 255859 of 25th April, 1896.

Henry Pieper had begun to make firearms at Liège, in Belgium, around 1866, and had pioneered the machine-manufacture of sporting guns with such success that the Liège plant was extended, during the 1870s, and an additional factory also had to be built at Nessonvaux.

Pieper himself was a man of great energy, who secured patents in fields unrelated to firearms (covering metals, electric brakes, and electric motors, amongst other matters) and was also associated with Louis Bachmann, of Etterbeck, Lez-Bruxelles, in the manufacture of small-arms ammunition, but he died in 1898, shortly after converting his business into that "Société Anonyme" earlier mentioned, and it is possible that his passing inhibited development of the Pieper Model 1890 "gas-seal" revolver described in Chapter IV.

After its founder's death the Pieper company (operating under its famous "Bayard" trade mark) continued to expand over those years of concern here, gaining awards at no less than six International Exhibitions between 1900 and 1913. An attempt to add bicycles and motor-cars to the firm's range of products was unsuccessful, but (after re-forming as the "Anciens Établissements Pieper") concentration upon the manufacture of small-arms and ammunition restored whatever financial ground had been lost by the previous venture.

Around 1905, indeed, manufacture of self-loading pistols and semi-automatic rifles was also commenced, under the patents of J. WARNANT (*q.v.*) or Nicolas Pieper, and with such success that the Liège and Nessonvaux plants were eventually consolidated into one large establishment, at Herstal.

PIRLOT & TRESART. Messrs. Pirlot & Tresart communicated to A. ARBENZ (*q.v.*) the subjects of his Br. Pat. 10974/1887, and in that Specification the communicants were described simply as

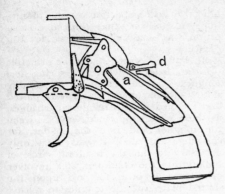

FIG. 60. *Pirlot & Tresart's safety-catch.*
(After Br. Pat. 10974/1887.)

"Gun Manufacturers", at Liège, Belgium.

As may be seen from Figure 60, the patent related to a rudimentary safety-device for revolvers, consisting of a flat spring "a", which could be forced down behind the hammer (by rotating a lever "d") to prevent "accidental explosions" through inadvertent pressure on the trigger. When "d" was turned upwards, "a" automatically sprang clear of the hammer, and the weapon could be fired. Like the designs of M. V. B. ALLEN (*q.v.*), Pirlot & Tresart's safety-catch was intended for use upon the cheapest revolvers, and it bears a strong external resemblance to a device used by the American firm of Hopkins & Allen (see Chapter I) which dispensed, however, with the flat spring "a" visible in Figure 60.

It is not known for how long the firm traded, but it is assumed that one partner was related to the Liège house of Pirlot Frères, which had (in the 1870s) controlled patents covering the "Chamelot Delvigne" service revolvers (described in Chapter II) at the time of their first general introduction into Europe.

PRAUNEGGER, F. Ferdinand Praunegger was joint-applicant with L. P. SCHMIDT (*q.v.*) for Br. Pat. 25561/1896; in the Specification, Praunegger was merely described as a "retired Imperial and Royal Local Commandant", of

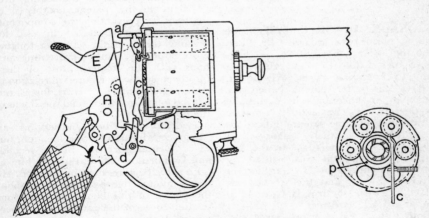

FIG. 61. *Praunegger & Schmidt's ejector.*
(After Br. Pat. 25561/1896.)

The hammer "A" (carrying a cartridge-case deflector "E") strikes a pin "a", which moves forward and pivots lever "b" which, in turn, pivots lever "c". Lever "c" has an ejector riding (beneath the cartridge rims) in an annular groove "p" cut at the rear of the cylinder, and thus ejects any cartridge in the "one o'clock" chamber. A disconnector "d" can be set to make "c" miss the relevant chamber at the first discharge of a fully-loaded pistol.

Graz, in the Austrian Empire. Since even less is known about his fellow-applicant, the subjects of Br. Pat. 25561/1896 are described here, but it must be accepted that Schmidt may in fact have been the designer of the idea patented.

As may be seen from Figure 61, Br. Pat. 25561/1896 related to a device for the automatic ejection of cartridge-cases from a (solid-framed) revolver, and the Specification set out three claims of novelty as to a hammer-operated ejector, a device for preventing ejection of a loaded cartridge on the first shot, and a removable side-plate giving access to the ejector mechanism.

Like the earlier design of H. A. SILVER (*q.v.*) and W. FLETCHER (*q.v.*), Praunegger & Schmidt's ejector consisted of a lever, pivoted in the standing-breech, which (on being struck at one end by the falling hammer) see-sawed to flip a cartridge-case rearward from each chamber as it rotated across the ejector; however, this Austrian device imparted the ejecting blow *via* a frame-mounted pin, and also had a deflection bulge on the right side of the hammer, so that the ejected case did not hit the firer in the face.

PRIDEAUX, W. DE C. William de Courcy Prideaux secured Br. Pat. 3560/1893 from 5 Fore Street, Wellington, Somerset, and Br. Pat. 22653/1914 from 12 Frederick Place, Weymouth, Dorset; this latter patent (when the Complete Specification was eventually accepted, in 1915) was actually a mosaic of features from three patent applications by Prideaux, namely, 22653/1914, 23670/1914 and 7100/1915. In the first patent, the applicant was assisted by London Patent Agent H. Gardner, of 166 Fleet Street, and the second was guided by a successor firm, H. Gardner & Son, at 173/5 Fleet Street.

Both Br. Pat. 3560/1893 and 22653/1914 related to a device for loading simultaneously all the chambers of a hinged-frame (see Plate 23) or swing-out cylinder (see Plate 1) revolver, and unlike the device of H. E. NEWTON (*q.v.*) the Prideaux "Magazine Loader" was successful. Specimens are common, even today, and many of them bear official British inspection or issue stampings, to confirm that official recognition was eventually achieved for this device.

Br. Pat. 3560/1893 stated the principle of the loader, whereby spring-steel tongues (passed through a suitably slotted circular metal plate) were paired and inclined to grip revolver cartridges, as these were slipped sideways between the tongues and into the loader, for carrying. At need, it was then only necessary to put the resultant circle of bullets into the chambers of a revolver cylinder and push forward upon the slotted plate, for the tongues to release their grip (as the plate forced them apart) and the plate to thrust the freed cartridges firmly into their chambers. Figure 62 shows the tongues "A" (screwed to a suitable mount "B") inserted through the slotted plate "C", together with a side elevation of a charger loaded with cartridges "E"; at the foot of the Figure is shown the method for loading Prideaux chargers, in the form in which these were eventually marketed.

Br. Pat. 22653/1914 was concerned with improvements to the loader proposed in the first patent, notably as to methods for preventing the components from becoming separated in use, for opening the cartridge-retaining tongues more positively, and for preventing mishaps with the loader. Most of these improvements were ignored in relation to those loaders made for H.M. forces, but can be found in commercial specimens of the device.

Prideaux described himself as an "Engineer" in the first Specification, but as a "Dental Surgeon" in the second, and Commander Chinn refers to him as a French citizen resident in England. He was a most active patentee throughout the period of this book, his inventions tending to be of the gadget variety personified by his magazine loader, but with a strong element of the practicable in all of them. He is credited (by Commander Chinn) with inventing the disintegrating metal-link belt used so successfully in Vickers aerial machine-guns (from around 1917), and his British Patent 15828 of 9th November, 1915, may be the one in point for that claim.

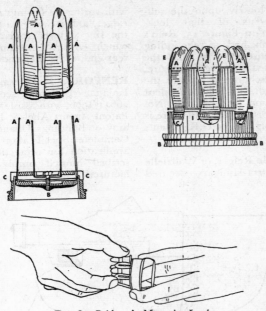

FIG. 62. *Prideaux's Magazine Loader.*
(After Br. Pats. 3560/1893 and 22653/1914.)

RANDALL, C. W. Charles Wells Randall was a Mining Promoter (of 2617 College Avenue, Berkeley, Alameda County, California, U.S.A.) and joint-applicant with I. H. RODEHAVER (*q.v.*) for Br. Pat. 6937/1911.

The two applicants were assisted to secure this protection (by London Patent Agents Gedge & Feeny, of 60 Queen Victoria Street), which had the special objective of providing a firearm with both shot-gun and rifle barrels, capable of firing either barrel by a single trigger.

To accomplish this objective, a gun with revolving cylinder and superimposed barrels was proposed, in which the cylinder had two concentric series of six shot-gun-calibre and six rifle-calibre chambers; the revolving arbor (which was keyed to the cylinder by a hexagonal rear section mating with a hexagonal socket in the cylinder) carried two ratchets at its rear end, and could be moved axially, at the firer's choice, to permit engagement of one or other of these ratchets by a conventional trigger-

mounted pawl. The hammer had two fixed firing-noses, and a user merely selected the appropriate ratchet to bring the cartridge of his choice (be it shot or ball) under the hammer.

REID, G. B. George Beauregard Reid, an Architect at Aberdeen, State of Washington, U.S.A., secured Br. Pat. 23659/1910, with assistance from Patent Agent P. R. J. Willis, of Fife House, Kingston-on-Thames; although Reid's application was not filed in the United Kingdom until 12th October, 1910, he was granted his protection as from 12th October, 1909 (a "Convention Date" see Appendix I), even though his Complete Specification was not accepted by the British Patent Office until 9th February, 1911.

The Specification to Br. Pat. 23659/1910 set out three claims of novelty for a concealed-hammer self-cocking lock-mechanism alleged to be adaptable to any type of small-arm, although a revolver was shown in the drawings. Based loosely upon the self-cocking components of that lock-mechanism shown in Figure 15, Reid's mechanism (which had a rebounding hammer) was constructed so that the hammer was cocked by trigger-pressure, but slipped for discharge as soon as the trigger was released. Reid held equivalent American protection (as U.S. Pat. No. 955436 of 19th April, 1910), but there is no evidence that his U.S. or U.K. patents were ever worked.

REIGER, E. Erwin Reiger, of Wollzielle 22, Vienna, Austria-Hungary, secured

with spring-steel wings to hold the cartridges, and it was rotated by a pawl on the ringed lever (operating the pistol) which engaged rotating teeth at the rear end of the magazine.

RENFORS, H. Herman Renfors, of Kajana, Finland, secured Br. Pat. 26611/1906, with assistance from London Patent Agents Abel & Imray, of Southampton Buildings, Chancery Lane; in the Complete Specification filed with his application for protection, Renfors described himself simply as a "Manufacturer".

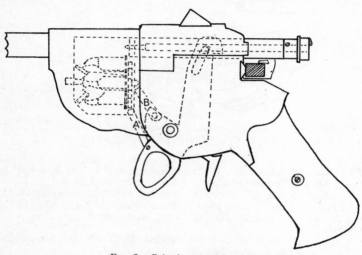

FIG. 63. *Reiger's magazine pistol.*
(After Br. Pat. 6360/1889.)

"A" = magazine pawl.   "B" = magazine bolt.

Br. Pat. 6360/1889, with assistance from London Patent Agents Herbert & Co., of 18 Buckingham Street, Strand.

The Specification to Br. Pat. 6360/1889 set out four claims of novelty for a lever-operated repeating pistol, with rotary magazine, of the type shown in Figure 63; this weapon bore some external resemblance to that protected by K. KRNKA's Br. Pat. 14088/1888 (*q.v.*), but may be distinguished from it by Reiger's preference for a manually-operated breech-bolt lock.

Reiger's rotary magazine was skeletal,

The patent claimed as novel the idea of fastening a revolver or other hand-gun to walking-sticks, or umbrellas, by the use of a variety of shell-clamps sketched in the Specification drawings. This idea was not new, for it had probably been anticipated by M. O'Mahoney's Br. Pat. No. 4146 of 12th October, 1880, and seems to have roused little interest in the United Kingdom.

REYES, B. Bernardo Reyes secured Br. Pat. 8761/1899 through P. R. J. Willis, a British Patent Agent. In the Specification to that patent, Reyes gave his residence as in Monterey, State of Nuevo Leon, Mexico, and his occupation as "Brigadier-General of the Mexican Army".

The subject of this protection is sketched as Figure 64, and was a pistol-sword comprising a sword-blade reduced at the tang to pass through a pistol butt, and into the sword-hilt; the hand-guard of this sword was arranged to protect the pistol-trigger, and a simple spring-catch united revolver to blade.

Pistol-swords were centuries old by 1899 (and see the combination arms of A. G. ARGLES, R. G. GORDON-SMITH, D. T. LAING, P. MONNERAT, E. PAUL, and G. TRESENREUTER), but Reyes's design had the merit (unusual in such weapons) that his pistol could be instantly drawn off the sword-tang, and used as a firearm, without the embarrassment of a blade to deflect the user's aim. It was, in fact, a highly desirable arm for any man who could wear a sword where even a holstered revolver might have caused com-

After he had been nearly two years in prison, the garrison of Tacubaya released Reyes to lead their march upon the National Palace at Mexico City, but on this occasion Madero was unforgiving, and the machine-gunners of the Palace guard killed Reyes, with nearly 200 followers and bystanders, on Sunday, 9th February, 1913.

Survivors of the attempted coup were doubtless comforted by subsequent events, for both Francisco Madero and Gustavo (his brother) were arrested nine days later. Their captor, General Huerta, put Gustavo to death immediately (but reputedly by torture at the hands of the Citadel guard), and the President was shot five days later, in transit to another prison, along with Pino Suarez, the Vice-President.

RICCI, C. Colombo Ricci, of Sant-arcangelo di Romagna, Italy, was a Mechanical Engineer resident in London, when he secured Br. Pats. 7003/1893 and

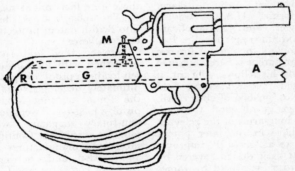

FIG. 64. *Reyes's Revolver Sword.*
(After Br. Pat. 8761/1899.)

The revolver and sword-guard "R" are formed as a unit, and secured to the tang "G", of the sword-blade "A", by a spring-push "M".

ment and, in the light of subsequent events, it is a pity that we shall never know if the inventor had occasion to test the versatility of his own design.

Reyes became Mexican Minister of War to the failing régime of President Porfirio Diaz, and when the latter fled Mexico (in May 1911) Reyes was unwise enough to oppose the successor, President Francisco Madero.

16272/1894, without assistance from a British Patent Agent. The Specifications to these patents mentioned addresses for Ricci at 85 Vincent Square, Westminster, 25 Tennison Street, Lambeth, and 28 Harwood Road, Walham Green.

Br. Pat. 7003/1893 made nine claims of novelty for a long-recoil magazine rifle, capable of automatic fire, which had a rotary magazine; only the cut-off and a device for tensioning the carrier-spring were specifically claimed as novel in relation to this magazine.

Br. Pat. 16272/1894 had a long Specification, and laid twenty-six claims of novelty to improvements for firearms; nineteen of those claims strictly related to "gas-seal" revolvers of a type discussed in Chapter IV (and see Fig. 28), whilst the remainder described a semi-automatic blow-back rifle, similar in principle to that covered by Br. Pat. 7003/1893, which had hammer-ignition and was adaptable to manufacture for use with rotary or box magazines.

These two patents were apparently Ricci's only ventures into the patenting of firearms in the United Kingdom, but W. H. B. Smith reported that Ricci did interest the U.S. Navy in testing a "gas-operated" revolver of his design, around the turn of the century, and this test-weapon may have been that shown in Figure 28.

RODEHAVER, I. H. Isaac Harrison Rodehaver (of East Auburn, Placer County, California, U.S.A.) was a Mining Engineer, and joint-applicant with C. W. RANDALL (*q.v.*) for Br. Pat. 6937/1911. Although the curious firearm covered by that patent is here described in remarks upon his fellow-applicant, it should be noted that Rodehaver held U.S. Patents Nos. 990669 of 20th April, 1911, and 1042145 of 22nd October, 1912, covering long-arms of the relevant type; a half-share in the later patent (which related to a "gas-seal" improvement upon that basic design covered by Br. Pat. 6937/1911) was held by James Toman, of Sutter Creek, California.

ROMANEL, R. C. Raphael Claudius Romanel, an Engineer, of 1 Dunning Terrace, Derby Rd., Ponders End, was joint-applicant with F. MARTIN (*q.v.*) and A. H. WILLIAMS (*q.v.*) for Br. Pats. 9998/1887 and 6994/1888; in the latter case, these applicants were assisted by London Patent Agent L. Lloyd Wise, of 46 Lincoln's Inn Fields.

Romanel was active as a patentee in various fields, during the 1890s, and it assumed that he designed (at any rate, in large degree) the subjects of these two patents, both of which aimed at producing a magazine rifle to be used or manipulated by persons familiar with the Martini-Henry single-shot rifle, and without special drill or training for them.

The first patent proposed to mount a rotary magazine in the stock-wrist (complete with cut-off) and to pass cartridges successively from it, into the rifle-breech, by merely lowering and raising the under-lever in normal fashion; the second patent increased the potential fire-power, by addition of another (twelve-round) magazine in the butt-stock of the rifle.

ROTH, G. Georges Roth was joint-applicant for Br. Pat. 19839/1901 with C. KRNKA (*q.v.*), under whose name the curious automatic rifle covered by that patent has already been described.

In the Specification to their patent, Roth was described simply as a "Manufacturer", of 50 Rennweg, Vienna (the address also given for his associate), but he does warrant more attention than those bare facts might suggest, although Br. Pat. 19839/1901 was his only venture into British patent protection for arms of concern here.

Between 1898 and 1900, Roth was concerned with four British patents for self-loading pistol designs, which were ultimately developed commercially into the 8-mm. ten-shot Model 1900 Roth pistol, a long-recoil weapon, with integral non-rotary magazine, which aroused some interest on the Continent. He was a substantial manufacturer of small-arms ammunition and, between 1912 and 1913, his company (the G. Roth Aktien Gesellschaft) also moved into the field of automatic-rifle design, but on lines more conventional than those proposed in Br. Pat. 19839/1901.

RUPERTUS, J. Jacob Rupertus (of 5519 Royal Street, Germantown, Philadelphia, Pennsylvania, U.S.A.) was described as a "Mechanic", in the Specification to Br. Pat. 17520/1899. This was his sole appearance as a patentee of revolving arms at British law, but he had (in the years between 1859 and 1899) secured five U.S. patents in the field, and John E. Parsons notices his activities in the 1870s as a patent litigant against Smith & Wesson, and as patentee of minor ejector improvements to a Forehand & Wadsworth revolver tested (but rejected) by the U.S. Ordnance Department. In the 1860s, he had been associated with the Tryon family of Philadelphian gunmakers, who had acted as sole agents for pistols and revolvers manufactured by the Rupertus Patent Pistol Manufacturing Co. at 120–122 North Sixth Street, Philadelphia. However, a decision by Edward K. Tryon Jnr. & Co. to act as "jobbers" (i.e. wholesale distributors) of standard arms by well-known U.S. makers, had apparently left Rupertus to carry on, alone, as a manufacturer of cheap single-action pocket rim-fire revolvers, which he sold under such names as "Empire" or "Hero". This venture seems to have ended in 1888, and probably as a result of competition from cheap machine-made double-action revolvers (of a type described in Chapter I) manufactured by factories at Norwich, Conn.

It is interesting to notice, therefore, that Br. Pat. 17520/1899 (for which the American equivalent was U.S. Pat. No. 633734 of 26th September, 1899) covered an ingenious self-cocking lock-mechanism, illustrated as applied to a hinged-frame self-ejecting revolver of that type which had ended Rupertus' earlier venture. In this design, the mainspring (when "at rest") held the enclosed hammer at full-cock; pressure on the trigger, however, diverted the thrust of the mainspring to one that would drive the hammer down on to a cartridge, and simultaneously withdrew a "dog" to permit the hammer to fall.

SABO, J. John Sabo (a "Mechanical Engineer") of 3402 Woodbine Avenue, Cleveland, County of Cuyahoga, Ohio, U.S.A.) secured Br. Pat. 1927/1910, with assistance from London Patent Agents Wheatley & Mackenzie, of 40 Chancery Lane.

Sabo (who did not appear again as a British patentee for firearms) proposed the use in rifles of rotary-drum magazines comprising a bundle of cartridge-containing tubes, rotating about an axis, which were embedded in the buttstock. Means for rotating the magazine, intermittently as each tube emptied, were claimed, along with devices for keeping cartridges in all the tubes except the one aligned with a delivery-tube to the breech, and Winchester Model 1903 (self-loading) or Model 1906 (pump-action) rifles were sketched as vehicles for the magazine.

SALVATOR, E. A. Emanuel Amodeo Salvator (of Washington, D.C., U.S.A.) secured Br. Pat. 12686/1886, with assistance from London Patent Agent G. F. Redfern, of 4 South Street, Finsbury, and this survived into years of concern here; see Table I.

This patent stated twenty claims of novelty for a lever-operated belt-fed rifle (with liquid-cooled barrel), a special rimless cartridge for use in it, and a belt-magazine which was strapped to the person using the arm, in similar fashion to that claimed by L. & S. S. YOUNG-HUSBAND (*q.v.*). Salvator's design abounded in such details as a knife (fixed to the breech-bolt) which tidily trimmed off the empty end of the cartridge-belt, after each shot, and it is improbable that many such arms were made.

SAVAGE, A. W. Arthur William Savage secured Br. Pat. 22901/1892 with assistance from Birmingham Patent Agent George Barker (of 77 Colmore Row) and Br. Pat. 19848/1899 with assistance from London Patent Agents Herbert Haddan & Co., of 18 Buckingham Street, Strand; in the first Specification, Savage was simply described as of Utica, Oneida County, New York State, whilst in the second Specification these details were expanded to include an address at 81 Howard Avenue, Utica, and the description of "Manufacturer".

Savage was apparently born in Jamaica (at Kingston), but educated in both England and the United States, and became something of an international traveller as a young man. Satterlee & Gluckman record that he eventually settled in Utica, N.Y., during the 1890s, and that he was for a while Manager of the Utica Belt Line Railroad. However, the route by which he came to an interest in firearms design (and an important place in these pages) remains obscure.

Clearly, however, Savage entered this field by the conventional path of patenting a promising idea, and his first patent application (which actually had to be renewed in February 1892) was filed in 1889, and related to a magazine rifle; he followed that application with others, in 1891, 1892 and 1899, being actions to which the following course of events can be related.

The application of 10th April, 1889 (which became, by later renewal, U.S. Pat. 502018 of 25th July, 1893) related to a lever-action rifle, with a rotary magazine; unlike the better-known weapon shown in Plates 34 and 35, the magazine in this rifle did not have a rotating carrier in which each round was carried by a separate cradle, but used instead a single rotary wing (similar to that shown in Figure 52) to urge the cartridges round an annular path, to the receiver. The patentee followed this application with those for U.S. Pats. 460786 of 6th October, 1891 (for a lever-action rifle, with a box-magazine outside the scope of these pages), 491138 of 7th February, 1893 (which was for a lever-action rifle and rotary magazine covered by the claims of Savage's Br. Pat. 22901/1892 referred to above), and by the above-mentioned revival of this 1889 application. It is noteworthy that (when applying for his U.S. patents of 1891 and 1893) Savage still described himself as "a subject of the Queen of Great Britain", and worth recording that his domicile was at Bay Ridge, Kings County, New York.

Early in 1892, Savage submitted two nine-round, lever-action rifles (with rotary magazines) for test by a U.S. Army Board. It is probably that these weapons were covered by the claims of his U.S. Patent Application of 1889 (i.e. the Application later renewed to become U.S. Patent 502018 of 1893), and that, although the Board did not recommend adoption for the 1892 arms, experience in this test prompted design improvements that became the subjects of Savage's Br. Pat. 22901/1892 and U.S. Pat. 491138 of 1893.

In 1895, this patentee became asso-ciated with the Savage Repeating Arms Co., at Utica, which sold a six-shot Model 1895 lever-action rifle (in both military and sporting versions, of ·303 Savage calibre) actually manufactured for it by the Marlin Firearms Co., of New Haven, Conn., being a weapon covered by the claims of Br. Pat. 22901/1892 and U.S. Pat. 491138 of 1893; since that U.S. patent (along with U.S. Pat. 502018 of 1893) was assigned by Savage to J. Morris Childs, Richard S. Reynolds and Edwin H. Risley, all of Utica, N.Y., it is assumed that these three men were the principal shareholders in the Savage Repeating Arms Co.

By 1898, however, a manufacturing plant was set up at Utica. Childs and Risley dropped out of the picture, and the company was then reorganized, as the Savage Arms Co., in 1899; A. W. Savage was not a director (Henry W. Millar being President, T. R. Proctor the Vice-President, and W. J. Green the Secretary and Treasurer of the Company) but he served as General Manager. With this reorganization, there was introduced an improved "Model 1899" rifle, which became justly famous, and is manufactured even today; this weapon was based upon the claims of Br. Pats. 22901/1892 and 19848/1899, or rather the U.S. equivalents thereof.

During most of the years in point here, the "Model 1899" rifle was primarily offered as a half-stocked weapon, which might be had with a round, half-, or full-octagon 26- or 22-in. barrel, although (see Plate 35) variant arms were available; however, any one of seven grades of engraving could be ordered, along with carved or fancy wood stocks, and the Savage Arms Co. catalogues made impressive reading, offering also a range of sights (five of them telescopic) and reloading tools to meet every taste. This rifle remained broadly based upon the Model 1895 arm, and was initially offered in ·303 Savage calibre only; six cartridges could be carried in the Model 1899 design, but the capacity of the rotary magazine (see Plate 35) was now only five rounds.

In fact (although the Specification contained eight specific claims of novelty),

Br. Pat. 19848/1899 was primarily concerned only with an "automatic mechanism in a hammerless rifle for indicating the position of the firing mechanism and . . . mechanism for retracting the firing-pin or hammer so as to render it safe against premature explosions, and so as not to interfere with the movements of the cartridges". It was noticeable (in this Specification) that both the mechanism for controlling movement of the cartridges from the rotary magazine and that magazine itself were regarded by the patentee as constituting "no part of this invention" and description of those parts was deliberately omitted from his Specification. The improvements of this patent therefore actually consisted in a small pivoted plate (mounted at the top forward end of the breech-bolt and visible in Plate 34) which was raised by the firing-pin when the latter was being cocked, so indicating to the firer that his rifle was loaded, and in the lever "L" (pivoted to the breech-bolt and visible in Plate 34, lower) which retracted the firing-pin slightly, as soon as the rear-end of the breech-bolt dropped, on re-loading.

Although the Model 1899 rifle came to be chambered for a variety of cartridges over those years of concern here (and such rounds as the ·30-30 or ·32-40 Winchester are examples), the inventor made great efforts to promote its use in his own ·303 Savage calibre. This ammunition (a rimmed round similar to the British ·303 cartridge) could therefore be obtained in a variety of loadings, suitable to various tasks. In 1904, for example, there were available the ·303-28 Smokeless ("Regular" or "Expanding" bullets), the ·303-40 Black Powder, the ·303-5 (lead bullet) or ·303-15 (metal-covered bullet) "Miniature", and ·303-20 Schuetzen Target (paper-patched lead bullet) cartridges, but the action of Savage's rifle proved so stout that (in 1912) a version handling the high-velocity ·22 Savage Hi-Power centre-fire cartridge was introduced, and this was followed (in 1913) by a model for the famous ·250-3000 Savage cartridge, propelling an 87-grain bullet at the then phenomenal velocity of 3000 f.p.s.

The principles of operation for the Model 1899 rifle may be grasped by reference to Plate 34, and it is worth recording that the breech-bolt, indicator, sear, firing-pin, hammer, extractor and retractor of the Model 1899 arm were intended to interchange with equivalent components from any Model 1895 rifle, so that older weapons could have the above-mentioned improvements added at will.

In Plate 34 (top), the breech-bolt "E" slides longitudinally in the action-body, and is either advanced and raised into the locked position (chambering a cartridge as it goes) or lowered and retracted to the rear (extracting and ejecting any chambered cartridge en route) by operating the pivoted finger-lever "A". It will be seen that "A" has a curved arm (concentric with the pivot of "A") which is connected to an extension of "E" by a transverse pin which travels in an inclined groove in the extension.

When, as shown in Plate 34 (top), the finger-lever "A" is depressed, the breech-bolt "E" (which is, when in the closed position, supported at the rear by the recoil-shoulder "U" in the standing breech, and from below by the frame-lump "H" engaging the nose of the curved arm on "A") is first lowered at the rear, to unlock it, and then withdrawn to the back of the action-body, extracting and ejecting any chambered cartridge, as it retreats. At the dropping of the rear end of the breech-bolt "E", the retractor "L" (which is a forked component then engaging the sear-screw "P" on the standing breech) is also depressed, and its rear-end sweeps down the face of a projection on the hammer "N" to retract the firing-pin slightly and prevent accidental discharge of the cartridge next to be loaded; this latter feature is, of course, one of the claims of Br. Pat. 19848/1899 described above.

On raising "A" from the lowered position shown in Plate 34 (top), the breech-bolt "E" is carried forward again by the curved arm on "A", and raised to lock into position against "U", for firing, as mentioned above; en route, it has picked up a cartridge from the magazine (the rotating-spring of which was put into tension by loading cartridges in through the top of the action, as shown in Plate 35 (top), whilst the breech-bolt was open), chambered it, and cocked the hammer "N" against the sear "K". Until the breech-bolt "E" is fully home, and locked, the inner edge of the curved arm on "A" immobilizes the trigger "R" completely, and when locking of the breech-bolt is complete, a recess in the top of the firing-pin (which is screwed on to the end of "N") tips up the loading indicator "Y", as claimed in Br. Pat. 19848/1899.

The topmost cartridge in the rotating magazine-carrier "G" is saved from spillage, when the breech-bolt "E" is opened, by an L-shaped lever or automatic cut-off "C" shown in Plate 35 (top). The lower end of that cut-off being pivoted with the spring-operated magazine-carrier spindle, the top arm of the cut-off therefore moves transversely to the line of travel for the breech-bolt "E", when that component is opened, but is brushed to one side again when "E" is levered forward to chamber a cartridge.

Similarly, the top arm of "C" may be swung to the left by finger-pressure, when the breech-bolt "E" is open, either to load an extra round into the breech when the carrier "G" is full, or when the user wishes to close the breech without chambering a cartridge; for either purpose, full retraction of the top arm "C", by the finger, retires the topmost cartridge in the carrier "G" below the line of travel of the breech-bolt "E", so that only a cartridge dropped deliberately into the breech-opening will be caught by "E" on its forward travel. It will be observed (in Plate 34) that a numerical indicator is stamped upon the front edge of the rotating carrier "G"; the indicator can be seen through a frame aperture, to establish the number of cartridges remaining in the magazine.

A. W. Savage (whose picture appears in Plate 37) made great efforts to secure some kind of service adoption for Model 1899 rifles of the type shown in Plate 35. He was successful in securing an unanimous recommendation by the New York State Board of Examiners that his rifle be adopted by the National Guard of that State, but the expense of such adoption made this recommendation a dead letter. A warm tribute by a Mexican Board of Army Officers (in June 1897) had proved equally useless in relation to his Model 1895 design, and the Model 1899 rifle never achieved, in official circles, that level of appreciation and use attained commercially.

SCHLUND, H. or H. A. Henry Schlund (from 28 Southampton Buildings, Chancery Lane, the address of London Patent Agent C. D. Abel) secured Br. Pat. 9084/1885; Henry Augustus Schlund (from 4 South Street, Finsbury, the address of London Patent Agent G. F. Redfern) secured Br. Pat. 11900/1886. Both patents related to revolvers (the later protection being for specific improvements to the inventions of the earlier) and both survived into that period of concern here, as shown in Table I. Although both Specifications mention the patentees as resident at "Aston Cross, Birmingham", it is still uncertain if H. Schlund and H. A. Schlund were actually different men, since several patents were secured in each name during the 1880s, and the *Abridgement of Specifications, Class 119* certainly treated those names as distinct.

Br. Pat. 9084/1885 covered the principal features of a hinged-frame self-extracting concealed-hammer revolver, with double-trigger lock-mechanism in which the hammer was cocked by pressure on a lower trigger (protruding beneath the trigger-guard) and released by pressure upon an upper trigger. Br. Pat. 11900/1886 improved the earlier weapon, by moving both triggers within the trigger-guard, and by ensuring that the hammer could not reach a cartridge until the barrel was properly latched.

Revolvers were produced in quite modest numbers (and under both of the above patents) between 1887 and 1890, with ·450 c.f. or ·380 c.f. versions of the improved arm being slightly more common, today, than any other models; the larger of these two examples was six-chambered, had a 6-in. barrel and an overall length of 11½ inches, whilst the smaller arms (also six-chambered) measured 8¾ inches overall and had 4-in. barrels. These weapons are almost invariably marked "Kynoch Gun Factory, Aston. Patent Model", without specific reference to the name of Schlund, and serial-numbers between 363 and 581 are the only ones so far observed by this writer.

The Kynoch Gun Factory was a venture by George Kynoch, M.P., and briefly manufactured Gras rifles and Schlund revolvers in the Aston Cross factory formerly operated by one of the great Birmingham revolver-makers, William Tranter. Kynoch died in 1890, and it is believed that the Kynoch Gun Factory venture (which must not be confused with the firm of ammunition-makers Kynoch Ltd., from which George Kynoch had departed in 1888) halted with his death, making the Schlund revolver a moribund design almost from the commencement of our period.

Henry Schlund (who lived at 21 Westminster Road, Birchfields, Birmingham in the 1890s) was a known engineer-associate of George Kynoch in a small ammunition-manufacturing venture called The Aston Arms Co., Ltd., which collapsed in 1891; he may have continued, in that line, with The British Munitions Co., Ltd. (of Northumberland Works, Millwall) for a year or two afterwards

Nothing is currently known of Henry Augustus Schlund, if that name actually existed distinct from Henry Schlund's, save as joint-applicant for other British patents, some of which were quite unrelated to small-arms.

SCHMIDT, L. P. Ludwig Philipp Schmidt (of Graz, Austrian Empire) was joint-applicant with F. PRAUNEGGER (*q.v.*) for Br. Pat. 25561/1896; the two men were assisted to secure this protection by London Patent Agent W. H. Beck, of 115 Cannon Street, E.C. As was remarked in the notes upon F. PRAUNEGGER (*q.v.*) nothing is known of Schmidt's background, or of the contribution that he made to the revolver-cartridge ejection device covered by Br. Pat. 25561/1896.

SCHMIDT, P. Paul Schmidt, a Police Lieutenant, of Oranienstrasse 119, Berlin, S.W.68, was joint-applicant with K. DOBSLAW (*q.v.*) for Br. Pat. 8353/1914; the electric sighting-and-lighting device covered by that patent has been described

in remarks upon K. DOBSLAW (*q.v.*), and Schmidt's contribution to the invention remains (like his fellow-applicant's) to be established.

SCHNEE, G. H. Gotthilf Heinrich Schnee (of 39 Goethe Strasse, Munich, Bavaria) was described as a "Retired Captain of the Prussian Army" in the Specification to his Br. Pat. 5607/1888, which he secured without assistance from a British Patent Agent, and which (see Table I) survived into years of concern here.

Br. Pat. 5607/1888 set out eleven claims of novelty for lever-and-rack operated magazine small-arms, which had horizontally-sliding cylindrical loading-bolts, backed up by vertically-sliding recoil-blocks. A skeletal revolving cartridge carrier (in a rounded mantle) picked up rounds loaded by the handful into a hopper or cartridge-box. Most of the claims of the patent related to rifles, but a pistol version (with its lock-mechanism mounted on the operating lever) was also envisaged.

SCHOENAUER, O. Otto Schoenauer communicated the subjects of Br. Pat. 5793/1884 to London Patent Agent G. E. VAUGHAN (*q.v.*) and that protection (which survived into years of concern here, as shown in Table I) covered a rotary magazine for use in bolt-action rifles; later, Schoenauer was joint-applicant with F. VON MANNLICHER (*q.v.*) for Br. Pat. 1567/1900 covering the similar (but more successful) magazine shown in Figure 51.

Essentially, the claims of Br. Pat. 5793/1884 proposed use of a cartridge carrier (mounted inside a cylindrical casing) which could rotate about a central spindle in a somewhat similar manner to that shown in Figure 52; at the rear end of the spindle were fixed two ratchet-wheels, one of which had a larger diameter than the other, and the smaller of which was engaged by a spring-stop. When the bolt-handle of the rifle was turned down (to close the rifle-breech behind a cartridge) a projection on the underside of the bolt was also rotated and this projection struck the larger ratchet-wheel of the magazine, to bring round the cartridges resting in the cartridge-carrier. On opening the bolt (to re-load), the spring-stop bearing on the smaller ratchet-wheel in the magazine caused the cartridge carrier to rotate a round completely into alignment with the breech, and then locked the cartridge carrier in that alignment, so that the bolt might pick up the round when thrust forward. A lever on the outside of the rifle could be worked to disengage the magazine drive, and permit use of this rifle as a single-loader.

Schoenauer (whose name may also be found spelled as "Schönauer" or even "Schoenhauer", in contemporary literature) was an employee and Manager of the OESTERREICHISCHE WAFFENFABRIKS-GESELLSCHAFT (q.v.) for many years, and Maclean records that he eventually became Technical Director of the Company, in 1896. During preceding years (and notably in that period from about 1879 until 1885) Schoenauer had been one of a sextet of designers involved in protracted experiments upon the use of rotary magazines in bolt-action rifles, as part of an immense series of tests aimed at producing an acceptable bolt-action magazine rifle for general adoption by the Austrian forces. In these pages, the names of F. VON MANNLICHER (q.v.) and J. SCHULHOF (q.v.) appear (with that of Schoenauer) from amongst this group, but Captain Kromar, Josef Spitalsky (Schoenauer's predecessor as Technical Director of the Steyr company) and Josef Werndl had all been also involved in these experiments, and each had developed rotary magazines for service trials, as indicated in earlier remarks upon the OESTERREICHISCHE WAFFENFABRIKS-GESELLSCHAFT.

In the event, however, Austrian forces adopted a clip-loaded Mannlicher rifle without a rotary magazine (see F. VON MANNLICHER), and it was not until 1900 that Schoenauer's name was at last linked to a successful magazine of this type, with development of the Mannlicher-Schoenauer design shown in Figures 51, and the joining of Schoenauer's name with that of von Mannlicher in the application for Br. Pat. 1567/1900, and its foreign equivalents.

SCHULHOF, J. Josef Schulhof secured, in his own name, Br. Pats. 9066/1886 10423/1887 and 10286/1888, which survived into the period of concern here (see Table I), and he also communicated to London Patent Agent A. J. BOULT (q.v.) the subjects of Br. Pat. 7490/1889; as to "communicated" British patents see, generally, Appendix I.

Schulhof (who mentioned an address at 4 Nibelungengasse, Vienna, in the Specification to Br. Pat. 7490/1889) was a fairly prolific patentee of firearms during the 1880s, and succeeded in arranging Austrian service tests for some rather curious bolt-action rifles (with non-rotary stock-magazines of unusually large capacity) in 1882 and 1883; subsequently, he turned his attention to rotary magazines for such arms, and Maclean notes that he secured really serious Austrian service attention (though not adoption) for a Model 1887 rifle with such a feature. At that time, however, Schulhof was competing with those designers mentioned in remarks upon O. SCHOENAUER (q.v.), and his design was discarded in favour of the clip-loaded rifles of F. VON MANNLICHER (q.v.) mentioned in remarks upon that inventor.

Schulhof's Br. Pat. 9066/1886 related to a straight-pull bolt-action rifle, with a spring-rotated magazine; in this design, a chain linked to the magazine loading-gate rotated the cartridge carrier, and put the carrier-spring into tension, when the loading-gate was opened. This design gave trouble, and Schulhof's Br. Pat. 10423/1887 proposed to replace the chain-operated tensioning of the carrier-spring by use of a rack on the inner end of the loading-gate, which rack engaged teeth on the carrier-spindle and rotated that component (tensioning its spring) when the gate was opened. This magazine was used in the Model 1887 Schulhof rifle mentioned above, and the tensioning feature somewhat anticipated that method proposed by Br. Pat. 14576/1900 of O. H. J. KRAG (q.v.) or Br. Pat. 19320/1900 of T.A. FIDJELAND and J. A. SCHWARZ (q.v.); Schulhof restated the principle (with minor improvements) in his Br. Pat. 10286/1888, and his Br. Pat. 7490/1889 merely proposed the use of a longitudinally-mounted spring for preventing premature spillage of cartridges, from rotary magazines of this type, during operation.

Schulhof was working in competition with those five other designers of rotary magazines mentioned in remarks upon O. SCHOENAUER (*q.v.*), and it has been suggested that the Austrian Army's decision not to adopt the Model 1887 Schulhof rifle was based upon the expense of such adoption, rather than any technical defect. Thus it is noticeable that Viglezzi listed that arm as in the hands of Belgian troops, and it is therefore possible that the design found abroad appreciation denied to it in Austria.

SCHWARZ, J. A. Johan Allum Schwarz, of Kristiassand, S., was a Captain in the Royal Norwegian Army, and joint-applicant with T. A. FIDJELAND (*q.v.*) for Br. Pat. 19320/1900. The claims of that patent are described in remarks upon Captain Schwarz's fellow-applicant.

SHEPHEARD, G. George Shepheard, an "Army Pensioner", of Nybridge, Devonshire, secured Br. Pat. 2214/1885 (which survived into years of concern here) with assistance from London Patent Agents Edwards & Co., of 35 Southampton Buildings, W.C.

Shepheard's Specification set out four claims of novelty for a six-shot fully-automatic radial rifle. In this weapon a clock-work device rotated a radially-chambered disc one-sixth of a revolution (to bring a fresh cartridge into alignment with the barrel), after the recoil of

discharge had freed the disc from arresting-teeth on the inner periphery of the disc-casing. A variant model was also claimed, in which the breech-end of the barrel seated successively in each cartridge-chamber, but no specimen of either model is known to have survived.

SILVER, H. A. Hugh Adams Silver was joint-applicant with W. FLETCHER (*q.v.*) for Br. Pat. 16078/1884, covering a cartridge-ejector shown in Plate 30, and described in remarks upon the latter applicant. These men traded as S. W. Silver & Co., on Cornhill, London (in Sun Court), until 1904, when Fletcher went into business on his own account.

During their association, the two men secured British patent or design protection covering several trifling improvements to conventional firearms, and their firm name is occasionally found upon various models of revolver, in the cheaper price-range.

STEERS, W. E. William Edward Steers, of "Hilltop", Whitehill, Caterham, Surrey, secured Br. Pat. 8910/1911 with assistance from London Patent Agents Marks & Clerk, of 57/58 Lincoln's Inn Fields.

Steers (who was described as a "Gentleman", in the Specification to his patent) proposed a sighting attachment, for small-arms, of that type shown in Figure 65, where the sights "c" and "d" of a revolver are mounted upon sliding or folding extension-pieces "a" and "b", in order to increase the distance between

FIG. 65. *Steer's pistol sight.*
(After Br. Pat. 8910/1911.)

the sights. This type of improvement (due to the ease with which it can be knocked out of truth) has never been very popular, but the late Sir Hugh B. C. Pollard had one Smith & Wesson "M & P" revolver in his collection, to which Steer's device, or something very like it, had been fitted to yield a sight-base of nearly eighteen inches.

SUNNGÄRD, H. Harald Sunngärd secured Br. Pat. 4395/1910 with the assistance of London Patent Agents Jensen & Son, of 77 Chancery Lane; in his Specification, Sunngärd was described as a Civil Engineer, of 33 Kongensgate, Christiania, Norway.

Br. Pat. 4395/1910 set out four claims relating to cheap detachable rotary drum magazines, for use with automatic rifles (or machine-guns), of the type shown in Figure 66; these drums could be loaded carelessly, with handfuls of cartridges,

being so proportioned that it was impossible for a cartridge to lie across a compartment and so to jam the magazine.

Principal features of Sunngärd's design were rotating spider "E", "F" (powered by a spiral spring inside "E", which was cranked into tension by an external handle), and the curved guides "G" and "H", which fed the outer row of cartridges up to the rifle-breech. This magazine probably unbalanced badly any rifle to which it was fitted, but was almost certainly intended for use with a gas-operated automatic rifle which (originally in the name of Harald Sundby) Sunngärd had patented as Br. Pat. 13824 of 12th August, 1908. The elaborate Specification to this patent (which is not included in Table II) indicated only that a magazine might be attached to the side or bottom of the rifle, but did not indicate the type of magazine actually proposed to be used.

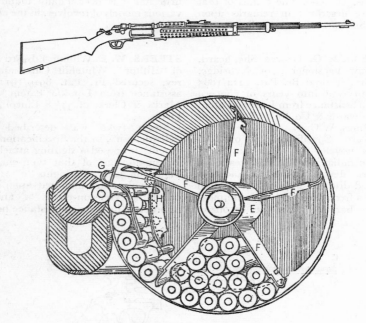

FIG. 66. *Sunngärd's rifle magazine.*
(After Br. Pat. 4395/1910.)

The Sundby-Sunngärd automatic rifle to which, it is suggested, the rifle-magazine above might have been applied.

TAMBOUR, J. Joseph Tambour, of Mathildenplatz XX, Vienna, Austria, ("Gentleman") secured Br. Pats. 22657/1901 and 20307/1902, with assistance from London Patent Agents Abel & Imray, of Southampton Buildings, Chancery Lane; he was a prolific patentee of safety-devices for small-arms, between 1899 and 1907, but only these two British patents are definitely in point here.

Br. Pat. 22657/1901 protected a hammer-locking device for small-arms, which was shown (in the Specification) as applied to that M/1898 Austro-Hungarian service revolver in Plate 12; by a modification to this weapon, a lever pivoted in the back-strap of the butt bore against the hammer to support this component at half-cock. When the arm was full-cocked, however, this lever engaged a hook-shaped projection on the hammer, and only correct grasping of the butt would then depress the lever and permit pressure on the trigger to drop the hammer.

The Specification to Br. Pat. 20307/1902 contained but a single claim of novelty, covering a direct locking-lever for engaging the sear of small-arms, which lever was to be disengaged by a pressure-piece, along similar lines to the first patent. A Webley-Fosbery recoil-operated revolver (see G. V. FOSBERY, and Plate 31) was both shown in the Specification drawing and mentioned in the text as suitable for Tambour's improvement, but this time having its grip-safety embedded in the front butt-strap.

TARGAN, R. Robert Targan was joint-applicant with the WAFFEN-TECHNISCHE GESELLSCHAFT "WESPI" (q.v.) for Br. Pat. 28924/1912; in the Specification to that patent Targan was described simply as a "Merchant" (of the same address as the "Wespi" company), and the claims of this patent are discussed in remarks upon the other patentee.

TASKER, V. C. Vernon Compton Tasker, a Mechanical Engineer at 909 Lafayette Street, Bridgeport, Conn., U.S.A., secured Br. Pat. 21276/1902 with assistance from London Patent Agents Marks & Clerk, of 57/58 Lincoln's Inn Fields. A Complete Specification was filed with Tasker's application for protection (suggesting that the relevant design was viable at date of application), and set out twenty-two claims of novelty for a self-cocking firing-mechanism for artillery, which was also claimed as applicable to small-arms. A revolver embodying a slightly modified version of this mechanism was both described and illustrated in the Specification to Br. Pat. 21276/1902, but was not (oddly enough) the subject of any specific claim of novelty.

No specimen revolver is known to exist, but one entry relating to an assignment, transmission or licence in respect of Br. Pat. 21276/1902 appeared in *The Official Journal of the Patent Office* in February 1908, and suggested that Tasker did interest somebody in the primary objective of the patent.

TATAREK, E. First Lieutenant Edmund Tatarek, of 11 Barcsay ut, Budapest, Hungary, was joint-applicant with J. VON BENKÖ (q.v.) for Br. Pat. 1928/1911 (which is discussed in remarks upon his fellow patentee), and also concerned with a group of Hungarian designers working upon gas-operated semi-automatic rifles, just prior to the First World War.

TAVERNIER, L. F. Louis Ferdinand Tavernier ("Gentleman"), of 17 Portsea Place, Connaught Square, London, secured Br. Pat. 16350/1890 in respect of the radial magazine-pistol shown in Figure 67; the Provisional Specification to this patent was filed by Henry J. Cooke, of 13 Victoria Street, London, who was probably (though not stated to be) a Patent Agent.

Tavernier's pistol followed the same basic pattern as that of E. FABRE (q.v.) and A. TRONCHE (q.v.), being a self-cocking arm, in which an endless chain of cartridges moved fore-and-aft within the action-body, and mated with a reciprocating barrel at the moment of discharge. The butt of Tavernier's pistol could be folded up (guarding the trigger and reducing the bulk of the weapon), and considerable ingenuity was expended in synchronizing mating of barrel and cartridge carrier, by use of recoil- or buffer-springs to keep the carrier-chain taut.

Although magazine pistols of this type have survived in some numbers, their fundamental similarity makes positive identification of Tavernier's variant a matter requiring detailed study, and no signed specimen of his design is known to this writer.

also associated with A. J. BOULT (q.v.) during the 1890s; soon after the turn of the century, however, his practice operated under the style "W. P. Thompson & Co.", and he may have retired or died around 1908. The firm survives today.

THOMSON, B. T. L. Benjamin Thomas Lindsay Thomson, an Engineer at 4 Altenburg Garden, Clapham Common, Surrey, was joint-applicant with

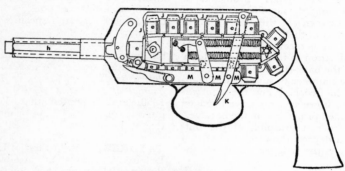

FIG. 67. *Tavernier's magazine pistol.*
(After Br. Pat. 16350/1890.)

Cartridges are inserted into the linked chambers "eee", via a removable side-plate. The trigger "K" is linked to one lever "JJJ" sliding in the top of the action-body, and to another "MMM" in the bottom of the pistol. When "K" is pressed, "JJJ" acts as a pawl, rotating the chain of chambers "eee" by engaging a ratchet "r"; simultaneously, "MMM" retracts the sliding barrel "h" to mate with the chamber aligned with it, and also cocks a hammer against the coiled springs shown in the Figure, and then releases it to fire the cartridge.

THOMPSON, W. P. William Phillips Thompson, F.C.S., M.I.M.E., was a well-known British Patent Agent of the "Agency for Foreign Patent Solicitors" at 6 Lord Street, Liverpool, 6 Bank Street, Manchester, 118 New Street, Birmingham, and 323 High Holborn, London. A Civil Engineer by training, it was to him that D. E. GRANT, T. F. TÖRNELL, and the IDEAL HOLSTER CO. (q.v.) respectively communicated the subjects of Br. Pats. 6541/1893, 8331/1888, and 22653 and 22654/1901, and he also assisted a number of other patentees listed in these pages to secure their protection; as to "communicated" British patents see, generally, Appendix I.

Thompson probably practised through most of the years in point here, and was

J. S. WALLACE for Br. Pat. 4205/1891, which was secured under guidance from London Patent Agents Haseltine, Lake & Co., of 45 Southampton Buildings. The Specification related to improvements in small arms, of the "Giffard" type, worked by compressed or liquefied gas, and included a claim for a revolving magazine to be used in such arms.

THORSEN, T. Theodore Thorsen, of 216 Dock Street, Philadelphia, U.S.A., communicated the subjects of Br. Pat. 4148/1902 to London Patent Agent H. H. LAKE (q.v.); in the Specification to this patent, Thorsen was described as a "Gun Maker".

Br. Pat. 4148/1902 protected a recoil-operated automatic rifle, in which the breech-bolt recoiled (after being un-locked from the barrel) deep into the butt, *via* an arcuate passage containing a return spring. The magazine was a "cylindriform" design, loaded by opening a hinged lid at the side of the rifle, in which the carrier-rotating spring was put into tension by a rack on that lid (engaging a pinion on the carrier-spindle), which tensioned the spindle as the lid was opened. This latter feature was not new in principle, having been anticipated by patents of O. H. J. KRAG (*q.v.*) and J. SCHULHOF (*q.v.*) above described.

TÖRNELL, T. F. Tor Fabian Törnell (of Carlsborg, Sweden) was a Lieutenant in the Swedish Army, who secured Br. Pat. 8331/1888 (which survived into our period), with the assistance of London Patent Agent W. P. THOMPSON (*q.v.*).

Törnell's aim by Br. Pat. 8331/1888 (for which he held equivalent Swedish and other patent protection) was to improve the Nagant M/1887 service revolver shown in Plate 21, with which he and his fellow officers were then armed. As Plate 21 will show, under scrutiny, the cylinder of this revolver is not positively bolted in alignment with the barrel, when the hammer is "at rest", so that it is possible for the cylinder to be accidentally rotated and thus to bring an empty cartridge-case under the hammer.

Törnell, sensibly enough, simply modi-fied the standard lock-mechanism (which is shown in Figure 19) to provide an extra cylinder-bolt engaging small addi-tional locking-slots milled or punched into the cylinder, just forward of the main locking-slots visible in Plate 21. By split-ting the trigger into two tandem parts, with front segment pivoted on rear, and forming a small tooth at the top of the foremost segment, Törnell supplied a bolt always engaged with the cylinder when the trigger was "at rest", but immediately withdrawn as soon as the trigger was pressed.

Cav. Capt. C. A. I. Belfrage (Curator of the *Kungl. Armémuseum*, Stockholm) has courteously advised that Swedish government permission to apply Törnell's improvement to M/1887 service revolvers

was granted in 1893, but that formal approval for general adoption did not ensue. As a result, specimen arms are rare today.

TRESENREUTER, G. Gustav Tresen-reuter (of Plan Ufer 60, Berlin S., Ger-many) secured Br. Pat. 921/1902, with assistance from London Patent Agents Boult, Wade & Kilburn; in the Specifica-tion to this patent, Tresenreuter was described as an "Engineer", and the protection was his only traceable venture into the field of firearm design under British law. Since the Pistols Act 1903 (which adversely affected sales of such ballistic toys as that patented by Tre-senreuter) was to be passed in the follow-ing year, the patentee's timing for his patent application was unfortunate.

Br. Pat. 921/1902 set out four claims of novelty for a small self-cocking revolver (fired by pressing its trigger forward), which was fitted entirely within the T-shaped handle of a walking-stick or umbrella; this weapon may be considered within the same category as those other combination arms described above in remarks upon A. C. ARGLES, R. G. GORDON-SMITH; B. KREITH, D. T. LAING, P. MONNE-RAT; E. PAUL, and B. REYES.

TRONCHE, A. Auguste Tronche was joint-applicant with E. FABRE (*q.v.*) for Br. Pat. 15771/1888, which survived into the period of this book; Tronche's address and occupation were stated (in the Specification to this patent) to be the same as those of his fellow-applicant. A magazine pistol covered by the claims of Br. Pat. 15771/1888 is briefly described in remarks upon Emile Fabre.

TURBIAUX, J. E. Jacques Turbiaux (of Paris, France) communicated the subjects of Br. Pat. 2731/1882 to E. C. BREWER (*q.v.*), and this protection sur-vived into years of concern here; as to "communicated" British patents see, generally, Appendix I.

Br. Pat. 2731/1882 covered the princi-pal features of a radial revolver shown in Figure 68, and Turbiaux held equivalent protection in Belgium (No. 58148 of 9th June, 1882), France (No. 149466 of 9th June, 1882) Italy (No. 14318 and 346 of

14th June, 1882), and the United States (No. 273644 of 6th March, 1883); his American patent (after assignment) was the basis for certain activities, earlier described, by P. H. FINNEGAN (*q.v.*).

As may be seen from Figure 68, Turbiaux proposed a small compact revolver, which was to be clenched in the right fist (with its barrel protruding between the user's index and third fingers), and fired by squeezing a rear-mounted trigger forward, with the palm of the hand; this movement rotated the radial cylinder (which had to be entirely removed for loading) and also cocked and released a firing-pin.

In France, Turbiaux's revolver was retailed in 6-mm. rim-fire (10-shot) or 8-mm. centre-fire (seven-shot) versions, with some of the latter arms chambered for a curious centre-primed cartridge used in a (non-rotary) *Gaulois* "squeezer" magazine pistol. Since the *Gaulois* arm was not even patented by E. Mimard and

P. Blachon until 1893, it seems possible that Turbiaux actually worked his Continental patents for a period comparable to that covering the activities of P. H. FINNEGAN (*q.v.*) under Turbiaux's above-mentioned U.S. patent, which Finnegan and his company had purchased.

The Continental Turbiaux arms measured about 4½ inches in overall length, and had barrels about 1½ inches long; markings varied, but could include three legends upon various components, namely, "Le Protector" (which name Turbiaux included in his patent Specifications), "Système E. Turbiaux", and "Bvte S.G.D.G. en France et à l'Étranger, Paris". Serial-numbers in a range up to nearly 8000 have been observed, but the basis for their allocation is not clear, and more arms may have been manufactured than the surviving serials would suggest. A sliding safety-catch was noted upon some revolvers with high serial-numbers.

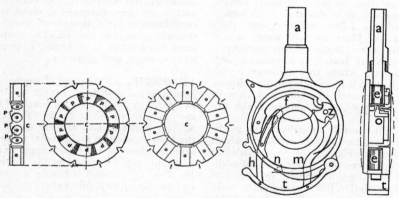

FIG. 68. *Turbiaux's revolver.*
(After Br. Pat. 2731/1882.)

"a" is the barrel, screwed into a casing and aligned with radial cartridge-chambers "eee" in the cylinder "c". A trigger "t" carries the pawl "h" (engaging a ratchet "ppp" on one side of "c") and the cocking-lever "m", which pushes against a tumbler "z", connected to a firing-pin "o" working against the tension of the mainspring "f". Another spring on the trigger "t" rests upon the cylinder-bolt "n" (engaging locking-notches "iii" around "c"), which is first overridden by the pressure of the pawl "h", but finally held home in a notch "i", at discharge, by the full compression of the spring on "t". Only self-cocking fire is possible; loading is accomplished by removing one of the side-plates of the casing, and shaking out the cylinder "c" into the user's hand for the insertion of cartridges.

TURNBULL, W. J. Walter Joseph Turnbull was an "Engineer" at 427 Carondelet Street, New Orleans, Louisiana, U.S.A., and joint-applicant with w. h. bofinger (*q.v.*) for Br. Pat. 19265/1902; as earlier stated, it is assumed (from his profession) that Turnbull designed the weapon protected by this patent, which is shown in Figure 69.

As may be seen from the Figure, Br. Pat. 19265/1902 described a manually-operated endless-chain magazine pistol,

ridge-chain. A grip-safety (embedded in the front butt-strap) was also proposed for use in this arm.

Farrow (publishing in 1904) wrote that "an accurate repeating revolver [*sic*], which fires sixteen shots without reloading, has been recently invented by W. J. Turnbull, of New Orleans. It has but three working parts, is light in weight, cannot possibly get out of order, and should any of the cartridges fail to fire, all that is necessary is to press the trigger again to bring another cartridge into

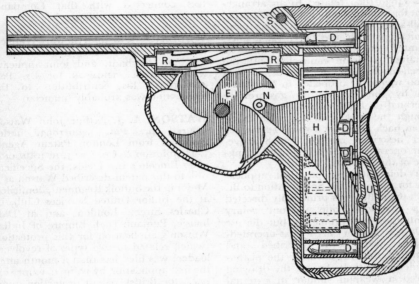

Fig. 69. *Bofinger & Turnbull's "revolver"*.
(After Br. Pat. 19265/1902.)

which had a number of trigger-arms "E" rotating radially within the trigger-guard; pressure on one of these arms caused the arm behind it to lift and release the hammer "H", as "N" slipped by, whilst the topmost arm (as it too was rotated forward) engaged a cam-slot in the spindle "R" rotating the chain-magazine, and so brought another cartridge "D" into alignment with the barrel. Discharge occurred *in situ*, within the magazine links, and the whole rear-section of the stock hinged upwards, for replacement or re-loading of the cart-

position and fire it . . . and therefore, the weapon can be fired as rapidly as the operator can press the trigger."

Although Farrow's paean of praise suggests that Turnbull alone was responsible for this design, and that it was quite novel, the "paddle wheel" trigger had been envisaged by Adamanthus Coray Houston (of Pickaway, West Virginia) a decade earlier; the latter's U.S. Patent No. 457278 of 4th August 1891 envisaged a solid-framed self-cocking revolver with just such a feature. However, Farrow's remarks do suggest that Turnbull at least got his design off the drawing-board, and it would be interesting to know if H. DANNER (*q.v.*) owed anything to this American patentee, in relation to his Br. Pat. 22131/1905.

UNGE, W. T. Captain Wilhelm Unge, of Valhallavagen 37, Stockholm N., Sweden, secured Br. Pat. 14639/1890 under guidance from London Patent Agents Haseltine, Lake & Co., of 45 Southampton Buildings.

Although there were nine other more detailed claims, the primary claim of Br. Pat. 14639/1890 related to an arrangement for automatically loading and firing small-arms, by means of a cylinder (communicating with the bore, *via* a port) mounted beneath the barrel, which also contained a piston connected with the breech-mechanism of the arm. This piston was to be propelled in one direction by the air- and/or gas-pressure generated on firing (which was fed to it through the port) and was then to be driven back again by a spiral spring (or other described means), which movement operated the loading- and firing-cycle of the lock-mechanism.

In demonstrating practical applications for this idea, the Specification to Br. Pat. 14639/1890 was principally directed to a magazine rifle without rotary ammunition-feed principles, but the use of Unge's system in a gas-operated-revolver was both described and illustrated therein; save for the piston-cylinder beneath its barrel, the drawing showed a weapon similar in external appearance to that Swedish M/1887 Army revolver shown at Plate 21, and most strongly suggested that it had been made by reference to a specimen arm, and not simply upon the drawing-board. Although operating in a fashion similar to that claimed by R. PAULSON (i.e. by an operating rod on the gas-piston, passing back through the arbor to strike the hammer), Unge's revolver was distinguished by the presence of a disconnector, to permit manual-operation of the weapon, and by direct linkage of the operating-rod to the hammer during use as a gas-operated firearm.

VAUGHAN, G. E. George Edward Vaug-

han was a well-known London Patent Agent (practising at 57 Chancery Lane), to whom the AUSTRIAN SMALL-ARMS MANUFACTURING CO. (*q.v.*) and O. SCHOENAUER (*q.v.*) respectively communicated the subjects of Br. Pats. 7989/1885 and 5793/1884, which survived into our period; as to "communicated" British patents see, generally, Appendix I.

Vaughan died or retired before that period in point here, but had apparently been the chosen London Patent Agent of the OESTERREICHISCHE WAFFENFABRIKS-GESELLSCHAFT (*q.v.*), and of other patentees connected with that Company, during most of the 1880s.

WALLACE, J. S. John Stewart Wallace, of Cliftonville Avenue, Belfast, was a Timber Merchant, and joint-applicant with B. T. L. THOMSON for Br. Pat. 4205/1891; his contribution to the transaction was probably financial.

WATSON, A. J. Arthur John Watson secured Br. Pat. 5420/1893, under guidance from London Patent Agents J. H. Johnson & Co. (see J. H. JOHNSON), of 47 Lincoln's Inn Fields; the Specification to this patent described Watson as a Major in the Suffolk Regiment, domiciled at the Junior United Services Club, in Charles Street, London, and at Dalhousie, Punjaub [*sic*], Empire of India. Watson's application for this protection (which related to two types of revolver-loader) was filed less than a month after the first application by W. DE C. PRIDEAUX (*q.v.*) for British patent protection upon a similar kind of device. These inventions were, however, quite distinct in their methods of operation, though both aimed to introduce a required number of cartridges into a revolver-cylinder in one motion.

Watson actually suggested two types o1 loader, one apparently intended to be thrown away after use, whilst the other could be re-charged an indefinite number of times. The first design (which this writer has not encountered) grouped cartridges around a vertically-grooved wooden core, and held them on that core by use of a soft-metal band, soldered around the assembly, which could be torn off (to release the rounds) after the circle of bullets had first been introduced into the chambers of a revolver.

The second type of loader was carried in a device attached to the user's sword-belt, and secured by a chain to prevent loss; it was a light cylindrical steel container for cartridges, which were secured inside it by projections on the partly-rotatable top. These projections engaged the cartridge-rims, and the user released that engagement (after inserting the bullets into the revolver-chambers) by a part-turn of the top of the loader, to the right. This model was quite energetically promoted, by THE WEBLEY & SCOTT REVOLVER AND ARMS CO., LTD. (q.v.).

Watson was born on 4th June, 1853, and commissioned a Sub-Lieutenant in the East Suffolk Regiment (12th) on 9th August, 1873, with the 2nd Battalion; at 12th February, 1880, he became a Lieutenant, Regimental Instructor of Musketry, and was gazetted as Captain on 14th April, 1883. He passed Staff College, and was then posted to the H.Q. Staff of the Army of India, as Deputy Assistant Adjutant General (for Instruction).

Between 1884 and 1885, he was a Brigade Major on the Bechuanaland Expedition (in which he received an Honourable mention in dispatches), and in 1886 he transferred to the 1st Battalion of his regiment, and was (two years later) involved in the Hazára expedition to the Taimani highlands of Afghanistan. In 1895, he was Road Commandant with the relief force in Chitral (where he secured the campaign medal, with Clasp) and became a Lieutenant-Colonel on 10th September, 1898. He was killed in action, at Rensburg, South Africa, on 6th January, 1900.

WEBLEY, H. Henry Webley was born in 1846, and was one of four sons born to Philip Webley, with whom Henry (and his brother T. W. WEBLEY; q.v.) traded as P. WEBLEY & SON, until his father's death in 1888; Philip Webley was a noted Birmingham gun-maker and revolver manufacturer, who may be fairly regarded as a joint-founder of THE WEBLEY & SCOTT REVOLVER AND ARMS CO., LTD. (q.v.), although that Company was not incorporated until 1897.

Upon the organization of this Company, Henry Webley retired from business, but was (in 1904) available to take a seat on the Board of Directors, at the retirement therefrom of John Rigby. Four years later (Dowell records), he was severely injured in an accident, and although he rendered signal service to his country (after 1914) under the press of war, he appears in these pages only by virtue of two patents which survived into the period of this book.

Br. Pat. 5143/1881 (see Fig. 20) was secured jointly with his brother, T. W. WEBLEY (q.v.), and probably under guidance from London Patent Agent W. E. Gedge; this patent related to ejector- and cylinder-dismount improvements to revolvers, and in a method for attaching a revolver cylinder to its axis in a manner preventing the clogging of rotation by fouling generated on discharge. All of these improvements were used in Webley "Improved Government" hinged-frame self-extracting commercial revolvers (which might be considered obsolete by 1889, as mentioned in Chapter III), and in Webley "Mark I" or "Mark II" Service revolvers of the type shown in Plate 23.

Br. Pat. 4070/1885 was secured jointly with J. CARTER (q.v.), and with the assistance of W. E. Gedge. It was an extremely important patent to the Webley firm (and its successor limited liability company), for the claims of this Specification covered a famous "stirrup" barrel-latch used on all Webley service revolvers, from the "Mark I" onwards, and on those fine commercial arms shown in Plates 25 and 26. Since, in addition, this patent protected a lock-mechanism used in early models of the commercial Webley "WG" Army and Target revolvers (see Fig. 23), it was maintained for its full permitted "life", as shown in Table I.

WEBLEY, T. W. Thomas William Webley (a brother of H. WEBLEY; q.v.) was born in 1838, and died in 1904; he was the eldest son of Philip Webley (see remarks to H. WEBLEY) and entered his father's business, in 1859 or 1860, after serving a full seven-year apprenticeship in the Birmingham gun-trade. Although joint-applicant with H. WEBLEY (*q.v.*) for Br. Pat. 5143/1881 (and holder of an earlier patent in the revolver field, long expired by 1889), T. W. Webley appears to have been more concerned with the running of the firm of P. WEBLEY & SON, and with selling its products, than with developing improvements to those arms of interest here. A most able business man, he was first Managing Director of THE WEBLEY & SCOTT REVOLVER AND ARMS CO., LTD. (*q.v.*), in which capacity he served until his death, and remarks upon that Company and its products will speak for his success.

WEBLEY, P. & SON and **WEBLEY & SCOTT REVOLVER AND ARMS CO., LTD., THE** later **WEBLEY & SCOTT LTD.** The Webley & Scott Revolver and Arms Co. Ltd. was joint-applicant with W. J. WHITING (*q.v.*) for Br. Pats. 18225/1900, 18294/1901, and 20430/1902, which applications were handled for these applicants by Henry Skerrett, a Patent Agent at 24 Temple Row, Birmingham. The reader's attention is directed to remarks upon G. V. FOSBERY (*q.v.*) for a description of that device protected by Br. Pat. 18225/1900 and applied to Model 1901 Webley-Fosbery "Automatic" revolvers; it should be noted, however, that the patent claimed general use, in revolvers, of an automatic cylinder-alignment device, to engage the cylinder when the weapon was opened, and to free it when the weapon was closed. There was, in other words, no limitation of claims to use of the patented device upon Fosbery revolvers only. The claims of Br. Pat. 18294/1901 are briefly noticed in remarks upon W. J. WHITING (*q.v.*), and related to various revolver-loaders, one of which was developed for use in Webley-Fosbery arms.

Br. Pat. 20430/1902 laid four claims of novelty to an improved double-action revolver lock-mechanism, in which undue rearward travel of the trigger was avoided (with its resultant disturbance of the finger-position), when thumb-cocking in single-action fire; whether in double- or single-action fire, the trigger maintained one position in the trigger-guard (unlike that in more conventional

lock-mechanisms), and so the shooter's "hold" and aim went undisturbed. To attain this end, the patentees simply modified a Schmidt-Galand lock mechanism (used in all Webley service revolvers of the period; see Fig. 33), exhibiting great ingenuity in confining the necessary alterations to but one component, namely, the trigger. However, there is no evidence that this patent was ever developed by the Company, and (see Table II) it was allowed to lapse quite early in its potential life.

In the face of Major W. C. Dowell's formidable work upon the various Webley firms, and their products, any summary of the Company's activities between 1889 and 1914 becomes difficult to phrase without needless repetition. However, Webley arms are such an important component of the story told here, that an outline of the firm's record must be attempted; in addition to these notes, the reader's attention is directed to those upon other patentees whose activities were linked with the Webley house (or its products), namely, J. CARTER (*q.v.*), W. FLETCHER (*q.v.*), G. V. FOSBERY (*q.v.*), H. W. GABBETT-FAIRFAX (*q.v.*), H. W. & J. F. LATHAM (*q.v.*), R. MORRIS (*q.v.*), J. TAMBOUR (*q.v.*), H. WEBLEY (*q.v.*), T. W. WEBLEY (*q.v.*), and W. J. WHITING (*q.v.*). Chapter III and Plates 22 to 27 and 31, are also in point.

The firm of P. WEBLEY & SON was founded in 1838, with the birth of T. W. WEBLEY (*q.v.*) to Philip Webley (a Birmingham gun-lock filer, established at 84 Weaman St., Birmingham, as a supplier of weapons, materials and components to the gun-trade), with the full firm-name being adopted in 1859, upon Thomas William Webley's coming-of-age; it appears likely that the trading style P. WEBLEY & SONS was sometimes used by the firm (after H. WEBLEY (*q.v.*) had attained his majority), but be it noted that the original trading-style is that normally found upon weapons dating from the period in point here.

By 1889, P. WEBLEY & SON were substantial suppliers of firearms and components to both the Birmingham and London gun-trades, and had secured a dominant position in the manufacture of revolvers in Great Britain. As remarks upon J. G. ACCLES (*q.v.*), E. C. GREEN (*q.v.*) or J. F. LATHAM (*q.v.*) will show, there were competitors to prevent a U.K.-monopoly, but such rivals worked on a scale too small to cause real embarrassment, so that P. WEBLEY & SON actually faced a more serious rivalry from the COLT'S PATENT FIREARMS MANUFACTURING CO. (INC.) (*q.v.*), and other American or Continental manufacturers noticed in Chapters I and II, in the civilian markets of the world, than from any British maker of hand-guns.

This type of competition also faced P. WEBLEY & SON where the arming of British officers was concerned, since possession of a commission carried with it the right to buy any revolver chambering service ammunition, and many Colt or Smith & Wesson revolvers were purchased. However, in the matter of arming British "Other Ranks" with revolvers, this firm enjoyed an unbroken monopoly from 1892 (see remarks to O. JONES) until it was swallowed up by the merger next to be described.

In 1897, a limited liability company called THE WEBLEY & SCOTT REVOLVER AND ARMS CO., LTD. was formed, which took over and merged the assets of three trading partnerships, namely, P. WEBLEY & SON, W. C. Scott & Sons and Richard Ellis & Son. The latter two firms also manufactured shot-guns and rifles in Birmingham (and were of such excellent reputation, that the new Company used their names as trade marks for many years afterwards), but are not known to have been involved in revolver manufacture at the time of this reorganization.

During most of the years of concern here, the Company not only had its main factory at 81–91 Weaman Street, Birmingham, but also maintained other premises at Lancaster Street and St. Mary's Row in that city, and had establishments in London, at 78 Shaftesbury Avenue, W.1 and (after 1907) at 55 Victoria Street, S.W. The Managing Director (until his death, in 1904) was T. W. WEBLEY (*q.v.*), who was assisted in that field of particular concern here by the efforts of J. CARTER (*q.v.*), G. V. FOSBERY (*q.v.*), H. WEBLEY (*q.v.*) and W. J. WHITING (*q.v.*); he was succeeded,

as Managing Director, by F. T. Murray.

Those various revolvers manufactured by THE WEBLEY & SCOTT REVOLVER AND ARMS CO., LTD. (or WEBLEY & SCOTT LTD., as it was formally re-named, in 1906) are described above in Chapter III, or in remarks upon G. V. FOSBERY (*q.v.*), H. WEBLEY (*q.v.*) or W. J. WHITING (*q.v.*), but it cannot be too strongly emphasized that the Company's business was not based upon revolvers, during any of those years in point here.

It is true (see Plates 22, 24 and 31) that a substantial range of such arms was offered by the Company, so that the 1914 pistol catalogue, for example, tendered details of a dozen models of revolvers, many of which could be had in several barrel lengths and alternative qualities. However, the same catalogue offered both self-loading pistols and single-shot target or signalling arms, and the total contents formed but a part of products listed in the Company's full catalogue of equivalent date, amongst shotguns (hammer or hammerless), rook and Martini-action rifles, bolt-action and falling-block rifles, ball-and-shot guns, Express rifles, or wild fowling guns of 4- and 8-bore calibres. In addition, the firm was widely advertised as a contractor to H.M. War Department, The Admiralty, India, The Colonies, the Chinese Navy, the Argentine Republic, the Royal Irish Constabulary, and the Dublin, Metropolitan, Cape Mounted, Lisbon, and Egyptian Police, as well as to various shipping companies.

The First World War drastically altered this situation by forcing the Company to concentrate upon manufacture (for H.M. Government) of revolvers, self-loading pistols, and signal pistols, to the exclusion of most of its pre-1914 products, but even this switch in emphasis occurred in 1915 or 1916, and is irrelevant to the points made above, namely, that the company (whilst enjoying a virtual monopoly of revolver manufacture in the United Kingdom and the British Empire) sold revolvers as part only of its normal manufactures, and not even the South African fighting, between 1899 and 1902, greatly affected that position.

In concluding these remarks upon the

T

Webley house, it may be helpful to note that use of the trading-style P. WEBLEY & SON was not immediately abandoned with the formation of a limited liability Company. It is therefore quite possible to find Webley revolvers marked with the earlier name, which either have serial-numbers higher than weapons of the same model marked with the Webley & Scott Ltd. company-name, or are of a model introduced after 1897, the date at which the limited liability company was incorporated. Noteworthy examples in the first category have been observed amongst "RIC" Model 83 arms, whilst "WP" and Webley-Fosbery revolvers have been noted, quite frequently, in the second classification.

"WESPI", WAFFEN-TECHNISCHE GESELLSCHAFT, M.B.H. The Waffen-Technische Gesellschaft "Wespi" m.b.H. (of Lindowerstrasse 18/19, Berlin, N.39) was joint-applicant with R. TARGAN (q.v.) for Br. Pat. 28924/1912; these applicants were assisted to secure their protection by London Patent Agents Wheatley & Mackenzie, of 40 Chancery Lane. Since Targan stated his address as that of the Company, it is assumed that he was a director or employee of it.

The Specification to Br. Pat. 28924/1912 set out four claims of novelty for improved methods in providing electricity to a luminous sighting-tube or gun-sight, which the W. T. G. "Wespi", R. Targan and A. Wiegel had originally patented as Br. Pat. No. 14269 of 18th June, 1912 (not in Table II); essentially, these improvements related only to providing a battery which was not an integral part of the sight.

Br. Pat. 28924/1912 should be considered (in these pages) with the inventions of K. DOBSLAW & P. SCHMIDT (q.v.), C. A. LEWIS (q.v.), and V. DE MARAIS & G. E. GARDNER (q.v.), but the Specification to it (by powers vested in the Comptroller of Patents, under s.7 (4) of the Patents & Designs Act, 1907) actually drew any reader's attention to the similarity between its claims and those in the Specifications of D. Abercrombie's Br. Pat. No. 11700 of 21st May, 1904; G. Daninger's Br. Pat. No. 10108 of 13th May, 1905; C. A. LEWIS (q.v.), and S. D.

Adair's Br. Pat. No. 8751 of 11th April 1910; and F. B. Prike's Br. Pat. No. 27658 of 9th December, 1911.

The patents concerned all related to gun- or rifle-sights outside the scope of these pages, and are not listed in Table II.

WESSON, D. B. Daniel Baird Wesson secured Br. Pats. 6184/1894, 24588/1901, and 24597/1901, with assistance from London Patent Agents Haseltine, Lake & Co., of 45 Southampton Buildings; he was described as a "Manufacturer" in all three Specifications, but as resident at 55 Stockbridge Street, Springfield, County of Hampden, Mass., U.S.A. in the first case and as at 50 Maple Street, Springfield, on the latter occasions. Wesson (b. 1825; d. 1906) was the driving-force behind the well-known firm of Smith & Wesson, who manufactured revolvers at Springfield, and these three British patents give little idea of his equivalent activity, as a patentee of improvements to revolvers, in America, where he secured no less than thirty-four such patents in his sole name, and was joined with others in successful applications for U.S. protection.

Br. Pat. 6184/1894 (to which U.S. Pat. 517,152, of 27th March, 1894, was the equivalent) stated eight claims of novelty for improvements to revolvers with double-action lock-mechanisms, and cylinders that were swung sideways out of the pistol-frame, on a crane or yoke, either for manual and simultaneous ejection of cartridges from their chambers or for re-loading; examples of such arms appear in Plates 5 or 36, and the patent aimed to provide (i) a safety-device preventing discharge of the arm unless the cylinder was first swung securely home into the frame, and (ii) an improved cylinder-crane, arbor, and ejector.

The patentee attained his first objective by ingenious use of that rolling motion necessarily imparted to the pivot of the cylinder-crane or yoke (the pivot being a stem longitudinally embedded in the front lower frame of the arm), when the cylinder was swung outwards for loading or unloading. This rolling motion cammed rearwards a small bolt (mounted along the crane-pivot), which was aligned with the trigger-nose and blocked the movement of the trigger, so that it could not be pressed, to fire the weapon, whilst the cylinder was swung out. Wesson's second improvement combined, as one component, the manually operated ejector and the latch by which the cylinder and its crane were locked into the frame; here, a small nib at the rear-end of the ejector-rod (which latter

Pat. 6184/1894 (and its American equivalent) were used by the firm of Smith & Wesson, when it introduced the "Model I" revolver of relevant type shown in Plate 5, although the methods used for such refinements either did not strictly follow apposite claims of the patents, or else were (in later versions of such arms) shortly superseded by improved methods for achieving the same ends.

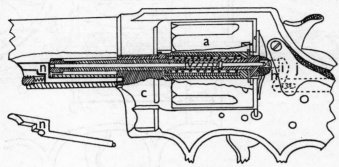

FIG. 70. *D. B. Wesson's cylinder-latch.*
(After Br. Pat. 24588/1901.)

The arbor of the cylinder "a" is carried on a side-swinging crane "c", permitting "a" to be swung outwards from the pistol-frame (*i.e.* towards the reader) for loading or cartridge-ejection.

The cylinder "a" is latched into the pistol-frame at three points, but is unlatched by a single lever, the thumb-piece "j". This is accomplished by forming a lug beneath the barrel which contains a spring-loaded sliding bolt "n" (also shown separately in the Figure) with projections on it engaging recesses in both the front of the ejector-stem and the front of the crane "c".

Pressure on "j" pushes forward (by the internal agency of "i") a spring-loaded rod passing entirely through "a" which rod normally latches the cylinder at its rear by engaging a recess cut in the standing-breech. Movement of that rod is directly transmitted to "n", disengaging it from the front locking-recesses in the ejector-stem and the crane, and thus leaving the cylinder "a" free to be swung outwards on the crane "c".

passed longitudinally through the arbor, to carry a star-shaped ejector on its rear end) was withdrawn from a securing-hole in the standing-breech, when the user pulled forward the front end of the ejector-rod, where it protruded forward beneath the barrel. This action having freed the cylinder to be swung clear of the frame, on its crane, a reversal of pressure on the ejector-rod then expelled the ejector at the rear of the cylinder, and dislodged the cartridges.

Both design-features claimed in Br.

Br. Pat. 24588/1901 (to which U.S. Pat. 688141 of 3rd December, 1901, was the equivalent) laid three claims of novelty to a system, shown in Figure 70, for securely latching into their frames the cylinders of revolvers designed to have that component swung out to the side of the arm, on a crane, for loading; it will be noted, from Figure 70, that the cylinder and crane were securely latched in no less than three places by this system. The device was used by Smith & Wesson in those heavy, but exquisitely-made,

"Model ·44 Hand Ejector (New Century)" revolvers discussed in Chapter I, and Br. Pat. 24588/1901 need not detain us here save to remark that (the highest degree of machining *finesse* being required to make such a latch on a production-basis) only Smith & Wesson ever manufactured it successfully, and that the type

Figure 71. Smith & Wesson had experienced some customer-complaint in respect of single-point latches of that type initiated by Wesson's Br. Pat. 6184/1894, due to the fact that they had adopted an anti-clockwise cylinder-rotation system in which the pawl tended to push the cylinder outwards (on its crane) from the

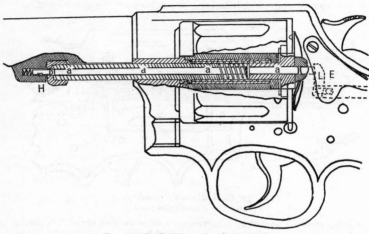

FIG. 71. *D. B. Wesson's cylinder-latch.*
(After Br. Pat. 24597/1901.)

The cylinder is mounted as described in Figure 70 (*i.e.*, so as to be swung outwards towards the reader, on a crane), but here is latched into the frame at two points only.

At the front, a lug beneath the barrel carries a spring-catch, which latches the front end of a spring-loaded rod "aaa" passing through the ejector-rod; at its rear-end, "aaa" forms the other latch, by engagement with a cavity in the standing-breech.

When the thumb-piece "E" is pressed down, "L" moves forward to thrust "aaa" forward in turn, thus unlatching the cylinder (by removing the rear end of "aaa" from the standing-breech, and using the front-end of "aaa" to unseat the front bolt at "H"), and freeing it to be swung out upon its crane.

of pivoted thumb-lever shown in the Specification drawings as suitable for operating this latch was never used in production arms. Instead, a sliding thumb-piece (developed for the S & W "·38 Military, Model 1899" revolver) was adopted.

Br. Pat. 24597/1901 (to which U.S. Pat. 689260 of 17th December, 1901 was the equivalent) protected a more simple form of cylinder-latch than that claimed by the previous patent, which is shown in

frame. Br. Pat. 24588/1901 was one answer to this problem (and remained in use for certain S & W models until 1915), but the two-point latch claimed under Br. Pat. 24597/1901 and shown in Figure 71 proved so satisfactory in use that it was used in all other post-1901 S & W swing-out cylinder centre-fire revolvers of concern here, and continues in use today.

To supplement these remarks upon D. B. Wesson, it is reasonable to conclude with brief mention of Smith & Wesson, the firm so ably headed by Wesson, until shortly before his death. Unlike the COLT's PATENT FIRE ARMS MANUFACTURING CO. (INC.) (*q.v.*), for example, this Springfield business was not apparently incorporated as a company of limited liability during most of the years of concern here, and (as a result) nowhere appears in Tables I or II as a patentee, yet it would be misleading to exclude mention of it from these pages, on that account.

The firm had begun to trade at Springfield, in October 1857, after the formation of a partnership between Horace Smith (b. 1808; d. 1893) and D. B. Wesson to manufacture breech-loading revolvers, and was successful from its inception. Control of Rollin White's U.S. Pat. 12648 of 3rd April, 1855 (covering the principle of the breech-loading revolver cylinder) gave Smith & Wesson an American monopoly in the manufacture and sale of such arms, which endured until 1869, and since that monopoly was backed by a firm both willing to enforce its patents and producing arms of good quality and at reasonable prices, success had been immediate and enduring.

In January 1874, Horace Smith had then sold his interest in the firm to D. B. Wesson, but the joint firm-name was maintained, and in years prior to 1889 the firm could be said to have pioneered the introduction into America of at least two really important improvements to revolving arms (namely, the hinged-frame self-extracting, and concealed-hammer grip-safety weapons), whilst also introducing a number of detailed advances to the art generally. Certain models introduced in years prior to 1889 continued to be marketed by the firm for some time thereafter (see Plate 5), and were widely imitated by Belgian, Spanish and other American makers, but Smith & Wesson also introduced solid-framed arms, with swing-out cylinders (of the type shown in Plate 5) during 1896, and devoted considerable attention to the manufacture of such arms. Some improvements are not readily discernible on casual examination, but few other revolver-makers paid so much attention to the elimination of wear in their products as was the case at Springfield.

As early as 1888 (D. B. Wesson's U.S. Pat. 377878 of 14th February) attention had been turned to the facing of bearing-surfaces with hardened steel to minimize wear, and this activity was followed (D. B. Wesson's U.S. Pats. 401087 of 9th April, 1889; 520468 of 29th May, 1894; 542745 of 16th July, 1895; and 684331 of 8th October, 1901, respectively) by incorporating hardened-steel inserts on the bearing-side of cylinder-locking notches, and the use of anti-friction bearings for, or shimming of, revolver-hammers. In those swing-out cylinder designs described at Chapter I, too, it eventually became normal practice for ratchet, ejector and ejector-stem to be made as one drop-forged component, to mount the cylinder (at both ends) in hardened-steel bearings, to latch the cylinder at two or more points (as described above, under Br. Pats. 24588/1901 and 24597/1901), and to embody hammer-blocking and rebounding devices to make accidental discharge virtually impossible.

Perhaps in light of its initial experience with Rollin White's valuable U.S. patent, the firm had early realized that value to be found in such protection, and having used before 1889 (by licence or assignment) important American patents held by F. H. Harrington, W. C. Dodge, C. A. King, G. W. Schofield, J. H. Bullard and W. Trabue, it further developed the practice, in years of concern here, to embrace that important network of such protection secured in the names of D. B. Wesson and Joseph Hawes Wesson, one of his sons.

As was the case with COLT'S PATENT FIRE ARMS MANUFACTURING COMPANY (INC.) (*q.v.*), Smith & Wesson preferred to sell their products to dealers, at home or overseas, but would accept individual orders from customers unable to secure what they needed from such sources. John E. Parsons records that business to most dealers was originally by discount and rebate (with commission paid only to a select number of representatives), which were allowed at publicized rates, and based entirely upon the quantities purchased. It is believed that this practice obtained over those years in point here, in alliance with the then permitted practice of enforced minimum retail prices. The factory both repaired and replated (or reblued, with its incomparable finish) S & W revolvers sent in by customers, and guaranteed its arms in uncompromising terms; cartridges, reloading-tools, sights, cases, stocks and spare parts could be purchased (by post), and revolvers could be finished in various grades of engraving and plating at costs (dependent upon the quality of the work) varying between $1.50 and $45, in 1900.

In the 1870s and 1880s, its hinged-frame self-extracting revolvers had been adopted as service sidearms by the Argentine, Russian and United States governments, as well as by the armed or police forces of other countries; with the introduction of its solid-framed swing-out cylinder arms, in 1896, the firm repeated this success in America (see Chapter I), and was to achieve a very large market indeed, from 1914 onwards. Success prior to 1914, however, was primarily achieved with the sale of police, target and pocket arms.

WHEELDON, I. Isaac Wheeldon (a Mining Engineer, at 335 Collins Street, Melbourne, Victoria, Australia) secured Br. Pat. 8045/1900, with assistance from London Patent Agents Herbert Haddan

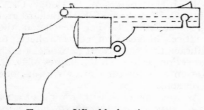

FIG. 72. *Wheeldon's wire-cutter.*
(After Br. Pat. 8045/1900.)

& Co., of 18 Buckingham Street. Six claims of novelty were laid to the idea of cutting barbed-wire by use of firearms. After 1914 this idea was quite extensively examined by various patentees, but Wheeldon was the first to file application for a British patent upon it.

Essentially, Wheeldon envisaged the forming of resistance surfaces (or "dies", as he termed them) by which the wire might be retained for cutting by a bullet. For revolvers (see Fig. 72) the resistance surfaces had to be formed in the barrel, but rifles (firing a bullet at higher velocities) might omit the foremost surface altogether, and merely use a guide to align wire with bore.

WHITING, W. J. William John Whiting secured Br. Pats. 1923/1886 (see Table I) 3427/1891, 17291/1896, 4924/1901, and 10072/1905, in his own name; he was also joint-applicant with J. CARTER (*q.v.*) for Br. Pat. 5778/1888 (which survived into years of concern here, see Table I), and with THE WEBLEY & SCOTT REVOLVER AND ARMS CO., LTD. (*q.v.*) for Br. Pats. 18225/1900, 18294/1901, and 20430/1902. His own patents mentioned three successive addresses, first at Sutton Coldfield (near Birmingham), and then at 153 Linwood Road and 53 Douglas Road, Handsworth, a Birmingham suburb; in his joint patent applications, the addresses mentioned were at Mona Terrace, Bracebridge Street, Aston Juxta, Birmingham, as to the first, and of Douglas Road, Handsworth, for the last three.

Whiting was, over the whole period in point here, associated with or wholly employed by Birmingham revolver-makers P. WEBLEY & SON (*q.v.*), or the successor limited liability Company, and his ascent into the management of that firm can be traced in those various descriptions of his then current occupation, successively recited in the Specifications to his patents. In the earliest (i.e. Br. Pat. 1923/1886), no description appeared, but the joint-application with J. CARTER (*q.v.*) described Whiting then as a "Tool Maker", and his Br. Pat. 3427/1891 saw him defined as a "Foreman of Works", which standing was transformed into that of "Works Manager", during the formalities of securing his Br. Pat. 17291/1896; status as a "Director of The Webley & Scott Revolver and Arms Company Limited" was noted with his application for Br. Pat. 10072/1905.

As to the subjects of these various British patents, five at least were of substantial value to Whiting's employers, in those special fields to which they related;

the patentee also secured other patents, outside the scope of this work, from which similar benefit accrued.

Br. Pat. 1923/1886 (see Table I) related to an anti-fouling sleeve for revolvers, which prevented penetration of smoke and dirt between cylinder and arbor; thus, a ferrule was turned at the front of the cylinder, around the arbor hole, and into the recess thus formed was slipped a metal sleeve, with a skirt formed circumferentially about it to engage the ferrule and so block off the arbor-hole completely. This device was used upon certain early Webley revolvers into the 1890s, but need for such protection lessened as smokeless powders superseded black-powder, and such application was abandoned before the turn of the century.

The Specification to Br. Pat. 5778/1888 (see Table I) contained fourteen claims of novelty for improvements to revolvers, and illustrated a solid-framed, concealed-hammer, self-cocking design, in which the hammer was automatically rebounded to full-cock, on releasing the trigger, after each shot. This arm was never manufactured commercially by P. WEBLEY & SON (q.v.), or by the successor limited liability Company, but a type of cylinder-bolt specifically claimed in this Specification was taken up by the firm, and extensively used by it. This device (shown in Figure 21, as manufactured) was embodied in all Marks of Webley service revolver relevant to these pages, and also incorporated by Webley "WS" Army and Bisley Target commercial revolvers introduced after Br. Pat. 5778/1888 had expired (see Table I); the operation of it is described in Chapter III, with the remarks upon such arms.

Br. Pat. 3427/1891 was yet another important patent for the Webley house, and related to devices for retaining (and releasing, when desired) the cylinders of revolvers with hinged-frames of the type shown in Plate 25 (top). As in the previous case of Br. Pat. 5778/1888, the subjects of Whiting's Br. Pat. 3427/1891 are discussed in Chapter III, with those civilian and service arms to which such improvements were applied.

Br. Pat. 17291/1896 was a patent of improvement to Whiting's Br. Pat.

3427/1891, and proposed two forms of cylinder-retainer (for use in hinged-frame arms of the type shown in Plate 25, lower) which were automatically withdrawn from engagement with the retaining surfaces on the cylinder when the barrel was latched (and the cylinder kept in place on its arbor by the standing-breech), but which were lifted into engagement to hold the cylinder upon the arbor, when the barrel was unlatched and tilted down upon its frame-hinge. One of these devices was of importance to the Webley house (see Fig. 22), and is described in detail in Chapter III.

Both Br. Pats. 18225/1900 (which was secured jointly with THE WEBLEY & SCOTT REVOLVER AND ARMS CO., LTD., q.v.) and Whiting's own Br. Pat. 4924/1901 have been earlier considered in remarks upon G. V. FOSBERY (q.v.). Although the cylinder-alignment or securing devices covered by these patents were applicable to conventional revolvers, they were in fact applied almost exclusively to Webley-Fosbery "Automatic" revolvers, of the type shown in Plate 31, and this situation developed also in regard to Br. Pat. 18294/1901, when that protection was secured by Whiting and THE WEBLEY & SCOTT REVOLVER AND ARMS CO., LTD. (q.v.). This patent claimed various types of cartridge-charger for the simultaneous loading of all chambers in a revolver, and most of the "coupler discs" (as the patentees termed their devices) were simply thin metal plates, drilled and recessed to take six rimmed revolver cartridges, which were inserted into (and ejected from) a revolver with their charge of cartridges in situ; one claim of novelty, however, related to a circumferentially-notched "coupler disc", into which rimless or semi-rimmed cartridges might be slid sideways (to be held by the notches around the plate engaging in their extraction-grooves), and this one form of revolver-charger was developed to become that highly characteristic device used for loading ·38 ACP semi-rimmed cartridges into the eight chambers of a Webley-Fosbery revolver made in that calibre.

Br. Pat. 20430/1902, taken by Whiting jointly with THE WEBLEY & SCOTT REVOLVER AND ARMS CO., LTD. (q.v.), related to an improved double-action revolver lock-mechanism (already described in remarks upon that Company), which was never commercially developed. The case was similar for Whiting's own Br. Pat. 10072/1905, which explored an idea still extensively used today by some American revolver-makers, namely, the use of spiral wire springs in place of flat or V-springs, for revolver lock-mechanisms; in Whiting's design, a single helical spring (trapped upon a rod, one end of which bore against the hammer, to power that component, and the other end of which operated the mainspring auxiliary lever) served as combination hammer-, trigger-, and pawl-spring, in a modified Schmidt-Galand double-action lock-mechanism of the basic type shown in Figure 33.

WHYTE, C. C. B. Charles Cecil Beresford Whyte ("Gentleman", of Hartley Manor, Carrick-on-Shannon, Co. Leitrim, Ireland) secured Br. Pat. 10651/1888, under guidance from London Patent Agents Abel & Imray, of 28 Southampton Buildings, and his protection survived into years of concern here, as shown in Table I. The Specification to Whyte's patent contained a single claim of novelty for a holder (attached to the user's belt or saddle) in which a revolver or other small arm might be carried, suspended by its trigger-guard from a boss formed between two ends of a spring, with the trigger bolted against accidental discharge.

WILKINSON, E. W. Edward William Wilkinson traded with C. O. ELLIS (*q.v.*) as Charles Osborne & Co. (at 12–14 Whittall Street, and 16/17 Sand Street, Birmingham), and was joint-applicant with his partner, and with F. CASHMORE (*q.v.*), for Br. Pat. 5151/1896.

The subjects of that patent, and the scope of activities in which Charles Osborne & Co. engaged, have been respectively examined in earlier remarks upon F. CASHMORE and C.O. ELLIS, (*q.v.*), to which remarks the reader's attention is directed.

WILLIAMS, A. H. Albert Henry Williams (of 13 John Street, Bedford Row, London) was joint-applicant with F. MARTIN (*q.v.*) and R. C. ROMANEL (*q.v.*) for Br. Pats. 9998/1887 and 6994/1888, which survived into the period of concern here, as shown in Table I. The subjects of these two patents are briefly discussed in earlier remarks upon R. C. ROMANEL (*q.v.*), and it is believed that Williams (who was described as a "Gentleman", in both Specifications) made a financial rather than technical contribution to them.

YOUNGHUSBAND, L. and S. S. Lancelot Younghusband (of Victoria Road, Darlington, Co. Durham) and Samuel Smith Younghusband (of Rose Villa, North Road, Darlington) were Engineers, and joint-applicants for Br. Pat. 3047/1886, which survived into years of concern here, as shown in Table I; they were assisted to secure their protection by London Patent Agents A. M. and W. Clark, of 53 Chancery Lane.

The Specification to Br. Pat. 3047/1886 described a trigger-operated self-cocking rifle, with rotary belt-feed, and a special rimless cartridge for use in it. The magazine for the cartridge-belt was (like that of E. A. SALVATOR, *q.v.*) strapped to the marksman, and it seems improbable that the Younghusbands' design was ever seriously considered by a British arms manufacturer.

APPENDIX III

ANNOTATED BIBLIOGRAPHY

Foreword

Wahl, P. & Toppel, D. *The Gatling Gun* (Arco Publishing Co., Inc. New York, 1965).

Allen G. C. *The Industrial Development of Birmingham and the Black Country. 1860–1927* (Frank Cass & Co. Ltd. London, 1966).

"Artifex" and "Opifex". *The Causes of Decay in a British Industry* (Longmans, Green & Co., 1907).

Birmingham & Provincial Gunmakers' Association. *The Gun Trade Hand Book* (Birmingham, 1906).

Rolt, L. T. C. *Tools for the Job* (B. T. Batsford Ltd. London, 1965).

Chapter I

"Artifex" and "Opifex". *op. cit.*

Sell, De W. E. *Collector's Guide to American Cartridge Handguns.* (The Stackpole Co., Harrisburg, 1963).

Gould, A. C. *Modern American Pistols and Revolvers* (Bradlee Whidden, Boston, 1894).

Farrow, E. S. *American Small Arms* (New York, 1904).

Serven, J. *Colt Cartridge Pistols* (California, 1952).

Parsons, J. E. *The Peacemaker and its Rivals* (William Morrow & Co. New York, 1959).

Kuhn, Lieut.-Col. R. C. *·45 Martial Revolvers* (The Gun Report. Illinois, May 1961).

Harrison, G. Charter, Jnr. *Colt "Peacemaker" Production by Years* (The Gun Collector, Issue 47. Madison, 1957).

National Rifle Association, The. *Illustrated Firearms Assembly Handbook* (N.R.A. Washington. *circa* 1961).

Radford, C. S. & Morgan, S. *Handbook on Naval Gunnery; Manual for Colt's Double-Action Navy Revolver* (2nd edn. New York, 1896).

Hatcher, Major J. S. *Pistols and Revolvers and their Use* (Small-Arms Technical Publishing Co. Delaware, 1927).

Mathews, J. H. *Firearms Identification* (The University of Wisconsin Press. Madison, 1962).

MacFarland, H. E. *Arms Production—Folsom Trade Branded Guns* (The American Rifleman. Washington, February 1969).

Satterlee, L. D. and Gluckman, Major A. *American Gun Makers* (Otto Ulrich Co. Buffalo, 1940).

Carey, A. M. *American Firearms Makers* (Thomas Y. Crowell Co. New York, 1953).

Webster, D. B., Jnr. *Suicide Specials* (The Stackpole Co. Harrisburg, 1958).

Berg, P. O. *The Hopkins & Allen Guns* (The Gun Report. Illinois, December 1961).

Smith, W. P. *Notes on the Manufacturers of Cheap Pistols (or Revolvers)* (The Gun Report. Illinois, December 1962).

Clede, B. *John Mahlon Marlin* (Shooting Times, 1969).

de Haas, F. *Meriden Model 10 Rifle* (The American Rifleman. Washington, January 1969).

Karr, L. K., Jnr. and C. R. *Remington Handguns* (Pennsylvania, 1956).

Parsons, J. E. *Smith & Wesson Revolvers; The Pioneer Single Action Models* (New York, 1957).

McHenry, R. C. & Roper, W. F. *Smith & Wesson Handguns* (Huntingdon, 1945).

Kuhn, Lieut.-Col. R. C. *Smith & Wesson Martials* (The Gun Report. Illinois, April 1956).

Smith, W. H. B. and Bellah, K. *Book of Pistols and Revolvers* (The Stackpole Co. Harrisburg, 1965).

Chapter II

Taylerson, A. W. F. *The Revolver, 1865–1888* (Herbert Jenkins. London, 1965).

Leleu, V. *Revolvers et Pistolets Automatiques Récents* (Paris & Nancy, 1903).

Blair, C. *Pistols of the World* (B. T. Batsford Ltd. London, 1968).

Hertslet, Consul-General Sir C. *Report on the Arms Industry of Liège. (No. 650 Miscellaneous Series. Diplomatic and Consular Reports. Belgium. Cmd. 2683–14)* (H.M. Stationery Office, 1906).

Anon. *Instruction sur les Armes portatives en usage dans les corps de l'Armée* (Brussels, 1906).

Karnop, K. P. *A Rare European Martial* (The Gun Report. Illinois, May 1966).

Hoff, Dr. A. *Danske Marinerevolvere* (Tøjhusmuseet. Copenhagen).

Smith, W. H. B. and Bellah, K. *op. cit.*

"J.O." *Französischer Armeerevolver Chamelot-Delvigne* (Deutsches Waffen-Journal. January 1968).

Josserand, M. H. *Les pistolets, les revolvers et leurs munitions* (Paris, 1966).

Anon. *Manualetto di tecnica militare* (Escrito e Nazione. May 1930. No. 5).

Anon. *Manuale per il Graduato* (Le Forze armate, 1931).

Anon. *Les Armes a Feu Portatives des Armées Actuelles et Leurs Munitions par Un Officier Superieur* (Paris, 1894).

Anon. *Les Armes a Feu Portatives des Armées Actuelles et Leurs Munitions par le Commandant Bornecque* (Paris, 1905).

Smith, W. H. B. *Small Arms of the World* (Military Service Publishing Co. Harrisburg, 1948).

Barado, F. and Génova, J. *Armas Portatiles de Fuego* (Barcelona, 1881).

Mathews, J. H. *op. cit.*

Parsons, J. E. *Smith & Wesson Revolvers. op cit.*

Skaar, F. C. and Nielsen, O. *Haerens Håndvåpen—Pistoler og revolvere 1814–1940* (Oslo, *circa* 1952).

Anon. *Colectia de toate legile, reglementele, decisiunile, Vol. II* (Bucharest, 1883).

Miclescu, G. *Arme portative.*

Anon. *L'Armée Roumaine* (Angers, 1900).

Fabal, Gen. J. E. R. *Historia de la Infanteria de la Marina Española* (Madrid, 1967).

Bosson, C. *Histoire et Description de l'Arme a Feu en Suisse. 1817–1957* (Geneva, 1958).

Schmidt, R. *Les nouvelles Armes à feu portatives.* (Paris 1889).

Chapter III
Anon. *The Kynoch Journal, Vol. 5* (Jan.–Dec., 1904).
Taylerson, A. W. F. *op. cit.*
Dowell, Major W. C. *The Webley Story* (The Skyrac Press. Leeds, 1962).
Birmingham and Provincial Gunmakers' Association. *op. cit.*
War Office, The. *Instructions for Armourers* (H.M.S.O., 1912).
Pemberton, W. B. *Battles of the Boer War* (B. T. Batsford Ltd., 1964).
Smith, W. H. B., Bellah, K. *op. cit.*

Chapter IV
Leleu, V. *Exposition Universelle de 1900 (à Paris); Armes à Feu Portatives de Guerre* (Paris/Nancy, 1902).
Mathews, J. H. *op. cit.*

Chapter V
Higgins, C. *A Concise Treatise on the Law and Practice of Patents for Inventions* (London, 1884).
Gordon, J. W. *The Statute Law relating to Patents of Invention and Registration of Designs* (London, 1908).

Appendix I
Anon. *The Official Journal of the Patent Office* (London, 1889–1924).

Appendix II
Anon. *Patents for Inventions. Abridgements of Specifications.*
        Class 119, Small-Arms.
        Period—A.D. *1889–92* (H.M.S.O., 1898).
        Period—A.D. *1893–96* (H.M.S.O., 1900).
        Period—A.D. *1897–1900* (H.M.S.O., 1903).
        Period—A.D. *1901–04* (H.M.S.O., 1907).
        Period—A.D. *1905–08* (H.M.S.O., 1911).
        Period—A.D. *1909–15* (H.M.S.O., 1922).
Blair C. *op. cit.*
Leleu, V. *Revolvers et Pistolets Automatiques Récents. op. cit.*
Serven, J. E. *op. cit.*
Parsons, J. E. *The Peacemaker and its Rivals. op. cit.*
Anon. *L'Armurerie Liègeoise* (Liège, 1909).
Bock, G. *Moderne Faustfeuerwaffen und Ihr Gebrauch.* (Neudam, 1922).
Farrow, E. S. *op. cit.*
Smith, W. P. *More on the History of Protector revolvers* (The Gun Report, January, 1967).
Dowell, W. C. *op. cit.*
Craig, C. W. Thurlow and Bewley, E. G. *Webley 1790–1953* (Birmingham, 1953).
    The material upon *Grenfell & Accles Ltd.* was compiled from the file of that company; Public Record Office, London (Ref: BT31/4996. No. 33442).
    The material upon O. JONES (*q.v.*) and A. T. DE MOUNCIE (*q.v.*) was compiled from material at the Public Record Office, London (Ref: SUPPLY/6/49).
Koch, G. *Die Jagd-Gewehre der Gegenwart* (Weimar, 1891).
National Rifle Association, The. *op. cit.*
Peterson, H. L. *Encyclopaedia of Firearms* (London, 1964).
Maclean, J. *Waffenschmied Europas. Arms in Austria 1867–1890.* (Guns Review. Harrogate, June–Oct. 1968).
Anon. *Musée Retrospectif de la Classe 51 a l'Exposition Universelle Internationale de 1900 a Paris; Armes de Chasse.*
Chinn, G. M. *The Machine Gun, Vol. I* (Washington, 1951).

Leleu, V. *Exposition Universelle de 1900. op. cit.*
Viglezzi, I. *Armi a Ripetizione* (Rome, 1890).
Taylerson, A. W. F. *op. cit.*
Simpson, L. B. *Many Mexicos* (University of California Press, 1952).
Webster, D. B., Jnr. *op. cit.*
Satterlee, L. D. and Gluckman, Major A. *op. cit.*
Lustyik, A. *Le Protector* (The Gun Report, October 1966).
Parsons, J. E. *Smith & Wesson Revolvers; The Pioneer Single Action Models. op. cit.*
Smith, W. H. B. *op. cit.*

INDEX

Numbers in **heavy type**-refer to pages with Plates or Figures upon them.